SECOND EDITION

D1458551

THE SEARCH
FOR
COMMUNITY POWER

5·20

Edited by
Willis D. Hawley
Duke University

Frederick M. Wirt
*University of Maryland,
Baltimore County*

PRENTICE-HALL, INC., ENGLEWOOD CLIFFS, NEW JERSEY

Library of Congress Cataloging in Publication Data

HAWLEY, WILLIS D., COMP.
  The search for community power.

  Bibliography: p.
  1. Community power—Addresses, essays, lectures.
I. Wirt, Frederick M., joint comp. II. Title.
HM136.H33 1974   301.15′5   73–18234
ISBN 0–13–796912–0

To our firstborn,
KAREN and LESLIE

PRINTED IN THE UNITED STATES OF AMERICA

10   9   8   7   6   5   4   3   2   1

PRENTICE-HALL INTERNATIONAL, INC., *London*
PRENTICE-HALL OF AUSTRALIA, PTY. LTD., *Sydney*
PRENTICE-HALL OF CANADA, LTD., *Toronto*
PRENTICE-HALL OF INDIA PRIVATE LTD., *New Delhi*
PRENTICE-HALL OF JAPAN, INC., *Tokyo*

Contents

iii

PART TWO

**Methodological Problems in Specifying Patterns of Community
Power   129**

CHAPTER THREE

Measuring the Relative Power of Groups and Individuals   139

CHAPTER FOUR

Issues and Non Issues: Where Does One Look for Community
Power?   167

CHAPTER FIVE

Locating Decisionmakers   209

Preface

That relationship among men which we call "power" has captured the imagination of scholars of western civilization for a period so long that "the memory of man runneth not to the contrary." From earliest times, records reveal inquiry into the nature of power and the ways in which it is obtained, secured, exercised, and lost. Since Plato, philosophers have mused over the question: Who should have power? To what ends should power be employed? Since Thucydides, historians have chronicled the ways of men in power. In the contemporary period social scientists have peeled off parts of the phenomena of power for specialized study. Sociologists have examined its social aspects, particularly in terms of class and status; economists have analyzed the amassing and organization of its economic aspects in institutional terms; political scientists have examined the formal and informal aspects of political power in both its institutional and behavioral modes.

Americans, scholars as well as laymen, seem to have a special fascination with the subject, a fascination often tinged with a certain fear. Our Constitution makers, reflecting the attitudes of their contemporaries, were repelled by the evil potential of political power and sought to restrain it in a systematic maze of checks and balances, divisions and separations. In the last part of the nineteenth century the development of highly concentrated economic power produced similar fears of this kind, which led to governmental restraints upon business. In our times the opinion surveys demonstrate that a fear of both political and economic "bigness" is widespread among the populace. At the same time, we seem to admire powerful and assertive people. For example, the popularity of the President increased during periods of new war initiative in Southeast Asia even while the public's approval of the war itself was declining.

With all this interest in power, it is curious that until very recently few scholars examined the structure of power at the community level. Local "place histories" abound from early times, but these are most often chronicles of good and bad periods, of population rise and economic growth—overlaid by polemics suggesting that the particular history demonstrated the favor of God or manifest destiny in the particular locale. The first American commentaries squarely focusing on the bases of power and the uses of power in the community are to be found in scattered newspaper attacks on corrupt political organizations after the Civil War. Entirely concerned with the machinations of political power, they offer little in the way of comparison, and hence, little theory about the subject.

One of the first consciously comparative analyses of communities was Lincoln Steffens' *Shame of the Cities*, published in 1904. It was a survey concerned less with developing a conceptual or empirical theory than with promulgating a normative attack on the mutually corrupting influences of local political parties and local business. Much of the community analysis which followed in the first quarter of this century was equally concerned with demonstrating that certain reforms in political machinery were all that were necessary in order to overcome corruption.

The first major departures from this tradition appeared in the late 1920s and mid-1930s with the publication of Robert and Helen Lynd's "Middletown" studies. For the first time the total community was in focus, not merely its political institutions. While the Lynds' emphasis upon the dominance of business leaders was not new, their interest in the way in which this control was exercised through many social structures (not least of which were community values) filled in for the first time details of the pervasive influence of a small group across a range of local issues. This analysis (in *Middletown in Transition*) of the dominance of a community by a single family provided a point of departure for the sociological study of community power elites. It is interesting to note that almost a decade earlier two novelists, Sherwood Anderson in *Winesburg, Ohio* and Sinclair Lewis in *Mainstreet*, portrayed systems similar to those found in "Middletown." In the 1940s other sociologists, W. Lloyd Warner in "Yankee City" and "Jonesville" being the most prominent, reached conclusions which paralleled those of the Lynds.

With the appearance of Floyd Hunter's *Community Power Structure* in 1953, however, a new phase in the search for community power commenced. In some respects the most sophisticated study to that time, Hunter's work clearly stated a method for detecting and studying local power structures. His book precipitated a reaction from some dissenting political scientists, setting off an interdisciplinary debate which has not yet run its course.

In the last few years there has been a growing interest among social scientists in the questions of how and by whom decisions are made in American communities. This interest is manifest in hundreds of articles, monographs, and books. The best of this literature has one or more of these distinguishing characteristics: it provides important insights into the problems of social research; it furnishes the conceptual or empirical basis on which social-system theory (especially political theory) can be developed; it contributes to the normative evaluation of the operation of our democratic society.

There is now a large number of studies which differ significantly in their conceptualization, research methods, and conclusions, so that the study of community power requires increasingly wide reading. In this book we have collected some of the more important commentaries on the search for power in American communities—commentaries which treat major aspects of this special field. Included are definitions, findings, methods, problems, and future research directions. Of course, reasonable scholars will differ with us about both the criteria of importance and the consequent selections in this book—but we do not pretend that what is offered here is necessarily the "last word" or the "best" writing in the field. We do believe that the selections herein represent a fairly comprehensive survey of the nature, quality, potential, and problems of community power research.

This revised edition is organized into three main parts each of which is preceded by an essay designed to place the material in that part in the context of the larger field of analysis and research to which it is related. In Part I we review two seminal commentaries on the nature of power and a number of the more significant community studies which set the stage for contemporary research. Part II surveys some of the more vexing methodological problems in the search for community power. Part III examines a number of recent comparative studies which seek to develop theoretical understandings of community power. Since the first edition was published in 1968, there has been a dramatic increase in the number of studies which are concerned with the policy consequences of different patterns of influence and this development is reflected in several of the articles in the third section of the book. Each selection has a short preface which introduces the reader to the ideas therein and suggests when appropriate, some important aspects of the material not included in the selection itself. In some cases footnotes have been omitted; those included in this edition have been renumbered.

The first edition included an extensive bibliography citing studies of community power. We have omitted that section from the revision because of space limitations and because other bibliographies are available. A list of these bibliographies is included here as Appendix A.

It seems to us that the study of community power has much to recommend it to social scientists. Its many methodological problems illustrate the complexity of social research. The problems of theory building suggested in the context of this study have consequence for an empirically based understanding of who gets what, when, and how in presumably democratic societies. The study of community power also helps to evaluate the normative theory of democracy by validating or invalidating the empirical aspects of such theory. In short, the lessons to be learned from the search for power in American communities are important in many ways, and we believe that they have substantial applicability to both larger and smaller social systems.

PART ONE

Early Concepts and Studies: Setting the Stage for Contemporary Research

The choice of a "beginning" of the search for community power is somewhat arbitrary. In one sense, Aristotle may be said to have been a student of the field in his analysis of the constitutions of Hellenic city-states. Certainly many classical political ideas dealt with the nature of power as it was evidenced in all institutions of society. Even the beginning of the study of *American* community power might be said to trace to De Toqueville or perhaps to Lincoln Steffens in *The Shame of the Cities*, published in 1902. Our selection of a beginning point, however, employs more narrow criteria, namely, when those regarded as social scientists advanced the first conceptualizations and empirical research geared to those concepts.

As a start, it is important to understand what is meant by "power." The concept of power has an elusive quality which has led scholars to wrangling since first they turned to its study. The average person has an intuitive grasp of its meaning, and, indeed, most of us use the concept in daily conversation without much thought, assuming that our listeners know what we mean. But like many other general terms by which we seek to encapsulate complex aspects of life, power has many dimensions of meaning.

Of citizen Jones we may say, "He is a powerful man," "Jones has a lot of pull," or "Jones runs things in this town." A thoughtful person may ask what it is that Jones possesses—what is this thing called "power"?

At minimum, power analysts agree that power is involved when one person or a group achieves compliance from others with respect to the disposition of a given value. The means used to secure compliance and the consequences for those involved are among the many aspects of the phenomenon of power. We can see some of the definitional problems if we look again at Jones.

Let us assume that Jones is a banker and Brown is seeking a loan. Ordinary usage would have it that Jones has power over Brown because he can affect Brown's life-opportunities by the decision to grant or not to grant the loan requested. But exactly what is this power and what are its sources? How is it applied? Does the power lie in the bank's funds which Jones may dispense, or in Jones's choice to lend or not to lend the money at his discretion? Does the power, if it lies in the bank's funds, exist independently of Jones and regardless of who is the banker? Is Jones's power *potential* power, in the sense of being latent even if it is not used? Or does his power exist only when it is employed? Further, how does the banker Jones's power in this case compare to that of the political ward leader who can swing her district's votes as she wills? Can power of one sort, for example, control over credit, be converted to power of a different sort, for example, making public policy? Is power *additive* in the sense that every use of it enhances the possessor's next use of it, or is it *depletive* in the sense that every use of it causes a power loss that cannot be replaced without effort? Many of these questions, as well as others, will be faced in the selections in this book.

We suggest that the various ways of analyzing the concept of power may be seen to fall on a continuum between two major approaches to the problem. The first of these approaches focuses on institutional bases of influence and attributes power to those who have access to these institutions. In other words, certain institutions—such as political parties, social classes, corporations, military groups, religious organizations, and the like—possess certain characteristics which may be regarded as *power resources*. These resources are used to secure from others compliance with the institution's purpose. Power resources might include wealth, votes, prestige, physical coercion, etc. Persons in a position to employ an institution's power resources are considered powerful. To oversimplify, *in this approach power is seen as inhering fundamentally in institutions rather than in people.* Thus, when kings were thought divine, power adhered to kingship whether in his use of power the incumbent was an idiot like George III or a genius like Peter the Great.

A second approach is to view power as the result of interpersonal rela-

tionships. Here, regardless of the power resource—money, military might, etc.—or the instruments by which the institutional base is effected—a loan, armament, etc.—what is common to all is a relationship between two people, one of whom induces the other to do the former's will. Potential power is relatively unimportant until it is translated into interpersonal transaction to achieve compliance. The qualities of the power holder are the main focus in this school, which is thought to explain why George III was not "really" powerful while Peter the Great was. In this view, it is imperative to discover how people act so as to understand how, among people possessing ostensibly equal power resources, one obtains compliance while another fails to or is unwilling to utilize his potential for obtaining compliance.

What we have said here is a simplification of quite sophisticated analyses. But it is offered as a basic observation to indicate what we believe is a major distinction between the ways in which power is defined. This distinction, though seldom as emphatic as we have described it, has influenced much of the analysis of community power which this book presents. If we believe that power is possessed only by a certain stratum of society, such as "the wealthy and well born," or "the bourgeoisie," then we may well view the distribution of power in the community or nation in terms of a pyramid. At the peak of the pyramid are concentrated the few who possess most of a community's resources and determine the life-opportunities for most others. Research based on this outlook involves finding the peak of the power pyramid and detailing the way in which those at the peak shape the lives of others.

On the other hand, our outlook may be that power adheres to specific individuals in specific situations involving particular values, bases, and means of power. Then we would view the community as composed of many peaks where different sets of leaders operate in different realms of decision making. Thus research is focused upon decisions, public and private, in which we can detect some persons compelling others to compliance. Further, this outlook, with its emphasis upon specification of the exact contours of a power matrix, implies the possibility of quantifying some of the relationships involved and hence of measuring the exact nature of the relationships.

Almost all recent studies of community power find that the actual distribution of power falls far short of the ideal type of democracy popularly (if erroneously) associated with Hellenic Athens, the nineteenth-century New England township, or the Swiss canton. And yet the conclusions of these studies differ in important ways, corresponding with what have been broadly labeled as "elite" and "pluralistic" systems. Elite rule implies that the key decisions in the community are dominated by a few whose interests are relatively cohesive and who enjoy substantial autonomy from potential claimants on their power. In addition, the concept of elite rule usually has a class component; that is, those who rule are economically or socially privileged. On the other hand, political pluralism implies that the distribution of power is somewhat dispersed and that class lines are not the assumed determinants of that distribution. Moreover, in a pluralist political system the balance of power is not invariable over time. It tends to adjust to new levels of equilibrium in response to demands from those who seek a greater share of the rewards that power brings.

Most contemporary students of social influence do not merely report things as they are; they accompany their findings with criticism or justification in normative terms. When criticism or justification is a component of community study, it seems that those authors who find elite systems are more likely to see their role as that of the critic or reformer; those who report pluralist findings, though not always satisfied with things as they are, seem more likely to view themselves as defenders of democratic theory. This possible distinction between community power analysts is interesting, and the literature on the normative aspects of this empirical work is extensive. We do not, however, treat it in this book.

Another difference between so-called elite and pluralist studies lies in the methodology generally utilized by the authors of each type. By and large, elite studies have sought to determine which individuals in the community have a reputation for being influential—"for getting things done." Sometimes such studies seek to identify those who hold positions thought to provide their incumbents with power resources. Cadres so identified are then shown to share similar values, which they protect or promote. Occasional incidents, frequently anecdotal in character, are utilized to illustrate the degree and manner in which this elite exercises its influence. The approach of what are conventionally referred to as pluralist studies, however, is to regard position and reputation as incidental, secondary, or even irrelevant, and to focus on concrete manifestations of influence in the process of political decision making.

Finally, elite studies seem to differ from pluralist studies in that the frame of reference of the former is often broader. Those who find elite rule are concerned with the exercise of power in social, educational, religious, political, and economic institutions, with greater emphasis often placed on the last of these. Pluralist studies on the other hand, tend to focus on the way in which social, economic, religious, and educational influences, etc., are manifested in more or less structured political decisions. As a result of these emphases, elite studies often center on economic dominants while pluralist studies often center on political dominants.

These distinctions, however, can easily be overstated. *As will become increasingly clear in this book, the distinctions between elite and pluralist systems are matters of degree rather than of mutually exclusive contrasts.*

Most of the research on community power prior to 1960 was conducted by social anthropologists and, especially, sociologists rather than political scientists or economists. The early dominance of the field by sociologists may be explained by a number of factors. First, with few exceptions, political scientists who worked in community settings tended to define politics somewhat narrowly and characteristically focused their attention on the form and structure of city and county governmental institutions.[1] Second, the study of local politics did not hold much status within the profession of political science and the research techniques and strategies of the so-called behavioral approach to politics—which were necessary to the systematic analysis of community—had not been widely adopted, especially by political scientists familiar with local affairs.[2] Third, the training and backgrounds of many sociologists may have led them to be more sensitive than political scientists to normative social theories and to ways of conceptualizing social systems, which resulted in a greater attention to class conflict and to their considering community study significant for analyzing society.[3]

As we have already suggested, many of the studies of community power which appeared in the 1950s and before—some of the most significant of which are excerpted in this section—concluded that public policy making in America's cities and towns was either directly or indirectly dominated by an elite with varying degrees of political autonomy and value consensus. But both the methodology and the findings of this earlier research increasingly came under attack, especially by political scientists.[4]

Despite this criticism, not until the 1960s did any sizable number of studies begin to appear which operationalized the methodological alternatives to these previous studies and provided empirical evidence to support the pluralist model of community power. While most early critics of the elite studies focused their attacks on the methodological aspects of this research, there was invariably an implicit—and often an explicit—alterna-

[1]See Lawrence Herson, "The Lost World of Municipal Government," *American Political Science Review* 51 (June 1957), 330–45.

[2]See Robert Dahl, "The Behavioral Approach to Politics: Epitaph for a Monument to a Successful Protest," *American Political Science Review* 55 (December 1961), 763–72.

[3]This point was initially brought to our attention by Steven Blutza. For a related view, see Nelson Polsby, *Community Power and Political Theory*, (New Haven: Yale University Press, 1963).

[4]Herbert Kaufman, and Victor Jones, "The Mystery of Power," *Public Administration Review*, 14 (Summer 1954), 205–12; Robert A. Dahl, "A Critique of the Ruling Elite Model," *American Political Science Review*, 52 (June 1958), 463–69; Nelson W. Polsby, "How to Study Community Power: The Pluralist Approach," *The Journal of Politics*, 22 (August 1960), 474–84, and his "Power in Middletown: Fact and Value in Community Research," *The Canadian Journal of Economics and Political Science*, 26 (November 1960), 592–603, and his "The Sociology of Community Power: A Reassessment," *Social Forces*, 37 (March 1959), 232–36, and his "Three Problems in the Analysis of Community Power," *American Sociological Review*, 24 (December 1959), 796–803; Raymond E. Wolfinger, "A Plea for A Decent Burial," *American Sociological Review*, 25 (October 1960), 636–44.

tive theoretical perspective in their writings. As noted above, they questioned the existence of a single center of power or a cohesive coalition of groups which wield power in most American communities. Instead, the critics proposed that there are usually (though not always) *multiple* centers of power, none of which is completely sovereign. In addition, these centers of power do not overlap or coalesce from issue-area to issue-area in any consistent way. The power of leaders is significantly limited by other leaders and by those whom they lead, although direct mass participation in decision making is not required or expected. Wallace Sayre and Nelson Polsby summarize the pluralist view this way:

> . . . in a wide range of community situations, participation in decision-making is limited to a relatively few members of the community, but only within the constraints of a bargaining process among elites and of an underlying consensus supplied by a much larger percentage of the local population whose approval is costly to secure.[5]

The theoretical assumptions of the pluralists also carry the implicit judgment that pluralist political systems are "better" (i.e., more democratic) than elite political systems. (Of course, those who have found elite rule also have often expressed their distaste for such structures.) While most of us would agree that a relatively broad dispersal of political power is preferable to the domination of community policies by the few, a pluralist structure of leadership is not in itself adequate evidence that the political system is serving the interests of the many. Indeed, a number of political scientists have recently become critical of those who have too readily equated pluralistic leadership structures with democracy. These scholars have warned that before we can begin to say that pluralism leads to democracy, it is minimally necessary to demonstrate, and not merely assert, that (1) a balance of power exists among competing interests and that, perhaps more important, (2) the leaders of competing groups are in some way responsible to the wishes of those they lead.[6]

In addition, because of the widespread and understandable tendency of democrats to view rule by the few as "bad" and pluralism as "good," or at least better, it may be useful to ask whether in some communities, especially small and homogeneous communities, dominance of decision making by an "elite" might not meet most of the demands of democratic

---

[5]Nelson W. Polsby, and Wallace S. Sayre, "American Political Science and the Study of Urbanization," in *The Study of Urbanization,* eds. Leo Schnore and Phillip Hauser (New York: John Wiley, 1965), 115–56.

[6]For example, see Grant McConnell, *Private Power and American Democracy* (New York: Knopf, 1966); Peter Bachrach, *The Theory of Democratic Elitism: A Critique* (Boston: Little, Brown, 1967); and E. E. Schattschneider, *The Semisovereign People* (New York: Holt, Rinehart & Winston, 1960).

theory. In the simplest case, upper-income citizens of homogeneous towns may place very few demands on local public facilities, except for the possible exception of demands for high-quality education, and the level of consensus on the quality and quantity of public services may be so high that the citizens knowingly (and even gratefully) relinquish political decision making to the few.[7]

Let us emphasize that there has been, at least until recently, an excessive tendency to dichotomize elitist and pluralist models of community power. The so-called "ruling elite" model has a number of variations, some of which seem not distinctly different from what other researchers might call pluralism. In short, there are no well-defined boundaries between elitist and pluralistic political systems. It may be too sharp a judgment, but there is much in the conclusion of Robert V. Presthus, after his analysis of competing methodologies, that "to some extent, where the sociologists found monopoly and called it elitism, political scientists found oligopoly but defined it in more honorific terms as pluralism."[8]

These concepts, methods and findings, which set the stage for more recent research, are reflected in the readings of this first part of the book. Chapter One includes two readings widely regarded as seminal contributions to the study of social and political power. Each emphasizes one of the two ways of looking at power which we have outlined—institutional and transactional. However, both authors would no doubt agree that one can neglect neither the bases and sources of power nor the ways in which those resources are utilized in analysis.

In the first selection, Max Weber, one of the intellectual fathers of modern sociology and political science, focuses upon the structural aspects of power, emphasizing such determinants as the control of markets or economic goods, honor or deference, and communal decisions. While he views power primarily in institutional terms, note the many careful distinctions he draws between bases and instruments of power, and the limitations he offers to an over-simplified Marxist interpretation of society. In the second article in Chapter One, Herbert Simon emphasizes the individual and interactional nature of power. He describes some of the special problems in the study of power which arise from the asymmetric nature of power relations and the phenomenon of anticipated reactions. This article previews many of the conceptual and methodological problems that community power analysts have faced in the years succeeding its publication in 1953.

The work of Weber and Simon indicates the complexity of a concept which may seem simple and clear at first consideration. Searching analysis

[7]See evidence of the latter in David W. Minar, "Community Basis of Conflict in School System Politics," *American Sociological Review*, 31 (1966), 822–35.

[8]Robert V. Presthus, *Men at the Top* (New York: Oxford University Press, 1964).

of the concept of power must not be viewed as academic nit-picking—an understanding of the components and dynamics of power is crucial to both sociology and political science, particularly the latter. Harold Lasswell and Abraham Kaplan put it succinctly: "The concept of power is perhaps the most fundamental in the whole of political science: the political process is the shaping, distribution, and exercise of power. . . ."[9] It is therefore immensely important that students of politics secure more agreement on the meaning of this most basic concept. As James March will suggest in Chapter Four, social scientists are far from clear when they use the word "power." Why this is so becomes clear in this chapter.

The six articles which comprise Chapter Two are arranged chronologically and reflect the increasing awareness of the complexity of political power that characterizes the literature in general. Although each of the first three selections concludes that the community studied was dominated by a "general purpose" political elite, the second and third note in various ways that such power is not exercised without some limits. These limits include competition, real or potential, as well as the sheer enormity of the task involved in exercising power. However, unlike the pluralist conclusion that leaders have constituencies to which they must be at least moderately responsive, those who find elite rule are more likely to see the relationship between leaders and the community as the relationship between "players" and "audiences." As in the theater, there is an interaction, but the audience rarely, if ever, pulls the player off the stage.

The first selection in Chapter Two is from the "Middletown" studies of Robert and Helen Lynd. The first of the well-known community studies utilizing the approach of social anthropology, *Middletown* and *Middletown in Transition* are now the classics in this genre. "Middletown" remains the prototype of the city in which one group—in this case the "X Family"— has a virtual monopoly in all aspects of community power.

Floyd Hunter's *Community Power Structure* is another landmark. In his study of Atlanta, Hunter describes a city seemingly controlled in all major decisions by financial and social elites, with a sub-layer of personnel who effectuate those decisions. While Hunter was not the first to employ panels of persons knowledgeable in community life who nominate decision makers, his particular technique was an important step in the systematic study of the community, and it led to much replication and refinement. This selection reveals the structure of power as Hunter found it, although his full discussion of the extensive sociometric work on which his conclusions were based has been abridged here.

The small town has been the subject of much glorification and abuse in the American myth system. For some, it embodies the best of our culture—

[9]Harold Lasswell and Abraham Kaplan, *Power and Society* (New Haven: Yale University Press, 1950).

warm, personal relationships, awareness and interest about issues affecting local life, freedom from the crushing pressures of an impersonal big city, and so on. For others, the small town is characterized by a homogeneity and conformity which cramp the spirit, by public apathy which allows a few old families or the wealthy to dominate public life, by the absence of cultural and social diversity, etc. Drama and literature have tended to emphasize the latter themes, although conventional wisdom has usually preferred the former. We present a selection from *Small Town in Mass Society* by Arthur Vidich and Joseph Bensman which reveals a community of shared values in which an elite can dominate by reflecting and reinforcing those values and by undercutting potential threats to its hegemony. But those who find in this a confirmation of their notion of small town America as a cheese press should also read Aaron Wildavsky's study of Oberlin, Ohio. There, diverse power bases and controversy exist, engendered by leaders who do not fit Vidich and Bensman's town; in short, pluralism can exist in small town life.[10]

Many Americans apparently believe (is it that we prefer to believe?) that "the country club set," "the big brass," "the best families," "city hall" (the one you can't fight), and the ubiquitous "they" are the people who *really* run things. It would appear that studies such as the first three presented in Chapter Two have either shaped or reinforced (and probably both) the popular notions of the distribution of privilege and prerogative in our society.

The first major book to appear which presented evidence that power in American cities was "pluralistic" in character (that is, broadly shared), was *Governing New York City*, in which Wallace Sayre and Herbert Kaufman examine the role of groups in the fragmented political system of the nation's largest city. A selection from that study is included in Chapter Two. Chapter Two also includes a rather lengthy excerpt from Robert Dahl's *Who Governs?* Dahl's study of New Haven, Connecticut, is probably the best known analysis of community power that supports the idea that city politics can be reasonably democratic. Most important, Dahl furnished the theoretical rationale upon which one might generalize his conclusions to other settings.

The final study in this chapter, *The Rulers and the Ruled* by Agger, Goldrich and Swanson, is significant because it is a forerunner to the comparative studies which characterize much of the theoretically oriented research of more recent years.[11] This study remains perhaps the most ambitious analysis of community power in terms of the scope and depth of its

[10]Aaron Wildavsky, *Leadership in A Small Town* (Totowa, N.J.: Bedminster Press, 1964). Also see Paul A. Smith, "The Games of Community Politics," *Midwest Journal of Political Science* 9 (February 1965), 37–60.

[11]Another important comparative study published during this period that deserves the student's attention is Presthus's *Men at the Top*.

substantive and theoretical concerns. It demonstrates both the promise and the difficulty of comparative longitudinal political inquiry. There is no way that an excerpt of the length permitted in this book could encompass the significant methodological and conceptual aspects of *The Rulers and the Ruled*. We have chosen to present those portions of the study which seek to develop a classification of community political systems. This excerpt places substantial emphasis on the important effects of community norms and values on patterns of influence. Unfortunately, few other scholars have followed them in pursuing the significance of such variables.

CHAPTER ONE

The Notion of Power

CLASS, STATUS AND PARTY

Max Weber

*The following selection, like many writings by its author, has had
great impact in shaping an intellectual approach to understanding social
life on the part of later scholars. With great appreciation of the subtlety
of distinctions in life, an historical sweep of supporting evidence which
can easily overpower, and a rigor of logic and argument, Max Weber
here explains the elements and dimensions of social influence. Many of
the institutions mentioned above in the introduction to this section are
analyzed to suggest how class, status group and party affect power's creation, distribution, and employment within a community.*

From Max Weber: Essays in Sociology, edited and translated by H. H.
Gerth and C. Wright Mills. Copyright 1946 by Oxford University Press, Inc.
Reprinted by permission.

1: ECONOMICALLY DETERMINED POWER
AND THE SOCIAL ORDER

Law exists when there is a probability that an order will be up-
held by a specific staff of men who will use physical or psychical compul-
sion with the intention of obtaining conformity with the order, or of
inflicting sanctions for infringement of it. The structure of every legal order
directly influences the distribution of power, economic or otherwise, within
its respective community. This is true of all legal orders and not only that
of the state. In general, we understand by "power" the chance of a man or
of a number of men to realize their own will in a communal action even
against the resistance of others who are participating in the action.

"Economically conditioned" power is not, of course, identical with
"power" as such. On the contrary, the emergence of economic power may
be the consequence of power existing on other grounds. Man does not
strive for power only in order to enrich himself economically. Power, including economic power, may be valued "for its own sake." Very frequently
the striving for power is also conditioned by the social "honor" it entails.
Not all power, however, entails social honor: The typical American Boss,
as well as the typical big speculator, deliberately relinquishes social honor.
Quite generally, "mere economic" power, and especially "naked" money
power, is by no means a recognized basis of social honor. Nor is power the
only basis of social honor. Indeed, social honor, or prestige, may even be
the basis of political or economic power, and very frequently has been.
Power, as well as honor, may be guaranteed by the legal order, but, at least
normally, it is not their primary source. The legal order is rather an additional factor that enhances the chance to hold power or honor; but it cannot
always secure them.

The way in which social honor is distributed in a community between
typical groups participating in this distribution we may call the "social
order." The social order and the economic order are, of course, similarly
related to the "legal order." However, the social and the economic order
are not identical. The economic order is for us merely the way in which
economic goods and services are distributed and used. The social order is
of course conditioned by the economic order to a high degree, and in its
turn reacts upon it.

Now: "classes," "status groups," and "parties" are phenomena of the
distribution of power within a community.

2: DETERMINATION OF CLASS-SITUATION BY MARKET-SITUATION

In our terminology, "classes" are not communities; they merely represent possible, and frequent, bases for communal action. We may speak of a "class" when (1) a number of people have in common a specific causal component of their life chances, in so far as (2) this component is represented exclusively by economic interests in the possession of goods and opportunities for income, and (3) is represented under the conditions of the commodity or labor markets. [These points refer to "class situation," which we may express more briefly as the typical chance for a supply of goods, external living conditions, and personal life experiences, in so far as this chance is determined by the amount and kind of power, or lack of such, to dispose of goods or skills for the sake of income in a given economic order. The term "class" refers to any group of people that is found in the same class situation.]

It is the most elemental economic fact that the way in which the disposition over material property is distributed among a plurality of people, meeting competitively in the market for the purpose of exchange, in itself creates specific life chances. According to the law of marginal utility this mode of distribution excludes the non-owners from competing for highly valued goods; it favors the owners and, in fact, gives to them a monopoly to acquire such goods. Other things being equal, this mode of distribution monopolizes the opportunities for profitable deals for all those who, provided with goods, do not necessarily have to exchange them. It increases, at least generally, their power in price wars with those who, being propertyless, have nothing to offer but their services in native form or goods in a form constituted through their own labor, and who above all are compelled to get rid of these products in order barely to subsist. This mode of distribution gives to the propertied a monopoly on the possibility of transferring property from the sphere of use as a "fortune," to the sphere of "capital goods"; that is, it gives them the entrepreneurial function and all chances to share directly or indirectly in returns on capital. All this holds true within the area in which pure market conditions prevail. "Property" and "lack of property" are, therefore, the basic categories of all class situations. It does not matter whether these two categories become effective in price wars or in competitive struggles.

Within these categories, however, class situations are further differentiated: on the one hand, according to the kind of property that is usable for returns; and, on the other hand, according to the kind of services that can be offered in the market. Ownership of domestic buildings; productive establishments; warehouses; stores; agriculturally usable land, large and small holdings—quantitative differences with possibly qualitative consequences—; ownership of mines; cattle; men (slaves); disposition over mobile instruments of production, or capital goods of all sorts, especially money or objects that can be exchanged for money easily and at any time; disposition over products of one's own labor or of others' labor differing according to their various distances from consumability; disposition over transferable monopolies of any kind—all these distinctions differentiate the class situations of the propertied just as does the "meaning" which they can and do give to the utilization of property, especially to property which has money equivalence. Accordingly, the propertied, for instance, may belong to the class of rentiers or to the class of entrepreneurs.

Those who have no property but who offer services are differentiated just as much according to their kinds of services as according to the way in which they make use of these services, in a continuous or discontinuous relation to a recipient. But always this is the generic connotation of the concept of class: that the kind of chance in the *market* is the decisive moment which presents a common condition for the individual's fate. "Class situation" is, in this sense, ultimately "market situation." The effect of naked possession *per se*, which among cattle breeders gives the nonowning slave or serf into the power of the cattle owner, is only a forerunner of real "class" formation. However, in the cattle loan and in the naked severity of the law of debts in such communities, for the first time mere "possession" as such emerges as decisive for the fate of the individual. This is very much in contrast to the agricultural communities based on labor. The creditor-debtor relation becomes the basis of "class situations" only in those cities where a "credit market," however primitive, with rates of interest increasing according to the extent of dearth and a factual monopolization of credits, is developed by a plutocracy. Therewith "class struggles" begin.

Those men whose fate is not determined by the chance of using goods or services for themselves on the market, e.g. slaves, are not, however, a "class" in the technical sense of the term. They are, rather, a "status group."

3: COMMUNAL ACTION FLOWING FROM CLASS INTEREST

According to our terminology, the factor that creates "class" is unambiguously economic interest, and indeed, only those interests involved in the existence of the "market." Nevertheless, the concept of "class-interest" is an ambiguous one: even as an empirical concept it is ambiguous as soon as one understands by it something other than the factual direction of interests following with a certain probability from the class situation for a certain "average" of those people subjected to the class situation. The class situation and other circumstances remaining the same, the direction in which the individual worker, for instance, is likely to pursue his interests may vary widely, according to whether he is constitutionally qualified for the task at hand to a high, to an average, or to a low degree. In the same way, the direction of interests may vary according to whether or not a *communal* action of a larger or smaller portion of those commonly affected by the "class situation," or even an association among them, e.g. a "trade union," has grown out of the class situation from which the individual may or may not expect promising results. [Communal action refers to that action which is oriented to the feeling of the actors that they belong together. Social action, on the other hand, is oriented to a rationally motivated adjustment of interests.] The rise of societal or even of communal action from a common class situation is by no means a universal phenomenon.

The class situation may be restricted in its effects to the generation of essential *similar* reactions, that is to say, within our terminology, of "mass actions." However, it may not have even this result. Furthermore, often merely an amorphous communal action emerges. For example, the "murmuring" of the workers known in ancient oriental ethics: the moral disapproval of the work-master's conduct, which in its practical significance was probably equivalent to an increasingly typical phenomenon of precisely the latest industrial development, namely, the "slow down" (the deliberate limiting of work effort) of laborers by virtue of tacit agreement. The degree in which "communal action" and possibly "societal action" emerges from the "mass actions" of the members of a class is linked to general cultural conditions, especially to those of an intellectual sort. It is also linked to the extent of the contrasts that have already evolved, and is especially linked to the *transparency* of the connections between the causes and the consequences of the "class situation." For however different life chances may be, this fact in itself, according to all experience, by no means gives birth to "class action" (communal action by the members of a class). The fact of being conditioned and the results of the class situation must be distinctly recognizable. For only then the contrast of life chances can be felt not as an absolutely given fact to be accepted, but as a resultant from either (1) the given distribution of property, or (2) the structure of the concrete economic order. It is only then that people may react against the class structure not only through acts of an intermittent and irrational protest, but in the form of rational association. There have been "class situations" of the first category (1), of a specifically naked and transparent sort, in the urban centers of Antiquity and during the Middle Ages; especially then, when great fortunes were accumulated by factually monopolized trading in industrial products of these localities or in foodstuffs. Furthermore, under certain circumstances, in the rural economy of the most diverse periods, when agriculture was increasingly exploited in a profit-making manner. The most important historical example of the second category (2) is the class situation of the modern "proletariat."

4: TYPES OF "CLASS STRUGGLE"

Thus every class may be the carrier of any one of the possibly innumerable forms of "class action," but this is not necessarily so. In any case, a class does not in itself constitute a community. To treat "class" conceptually as having the same value as "community" leads to distortion. That men in the same class situation regularly react in mass actions to such tangible situations as economic ones in the direction of those interests that are most adequate to their average number is an important and after all simple fact for the understanding of historical events. Above all, this fact must not lead to that kind of pseudoscientific operation with the concepts of "class" and "class interests" so frequently found these days, and which has found its most classic expression in the statement of a talented author that the individual may be in error concerning his interests but that the "class" is "infallible" about its interests. Yet, if classes as such are not communities, nevertheless class situations emerge only on the basis of communalization. The communal action that brings forth class situations, however, is not basically action between members of the identical class; it is an action between members of different classes. Communal actions that directly determine the class situation of the worker and the entrepreneur are: the labor market, the commodities market, and the capitalistic enterprise. But, in its turn, the existence of a capitalistic enterprise presupposes that a very specific communal action exists and that it is specifically structured to protect the possession of goods *per se*, and especially the power of individuals to dispose, in principle freely, over the means of production. The existence of a capitalistic enterprise is preconditioned by a specific kind of "legal order." Each kind of class situation, and above all when it rests upon the power of property *per se*, will become most clearly efficacious when all other determinants of reciprocal relations are, as far as possible, eliminated in their significance. It is in this way that the utilization of the power of property in the market obtains its most sovereign importance.

Now "status groups" hinder the strict carrying through of the sheer market principle. In the present context they are of interest to us only from this one point of view. Before we briefly consider them, note that not much of a general nature can be said about the more specific kinds of antagonism between "classes" (in our meaning of the term). The great shift, which has been going on continuously in the past, and up to our times, may be summarized, although at the cost of some precision: the struggle in which class situations are effective has progressively shifted from consumption credit toward, first, competitive struggles in the commodity market and, then, toward price wars on the labor market. The "class struggles" of antiquity—to the extent that they were genuine class struggles and not struggles between status groups—were initially carried on by indebted peasants, and perhaps also by artisans threatened by debt bondage and struggling against urban creditors. For debt bondage is the normal result of the differentiation of wealth in commercial cities, especially in seaport cities. A similar situation has existed among cattle breeders. Debt relationships as such produced class action up to the time of Cataline. Along with this, and with an increase in provision of grain for the city by transporting it from the outside, the struggle over the means of sustenance emerged. It centered in the first place around the provision of bread and the determination of the price of bread. It lasted throughout antiquity and the entire Middle Ages. The propertyless as such flocked together against those who actually and supposedly were interested in the dearth of bread. This fight spread until it involved all those commodities essential to the way of life and to handicraft production. There were only incipient discussions of wage disputes in antiquity and in the Middle Ages. But they have been slowly increasing up into modern times. In the earlier periods they were completely secondary to slave rebellions as well as to fights in the commodity market.

The propertyless of antiquity and of the Middle Ages protested against monopolies, pre-emption, forestalling, and the withholding of goods from the market in order to raise prices. Today the central issue is the determination of the price of labor.

This transition is represented by the fight for access to the market and for the determination of the price of products. Such fights went on between merchants and workers in the putting-out system of domestic handicraft during the transition to modern times. Since it is quite a general phenomenon we must mention here that the class antagonisms that are conditioned through the market situation are usually most bitter between those who actually and directly participate as opponents in price wars. It is not the rentier, the share-holder, and the banker who suffer the ill will of the worker, but almost exclusively the manufacturer and the business executives who are the direct opponents of workers in price wars. This is so in spite of the fact that it is precisely the cash boxes of the rentier, the share-holder, and the banker into which the more or less "unearned" gains flow, rather than into the pockets of the manufacturers or of the business executives. This simple state of affairs has very frequently been decisive for the role the class situation has played in the formation of political parties. For example, it has made possible the varieties of patriarchal socialism and the frequent attempts—formerly, at least—of threatened status groups to form alliances with the proletariat against the "bourgeoisie."

5: STATUS HONOR

In contrast to classes, *status groups* are normally communities. They are, however, often of an amorphous kind. In contrast to the purely economically determined "class situation" we wish to designate as "status situation" every typical component of the life fate of men that is determined by a specific positive or negative, social estimation of *honor*. This honor may be connected with any quality shared by a plurality, and, of course, it can be knit to a class situation: class distinctions are linked in the most varied ways with status distinctions. Property as such is not always recognized as a status qualification, but in the long run it is, and with extraordinary regularity. In the subsistence economy of the organized neighborhood, very often the richest man is simply the chieftain. However, this often means only an honorific preference. For example, in the so-called pure modern "democracy," that is, one devoid of any expressly ordered status privileges for individuals, it may be that only the families coming under approximately the same tax class dance with one another. This example is reported of certain smaller Swiss cities. But status honor need not necessarily be linked with a "class situation." On the contrary, it normally stands in sharp opposition to the pretensions of sheer property.

Both propertied and propertyless people belong to the same status group, and frequently they do with very tangible consequences. This "equality" of social esteem may, however, in the long run become quite precarious. The "equality" of status among the American "gentlemen," for instance, is expressed by the fact that outside the subordination determined by the different functions of "business," it would be considered strictly repugnant—wherever the old tradition still prevails—if even the richest "chief," while playing billiards or cards in his club in the evening, would not treat his "clerk" as in every sense fully his equal in birth right. It would be repugnant if the American "chief" would bestow upon his "clerk" the condescending "benevolence" making a distinction of "position," which the German chief can never dissever from his attitude. This is one of the most important reasons why in America the German "clubby-ness" has never been able to attain the attraction that the American clubs have.

6: GUARANTEES OF STATUS STRATIFICATION

In content, status honor is normally expressed by the fact that above all else a specific *style of life* can be expected from all those who wish to belong to the circle. Linked with this expectation are restrictions on "social" intercourse (that is, intercourse which is not subservient to economic or any other of business's "functional" purposes). These restrictions may confine normal marriages to within the status circle and may lead to complete endogamous closure. As soon as there is not a mere individual and socially irrelevant imitation of another style of life, but an agreed-upon communal action of this closing character, the "status" development is under way.

In its characteristic form, stratification by "status group" on the basis of conventional styles of life evolves at the present time in the United States out of the traditional democracy. For example, only the resident of a certain street ("the street") is considered as belonging to "society," is qualified for social intercourse, and is visited and invited. Above all, this differentiation evolves in such a way as to make for strict submission to the fashion that is dominant at a given time in society. This submission to fashion also exists among men in America to a degree unknown in Germany. Such submission is considered to be an indication of the fact that a given man *pretends* to qualify as a gentleman. This submission decides, at least *prima facie*, that he will be treated as such. And this recognition becomes just as important for his employment chances in "swank" establishments, and above all, for social intercourse and marriage with "esteemed" families, as the qualification for dueling among Germans in the Kaiser's day. As for the rest: certain families resident for a long time, and, of course, correspondingly wealthy, e.g. "F.F.V., i.e. First Families of Virginia," or the actual or alleged descendants of the "Indian Princess" Pocahontas, of the Pilgrim fathers, or of the Knickerbockers, the members of almost inaccessible sects and all sorts of circles setting themselves apart by means of any other characteristics and badges . . . all these elements usurp "status" honor. The development of status is essentially a question of stratification resting upon usurpation. Such usurpation is the normal origin of almost all status honor. But the road from this purely conventional situation to legal privilege, positive or negative, is easily traveled as soon as a certain stratification of the social order has in fact been "lived in" and has achieved stability by virtue of a stable distribution of economic power.

7: "ETHNIC" SEGREGATION AND "CASTE"

Where the consequences have been realized to their full extent, the status group evolves into a closed "caste." Status distinctions are then guaranteed not merely by conventions and laws, but also by *rituals*. This occurs in such a way that every physical contact with a member of any caste that is considered to be "lower" by the members of a "higher" caste is considered as making for a ritualistic impurity and to be a stigma which must be expiated by a religious act. Individual castes develop quite distinct cults and gods.

In general, however, the status structure reaches such extreme consequences only where there are underlying differences which are held to be "ethnic." The "caste" is, indeed, the normal form in which ethnic communities usually live side by side in a "societalized" manner. These ethnic communities believe in blood relationship and exclude exogamous marriage and social intercourse. Such a caste situation is part of the phenomenon of "pariah" peoples and is found all over the world. These people form communities, acquire specific occupational traditions of handicrafts or of other arts, and cultivate a belief in their ethnic community. They live in a "dispora" strictly segregated from all personal intercourse, except that of an unavoidable sort, and their situation is legally precarious. Yet, by virtue of their economic indispensability, they are tolerated, indeed, frequently privileged, and they live in interspersed political communities. The Jews are the most impressive historical example.

A "status" segregation grown into a "caste" differs in its structure from a mere "ethnic" segregation: the caste structure transforms the horizontal and unconnected coexistences of ethnically segregated groups into a vertical social system of super- and subordination. Correctly formulated: a comprehensive societalization integrates the ethnically divided communities into specific political and communal action. In their consequences they differ precisely in this way: ethnic coexistences condition a mutual repulsion and disdain but allow each ethnic community to consider its own honor as the highest one; the cast structure brings about a social subordination and an acknowledgment of "more honor" in favor of the privileged caste and status groups. This is due to the fact that in the caste structure ethnic distinctions as such have become "functional" distinctions within the political societalization (warriors, priests, artisans that are politically important for war and for building, and so on). But even pariah people who are most despised are usually apt to continue cultivating in some manner that which is equally peculiar to ethnic and to status communities: the belief in their own specific "honor." This is the case with the Jews.

Only with the negatively privileged status groups does the "sense of dignity" take a specific deviation. A sense of dignity is the precipitation in individuals of social honor and of conventional demands which a positively privileged status group raises for the deportment of its members. The sense of dignity that characterizes positively privileged status groups is naturally related to their "being" which does not transcend itself, that is, it is to their "beauty and excellence" [(καλο-κἀγαθια)]. Their kingdom is "of this world." They live for the present and by exploiting their great past. The sense of dignity of the negatively privileged strata naturally refers to a future lying beyond the present, whether it is of this life or of another. In other words, it must be nurtured by the belief in a providential "mission" and by a belief in a specific honor before God. The "chosen people's" dignity is nurtured by a belief either that in the beyond "the last will be the first," or that in this life a Messiah will appear to bring forth into the light of the world which has cast them out the hidden honor of the pariah people. This simple state of affairs, and not the "resentment" which is so strongly emphasized in Nietzsche's much admired construction in the *Genealogy of Morals,* is the source of the religiosity cultivated by pariah status groups. In passing, we may note that resentment may be accurately applied only to a limited extent; for one of Nietzsche's main examples, Buddhism, it is not at all applicable.

Incidentally, the development of status groups from ethnic segregations is by no means the normal phenomenon. On the contrary, since objective "racial differences" are by no means basic to every subjective sentiment of an ethnic community, the ultimately racial foundation of status structure is rightly and absolutely a question of the concrete individual case. Very frequently a status group is instrumental in the production of a thoroughbred anthropological type. Certainly a status group is to a high degree effective in producing extreme types, for they select personally qualified individuals (e.g. the Knighthood selects those who are fit for warfare, physically and psychically). But selection is far from being the only, or the predominant, way in which status groups are formed: Political membership or class situation has at all times been at least as frequently decisive. And today the class situation is by far the predominant factor, for of course the possibility of a style of life expected for members of a status group is usually conditioned economically.

8: STATUS PRIVILEGES

For all practical purposes, stratification by status goes hand in hand with a monopolization of ideal and material goods or opportunities, in a manner we have come to know as typical. Besides the specific status honor, which always rests upon distance and exclusiveness, we find all sorts of material monopolies. Such honorific preferences may consist of the privilege of wearing special costumes, of eating special dishes taboo to others, of carrying arms—which is most obvious in its consequences—the right to pursue certain non-professional dilettante artistic practices, e.g. to play certain musical instruments. Of course, material monopolies provide the most effective motives for the exclusiveness of a status group; although, in themselves, they are rarely sufficient, almost always they come into play to some extent. Within a status circle there is the question of intermarriage: the interest of the families in the monopolization of potential bridegrooms is at

least of equal importance and is parallel to the interest in the monopolization of daughters. The daughters of the circle must be provided for. With
an increased inclosure of the status group, the conventional preferential opportunities for special employment grow into a legal monopoly of special
offices for the members. Certain goods become objects for monopolization
by status groups. In the typical fashion these include "entailed estates" and
frequently also the possessions of serfs or bondsmen and, finally, special
trades. This monopolization occurs positively when the status group is exclusively entitled to own and to manage them; and negatively when, in
order to maintain its specific way of life, the status group must *not* own
and manage them.

The decisive role of a "style of life" in status "honor" means that status
groups are the specific bearers of all "conventions." In whatever way it may
be manifest, all "stylization" of life either originates in status groups or is at
least conserved by them. Even if the principles of status conventions differ
greatly, they reveal certain typical traits, especially among those strata
which are most privileged. Quite generally, among privileged status groups
there is a status disqualification that operates against the performance of
common physical labor. This disqualification is now "setting in" in America
against the old tradition of esteem for labor. Very frequently every rational economic pursuit, and especially "entrepreneurial activity," is looked
upon as a disqualification of status. Artistic and literary activity is also considered as degrading work as soon as it is exploited for income, or at least
when it is connected with hard physical exertion. An example is the
sculptor working like a mason in his dusty smock as over against the
painter in his salon-like "studio" and those forms of musical practice that
are acceptable to the status group.

9: ECONOMIC CONDITIONS AND EFFECTS OF STATUS STRATIFICATION

The frequent disqualification of the gainfully employed as such
is a direct result of the principle of status stratification peculiar to the social
order, and of course, of this principle's opposition to a distribution of
power which is regulated exclusively through the market. These two factors
operate along with various individual ones, which will be touched upon
below.

We have seen above that the market and its processes "knows no personal distinctions": "functional" interests dominate it. It knows nothing of
"honor." The status order means precisely the reverse, viz.: stratification
in terms of "honor" and of styles of life peculiar to status groups as such.
If mere economic acquisition and naked economic power still bearing the

stigma of its extra-status origin could bestow upon anyone who has won it the same honor as those who are interested in status by virtue of style of life claim for themselves, the status order would be threatened at its very root. This is the more so as, given equality of status honor, property *per se* represents an addition even if it is not overtly acknowledged to be such. Yet if such economic acquisition and power gave the agent any honor at all, his wealth would result in his attaining more honor than those who successfully claim honor by virtue of style of life. Therefore all groups having interests in the status order react with special sharpness precisely against the pretensions of purely economic acquisition. In most cases they react the more vigorously the more they feel themselves threatened. Calderon's respectful treatment of the peasant, for instance, as opposed to Shakespeare's simultaneous and ostensible disdain of the *canaille* illustrates the different way in which a firmly structured status order reacts as compared with a status order that has become economically precarious. This is an example of a state of affairs that recurs everywhere. Precisely because of the rigorous reactions against the claims of property *per se*, the "parvenu" is never accepted, personally and without reservation, by the privileged status groups, no matter how completely his style of life has been adjusted to theirs. They will only accept his descendants who have been educated in the conventions of their status group and who have never besmirched its honor by their own economic labor.

As to the general *effect* of the status order, only one consequence can be stated, but it is a very important one: the hindrance of the free development of the market occurs first for those goods which status groups directly withheld from free exchange by monopolization. This monopolization may be effected either legally or conventionally. For example, in many Hellenic cities during the epoch of status groups, and also originally in Rome, the inherited estate (as is shown by the old formula for indiction against spendthrifts) was monopolized just as were the estates of knights, peasants, priests, and especially the clientele of the craft and merchant guilds. The market is restricted, and the power of naked property *per se*, which gives its stamp to "class formation," is pushed into the background. The results of this process can be most varied. Of course, they do not necessarily weaken the contrasts in the economic situation. Frequently they strengthen these contrasts, and in any case, where stratification by status permeates a community as strongly as was the case in all political communities of antiquity and of the Middle Ages, one can never speak of a genuinely free market competition as we understand it today. There are wider effects than this direct exclusion of special goods from the market. From the contrariety between the status order and the purely economic order mentioned above, it follows that in most instances the notion of honor peculiar to status absolutely abhors that which is essential to the market: higgling. Honor abhors higgling among peers and occasionally it taboos higgling for the members of a status group in general. Therefore, everywhere some status groups, and usually the most influential, consider almost any kind of overt participation in economic acquisition as absolutely stigmatizing.

With some over-simplification, one might thus say that "classes" are stratified according to their relations to the production and acquisition of goods; whereas "status groups" are stratified according to the principles of their *consumption* of goods as represented by special "styles of life."

An "occupational group" is also a status group. For normally, it successfully claims social honor only by virtue of the special style of life which may be determined by it. The difference between classes and status groups frequently overlap. It is precisely those status communities most strictly segregated in terms of honor (viz. the Indian castes) who today show, although within very rigid limits, a relatively high degree of indifference to pecuniary income. However, the Brahmins seek such income in many different ways.

As to the general economic conditions making for the predominance of stratification by "status," only very little can be said. When the bases of the acquisition and distribution of goods are relatively stable, stratification by status is favored. Every technological repercussion and economic transformation threatens stratification by status and pushes the class situation into the foreground. Epochs and countries in which the naked class situation is of predominant significance are regularly the periods of technical and economic transformations. And every slowing down of the shifting of economic stratifications leads, in due course, to the growth of status structures and makes for a resuscitation of the important role of social honor.

10: PARTIES

Whereas the genuine place of "classes" is within the economic order, the place of "status groups" is within the social order, that is, within the sphere of the distribution of "honor." From within these spheres, classes and status groups influence one another and they influence the legal order and are in turn influenced by it. But "parties" live in a house of "power."

Their action is oriented toward the acquisition of social "power," that is to say, toward influencing a communal action no matter what its content may be. In principle, parties may exist in a social "club" as well as in a "state." As over against the actions of classes and status groups, for which this is not necessarily the case, the communal actions of "parties" always mean a societalization. For party actions are always directed toward a goal which is striven for in planned manner. This goal may be a "cause" (the party may aim at realizing a program for ideal or material purposes), or the goal may be "personal" (sinecures, power, and from these, honor for the leader and the followers of the party). Usually the party action aims at all these simultaneously. Parties are, therefore, only possible within communities that are societalized, that is, which have some rational order and a staff of persons available who are ready to enforce it. For parties aim precisely at influencing this staff, and if possible, to recruit it from party followers.

In any individual case, parties may represent interests determined through "class situation" or "status situation," and they may recruit their following respectively from one or the other. But they need be neither purely "class" nor purely "status" parties. In most cases they are partly class parties and partly status parties, but sometimes they are neither. They may represent ephemeral or enduring structures. Their means of attaining power may be quite varied, ranging from naked violence of any sort to canvassing for votes with coarse or subtle means: money, social influence, the force of speech, suggestion, clumsy hoax, and so on to the rougher or more artful tactics of obstruction in parliamentary bodies.

The sociological structure of parties differs in a basic way according to the kind of communal action which they struggle to influence. Parties also differ according to whether or not the community is stratified by status or by classes. Above all else, they vary according to the structure of domination within the community. For their leaders normally deal with the conquest of a community. They are, in the general concept which is maintained here, not only products of specially modern forms of domination. We shall also designate as parties the ancient and medieval "parties," despite the fact that their structure differs basically from the structure of modern parties. By virtue of these structural differences of domination it is impossible to say anything about the structure of parties without discussing the structural forms of social domination *per se*. Parties, which are always structures struggling for domination, are very frequently organized in a very strict "authoritarian" fashion . . .

Concerning "classes," "status groups" and "parties," it must be said in general that they necessarily presuppose a comprehensive societalization, and especially a political framework of communal action, within which they operate. This does not mean that parties would be confined by the frontiers of any individual political community. On the contrary, at all times it has been the order of the day that the societalization (even when it aims at the use of military force in common) reaches beyond the frontiers of politics. This has been the case in the solidarity of interests among the Oligarchs and among the democrats in Hellas, among the Guelfs and among the Ghibellines in the Middle Ages, and within the Calvinist party during the period of religious struggles. It has been the case up to the solidarity of the landlords (international congress of agrarian landlords), and has continued among princes (holy alliance, Karlsbad decrees), socialist workers, conservatives (the longing of Prussian conservatives for Russian intervention in 1850). But their aim is not necessarily the establishment of new international political, i.e., *territorial*, dominion. In the main they aim to influence the existing dominion.*

*The posthumously published text breaks off here.

NOTES ON THE OBSERVATION
AND MEASUREMENT OF POLITICAL POWER

Herbert A. Simon

In this selection we shift from an emphasis on the bases or sources of power to a discussion of the problems of defining and assessing power. Herbert Simon conceives of power in terms of causation, i.e., power is causing change in behavior. He is fundamentally concerned with understanding the interpersonal action involved in a power situation and with proposing ways in which such interaction may be quantified. As the reader proceeds to subsequent selections in this volume, he will note that Simon's statement of the three requirements of observable data in power analysis is later to be translated into three methods of analyzing community power systems, i.e., in order, the decision-making analysis, the stratified distribution of the resources of influence, and the reputational methods. This article was a pioneering effort to quantify the interpersonal elements of power. The basic concepts it develops preview a substantial body of later theorizing, especially by political scientists, as we shall see in later selections.

If political power is taken as one of the central phenomena to be explained by political science, then the propositions of political science will necessarily contain sentences and phrases like "the power of A is greater than the power of B," "an increase (or decrease) in the power of A," "the distribution of political power," and the like. And if the empirical truth or falsity of such propositions is to be tested, there must be agreement as to the operational definition of the term "power" and the operational means that are to be used to determine the degree of its presence or absence in any situation.

All of this is elementary enough—but how far has the task been carried out; to what extent have the operational tools of observation and measurement been provided us? That a great deal remains to be done can be made

From Herbert Simon, "Notes on the Observation and Measurement of Power," *Journal of Politics*, XV (November, 1953), 500–512, 514–516. Reprinted by permission of the publisher and the author.

clear, I think, by an outrageous example. Suppose that, in the presence of a boorishly critical skeptic, we were to assert: "Peron holds a monopoly of power in Argentina." Suppose that our skeptic were to reply: "Prove it." We could, of course, adopt the tactics of Dr. Johnson who, when asked to prove the existence of the table at which he was sitting, suggested that his disputant kick it. While this reply has never been adjudged entirely adequate by metaphysicians, kicking a table would certainly settle the question of its existence to the satisfaction of most empirical scientists. But how, precisely, does one "kick" a dictatorship to find out if it exists? If I kicked Peron, I would go to jail; but I would also if I kicked the King of England, who is not usually regarded as a dictator.

Now I do not doubt that Peron is dictator of Argentina; nor (a slightly more difficult point to establish) that the King is not dictator of England; nor (an even more subtle point) that Stalin was dictator of Russia at a time when he held no official governmental position whatsoever. Nor will I ask the reader to doubt these propositions. I will ask the reader, however, to join me in an inquiry into the meanings of propositions like those just stated, and into the means for establishing the truth of such propositions—which truth, in spite of the appearance of self-evidence, can certainly be confirmed only by empirical data. In general, our inquiry may be regarded as a series of footnotes on the analysis of influence and power by Lasswell and Kaplan in *Power and Society*, which we will take as the starting point.

SKETCH OF A DEFINITION OF THE TERM "POWER"

Like Humpty Dumpty, we will insist that a word means what we want it to mean. But if our aim is to construct a body of science, and if we already have in view the general range of phenomena to be explained, our definitions may be willful, but they must not be arbitrary. If we were to say that we would measure a man's power by his height, this would be an internally consistent definition, but one hardly useful in exploring the phenomena referred to in common speech as the phenomena of power. If we were to say that we would measure a man's power by his wealth *or* his ability to influence the behavior of others, the definition would not even be internally consistent, for these two criteria might in fact be only imperfectly correlated.[1]

---

[1]As we shall see, Harold D. Lasswell and Abraham Kaplan, in their otherwise very incisive analysis of power in *Power and Society* (New Haven: Yale University Press, 1950) came dangerously close to this latter error, being saved from it only by distinguishing between "influence" and "exercise of influence." Since their terminological convention is certainly inconvenient and confusing, I shall not follow it. Instead, I shall retain "value position" and "value potential" in place of their "influence," and use "influence" for their "exercise of influence."

Power and value position. I think that definitions which equate influence or power[2] with the values an individual possesses are unsuitable for political science. The difficulty is revealed when we try to state what we mean by a "value." If we list specific values—wealth, wisdom, or what not —then the statement that "A possesses certain of these values" is not what we mean when we say "A has power." For if these two statements are regarded as identical by definition, then a proposition like "the wealthy are the powerful"—dear to Marxists and anti-Marxists alike—ceases to be an empirical proposition in political science, and becomes true simply by definition.

A second defect of such definitions is that they confront us with the necessity of inventing new values to account for persons whom we wish to regard as powerful, but whose values lie outside the usual lists—Gandhi is a good example.

The situation becomes even worse if we admit power into the list of social values that define power. That power is a value, i.e., something desired and valued, is generally admitted; but if so, to define power as value position renders meaningless propositions like: "We can measure a person's power by his ability to acquire power."[3]

To summarize, I propose to define power and influence in such a way as to distinguish these concepts from value position. In doing so, I believe I am conforming to common usage, because (a) propositions, intended to be empirical, are often asserted with respect to the relation between power and value position, and (b) power is often asserted to be a value (but not the only value) that is desired.

If, having made a distinction between power and value position, we are able to establish an empirical relationship between the two, we can then use value position as an *index* of power—which is something quite different from using it as the defining operation. I think that we can conjecture what the relationship is likely to be. When a society is in a state of stable equilibrium, there is likely to be a close correspondence between the distribution of power and the distribution of value. If this is so, then, *in equilibrium situations*, we can use the value distribution as an index of the power distribution when the latter is difficult to ascertain directly.

Power and value potential. Objections similar to those just mentioned can be raised against defining power or influence as synonymous with value potential. Value potential (see Lasswell and Kaplan, p. 58) is simply value position referred to some future date. As before, such a definition would transform from empirical propositions to definitional identities such statements as: "Those who have power will employ it to improve their value

---

[2] It is not necessary, for present purposes, to distinguish between influence and power, and I shall continue to use the two words as synonyms.

[3] On the other hand, if power is independently defined, this proposition becomes an empirical statement about the dynamics of power.

position"—which is roughly equivalent to: "Those who have power have high value potential."

In fact, the two definition proposals examined thus far—relating power to value position and value potential, respectively—reveal that even at the empirical level we are not certain as to the relationship between the possession of values and of power. Does possession of power imply high value position or high potentiality of improving value position? In the previous section I suggested that, in equilibrium situations, we assume an empirical relationship to exist between value *position* and power in order to predict the latter from the former. In non-equilibrium situations, we often employ an assumed relationship between power and value *potential* to predict the latter from the former. These empirical dynamic relations may be represented diagrammatically thus:

Value Position → Power → Value Potential (Future Value Position).

An alternative definition. As an alternative to the definitions just discarded, we propose the definition of "influence process" employed by Lasswell and Kaplan: "The *exercise of influence* (influence process) consists in affecting policies of others than the self."

This definition involves an asymmetrical relation between influencer and influencee. Now we are wary, in the social sciences, of asymmetrical relations. They remind us of pre-Humeian and pre-Newtonian notions of causality. By whip and sword we have been converted to the doctrine that there is no causation, only functional interrelation, and that functional relations are perfectly symmetrical. We may even have taken over, as a very persuasive analogy, the proposition that "for every action, there is an equal and opposite reaction." If, in spite of this, we persist in thinking that there is something asymmetrical about the influence (or power) relation, it may be reassuring that quite similar relations can be introduced into the most respectable of physical systems.

It should be noticed also that the Lasswell-Kaplan definition refers to processes of change rather than to a state of equilibrium. Presumably, we observe the influence of A over B by noting the differences between the way B actually behaves and the way he *would* behave if A were not present (or if A's desires changed). Influence belongs to the theory of dynamics, or of comparative statics, rather than to the theory of equilibrium.

ASYMMETRY OF THE POWER RELATION

The notion that the power or influence relation of A to B is asymmetrical carries with it some implication as to how the phenomenon of power can be observed and measured. Let us first consider the case where the asymmetry is supposed to be complete; i.e., A influences B, but B does not influence A at all. Then, if we are dealing with a determinate system, the behavior of A can be predicted without any reference to his relation to B, while the behavior of B follows once we know the behavior of A. Stated otherwise, the social system as a whole must contain a subsystem, that determines the behavior of A, but in which B does not appear (or at least B's reactions to A's behavior do not appear).

Now to determine the influence of A upon B, we simply observe a number of situations in which the behavior of A varies, and note what is the concomitant variation in B's behavior. As a concrete example, let us suppose that a dictator is "unilaterally coupled" to his subjects—his decisions determine their behavior, but there is no "feedback" from their behavior to his. Then, if by manipulating the variables that determine his own expectations or desires we can change his decisions, we can also observe what changes this brings about in the behavior of the subjects.

Power in the presence of feedback. It will immediately be objected that we are never faced with a situation involving unilateral coupling in this extreme sense—that there is always some feedback from the influencee to the influencer. This difficulty can be handled in either of two ways: (1) we can give up the idea that the relation is asymmetrical; or (2) we can add an asymmetrical relation operating in the opposite direction from the first. *If the processes of influence take time,* and particularly if the time lags associated with the two asymmetrical relations are different, there is at least the possibility that we can make separate empirical observations of the two relations.

If, in our previous example, our dictator makes a decision, and if he is sensitive to public approval and disapproval, then we will observe in sequence: (1) the decision, (2) subsequent changes in behavior of the subjects, (3) expressions of approval or disapproval by the subjects, and (4) modifications in the decision if it proves to be unpopular. In favorable cases, the feedback may involve large time lags. If, instead of a dictator, we have an elected president, the feedback might take the form of a change in the holder of the office at the next election.

Now, if there is any feedback at all, measurement of influence requires the observation of disequilibrium as well as equilibrium. In a state of equilibrium in the case of the elected president, the last previous election would have already put in office a president whose decisions would be acceptable to the citizens—it would be impossible to determine whether the chicken was mother or daughter of the egg.

The role of anticipated reactions. But an even graver difficulty must be admitted. Because of the phenomenon that Friedrich has christened "the rule of anticipated reactions" and that the servomechanism engineer calls "anticipatory control," the time lags upon which we depend for measurement may be destroyed. If the President is elected, his decisions may be affected not only by what the citizens did in the last election, but also by his expectations of what they will do in the next.

I think it can be seen that the possibility of measuring the separate links in the chain of influence depend, in this instance, on the presence of some ignorance in the system. So long as the President is able to form exact expectations of the citizens' reactions, and they of what a candidate will do if elected, his influence on them cannot be distinguished from their influence on him, but let his or their forecasts be in error and the possibilities of disentangling the relations are re-established.

Fortunately for political scientists—who would otherwise be largely debarred from observation of the central phenomenon of their science—the members of the body politic are often far from accurate in their predictions. If President Roosevelt had foreseen the outcome of the 1938 "purges" he might not have undertaken them, and we should have been deprived of valuable information about influences on voting behavior. If the assassination of Lincoln had been anticipated, we would have lost instructive insights into the relative powers of President and Congress provided by the administration of Andrew Johnson. The unpredicted and the unexpected provide a break in the usual chain of intended connections and, serving as something of a substitute for controlled experimentation, permit us to observe the construction of the separate links.

Implications of the definition. Apart from the question of measurement, the habit of viewing a social structure as a network of (generally) asymmetrical relationships can help to clarify some of the ambiguities that are commonly found in statements of power relationships. This formulation teaches us that, when we wish to speak of the influence of a particular element in a social system upon that system, we must specify whether we mean the influence of the element considered as independent, with all the reverse feedback relations ignored, or whether we mean the net influence of the element, taking into account all the reciprocal influences of other elements upon it. Concretely, how powerful we consider the President to be depends on whether we ignore, or take into consideration, the fact that he is an elected official, and the fact that he is advised by a corps of permanent civil servants.

If we regard the President as an "independent variable," then we arrive at one assessment of his influence. If we add to our system the environmental influences created by the administrative bureaucracy, which greatly restrict the variability that differences in personal qualities and beliefs would otherwise produce in the behavior of different presidents, we arrive at a smaller estimate of the influence of those personal qualities and beliefs.

As an exercise for developing his skill in handling both this distinction and the rule of anticipated reactions, the reader may like to test his wits on the proposition: "The power of the President can be measured by the number of bills he vetoes where the veto is not overridden."

The interpretation of influence as unilateral coupling corresponds reasonably well with our everyday intuitive notions. We would ordinarily argue that it makes a greater difference to events in the United States if a Justice of the Supreme Court or a United States Senator is replaced than if John Jones, an Idaho potato farmer, retires and turns over his farm to his son. What we are saying here is that the personal characteristics of the individual occupying a particular position (a judgeship or a senatorial seat) constitutes a variable upon which other variables in the system depend. The influence of any position, according to this notion, is proportional to the amount of change induced throughout the system by a change in the characteristics of the individual occupying the position in question.

THE EXERCISE OF INFLUENCE AND THE INFLUENCE BASE

Direct measurements of influence are obtained when we can observe the ratio of change in behavior of influence to change in behavior of influencer. If, starting with such measurements, we are able to determine empirically the conditions that make for influence—the characteristics of individuals and situations that permit us to predict that the influence of a particular individual will be large—then we can derive from these empirical relationships additional indirect measurements of influence. In particular, if we can measure the magnitude of the influence *base*, we can infer from this the magnitude of the influence. (E.g., if wealth is the principal influence base in a particular situation—the principal means for exercising influence—then in that situation we may measure influence by wealth.)

Dynamic relationships. Now there are generally intricate relationships among the bases of influence and the values that are sought. In the first place, influence is the means, in rational social behavior, of securing the values that are desired. Hence, influence itself, and consequently the bases of influence also become something valued as means to other values. Moreover, many of the bases of influence may be valued *both* as means for the exercise of influence and for other reasons as well.

Wealth will serve as an example. Wealth, in most societies, is a base of influence, hence, a means for securing values. But wealth is also valued for the consumption it permits and the deference it commands. Now consider the extreme case of a society in which wealth is the only influence base, and where consumption and deference are the only values. In such a society, *investment* is the use of influence to augment the influence base, *consumption* is the use of influence to augment other values without increase in the influence base.

Similar dynamic relationships apply to influence bases other than wealth. Political power, too, can be "invested"—control of a legislature may be employed to gerrymander legislative districts in order to ensure continued control. It can also be consumed, to obtain desired legislation, sometimes at the expense of future power.

I have spelled out these dynamic relationships to emphasize the point made earlier that it is essential to distinguish between the operations that measure influence directly, and the indirect estimates of influence that can be inferred from measurements of the influence base. It is often true that influence is used to obtain value. (This accounts for the relationship between influence and value potential.) It is often true that value position provides the influence base. (This accounts for the relationship between influence and value position.) It is often true that influence is employed to augment future influence. In the scheme proposed here, these are all empirical relationships that should not be confused with definitional identities.

Comments on the nature of the influence base. The term "influence base" has been used here to refer to the conditions for the exercise of influence. The influence base is by no means synonymous with the value position, although there are two significant connections between them. First, when values are exchangeable, they can be given to others in return for desired behavior. It is in this sense that values provide a base for influence. Second, any condition that gives its possessor influence is likely to become a desideratum—a value. It is not because being a Supreme Court Justice is valued that such a Justice has influence; but, conversely, it is because he has influence that the position is valued.[4]

Because the connection between influence base and value is not always the same, a classification of influence bases in terms of the values related to them is rather superficial. A more fundamental basis for classification is with respect to the motivation of the influences that leads him to accept influence. On this basis, Lasswell and Kaplan define three successively narrower terms: (a) influence (encompassing all motivations for acceptance); (b) power (acceptance motivated by sanctions); and (c) authority (acceptance motivated by attitudes toward legitimacy).

There has been some tendency in the literature of political science to regard ordinary sanctions, like money and physical force, as the bases of "effective" power, and legitimacy as the base of "formal" power. The implication of this kind of language is that "effective" power is what determines actual behavior, while "formal" power is some kind of epiphenomenal rationalization of the power structure—window-dressing, so to

---

[4]To be sure, the connection can be even more complicated in a society where persons having a high value position are regarded as possessing the legitimate right to exercise influence. An example would be a prestigious scientist whose pronouncements on theology and politics are given respectful attention. But, properly speaking, the influence base in this case is not prestige but the rules of legitimacy in the society. I think the point will be clear after we have discussed, in the next paragraphs, the concept of legitimacy.

speak.[5] Some political scientists, however, Charles Merriam being a notable example, insist on legitimacy as an important independent motivation for the acceptance of power.

Which of these viewpoints is correct—and to what extent—is an empirical question. The definitions we have thus far constructed indicate, at least schematically, what kinds of data would be needed to answer the question. What is required is a situation in which we can observe: (a) the distribution of power as indicated by behavior changes of influencees as a function of behavior changes of influencers; (b) the distribution of monetary, physical, and similar sanctions among the influencers; and (c) the attitudes of influencees toward legitimacy, and their beliefs as to where legitimate power lies. Situations where there is the greatest possible discrepancy between the possession of sanctions and the possession of legitimacy would be the most rewarding. Many clearcut examples of the discrepancy between power bases can be found, of course, in revolutions. An example of a more subtle situation that could profitably be examined from this viewpoint is the behavior of the United States Senate in the 1937 fight over the Supreme Court bill. I will not try to prejudge the evidence except to state my personal conviction that legitimacy will turn out to be a far from epiphenomenal aspect of the power structure.

Expectations and the power base. An empirical study of this problem will not proceed very far without disclosing another crucial behavioral variable: the *expectation* of each of the participants about the behavior of the others. I refer not merely to the obscuring effects of the rule of anticipated reactions, discussed earlier, but to the fact that the consequences an individual thinks will follow on his actions depend on what action he thinks other individuals will take.

A political régime prescribes appropriate behavior rôles to its participants; these rôles include appropriate actions to constrain any particular participant (or small group of participants) who departs from his rôle. But the constraints will be applied only if the remaining participants (or most of them) continue to play their rôles. Hence, most of the sanctions a political régime has at its disposal—whether they consist of money, force, attitudes toward legitimacy, or what not—disappear at once when a large number of the participants act in concert to depart from their rôles.

To each individual in a political régime, consequently, the régime looks exceedingly stable so long as he expects the other individuals to support it; it looks exceedingly unstable when he pictures himself as acting in concert with a large number of others to overthrow it. Hence, estimates of the stability of a political structure depend not only on observation of the distribution of actual power, or of the distribution of the power base; but equally upon estimates of the capacity of subgroups for co-ordinated action.

It follows from this that power and influence, measured in terms of the definitions we have proposed, are not additive quantities. Every observation of a power relationship makes an assumption, whether explicit or implicit, as to the pattern of expectation and of group co-ordination. Such an observation will have predictive value, in general, only so long as this assumption holds.

To take a specific example, if we were to make some observations as to the power of a political party to discipline an individual member, we would probably reach conclusions that would be completely inapplicable to the question of the party's power to discipline an organized dissenting clique.

Expectations as a means of measuring power. At this point we might revert to a point raised at the beginning of this paper: how do we know that Peron is dictator of Argentina? If we accept the proposition we have just been urging, that expectations of consequences are a major determinant of behavior, then we can use such expectations, so long as the situation remains stable, to estimate where power lies.

We are faced here with an example of a self-confirming prophecy. Suppose we are able to ascertain that the people of Argentina really believe that Peron is dictator. It follows that they will expect sanctions to be applied to themselves if they do not accept the decisions of the Peron régime. Hence, so long as these expectations remain they will behave as if Peron were dictator, and indeed, he will be.

It seems to me that this is the valid core of the naive method we commonly employ as political scientists when, seeking to determine the power structure in a particular situation, we ask the participants what the power structure is. This procedure is valid to the extent that the expectations of the participants constitute the power base. It gives us, in fact, an indirect measure of influence in the same way that data on wealth, or on attitudes of legitimacy, give us indirect measures of influence.

Now if this technique of observation is to be used sophisticatedly, certain cautions must be observed. First, such observations fail to reveal wheels within wheels in the power mechanism. Peron decides for Argentina, but who decides for Peron? Second, when expectations diverge from the other elements in the power base, they may conceal the fragility of the power structure. We have seen that revolution involves, above all, a change in the expectations, and this will be revealed only at the moment of revolution.

Both of these points can be illuminated by looking at the phenomenon of the "figurehead." The holder of power begins to move toward the status of figurehead when his behavior is no longer an "independent variable" but is itself determined by his submission to power. This can take place in at least two ways. First, he may be aware of sanctions to which he is subject that are not apparent to others (if he makes the wrong decision, the secret police will assassinate him, or his mistress will refuse to sleep with him). In this case, he becomes a figurehead when the existence of these sanctions becomes known, for this knowledge will alter the expectations to conform to the "real" power structure. (Of course, other power bases enter to modify the course of events—he may continue to wield power because feelings of legitimacy attach to him.)

Second, the power holder may sense that the system of expectations is fragile—that revolution is imminent unless he anticipates the reactions to his exercise of power and restrains it within limits. Again, when awareness develops of his self-restraint, expectations will begin to change and he will begin to lose his power. It can hardly be doubted that this was a central process in the movement of England from a monarchical to a democratic government.

With this we may close our comments on the influence base—the conditions for the exercise of influence. We have seen that influence and the bases of influence are distinct and separately observable concepts; and that independent observation of them is required to assess the relative effectiveness of various influence bases in the influence process. Finally, we have seen that observations of the exercise of influence must, to be meaningful, be accompanied by observations of the expectations and capacities for cooperative action of the various subgroups acting in the power arena.

THE UNITS OF OBSERVATION

Our definition of influence leaves quite ambiguous the kinds of units in which degrees of influence might be expressed. The quantities with which we are most familiar are those measured in *cardinal numbers:* A weighs 200 pounds; he weighs twice as much as B. Sometimes we deal with a "weaker" kind of number, the *ordinal number*, which permits us to say that: "A is cleverer than B," but not: "A is twice as clever as B." We may also be aware of quantities that are not single numbers but pairs, triples, or n-tuples of numbers (usually called *vectors*). If A has five oranges and three apples, we may denote his possessions by the vector (5,3). We can say that A has more than B, who has (4,2); but we cannot compare A with C, who has (4,5). We cannot say that D has twice as many as A unless he has exactly twice as many apples *and* twice as many oranges.

All of these kinds of quantities, and others as well, occur in the physical sciences. Mass is a cardinal number, hardness an ordinal number, and force a vector. We should expect to find at least as rich a variety of quantities in the social sciences. Hence, we must ask ourselves what "kind" of a quantity best represents influence and power.[6]

I do not propose to tackle the problem in all its generality, but will, instead, examine one broad class of situations that I think is of significance. The particular class of power relations with which I shall be concerned is usually denoted by the term "authority," and I shall retain that term although it is used in a very different sense by Lasswell and Kaplan.[7]

We will say that an individual accepts *authority* when his choice among alternative behaviors is determined by the communicated decision of another. The acceptance of authority may stem from any combination whatsoever of the bases of power—monetary inducements, force, legitimacy, or any others. Authority is never unlimited—the range of alternative behaviors from which the superior may select the particular choice he desires of the subordinate is a finite range. The limits within which authority will be accepted we will call the *zone of acceptance*.

It is clear from the definition that authority is a form of influence: when A exercises authority over B, he exercises influence over B. Hence, a measurement of authority will be a measurement of at least one form of influence.

Let us regard each possible behavior that B can perform as an element in a set, and let us designate the set of all such possible behaviors by V. The set of behaviors that B will perform at A's command (the subset of V corresponding to B's zone of acceptance) we will designate by S. Then we can use the size of the set S as a measure of A's authority over B.

But what kind of a quantity is the size of S? Suppose that at one time B will accept any order in the set S, but at some later time he will only accept orders in S', which is a part of S. Then we are surely justified in saying that A's authority has decreased. Under such circumstances, comparisons of "greater" and "less" are possible. But it may happen that the zone of acceptance changes from S' to S'' where these are intersecting (overlapping) sets neither of which entirely includes the other. In this case we cannot say that A's authority has increased or that it has decreased—our sets are not completely ordered. The kind of quantity that appears most suitable for measuring the degree of authority of A over B is what the mathematician would call a "partial ordering."

Now this may seem a disappointing result—we started off with brave

[6]I believe that most of the arguments against "quantitizing" or "measuring" the "qualitative" variables encountered in the social sciences stem from ignorance of how flexible the concept "quantity" is, and how indefinite the lines between quantity and quality. Such arguments are particularly suspect when it is asserted in one sentence that a particular variable is "essentially qualitative" and in the next that the adjectives "more" or "less" can be predicated of it.

[7]As has been stated previously, in *Power and Society*, authority denotes power based on legitimacy.

talk about "measuring" and have ended with some statements about more or less inclusive sets. The point is that whatever quantities we construct must reflect the characteristics of the phenomena we propose to measure with them. Ordinary cardinal (or even ordinal) numbers possess the property that they are completely ordered. If power relations are only partially ordered, then we shall certainly end up by talking nonsense about them if we insist that they should be represented by cardinal numbers, or that we should always be able to predicate "greater" or "less" of them. If we feel disappointment, it should be directed at the phenomena with which we are confronted rather than at the kind of quantity that appears to represent them.

I must hasten to point out that the above discussion does not in any sense prove that it is impossible to associate cardinal numbers with authority relations. It often happens that, starting with sets of elements, we can associate a cardinal number with each set in such a way that the resulting complete ordering is consistent with the partial ordering defined by the sets themselves. (The cardinal number associated with each set measures, in some sense, its "size.") This is precisely what the tax assessor does when he associates with Jones' set of tangible possessions a number that represents the (presumed) amount of money for which these possessions could be exchanged in the market.

Putting aside the question of using cardinal numbers to measure the "sizes" of different zones of acceptance, we may ask how the sets themselves may be observed and measured. The procedure is relatively straightforward; we observe what kinds of decisions are accepted and what kinds are not. If His Majesty's first minister decides that several hundred additional lords shall be created to establish the supremacy of the House of Commons, will His Majesty accede to the request? The observation falls within our general definition of influence: how does the behavior of the influencee vary with the behavior (in this case the decision) of the influencer?

The difficulties that are generally involved in the observation of influence are present here also. Because of the rule of anticipated reactions, the influencee may behave in accordance with the anticipated decision, never expressed, of the influencer; and the influencer will seldom issue commands that he knows in advance lie outside the zone of acceptance of the influencee—the limits will seldom be observed except when predictions are faulty. Because of the effect of expectations, the zone of acceptance may be suddenly narrowed when the influencee judges that he will be joined in resistance to authority by others.

To pursue these matters further would carry us rapidly into some rather difficult mathematical questions. If we attempted to construct mathematical models for formulating and analyzing authority relations we would be led,

I think, to models resembling very closely those employed by von Neumann and Morgenstern in their *Theory of Games and Economic Behavior.* . . .

CONCLUSION

Let us now draw together the threads of our discussion. The problem posed at the outset was how we can make observations and measurements of the distribution of influence and power. The definition of the key terms—"influence" and "power"—is the first step toward an answer. The position taken here is that the phenomenon we wish to measure is an asymmetrical relation between the behavior of two persons. We wish to observe how a change in the behavior of one (the influencer) alters the behavior of the other (the influencee).

We have seen that in most situations, all sorts of reciprocal power relations are present, and that their observation is complicated by the anticipation of reactions. The more accurate the predictions of participants in the system of the reactions of others, the more difficult it becomes to observe influence. Our main hope must be that human beings will remain fallible in their predictions.

To the extent that we can establish empirically the conditions for the exercise of power, these conditions, or influence bases, provide an indirect means for measurement. Observations of the distribution of values and of attitudes regarding legitimacy constitute two significant kinds of indirect evidence about the distribution of power. A third, of critical significance, are the expectations of the participants in the power situation.

In a final section we examined the types of units in terms of which measurement might be expressed. Our principal conclusion here is that we must be prepared to admit into our measurement schemes many other kinds of units besides cardinal numbers. In particular, certain notions from set theory, such as the concept of partial ordering among sets, may be suggestive of fruitful schemes of measurement.

CHAPTER TWO

Alternative "Models" of Local Power Systems: Some Significant Community Studies

MIDDLETOWN'S "X" FAMILY: A PATTERN OF BUSINESS-CLASS CONTROL

Robert S. and Helen M. Lynd

Robert and Helen Lynd's studies of Muncie, Indiana (population 35,000 at the time of research), were among the first efforts to understand in depth the culture of an American community and to describe how that culture is affected by, and shapes the lives of, its people. The studies continue to be widely read and are almost unrivaled in the scope of their concern. The Lynds were not explicit about their research design except to say that they sought to examine all aspects of life in the community. The data upon which their conclusions were based were ob-

tained primarily from observations by the authors and three associates, from personal interviews, and from the study of records, maps, and newspaper accounts of life in Muncie. While the Lynds denied that there was any such thing as a "typical" American community, Muncie was selected because it was, in their judgment, "as representative as possible of contemporary American life."

The first report on Muncie appeared in 1929 under the title Middletown *and was based on research undertaken in 1925. The Lynds returned to Muncie in the mid-1930s to assess the impact of the depression on the life of that community. They found, among other things, that it was controlled much as it had been a decade earlier, by a small business elite which in turn was dominated by one family. In the selection below, taken from their second report,* Middletown in Transition, *the Lynds show the extent of the "X Family's" influence in Middletown and the ways in which that influence is exercised and maintained.*

"If I'm out of work I go to the X plant; if I need money I go to the X bank, and if they don't like me I don't get it; my children go to the X college; when I get sick I go to the X hospital; I buy a building lot or house in an X subdivision; my wife goes downtown to buy clothes at the X department store; if my dog stays away he is put in the X pound; I buy X milk; I drink X beer, vote for X political parties, and get help from X charities; my boy goes to the X Y.M.C.A. and my girl to their Y.W.C.A.; I listen to the word of God in X-subsidized churches; if I'm a Mason I go to the X Masonic Temple; I read the news from the X morning newspaper; and, if I am rich enough, I travel via the X airport." (*Comment by a Middletown man, 1935.*)

Since *Middletown* was published, some local people have criticized it for underplaying the role of the X family in the city's life. This group of wealthy families, along with four or five others, was not characterized as an "upper class" in 1925, because "these families are not a group apart but are merged in the life of the mass of the businessfolk." Whether or not the earlier study was entirely right in so largely grouping them with the rest of the business class, certainly no local prompting was necessary in 1935 to call attention to their overshadowing position. For, after ten years' absence from the city, one thing struck the returning observer again and again: the increasingly large public benefactions and the increasing pervasiveness of the power of this wealthy family of manufacturers, whose local position since 1925 is becoming hereditary with the emergence of a second generation of sons. . . .

In and out of the picture of Middletown in 1925 wove the influence of this family of brothers who had come to the city with the gas boom, begun with modest capital and become millionaires, and had ever since held an unostentatious but increasingly influential place in the city's life. . . .

Half a dozen other family names in Middletown are associated with the city's industrial development, but none of them so completely symbolizes the city's achievements. Of the original five brothers, four remained in 1924; and when shortly thereafter another died, the entire business of the city stopped during his funeral. Two of the brothers remain today, both men in their seventies, alert, capable, democratic, Christian gentlemen, trained in the school of rugged individualism, patrons of art, education, religion, and of a long list of philanthropies; men who have never spared themselves in business or civic affairs; high exemplars of the successful, responsible manipulators of the American formulas of business enterprise. In their conscientious and utterly unhypocritical combination of high profits, great philanthropy, and a low wage scale, they embody the hard-headed *ethos* of Protestant capitalism with its identification of Christianity with the doctrine of the goodness to all concerned of unrestricted business enterprise. In their modesty and personal rectitude, combined with their rise from comparative poverty to great wealth, they fit perfectly the American success dream.

Every American city has its successful businessmen, but the American success story has been kaleidoscopic in recent years. Local giants, the boys who have grown up with the town and made good, have shrunk in stature as rapid technological changes, the heavy capital demands of nation-wide distribution, and shifts in the strategic centers for low-cost production in a national market have undercut their earlier advantages of location, priority in the field, or energy; and as Eastern capital has forced them out or bought them out and reduced them to the status of salaried men, or retired them outright in favor of imported managements. One can classify American small manufacturing cities into two groups: those in which the industrial pioneers or their sons still dominate the local business scene, and those in which "new blood" has taken over the leadership; and it is likely that a census would show today a numerical predominance of the second group among cities containing major industries.

Middletown is, therefore, probably a minority city in this respect. The two remaining X brothers, reenforced by the active entry into the family business of four of the sons and two of the sons-in-law of the family, not only still own and control completely their wide business interests, but have become, amidst the local havoc of the depression, far more locally influential than ever before. It so happens that their industry, the making of glass fruit jars, is one that thrived on the depression; the great plant was not only kept busy, often employing night shifts throughout the lean years, but it returned profits reported to have been among the largest in their forty-five years of business. As the general level of the surrounding ground fell away in the depression, their preeminence increased. Their financial liquidity has been such that, with their public spirit, they have been able to cushion the local impact of the depression at a number of points; and a by-product of their strength in the midst of general weakness has been a marked increase in their banking and personal penetration into a number of areas of the city's business life. Both because of their generous help and this resulting increase in control, and because of a very human awe in the presence of a prestidigitator who can make money out of a business depression, the power and prestige of the X family among the business class in Middletown has grown decidedly with the depression. The fact that a local citizen could, late in 1934, characterize as "the one big point about this town" the fact "that the X's dominate the whole town, *are* the town, in fact" suggests the reason for the separate treatment of the family in this chapter.

Middletown has, therefore, at present what amounts to a reigning royal family. The power of this family has become so great as to differentiate the city today somewhat from cities with a more diffuse type of control. If, however, one views the Middletown pattern as simply concentrating and personalizing the type of control which control of capital gives to the business group in our culture, the Middletown situation may be viewed as epitomizing the American business-class control system. It may even foreshadow a pattern which may become increasingly prevalent in the future as the American propertied class strives to preserve its controls.

The business class in Middletown runs the city. The nucleus of business-class control is the X family. What the web of X wires looked like in 1935 may be seen from the following necessarily incomplete pattern of activities lying more or less on the surface of the city's life:

1. GETTING A LIVING

(a) *Banking.* . . . On the board of directors of the one remaining bank are three members of the X family, with one of them as chairman; while on the board of the trust company are the X member who is chairman of the bank's board, one of the sons, and a son-in-law. In addition to the members of the X family, seven of the remaining eleven members of the board of the trust company are also members of the board of the bank. Middletown's credit facilities are therefore very centrally controlled. In addition, one son is a director in one of the city's building-and-loan associations and two other sons are directors in a small "Morris Plan" loan company.

The ramifications of this banking control of the community's credit resources are wide and subtle. Only the insiders know its details, but one picks up constantly the remark in conversation that "The banks now control the Jones plant"—and the Smith plant and the Brown plant. There is probably some measure of truth in the statement by a businessman, who in the earlier study had always proved a reliable source of information, that "If you don't join up with the inner ring, you can't work with them and you can't work against them, and you won't get the credit to run your business if they are not for you." Another member of the business class commented: "It's a one-bank town now. People don't dare complain about the way the Community Fund and other local affairs are run because all of these stem straight back to the people who control our local credit resources."

Remarks like these must not be taken too literally and sweepingly, and it would be grossly unfair to read into the situation personal malevolence, least of all on the part of the X's at the center of the local control group. This inner financial group is simply the hub of a wheel engaged in running a city.

(*b*) *Legal talent.* Middletown's best law firms are retained in one or another of the interests of the X family. This renders understandable the comment of a local paper during the depression that "Lawyers and banks get along here. They maintain a happy relationship here as compared with their conflict in other cities." The personal attorney of a leading member of the X family is city attorney.

(*c*) *Industry.* The X family has not followed a policy of deliberately seeking financial control of other industries in the city. While they have an interest, direct or indirect, in some of the city's industrial plants other than their glass plant, paper-board plant, and the city's interconnecting trunk railways (which they own entirely), their power in Middletown industry is otherwise largely banking power and the commanding power of prestige and example. No secretary of the Chamber of Commerce could hold his position against X opposition. . . .

(*d*) *Retailing.* During the depression Middletown's largest department store failed. Since it occupied a building owned by the X family, the most conspicuous retail building in the city, the family has reopened it as the "X Store." And, like all X activities, it is a far better store than it was ten years ago under the former management, and a decided asset to the city. The family is reported to have an active interest in at least one other retail business, the leading furniture store in which one of the X brothers is a director, while its indirect banking controls in the retail field are particularly pervasive. Two dairies, run as playthings by younger members of the X family, squeezed the local milk market by pressing X milk into use in local institutions supported in part by X charity, and in 1934 a large independent dealer capitulated and sold out his business to the X's and became the manager for them. This kind of move, again, represents a specific gain to Middletown, as some of the city's milk is bad while the X milk is very superior. The output of a brewery in a neighboring city, in which the X family has a large interest as an outlet for its glass bottles, is said to be heavily pushed against all rivals in the local market.

2. MAKING A HOME

Since 1925 the X family has literally moved the residential heart of the city. An outstanding change in these ten years is the development of the northwest section of the city, the section where the X's live and the section most remote from local industrial plants, into the outstanding residential section. This shift has been carefully engineered by members of the X family. . . .

The X residential development in the West End is related to two other major developments engineered by the X's in that section, adjoining the new subdivisions: the purchase and transformation by the X's of the haggard old normal school into a cluster of beautiful buildings now bearing the name "X State Teachers College," with an associated handsome new laboratory grade and high school that is the envy of the rest of the school system; and the location, adjoining the college, of the new million-and-a-half-dollar hospital, an outright gift to the city by the X family. These combined developments give a distinction to Middletown's West End which no section of the city, grimy with soft coal smoke, had in 1925.

And yet, as one watches this flowering forth of the city under the guiding hand of the X family, one must bear in mind the comment of a local man that "The X's are about the only people I know of who have managed to augment their fortune by the art of philanthropy." . . .

3. TRAINING THE YOUNG

A member of the family is president of Middletown's school board, and a prominent X attorney is school attorney. Middletown feels comfortable with a member of this family at the head of its schools. An editorial comment in June, 1936, says: "There is still a feeling among women's organizations that there should be one woman on the [school] board, but that it is not likely to come about until a year hence, if then, or ever. Mr. X's term will expire a year hence *and there is no likelihood of replacing him if he still wants the job. . . ."* (Italics ours.)

The local college, though a State institution, is said to be X controlled both in its larger policies and in occasional small details. From both faculty and students, very guardedly in the former case and more openly in the latter, one heard of the pressure from the X's against radicalism in the college. . . .

It is not intended here to suggest that X State Teachers College is under deliberate repressive control. Its student body contains the most politically liberal force in the city. What is here suggested is that the college, though a State institution, is so closely watched by the X family and is so dependent upon their power and influence that it tends to follow officially their intellectual and political emphases. This does not, however, mean that all liberal teaching is stifled.

The family's authority in local educational matters is enhanced by the fact that it has also given $1,000,000 to the State University. One brother is president of the University's board of trustees.

4. Spending Leisure

Both the Y.M.C.A. and the Y.W.C.A. buildings are X philanthropies. . . .

Personnel and policies in the case of both "Y's" are closely controlled by members of the X family. . . . The family's other contributions to the leisure-time activities of the city are . . . extensive. . . .

5. Religion

A number of local churches, including working-class churches, have been helped in their building programs by X generosity. The X family, particularly the older generation, believes in the goodness of religion and in steady churchgoing. The influence of the older generation is, on the whole, theologically conservative. It would be unfair to say that their aid to local churches—from contributions to building programs to playground equipment—is given in order to influence these churches' teachings. Their gifts are undoubtedly prompted by a desire to make Middletown a better place in which to live, and to them as people of long religious tradition the church is an important community civilizing agency. But, though not so intended, their philanthropy here as elsewhere operates as part of the local business-class control system. All of business-class Middletown, including its ministers, hesitates to come out in the open against X causes or X points of view. One stubborn "liberal" minister is reported to have been "broken" by the family ten years ago. . . .

6. Government

. . . Middletown is a Republican stronghold. The business leaders tend to be solidly Republican, and in this the X family sets them a conspicuous model. A member of the family is Republican National Committeeman for the state; the family contributes heavily to Republican campaign funds and to the Liberty League; and they pull a consistently heavy oar financially and personally for the G.O.P. ticket, national, state, and local.

In the face of this established situation, a small sensation was created among Middletown Democrats when, after the turning of the state and nation to the Democratic party in 1932, one of the abler members of the second generation of X's suddenly bobbed up as an influential local Democratic leader and head of the (Democratic) Governor's Commission on Unemployment. The Democratic weekly paper commented in the summer of 1935:

> Young X has done pretty well for a new Democrat who voted the traditional X Republican ticket as late as the last general primary. He has laid himself up a job on the school board, as a Democrat, controls the Democratic mayor and county chairman, is the final word in hiring hands in relief work in ten counties, and the acknowledged boss of the Democratic party hereabouts.

This paper, the erratic personal organ of an old-time swashbuckling editor who was mayor from 1930 through 1934, and the one paper in town that deals baldly with messy local affairs, headlined this situation with characteristic colorfulness:

> Democratic Party Here Now a Possession of the Mighty X Kin: Ruthless in Business and Piratical Forays in Realms of Finance, They Play Both Political Parties on Theory That Heads We Win, Tails You Lose; [and again, in a later issue:] Smooth-running Politics Makes New-fledged Democrat President of School Board; Strides Past D— and Keeps G—, Republican, as School Attorney over Weak Protest of the Mayor; Young X Tells the Democrats Where to Get Off, but His Millions and Influential Family Surround Him With Groveling Servitors.

The present mayor, a Democrat who was reelected in the fall of 1935, after having served as mayor fifteen years earlier, is now sometimes spoken of as "X-controlled." . . .

On their part, the X family does not seek to exploit Middletown politically in the sense familiar to students of American municipal administration, nor need one read skulduggery, as one local commentator suggested, into the refund of a $52,000 income-tax overpayment by the Hoover administration in December, 1932, to the one of the X's who is a Republican National Committeeman and a heavy contributor to Republican campaign funds. It seems more probable that we are simply confronted here by a situation of conflict between two ostensibly separate but actually interdependent sets of cultural institutions: on the one hand, a set of lagging political institutions fallen into disrepute because of the meager calibre of the men who find it financially worthwhile in this culture to run for municipal office and because of the patent waste and graft incident to their operation; and, on the other hand, a set of economic institutions more ably manned by the best abilities in the male population, somewhat more efficient, and more central to the concern of an industrial community. The operators of the economic institutions do not want to bother with the political institutions; but, on the other hand, they do not want too much interference with their central economic concerns from the political institutions. They, therefore, bother to inject just enough control over the confusion of local politics to insure a tolerable tax rate, support for "sound" municipal cooperation in maintaining an open-shop town, control over the numerically dominant working class, and similar broad policies calculated to enable their central business of money-making to go forward without too much interference. And all of this is done by men like the X's with a strong sense of their actions being "in the public interest."

7. CARING FOR THE UNABLE

The strong arm of X philanthropies supports all Middletown charities.

8. GETTING INFORMATION (THE PRESS)

The X family has held for some years a powerful stock interest, loosely described locally as "controlling," in Middletown's morning paper. This paper is sometimes spoken of locally as "the X paper." The family also has an interest in a leading daily in the state capital.

In connection with the dissemination of information, one other point deserves note. A local labor man pointed out in 1935 that the X's now control, through their connection with the school board, Masonic Temple, and college, all the large meeting halls in Middletown. Such "control" is at present incidental and inconsequential. This type of situation can, however, assume real significance if, for instance, a labor or radical movement should become marked in Middletown. . . .

The picture of family-wise control by the X's presented in the preceding pages may have given the impression of close, coordinated planning among the members, old and young, of the family. The situation is actually much more informal than this. Even within the family a considerable degree of rugged individualism exists. There is a common sense of direction, but no family "general staff" mapping the strategy of investment and control. . . .

We obviously confront here a highly complicated situation regarding which no positive summary judgments are possible. It is the impression of the investigator:

> That the lines of leadership and the related controls are highly concentrated today in Middletown.
>
> That this control net has tightened decidedly since 1925 and notably with the depression.
>
> That the control is at very many points unconscious and, where conscious, well-meaning and "public spirited," as businessmen interpret that concept.
>
> That the control system operates at many points to identify public welfare with business-class welfare.
>
> That there is little deliberate effort from above to organize local bankers, businessmen, and leaders of opinion into a self-conscious "we" pressure group; but that this sharply centripetal tendency of Middletown's businessmen is normal behavior in a capitalist, credit-controlled culture where there is a potential control-center in the form of vast personal resources of demonstrated willingness to lend a friendly hand.
>
> That, so long as the owners of such vast personal resources exhibit a public-spirited willingness to help with local problems, leadership and control tend to be forced upon them by circumstances, and their patterns tend to become the official guiding patterns.
>
> That, viewed at any given time as a going concern, this centrally-hubbed control agency both may and does operate in many subtle and even ordinarily unintended ways to "welcome little fishes in with gently smiling jaws," with an accompanying loss to the latter of independent leadership. Those who try to be independent tend to be regarded, as the local phrase puts it, as "gumming the works." As the local Democratic editor, who loves mischievously to pin his victims to the wall not with pins but with broadswords, remarked editorially: "The ownership of banks, factories, colleges, breweries, dog pounds, hospitals, mayors, and county chairmen, centered in this millionaire group, has produced an appalling economic pressure on citizens who find themselves in the house of bondage. However, it is a benevolent protectorate extended over all who come into camp gracefully. But the stuffed club is always at hand, to penalize dissenters. 'Treat 'em right and they'll be good to us' has been preached here long enough."

What the future of this X control system will be is hard to guess. Within another decade the two remaining giants of the first generation will probably be out of active life. At present the policy of the family seems to be that it may as well give away a generous part of its income because it would be taken in taxes anyway. But the family's wealth will pass along fairly intact to the four sons and two sons-in-law now in their early thirties and forties. There is more diversity among these second-generation men, and one gathers that the intentness upon business that characterized the pioneering first generation is finding competition among the second generation from political ambition, activities involved in living as country gentle-

men, and other distractions. The second-generation men are in no sense
mere "rich men's sons" or "wasters," but are alert, able, and responsible.
The fact that they have not removed to larger cities but remain in Middletown, taking their places as wheel horses in the family team, suggests the
carrying forward of the *ancien régime.* A local minister expressed the belief
that the younger generation of the X's is "even better than the old," though
two businessmen concurred in stating that "The younger generation of X's
don't stack up in ability with the fading generation." The supporting power
of their wealth will remain, but one suspects that the intensity of devotion
to local causes will inevitably be somewhat less among these younger families that have not fought shoulder to shoulder with the city's business
pioneers to build a city from the boom town of the 1880's. Meanwhile,
hereditary, as over against first-generation, wealth offers Middletown the
possibility of increasing class stratification and the softening of local fiber
that tends to accompany the passage of first-generation wealth into second-
generation power. . . .

COMMUNITY POWER STRUCTURE

Floyd Hunter

> *Whereas the Lynds found that "Middletown" was dominated by a single family, Floyd Hunter found, almost twenty years later, that "Regional City" (Atlanta, Georgia) was controlled by a small, relatively cohesive, economic elite. Hunter's study of this city of over 300,000 persons (in 1950–51 when the research was carried out) was a seminal contribution to the study of community power. Indeed, the study's title, Community Power Structure, has become a common term, used by scholar and layman alike, and has had an important effect on the impression many have of the way cities and towns are "run."*
>
> *But the importance of Hunter's research lies not so much in his picture of the distribution of power in Atlanta, as in the methods he employed to identify and describe the pattern of influence which he reports. He sought to develop an operational and economical research technique which would lend itself to quantification. His basic approach, described in the opening paragraphs of this selection, is to ask presumably knowledgeable persons to identify those individuals who are most "influential" and to ascertain the relationship between these individuals. This technique, which has come to be called the "reputational" method, and which has undergone substantial refinement in recent years, has been the focus of considerable controversy which we will examine in Chapter 5.*

. . . No pretense is made that the group to be discussed represents the totality of power leaders of the community, but it is felt that a representative case sample is presented, and that the men described come well within the range of the center of power in the community.

The leaders selected for study were secured from lists of leading civic, professional, and fraternal organizations, governmental personnel, business leaders, and "society" and "wealth" personnel suggested by various sources.

From Floyd Hunter, *Community Power Structures* (Chapel Hill, N.C.: University of North Carolina Press, 1953), excerpts from Chapter 4. Reprinted with permission of the publisher.

These lists of more than 175 persons were rated by "judges" who selected by mutual choice the top forty persons in the total listings.* These forty were the object of study and investigation in Regional City. Some data were collected about the total number. Twenty-seven members of the group were interviewed on the basis of a prepared schedule plus additional questions as the investigation proceeded. Any figures used in the study will need to be tied fairly rigidly to the twenty-seven members on whom there are comparable data. Thirty-four Negro citizens are included in the study. The fourteen under-structure professionals in civic and social work who were interviewed have also provided data which may be considered comparable. . . .

The system of power groups which is being examined may not be called a closed system. The groups are links in a total pattern, which may offer suggestive clues to total power patterns in the operating system of Regional City. There are gaps in the power arc which investigation may not be able to close. Actually the discussion here is primarily concerned with the structuring of power on a policy-making level. Only a rudimentary "power pyramid" of Regional City will be presented. One may be content to do this because I doubt seriously that power forms a single pyramid with any nicety in a community the size of Regional City. There are *pyramids* of power in this community which seem more important to the present discussion than *a* pyramid. Let me illustrate this point.

In the interviews, Regional City leaders were asked to choose ten top leaders from the basic list of forty. The choices of the twenty-seven persons answering this question showed considerable unanimity of opinion. One leader received twenty-one votes out of a possible twenty-seven. Other leaders received nearly as many votes. Some received no votes at all. One could pyramid the forty leaders on the basis of the votes cast for them . . . but the pyramid is not a true expression of the existing relationships between the top leaders of the community. George Delbert, for example, was chosen eight times more than Charles Homer, and Homer is consequently six places down the scale from Delbert. Delbert is considered a "big man" in Regional City affairs, but he is not as big as Homer, according to most of the informants in answer to the simple question, "Who is the 'biggest' man in town?"

The question on which Delbert came to the top of the voting poll was phrased, "If a project were before the community that required *decision* by a group of leaders—leaders that nearly everyone would accept—which *ten* on the list of forty would you choose?" Delbert came out on top in this question, but not on the one related to who is the biggest man in town.

---

*Ed. note: There were fourteen judges, selected by the author, who represented three religions, were male and female, young and mature people, business executives and professional people, and Negro and white.

Thus the pyramid scheme suggested by the voting poll of leaders, related to making projects move, must be modified in relation to the factors which weigh in Homer's favor in other areas related to power. Quite possibly some of these factors are Homer's wealth, his social position, and his business position. . . .

The validity of the question concerning who might be chosen to "decide" on a community project cannot be measured purely in terms of a pyramid-structuring. Its validity for this study lies in the fact that the question determined, in some degree, "how near the center" this group was that could "move things" in the affairs of the community. Each man interviewed was asked to add names of persons he considered as powerful as or more powerful than the men listed. Sixty-four names were added to the list. Thirty-seven of the additional names were mentioned but once by informants. Sixteen were mentioned twice; five, three times; five, four times; and one, five times. Eleven informants added names, but there was general agreement that the list was a fairly comprehensive one as it stood, with the exceptions mentioned.

The high consensus regarding the top leaders on the list of forty, plus the lack of any concerted opinion on additional individuals, would indicate that the men being interviewed represented at least a nucleus of a power grouping.

The question was also put to interviewees, "How many men would need to be involved in a major community project in Regional City 'to put it over'?" The answers to this question varied from, "You've got the men right here on this list—maybe ten of them," to "fifty or a hundred." . . .

. . . [T]he "men of independent decision" are a relatively small group. The "executors of policy" may run into the hundreds. This pattern of a relatively small decision-making group working through a larger under-structure is a reality, and if data were available, the total personnel involved in a major community project might possibly form a pyramid of power, but the constituency of the pyramid would change according to the project being acted upon.

In other words, the personnel of the pyramid would change depending upon what needs to be done at a particular time. . . . The men in the under-structure may have a multiplicity of individual roles within the totality of the community structure which can be set in motion by the men of decision.

As I became familiar with the list of forty names through the interviewing process, it became evident that certain men, even within the relatively narrow range of decision leaders with whom I was dealing, represented a top layer of personnel. Certain men were chosen more frequently than others, not in relation to who should be chosen to decide on a project, as has already been indicated, but the same men interacted together on committees and were on the whole better known to each other than to those outside this group. Through analyzing the mutual choices made by those interviewed, it will be shown that there is an *esprit de corps* among certain top leaders, and some of them may be said to operate on a very high level of decision in the community; but this will not necessarily mean that one of the top leaders can be considered subordinate to any other in the community as a whole. On specific projects one leader may allow another to carry the ball, as a leader is said to do when he is "out front" on a project which interests him. On the next community-wide project another may carry the ball. Each may subordinate himself to another on a temporary basis, but such a structure of subordination is quite fluid, and it is voluntary. . . . It would seem from this evidence that the under group defers to the upper group, and that there is some solidarity in the upper echelons of policy-makers.

As shown earlier, power has been defined in terms of policy leadership, and the data given in the present chapter make a beginning at defining structural power relations. A group of men have been isolated who are among the most powerful in Regional City. It has been shown that they interact among themselves on community projects and select one another as leaders. Their relations with one another are not encompassed in a true pyramid of power, but some degree of ranking, even in the top-level policy leadership group, has been indicated. Let us now look at policy personnel patterns in another way.

In sizing up any individual one often asks, "What do you do for a living?" The reply to this question allows one rather quickly to rank another in a rough scale of social values. The men under discussion hold commercial, industrial, financial, and professional positions in Regional City that tend to classify them in the minds of any observer. . . .

. . . [M]ost of the leaders hold positions as presidents of companies, chairmen of boards, or professional positions of some prestige. Generally speaking, the companies represented in the listing are of major enterprise proportions. More than half the men may be said to be businessmen, if the term is used broadly. The major economic interests of the community are overwhelmingly represented in the listing. The pattern of business dominance of civil affairs in Regional City is a fact. No other institution is as dominant in community life as the economic institution. . . .

[One informant] was asked to tell how [decision-making groups] would operate in relation to one another on a community-wide project, and he outlined the procedure very clearly. . . . [R]epresentatives from each [group] are drawn into any discussion relative to a major community decision. Each man mentioned as belonging to a [group] also belongs to a major business enterprise within the community—at least the clique leader does. His position within the bureaucratic structure of his business almost automatically makes him a community leader, if he wishes to become one. The test for admission to this circle of decision-makers is almost wholly a man's position in the business community in Regional City. The larger business enterprises represent pyramids of power in their own right, as work units within the community, and the leaders within these concerns gather around them some of the top personnel within their own organization. They then augment this nucleus of leadership by a coterie of selected friends from other establishments to form knots of interest called "crowds" by [the informant]. The outer edges of any crowd may pick up such men as Percy Latham, the dentist, who in turn picks up others in relation to any specific activity in which the crowd may be interested. The top men in any crowd tend to act together, and they depend upon men below them to serve as intermediaries in relation to the general community. . . .

Several of the top leaders within the crowds would "clear with each other" informally on many matters. The older men, as mentioned earlier, tended to get their heads together on most matters, as did the younger group, but such relationships were not completely stable. Each man at the top of a "crowd pyramid" depended upon those close to him in business to carry out decisions when made. An older man, for example, could not command another older man to do something, but within his own crowd there would be a hierarchy he could put to work. In most instances decision-making tended to be channeled through the older men at some point in the process of formulation, but many things may be done on the initiative of any combination of several powerful leaders in the crowds named. None of the leaders indicated that he could work alone on any big project, nor did any feel that there was any man in the community with such power. The individual power leader is dependent on others in Regional City in contrast to mill or mining company towns where one man or one family may dominate the community actions which take place.

Society prestige and deference to wealth are not among the primary criteria for admission to the upper ranks of the decision-makers according to the study of Regional City. The persons who were included in the listing of forty top leaders purely on the basis of their wealth or society connections did not, with three or four exceptions, make the top listing of persons who might be called upon to "put across a community project." As has been mentioned before, a distinction is made between persons of wealth and social prestige who engage in work and those who do not. The persons of wealth are perhaps important in the social structure of the community as symbolic persons. They may be followed in matters of fashion and in their general manner of living. Their money may be important in financing a given project, but they are not of themselves doers. They may only be called decisive in the sense that they can withhold or give money through others to change the course of action of any given project. . . . If there is power in the charitable foundation structures, it resides in the lawyers who operate them, rather than in the donors who are largely inactive in the affairs of the foundations.

Political eminence cannot be said to be a sole criterion for entry into the policy echelons of Regional City's life, generally speaking. The two exceptions to this statement are embodied in Mayor Barner and County Treasurer Truman Worth. Both Barner and Worth were successful businessmen before becoming involved in local politics to the point of seeking public office. Their interests may be said to be primarily business in the strict sense of the word. Both have a popular following that has kept them in office, but their close associates are businessmen. Mayor Barner had only one picture in his office—that of Charles Homer, the biggest businessman in the community. Both Barner and Worth look to businessmen constantly for advice before they make a move on any project concerning the whole community. Furthermore, they do not ordinarily "move out front" on any project themselves, but rather follow the lead of men like Delbert, Graves, or any one of the other leaders of particular crowds.

The point made at this turn of the discussion is not a new one. Businessmen are the community leaders in Regional City as they are in other cities. Wealth, social prestige, and political machinery are functional to the fielding of power by the business leaders in the community. . . .

In the general social structure of community life social scientists are prone to look upon the institutions and formal associations as powerful forces, and it is easy to be in basic agreement with this view. Most institutions and associations are subordinate, however, to the interests of the policymakers who operate in the economic sphere of community life in Regional City. The institutions of the family, church, state, education, and the like draw sustenance from economic institutional sources and are thereby subordinate to this particular institution more than any other. The associations stand in the same relationship to the economic interests as do the institutions. We see both the institutions and the formal associations playing a vital role in the execution of determined policy, but the formulation of policy often takes place outside these formalized groupings. Within the policy-forming groups the economic interests are dominant.

The economic institution in Regional City, in drawing around itself many of the other institutions in the community, provides from within itself much of the personnel which may be considered of primary influence in power relationships. A lengthy discussion on institutions per se is not proposed. Their existence as channels through which policy may be funneled up and down to broader groups of people than those represented by the top men of power is easily recognized. . . .

The idea was expressed several times by interviewees that some minister *ought* to be on the listing, but under the terms of power definitions used in the study they did not make "top billing." It is understood, however, that in order to get a project well under way it would be important to bring the churches in, but they are not, as institutions, considered crucial in the decision-making process. Their influence is crucial in restating settled policies from time to time and in interpreting new policies which have been formed or are in the process of formulation. Church leaders, however, whether they be prominent laymen or professional ministers, have relatively little influence with the larger economic interests.

One cannot, in Regional City at least, look to the organized institutions as policy-determining groupings, nor can one look to the formal associations which are part of these institutions.

None of the men interviewed considered any of the associational groupings [private clubs] crucial in policy determination. Their role, like that of the organized institutional groupings, is one of following rather than leading. They may provide a forum for discussing and studying community issues, needs, and policies; but, when decision is called for, another structure must come into play before action becomes the order of the day. The organizations may serve as training grounds for many of the men who later become power leaders. Most of the leaders had "graduated" from a stint in the upper positions of the more important organizations. Most associational presidents, however, remain in the under-structure of the power hierarchy. The organizations are not a sure route to sustained community prominence. Membership in the top brackets of one of the stable economic bureaucracies is the surest road to power, and this road is entered by only a few. Organizational leaders are prone to get the publicity; the upper echelon economic leaders, the power. . . .

One more organizational component must be analyzed before tying together the units of the community structure. This component is what may be termed a fluid committee structure.

The committee is a phenomenon which is inescapable in organized community life in American hamlets, villages, small cities, and great metropolitan centers. Almost every activity of any importance in our culture must be preceded by committee work, carried on by committee work, and finally posthumously evaluated by a committee. Regional City is no exception to the general rule. . . .

Meetings are often a substitute for group action. As one Regional City professional phrased it, "There are those who believe in salvation by luncheon!" There is great faith manifest in certain quarters of our society that if people can just be got together in a meeting all problems will be solved. And there is some justification for this faith, since so many matters of community business, as well as private transactions, are brought to successful conclusions in meetings.

Meetings have the functions of clarifying objectives of a group and of fixing and delegating responsibilities for action on any matter. They may in like manner hold action in abeyance. Decisions reached in meetings may be solemnly binding, or they may not be. Decisions arrived at in one meeting may be changed in the next meeting. Responsibilities may be shifted and membership changed according to the will of the group as a series of meetings proceeds. Rarely are committee meetings bound by "constitutional" prohibitions or heavy legalistic trappings which characterize so many associational and institutional gatherings. The outstanding characteristic of the ordinary committee meeting is its fluidity and its adaptability in adjusting to changing conditions, which are so essentially a part of our modern urban culture. The importance of the committee in power relations cannot be overstressed.

While it is important to stress the fluidity of committee structure, it must also be pointed out that here is a stable base of personnel who are seen time and again in a variety of committee meetings. There are men in any community who devote large portions of their waking hours to attendance at one meeting or another. Public-relations men in industry and associational secretaries are paid to devote considerable of their time to meeting attendance. It becomes commonplace among this latter personnel group to see one another at committee mettings, and such personnel become familiar with community leaders who operate on a similar level with them. There is a tendency to judge the importance of these meetings by who is in attendance.

Most of the top personnel of the power group are rarely seen at meetings attended by the associational understructure personnel in Regional City. The exception to this general statement may be found in those instances in which a project is broad enough so that the "whole community needs to be brought in on the matter." Such meetings as bring in the under-structure personnel are usually relatively large affairs, rather than the smaller, more personal meetings which characterize policy-determination sessions. The interaction patterns of the two groups discussed here have shown a much higher rate of interaction among the top group than between the top and lower groups.

In matters of power decision the committee structure assumes keystone importance. The committee as a structure is a vital part of community power relationships in Regional City. Let us illustrate graphically in Figure 1 the place of two hypothetical policy committees in relation to institutional, associational, and corporate groups. . . .

We have also indicated in the figure that some institutions and associations are more frequently drawn upon for power personnel than others. The dotted lines represent those groups that are potential contributors to the policy-making structure. The cultural association group has been so designated, for example, since policy is formulated around some cultural activities which may have bearing on power relations. As an illustration, the status factor operating when a leader becomes a patron of the arts may have some relation to his general power position.

A few generalized remarks may be made concerning Figure 1, using a hypothetical example. . . .

If a project of major proportions were before the community for con-

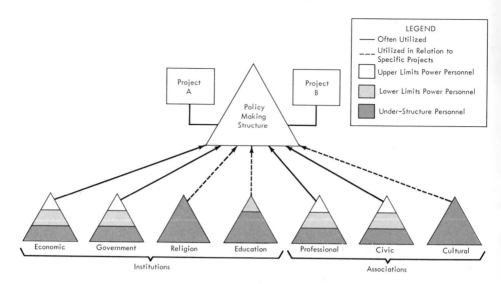

FIGURE 1. Generalized Pattern of Policy Committee Formation Utilizing Institutional and Associational Structures.

sideration—let us say a project aimed at building a new municipal audito-
rium—a policy committee would be formed. This may be called Project
Committee A. Such a policy committee would more than likely grow out of
a series of informal meetings, and it might be related to a project that has
been on the discussion agenda of many associations for months or even
years. But the time has arrived for action. Money must be raised through
private subscription or taxation, a site selected, and contracts let. The time
for a policy committee is propitious. The selection of the policy committee
will fall largely to the men of power in the community. They will likely be
businessmen in one or more of the larger business establishments. Mutual
choices will be agreed upon for committee membership. In the early stages
of policy formulation there will be a few men who make the basic decisions.
As the project is trimmed, pared, and shaped into manageable proportions
there will be a recognition that the committee should be enlarged. Top-
ranking organizational and institutional personnel will then be selected by
the original members to augment their numbers, i.e., the committee will be
expanded. The civic associations and the formalized institutions will next
be drawn into certain phases of planning and initiation of the project on a
community-wide basis. The newspapers will finally carry stories of the
proposals, the ministers will preach sermons, and the associational members will hear speeches regarding plans. This rather simply is the process,
familiar to many, that goes on in getting any community project under way.

Project B might be related to changing the tax structure of the community. Much the same organizational procedure will be repeated, but different associations may be drawn into the planning and execution stages. The policy-making personnel will tend to be much the same as in Project A and this is an important point in the present discussion. There will be a hard core of policy leadership on Policy Committee B that was also present on Project Committee A. This relative stability of the top policy-making group is a pattern quite apparent in Regional City civic affairs. A similar pattern of stable committee membership exists in the under-structure of the associational and corporate bureaucracies in the community which interact in a chain of command with the top power leaders on given projects.

It must be stressed that the same policy leaders do not interact repeatedly with the same under-structure personnel in getting projects put over. The interaction is based entirely upon a given project that is under consideration at a given time. The under-structure personnel may be likened to a keyboard over which the top structure personnel play, and the particular keys struck may vary from project to project. The players remain the same or nearly so, however.

A variation in the pattern of structuring a top-decision committee may be found in those policy committees in which the decision is made by individuals who are not to be out front on the project. In other words, the men of policy may wish to remain anonymous in relation to the action phases of the program in question. In such cases, the policy group remains informally intact, and "second-rate" or "third-rate" men are advertised as the sponsors of the particular project. This pattern may occur when a project is somewhat questionable as to its success. The policy-forming group is just as real, however, as if it were named publicly. The men upon whom falls the burden of carrying the project into its action stages are well aware of the persons who chose them. . . .

Of course the affairs of the community do not stop at its borders. There are relationships between personnel in the city and persons in state and national power groups. Robert K. Merton has observed that community leaders fall into "cosmopolitan" and "local" groupings.[1] This generalized concept seems to hold true in Regional City. Some men tend to confine their activities almost entirely within the community, while others are active on state and regional matters. . . .

The community politicians almost entirely operate locally on boards and committees, but the Mayor has many individual contacts with the two levels of government above him on a less formalized basis than boards and committees of policy would imply. . . . He is not the most influential man

---

[1] Paul Lazarsfeld and Frank N. Stanton, (eds.), *Communications Research* (New York: Harper and Brothers, 1949), p. 192.

in Regional City in local-national policy matters, and when the dynamics of the power structure is elaborated upon, this will become apparent. The Mayor denies much influence in state matters. . . . State and local politics are differentiated, but not entirely distinct. As in the other states where a large metropolitan center is located there is much friction and conflict of interest between the two political groupings. The two are joined often at that point at which major economic interests are involved, and the leaders of economic bureaucracies have much personal influence in bridging the formal structural gaps between the levels of government on specific matters.

In one of our postulates it is stated that, "Power is structured socially, in the United States, into a dual relationship between governmental and economic authorities on national, state, and local levels." In the light of the present analysis, there is less of a "dual" relationship than had been assumed. This is particularly true in Regional City, where the dominant factor in political life is the personnel of the economic interests. It is true that there is no formal tie between the economic interests and government, but the structure of policy-determining committees and their tie-in with the other powerful institutions and organizations of the community make government subservient to the interests of these combined groups. The governmental departments and their personnel are acutely aware of the power of key individuals and combinations of citizens' groups in the policy-making realm, and they are loathe to act before consulting and "clearing" with these interests. . . .

There is evidence, too, that the local economic interests tie into larger groupings of like interests on the state and national levels which tend to overshadow the policy-making machinery of government at all levels. The structure is that of a dominant policy-making group using the machinery of government as a bureaucracy for the attainment of certain goals coordinate with the interests of the policy-forming group. . . .

The structural relationships between the economic policy-determining groups and the operating units of government have often been looked upon as inherently immoral. The ethical implications of the domination by one set of men in manipulating government for specific and limited purposes may be avoided, but some concern must be expressed in relation to a functional difficulty which such domination presents in our society. . . . There are gaps in the power arc which are closed on many issues by the narrower-interest groups. In other words, it has been pointed out that the power personnel do not represent a true pyramid of political power. The power personnel may decisively influence most policies that concern legislative groups, and they are acutely aware of their own interests in such policy matters. However, on many issues they are not interested, and there is consequently no continuing structure which may transmit to the legislative bodies the general interests of the underlying groups within the body politic. This is no new problem, but it is a structurally significant one. If the formalized structures of government are under the domination of a group of policy leaders who are isolated from direct responsibility to the mass of people in a democratic society, then, values aside, the scheme is at best dysfunctional. No patent remedy is suggested in this writing but there is a structural weakness in the policy-making machinery and power-wielding mechanism as it has been observed in a particular locality. Correction of the difficulty may come from an open recognition of actual operating elements in power relations unobscured by abstract value descriptions which do not fit reality. Simply put, power structure is looked at here, not from the point of view of what one may think we have, or what one may think we ought to have, but rather in terms of what we've got. . . .

[A]n obvious question is, "What holds the system together?" This question was asked of our informants. The question was put in this way: "It is evident that we are dealing with a small group of policy leaders in this study, but the whole community of Regional City is comprised of some half million persons. What holds the whole group together in relation to the influence exerted by so few leaders?" . . .

Within the primary groups, or separate crowds clustered around specific interests, it is evident [from the answers to the previous question] that similar interests and resulting common sentiments have a great deal to do with holding the groups together. Men who work together over a long period of time become comfortable in their working relationships with one another. Mutual sentiments of liking will grow up between them, and these sentiments in turn will lead to further interactions.[2] The ability of a top leader to retain a position of prestige depends to some extent on how well he conforms to the norms of the group he leads. The men of Regional City tend to be exponents of the "common man" in appearance and manner of speech, at least during the workday. Some of the men of top wealth and position are spoken of as "common as an old shoe." Their private lives hidden from the general mass of people may be uncommon, but their everyday behavior tends toward a confirmation of what one Regional City professional in the under-structure has called the "patched pants theory." "The biggest ones act like they have patches on their pants," he said. . . .

Common interests, cutting across the lines of all separate crowds, tend to hold the community structure intact. . . . [M]oney represents power in a stable economy when it is backed by tangible resources. With this limitation noted, it must be admitted that money still has meaning in power terms in Regional City. It is an important element.

Force is also an element of power but it is not an independent element.

---

[2]George C. Homans, *The Human Group* (New York: Harcourt, Brace and Co., 1950), p. 112.

. . . One must look deeper than the elements of money or force to analyze adequately the power structure of Regional City. Both of these elements have their place, but both are interconnected with a complex set of habitual relationships of men which are described in terms of group relations. . . .

The leaders of Regional City tend to protect themselves from too many demands by channeling policy execution through an under-structure on matters of policy. This under-structure is not a rigid bureaucracy, as has been pointed out, but is a flexible system. It has elements of stability and tends to operate by levels. The men at each level are spoken of as first, second, third and fourth rate by the power leaders, who operate primarily in conjunction with individuals of the first two ratings. The types of personnel which may be found in each rating by a sample classification are as follows:

Examples of Personnel from First to Fourth Rate in Regional City

First Rate: Industrial, commercial, financial owners and top executives of large enterprises.

Second Rate: Operations officials, bank vice-presidents, public-relations men, small businessmen (owners), top-ranking public officials, corporation attorneys, contractors.

Third Rate: Civic organization personnel, civic agency board personnel, newspaper columnists, radio commentators, petty public officials, selected organization executives.

Fourth Rate: Professionals such as ministers, teachers, social workers, personnel directors, and such persons as small business managers, higher paid accountants, and the like.

These ratings might be expanded. They are given simply to indicate a suggested ranking of selected personnel who operate below the policy-making leaders in Regional City. The first two ratings are personnel who are said to "set the line of policy," while the latter two groups "hold the line." . . . The top leaders are conserving their time and energies for the primary role they play—policy-determination. They are also interested in holding a balance of power in the community. . . .

The "little fellows" are continually moved to perform their proper tasks by those above them. The roles defined for the under-structure of power personnel are carefully defined in keeping with the larger interests. Their movements are carefully stimulated and watched at all times to see that their various functions are properly performed.

Stability of relationships is highly desirable in maintaining social control, and keeping men "in their places" is a vital part of the structuring of community power. . . . If one of [the] under-structure men should be presumptuous enough to question policy decisions, he would be immediately considered insubordinate and "punished," first by a threat to his job security, followed possibly by expulsion from his job if his insubordination continued. . . .

There may be isolated dissatisfactions with policy decisions in Regional City, but mainly there is unanimity. The controversial is avoided, partly by the policy-making group's not allowing a proposal to get too far along if it meets stiff criticism at any point in decision-making. A careful watch is kept for what "will go" and for what "will not go. . . ." When criticism is open it is generally directed toward some of the under-structure men who are fronting for the larger interests. If criticism is directed toward the top leaders, the critic is liable to job dismissal in extreme cases or more subtle pressures in less flagrant cases. The omnipresent threat of power sanctions used against recalcitrant underlings is recognized by the lower echelons of power, and they generally go along with most decisions, grumbling in private with close associates, if at all. Most of these third- or fourth-rate leaders rationalize their behavior—particularly when upper decisions are in conflict with their professional or private value systems. . . .

SMALL TOWN IN MASS SOCIETY

Arthur J. Vidich and Joseph Bensman

Arthur Vidich and Joseph Bensman studied the daily life of "Spring-dale," a small town of 2500 people in upstate New York, during a period of three years. Their research design was closer to that employed by the Lynds than by Floyd Hunter. Like both "Middletown" and "Regional City," "Springdale" was apparently dominated by a small elite whose values were quite congruent.

While Vidich and Bensman's findings and approach are similar in many ways to those of the earlier studies, their analysis of the elements of power and the manner of its exercise adds important elements to the literature. Their use of leadership "roles" provides a foundation for comparative study, and their attention to the "costs" of leadership suggest some ways of conceptualizing the limits on personal power. The authors illustrate that those with power maintain their influence not only through their own energy and the skillful exercise of their resources, but also by meeting the general needs of the community—at least to the extent that effective opposition to their hegemony cannot be mobilized. In many respects their picture of small-town life fits the popular notion of the homogeneous community in which the maintenance of harmony is a fundamental objective of community leaders.

. . . The interlocking, duplication and overlapping of leadership roles tend to channel community policy into relatively few hands, and it results, at the level of the personalities of the leaders, in some degree of community coordination. That is, a wide range of community activities are coordinated simply because a small number of individuals are engaged in a wide range of leadership positions.

The extent to which this coordination is effective, however, is an interesting question which is open to exploration on the basis of our data. Moreover,

From Arthur J. Vidich and Joseph Bensman, *Small Town in Mass Society*, revised edition (Princeton, N.J.: Princeton University Press, 1968), pp. 258–267, 272–284. Reprinted by permission of the publisher.

the roles of leaders and would-be leaders that are not coordinated is also an important part of the leadership process since the activity represented by these roles may help to account for innovation, diversity and change.

Four of Springdale's leaders have appeared and reappeared in almost all contexts in our previous discussion. The leaders are Jones, Lee, Flint and Young. Jones is the farm feed and mill operator, Lee the editor of the paper and town clerk, Flint the lawyer and legal counsel to organizations, and Young the county committeeman and high-order Mason.

When one reviews the organized public life of the community from the perspective of leadership, it is quickly apparent that this small number of individuals occupies a great many of the available positions. In fact, one encounters the same faces over and over again in almost every community context. This is as true for the political, educational and religious spheres already described as it is true for other community activities. . . .

The extent to which such overlapping of leadership constitutes domination, the extent to which some areas of community life are free from the influence of this central leadership group and the extent to which different leadership groups appear to dominate in different institutional spheres—all these are separate problems subject to special analysis. However, looking only at the summation of such leadership roles, we can gain another view of the structure of the public life of the community.

Primary and Secondary Leadership Roles

Not all of the positions which the dominant leaders hold are equally important. Some can almost be called honorary positions which an individual gains by being dominant in other positions. When Lee is elected to the presidency of the Community Club and when Flint is made president of the business bureau, they are being given a form of social recognition for their community work in general. A nominating committee decides that "it is about time Lee is made president because of everything he's done." In this sense such positions are honorary and are thrust upon "generalized leaders," even though their occupancy involves work and even though it may be flattering to receive such recognition.

While a given leader may occupy a great many positions, not all positions are of equal importance to him. The occupancy of some serve simply as legitimations for the occupancy of still other positions. Being a church member and a lay church leader establishes prestige and an identification with an institution whose purposes are held to be materially disinterested. All of the generalized leaders maintain church affiliations. Moreover, they carry this identification further by giving financial and verbal support to almost any religious activity. Similarly, they occupy positions in charitable money-raising drives and community projects designed to "benefit the whole community." As individuals they feel they must occupy these positions not because of the positions themselves but because of other dominant positions: Flint's church and charitable activities support his party and village board positions, Lee's community work and fire-fighting activities support his town board position.

It can be said that of the numerous positions an individual may occupy some are master positions in the sense that they account for the dominance of a public personality. The other positions—the honorary and the legitimizing and the unwanted positions—are mere reflections of the master positions. The secondary positions are meaningful because they support and sustain the positions of generalized leadership. In order to understand the leadership dynamics of the community, it is always important to locate and distinguish one type of leadership position from the other.[1]

The Dynamics of Secondary Leadership Roles

The qualifications for leadership in a given sphere are to a certain extent based on an individual's being situated in a special set of circumstances so that it is strategically possible for him to be available, prepared and, perhaps, indispensable for a number of different positions. Moreover, once an individual has acquired the halo of being a public leader, he is drawn into additional positions just because he is known as a leader.

Men like Lee, Flint, Jones and Young, simply on the basis of past experience, are walking libraries of community history, of similar organizational problems encountered in the past and of other people's capabilities and personal problems. They are experts on legal procedures and policy matters and have an experiential basis of judgment in such matters; and they are recognized by others as having such attributes. They are in a position to put specific issues, policies and conflicts in the broad framework of the total community and its past and, because of this, lesser individuals will not or are not able to act without them. As a result of these processes, leadership accumulates leadership even when the individual does not desire the position of leadership. Flint, particularly because of his knowledge of legal forms, is constantly called upon to serve in advisory capacities in a great variety of organizations. He is called in as a consultant, for example, by almost all the committees of the Community Club, by the fire companies and by the library association, and he accepts all such calls either by attending the meeting or by conferring with committee and organizational heads. Although

---

[1]Floyd Hunter, *Community Power Structure: A Study of Decision Makers* (University of North Carolina Press, Chapel Hill, N.C., 1953), and H. H. Gerth and C. Wright Mills, *Character and Social Structure* (Harcourt, Brace and Co., N.Y., 1953).

he complains about these demands on his time, he is forced to accept such secondary duties, even when they are not desired, in order to sustain and follow through on what he regards as his primary positions. He tries to resist such demands on his time and frequently publicly complains about being overburdened and overworked, but invariably he accedes "because I know nobody else will do the job—there aren't enough leaders in this town."

Thus it happens that the general leader is called into consultations and discussions in which he is not *primarily* interested. Were he to refuse such demands over a period of time, he would not possess the knowledge of community affairs necessary to the leadership positions which he regards as important, especially the various governing boards and the Republican committee.

Community leaders, regardless of their reluctance to extend their leadership into secondary positions, are forced to submit to pressures to become involved in unwanted and alien activities because, if they do not accept such secondary positions, they are likely to be thought of as selfish power grabbers who want only to take and not to give. Hence, there is always the risk of losing power in the primary spheres if they refuse to extend themselves into secondary spheres. Seen from their own perspective, however, this is not a coldly and rationally derived calculus. It is important to note that these community leaders believe in social participation and public service as a basic form of self-legitimation; though they may complain of overwork and burdensome responsibility, these are also statements of self-justification which reveal the psychological importance of the activity for the self-image.

However, this overwhelming occupancy of so many important positions by so few men places stresses on other potential leadership groups. People who aspire to generalized leadership or people who are interested in leadership in only one area find access to preferred positions blocked by generalized leaders who are frequently not primarily interested in holding the positions to which the potential leadership aspires. . . .

Supporting Leadership Positions

The multiplication of leadership roles by a relatively small number of unspecialized leaders has a further consequence. Simply because these top leaders are involved in such a wide and continuous range of activities— literally day and night—the amount of time they can give to any one activity is necessarily limited. That is, they are not in a position to do leg work, administration and other forms of detailed work. Their leadership tends to involve the intangibles of consultation, policy discussions, advising and the informal bringing together of information and data based on all their "positions" as all of their background bears on a particular situation. This is simply to say, for example, that Flint in his role as village counsel or Lee in his role as town clerk is able to coordinate in his own person all facts and factors in the total life of the community which bear on the particular problem being considered. At any one time Flint is the only man who is in a position to coordinate the decisions of the Community Club and the village board. Indeed in the combination of Flint, Lee, Jones and Young one could gain almost a complete picture of the major activities, plans, personnel and decisions that make up the life of the community at any given moment.

In order for such a leadership complex to operate, a secondary type of role complex exists which supports and sustains and makes possible the efficient leadership of top leaders. These are the roles of the workers, the doers and the executors. When decisions are made, when top leaders have decided upon a course of action, they call upon others to do the actual work: they themselves are concerned only with checking work as it is done, and are continuously involved in a succession of other policy matters in other spheres of community life. For them leadership is a continuous shifting between receiving reports on actions relevant to past decisions and making new decisions which result again in receiving new reports. Below the top layer of leadership there exists a varied assortment of people upon whom generalized leaders can rely to carry out programs. These consist of professionals, particularly teachers, young wives of industrial workers who are willing to spend part of their day in organizational activities, a few industrial workers and a host of people with specialized interests in sports, education, culture, community betterment and so forth. In other instances they may be people (particularly women) who are simply known to have time and an interest in getting out and doing something. Each community leader knows who these people are and to a certain extent each has his own private constituency of workers whom he can call upon when necessary. . . .

This second group of technical leaders enlarges and magnifies the number of individuals that constitute the leadership corps of the town. They are selected and recruited on a number of bases. Each of the aspirants to such indispensable but secondary positions is assessed and scrutinized in his various capacities as he performs a successive number of technical tasks. On the basis of past performance, an image of him as an organizational personality arise in the "leadership mind" and in the "public mind." Once this image forms and crystallizes, he wears it as a public definition and as a yoke for the rest of his life in the community. . . .

FORMAL LEADERSHIP AND ORGANIZATIONAL POWER

There is no clear relationship between technical or secondary positions in formal "offices" or chairs and the actual control of policy within the community. The highest political leaders in the community, for example, may have no formal political positions, though they may have a position in a church. Jones and Young hold no political office and Flint is only the appointed clerk of the village board. Similarly, many of those who are simply technical implementers and who make no major policy decisions may occupy what appear to be the top official positions. The mayor, for example, and frequently the president of the Community Club are persons who have no voice in the determination of community affairs. There is, hence, no way to decipher the relationship between position and power except by detailed ideographic examination of the lines of decision making and policy formulaton.

SPECIALIZED LEADERSHIP ROLES

The appearance that power is monolithic, even within the limitations noted above, would be false if we did not consider the community's specialized leadership roles. There are a great many leaders who are interested in and oriented to only one institutional sphere. In a sense, for such leaders, the interest in leadership flows from an interest in that sphere rather than from an interest in leadership itself. For instance, the interest may be purely occupational; a given occupational position qualifies an individual for a position as a leader for roles surrounding and appropriate to that occupation. Leadership stops at the limits or at the boundary of the impact of the occupation. Teachers and ministers both fall within this category. . . .

SPECIALIZED LEADERSHIP AND SOCIAL CHANGE

Although the organizational powers of specialized leaders are limited, power takes many forms in addition to the organization. As noted previously, the power and influence of specialized leaders is very great in effecting diffused styles of life, patterns of taste and consumption, agriculture, religion and education—all of the higher levels of values—but it does not effectively penetrate the channels of organizational control and policy making. *It is for this reason that the more diffused collective life of the town has a different dynamic than does its organized life. For this reason the town can change in its external appearances, in its demographic composition, in its cultural content and in the whole nature of its public life and character without experiencing any change in the individuals and groups who exercise organizational and political control.*

But, in addition, there are definite processes which account for changes in the importance of generalized leaders in the community. Unlike more diffuse changes which result from the activities of specialized leaders, those changes which affect the character of social classes always affect the character of life and the image of it which general leaders mirror. Thus the recent rise to dominance of farmers colors the community's self-image, though this is only in degree. At the political level this is expressed in the predominance of farm-oriented leaders in all important aspects of the organized life of the community. The relative decline in the social and political influence of businessmen in the last forty years goes hand in hand with the increasing influence of farmers and the social, but not organizational, influence of the consumption-minded middle class: all this leads to a reshaping of the community's character. Although the pyschological characteristics of the businessmen are still present, they do not dominate community life except in the purely political segments of village politics. . . . The psychological characteristics of the farmers have percolated through almost all aspects of the public life. The farmer's importance is seen in purest form in the general symbolization of the community as an agricultural community, the equation of the town with the farmers and their interests and the belief that the prosperity of the town rests on the prosperity of the prosperous farmers. At the interpersonal level this is reflected in the willingness of all groups to talk to the farmer in his language and on his terms even when this is alien to one's own language and life circumstances.

CLASS AND LEADERSHIP

The Businessmen

A number of small businessmen occupy formal leadership positions, but it is precisely they who are not the real leaders. Yet it is remarkable that in politics, at least at the village level, the political perspective of the small businessman is the dominant one. The gap between their lack of actual leadership while holding formal political positions and the dominance of their perspective in village politics is bridged by the political brokers. Flint and Jones are the primary brokers for the businessmen, though it is Flint who is most exclusively oriented to the business community.

From the standpoint of the leadership process it is important to consider the special characteristics of the political broker. What precisely is his function? To what extent is he an errand boy and to what extent does he impose his leadership? How does he respond to various types of tensions and pressures?

Economically Flint is dependent on the businessmen since they constitute an important part of his legal clientele and since he receives fees from public funds which they administrate, but this does not mean that he is an errand boy. For any specific issue the businessmen do not actually know what they want or how to get it. They do know, in a general way, what kind of end result would be satisfactory. It is Flint who has to tell them what is desirable from their point of view in specific situations. Moreover, he definitely and indispensably is the only person who can tell them what are the most efficient techniques for reaching their goals. When the railroad announced a plan to eliminate its Springdale service it was Flint who coordinated their views, convinced them that the issue pertained to them and provided them with the technical know-how for organizing and conducting their defense before the Public Service Commission.

What is more, Flint talks more to the individual businessmen than they talk to each other, so that at any given time he has more information about them than they have of each other. He knows more what they think as a group than any one of them. He sees issues and events from a perspective which includes all the individual perspectives of the businessmen, while each businessman has a perspective which arises from the peculiarities of his own position. This means that Flint more than any single businessman is in a position to create a favorable atmosphere for one or another side of an issue. He can give a businessman ideas which the businessman otherwise would not have had and, by knowing beforehand what each individual business-man thinks, he can compromise the conflicting views of different business-men before they individually know that they have differences of opinion. In this way he creates an *atmosphere* by creating a business viewpoint on an issue where without him such a viewpoint might not come into being.

This, of course, does not mean that the broker possesses unlimited power. The major limit on his power as a broker is that he cannot be obviously and demonstrably wrong in a way that the error can be definitely attributed to him. That is, the ultimate check on his power and leadership is the possibility of not being able to cover up his mistakes. It must be remembered that his power and leadership is largely informal and hence rests simply in the confidence of the conferring group.

However, the business group is only one of the reference groups that Flint faces. The other referent group that he faces is, as it were, a referent group of one, namely, Jones, who is the gatekeeper to almost all upper levels of politics. Jones, himself a businessman but an economic giant among midgets, is much more than a businessman. Because of his peculiar position, as we have noted, he faces all groups in the community. But, as we have also noted, Jones does not deal directly with the businessmen, but rather deals with them through Flint. This is necessary for him because he cannot afford to be identified with any one faction in the town. It is for this reason that Flint is placed in the position wherein he has "to clear it with Jones."

The test case in political dominance arises when Flint is placed in such a position that his interests as a representative of the business group are at odds with the interests of Jones as a representative of other groups. Such conflicts ordinarily revolve around the town tax rate or some indirect expression of the tax rate such as an appropriation for roads or road equipment. The question is: How does Flint resolve the conflict? First, he attempts to mediate the two sets of interests and to placate both—to assure the businessmen that a proposed new road will improve business and to encourage attempts to build the road without a noticeable tax increase. But when conflicts cannot be resolved at this level, Flint must defer to Jones and, what is more, he must justify his action to the businessmen. This is not always difficult since the businessmen recognize the dominance of the other interests represented by Jones.

The Prosperous Farmers

Lee operates at almost the same level with reference to the farmers, but in this case both Lee and Jones face the farmers directly. Both meet them personally, but they do not necessarily compete with each other. Lee deals with the farmers as a political figure who makes political contacts. The farmers identify him as a political figure and his concerns are the immediate and direct issues in the politics of the town board.

Jones, the dominant political figure in the community, does not have to discuss politics with the farmers. His relations with the farmers and their relations with him take place in what appear to be non-political contexts. He circulates among farmers both in his place of business and in visits to farmers' homes on occasions which are quite natural to the conduct of his business and to his personal likes and dislikes. Since he occupies no political office, no one has any direct excuse to approach him on purely political terms except Flint, Lee and Young. This means that he does not have to discuss politics publicly at the level of immediate issues and procedural conflicts. Yet, through his "non-political" contacts and discussion and from reports from others, he continuously "knows" and understands the big political picture for the entire area. There is thus no occasion for him to be publicly political except to those others who are openly identified with the public process of politics. This has numerous consequences.

Everyone in the community knows that Jones is the most powerful man in town and that he is the political boss, but only a few can deal with him directly as a political boss. His personality reinforces his unapproachability. He is a shy, quiet, unassuming man who never appears to stand out in public situations. This role of political unapproachability and "open public anonymity" has the following political consequences:

1. There are almost no occasions on which he is forced to play a public political role (to "stick out his public neck") in conflicts between the

various interests he represents. His subordinates are forced to fight publicly among themselves, and when the issue is resolved in favor of one group, he has never been openly involved even though the resolution of the conflict could not occur without his private intervention. Only on the rare occasion when his machine is directly threatened by outsiders like West will he show his hand publicly. An open public gesture on his part is a formidable act and is understood by all as a *caveat*. Jones acts publicly only when his own political existence is threatened.

2. In instances where unanimity is achieved by all parties to a conflict or where there is no conflict, Jones identifies himself with the unanimity and publicly takes his stand. He avoids a public stand on any divisive issues.

3. Due to these factors, Jones appears to have very little shape or form to most segments of the population. Groups who wish to influence policy or share power recognize that Jones is the major blockage, but, because of the very shapelessness of his political profile and his apparent abstinence from politics, he is not even accessible for public attack. Since he cannot be explicitly linked with politics, it is impossible to organize opposition against him—there is nothing explicit that can be opposed—and it is futile to attack his subordinates because they do not have the power.

4. As a further consequence of the formlessness of his political sway, it is not easy to place limits on the extent of his power. It is not even possible for an opposition group to estimate and assess the extent and limits of his power and knowledge within his private sphere of operations. For this reason it is just as easy for groups who would be inclined to oppose Jones to overestimate his authority as to underestimate it. All groups and individuals overestimate his authority, but by this very fact they increase his power, since they act on the basis of their estimation.

Different groups and individuals respond differently to the structure of Springdale's politics. Most groups who are interested in politics simply accept the fact of Jones's authority without attempting to measure it. They rather attempt to work within it by attempting to influence Flint and Lee. Neighborhood groups in rural areas approach Lee when they are interested in road improvements. In all matters pertaining to the village it is almost automatic for people to see Flint.

THE POLITICAL INNOVATOR

The only group which attempts to measure Jones's authority is the "community improvement" group, composed largely of the professional segment of the middle class. This is not a permanent political group, but rather a loose temporary grouping whose personnel changes with changes in issues. Different individuals from within this class organize temporarily around issues in which they have a highly specific interest—the youth recreation program, the swimming hole. The leadership for such temporary interest groupings is not formalized, but, again, varies to a certain extent according to issues. . . .

With the exception of the old aristocratic families who largely serve only in ceremonial functions, this exhausts the groups who provide leadership for the community at any significant level. However, individual members of all the classes, except the shack people, can become workers in the organized social activities of the community:

1. *Traditional farmers* may hold ceremonial positions in the Grange and may serve on various work committees in the churches or the Grange.
2. *Prosperous farmers* may hold higher ceremonial positions in the Grange and the Masons, may occupy some of the higher lay positions in the churches and occasionally serve on committees in the Community Club, or, as in one case, can be its president. When prosperous farmers do not occupy higher positions it is not because they cannot but rather because they are reluctant and feel they do not have time.
3. *The businessmen* carry on the routine program of the business bureau— plan the dinner meetings, secure the speakers and chair the committees concerned with business ethics and outside competition. Some assist in church canvasses and others help on Community Club projects and programs; they may be on a program committee or they may act in plays. Some of their wives are in the ladies' aids and book clubs.
4. *Professionals* and *skilled workers* carry the major burden of the work load in the churches, the Community Club, the P.T.A., the Masons, the library and the dramatic and choral activities.
5. *The marginal middle class*, particularly the aspiring investors and hard-working consumers, carry out the projects and programs of the American Legion and also occupy its higher positions. They also almost exclusively staff and man the positions and activities of volunteer fire companies.

The description of such positions and the classes that fill them tell something about the nature of the organizations, but it tells very little about the dynamics of the community. Primarily, this is because at the very point where important decisions affecting the structure of the community are made the real decision-makers occupy no important formal positions which are relevant to the decision. The decision-makers may occupy positions which are only a *reflection* of the informal positions they hold, and which are not the position which announce the decisions.

LEADERSHIP AND SOCIAL CHANGE

Decision-making in the community is not a specialized function. The decisive leaders of the community do not occupy any specialized positions and are not limited in their decision-making to decisions whch affect only one sphere of the life of the community. Rather the same individuals, some of whom occupy no formal positions, are involved in making decisions which affect all aspects of the community. They shift their focus of attention from sphere to sphere as decisions in one particular sphere affect different aspects of the community is different ways.

As a permanent "policy" (although policy is too calculating an expression since they are simply following the logic of their attempt to maintain control) they attempt to limit the areas in which specialized leaders can exercise authority and influence the community. They attempt to restrict the activities of all specialized expert groups except the political expert, that is, themselves. It must be remembered, however, that this attempt to control is with respect to local affairs only. They attempt to retain control within the local community at the same time that the local community is changing and is influenced by the outside world. In spite of the complexities of the problems of local control, these amount to almost nothing in comparison to the changes the community is undergoing with reference to and as a product of the outside world. In a sense, then, the opposition to the local leadership does not consist of dissident groups within the community but rather the whole trend of mass society which impinges on the local arena. In his attempts to deal with such larger trends in modern society, the hardboiled realistic politician takes on as his adversary the major currents of change in modern society that affect the small town. Seen in this light, the political realists become genuine romanticists, and so it appears that it is precisely such romanticism which seems to keep the local society functioning regardless of the stresses and strains under which it operates.

However, one must not overlook the fact that their control in the local community is exercised from the standpoint of a number of real political bases. They draw their support from all the dominant groups in the town. From one point of view, then, it is not their own narrow class interest that they express, though this is not always as clear in the case of Jones, but even he goes much beyond his own immediate class interests in his political concerns. To a certain extent, then, politics and the direction of community affairs have an autonomy of their own. Perhaps this is simply because those who are concerned with politics become submerged in the aesthetics and the sheer rhythm of politics.

But even when they are not directly concerned with their own class interests, the political managers must take into account the class interests of the significant economic groups that impinge upon politics and they must weigh and balance the interests of these groups. They must develop programs which are combinations and compromises that reflect the weight, the interests, the activity and the intensity of feeling of these groups. In a sense the political managers, then, are actors who play to a passive audience and who, after all their histrionics, depend on their ability to please and entertain groups which frequently appear to be only observers. The players aim all their acting at the audience and the audience acts only to approve or reject. Only in extreme situations is the audience seen as the instigator in the interchange between player and audience, but if one follows the plays performed and the manner in which they are played, one can see the relationship between the player and the audience. However, to account for changes in the play and in the acting, it is always necessary to account for changes in the composition of that part of the audience which has the interest and the price of a ticket. At some points the audience changes to the point where certain actors lack the ability and the skills to please it, and these are the crucial points in the history of the town. The dynamics of the town which change the composition and character of the political audience thus, while hidden, are decisive in determining the scene, the cast and the play.

GOVERNING NEW YORK CITY

Wallace S. Sayre and Herbert Kaufman

The notion that the giant cities of today are run by some monolithic political "machine" or "interests," economic or otherwise, should be cast into serious doubt by a thorough reading of the volume from which this selection is taken. Sayre and Kaufman provide us with a clear, systematic statement of the competitive, multicentered nature of decision making in New York City. Policy seems not so much to be made as to be extruded from the crevices between semi-autonomous centers of influence. That New York City is not unique in this pluralist pattern may be judged from other volumes dealing with Chicago and Syracuse. The counterpoised fears of these decision makers in New York prevent the development of a cohesive, internally consistent elite who "run the town." The decision centers are numerous and they are kept from flying apart by a series of "balance wheels" in the system.

Sayre and Kaufman examine the election process, the distribution of city positions, and the outcome of specific issues. In addition, they study, over a period of time, the activities of groups and institutions which they identify as key participants in the political process. Basing their selections on historical data and other evidence, the participants they designate are: administrators of line agencies and other key bureaucrats; special authorities and certain agencies; parties and nongovernmental groups; the courts; officials of other governments; the city council; the Board of Estimate; and the Mayor's office.

A full view and a fair judgment of New York City's many-faceted politcal and governmental system has been a matter of national as well as local debate for at least a century and a half. Historians and journalists, statesmen and politicians, social scientists and other analysts, writers in verse and prose have all been fascinated by the power, the variety, the size, and the significance of the city, its politics, and its government. But they have not achieved

Excerpted from Chapter 19, "Risks, Rewards, and Remedies," in *Governing New York City*, by Wallace S. Sayre and Herbert Kaufman, © 1960 by Russell Sage Foundation, New York.

consensus. The city in the nation, the city in the state, the city in its metro-politan region, the city as a city, the quality of its political and govern-mental life—all these remain, and will continue, as matters of debate and discussion, of interest and concern—for the nation as well as for the city.

The most striking characteristic of the city's politics and government is one of scale. No other American city approaches the magnitude, scope, variety, and complexity of the city's governmental tasks and accomplish-ments. Nor does any other city represent so important a political prize, in its electorate and its government, in the national party contest. Nor can any other city match the drama, the color, and the special style of the city's own politics. In all these respects the city is imperial, if not unique, among American cities.

The city's politics and government have been more widely known for their defects than for their claims to excellence. This notoriety rather than fame for the city has been the product of many causes. There has been the city's high visibility as the nation's largest urban center. There have been the effective processes of exposure built into the city's political system. There have been the highly articulate voices of dissent and criticism always pre-sent in the city. There have been, too, the scale and theatrical qualities of the defects in the city's political system. And the citizens of the city have themselves been more given to eloquence in their indignation at "failures" than in their pride over "successes." Notoriety is, in this sense, perhaps itself a valid claim to fame for the city: the city's political and governmental system has never produced contentment, acquiescence, or a sense of lasting defeat among its critics. The voice of the critic has often had the most attentive audience.

The city's political system is, in fact, vigorously and incessantly competi-tive. The stakes of the city's politics are large, the contestants are numerous and determined, the rules of the competition are known to and enforced against each other by the competitors themselves, and the city's electorate is so uncommitted to any particular contestant as to heighten the competition for the electorate's support or consent. No single ruling élite dominates the political and governmental system of New York City.

A MULTIPLICITY OF DECISION CENTERS

The decisions that distribute the prizes of politics in New York City issue from a large number of sources.

Each source consists of two parts: a "core group" at the center, invested by the rules with the formal authority to legitimize decisions (that is, to promulgate them in the prescribed forms and according to the specified procedures that make them binding under the rules) and a constellation of "satellite groups," seeking to influence the authoritative issuances of the core group. The five large categories of participants in the city's political contest whose roles have been described in this volume—the party leaders, the elected and appointed public officials, the organized bureaucracies, the numerous nongovernmental associations (including the mass media of communication), the officials and agencies of other governments—play their parts upon the many stages the city provides. The most visible of these stages are those provided by the formal decision centers in each of which a core group and its satellite groups occupy the middle of the stage. Every center (every core group and its satellite groups), whatever its stage, must also continuously acknowledge the supervising presence of the city's electorate, possessing the propensity and the capacity to intervene decisively in the contest on the side of one contestant or the other.

Party leaders are core groups for nominations. They function as satellites, however, in many decisions about appointments, and in connection with substantive program and policy decisions in their role as brokers for other claimants. The city's electorate is the core group for electoral decisions, where it has a virtual monopoly. Other participants in the contest for the stakes of politics may exert considerable influence on the electorate, but only in the same fashion as satellite groups in other special areas influence each appropriate core group.

In all other decision centers the core groups are composed of officials. Most prominent among these core groups are the officials presiding over the decision centers of the general organs of government—the Mayor, the Board of Estimate, the Council, and the legislators and executives at the higher levels of government. Their decisions spread across the entire spectrum of the city's governmental functions and activities; consequently, all the other participants in the political process are, at one time or another and in varying combinations, satellite groups to these central core groups, trying to influence their actions. Each of their decisions, it is true, evokes active responses only from those participants particularly interested in the affected sphere of governmental activity, but most of their decisions prove to be of interest to some participants in all the five major categories (though rarely to all participants in all categories). In the course of time, most groups taking part in the city's politics apply leverage to the core groups in the general governmental institutions in efforts to secure favorable decisions. The courts are also general organs, and therefore the judges as the core group in that arena are of interest to most contestants at one time or another, but the modes of influence exerted on them are somewhat more restricted and institutionalized than those exerted on the core groups of other general organs.

Functionally specialized officials constitute the core groups for decisions in particular functional areas of governmental action, whether these are in line agencies (such as the Board of Education, the Department of Welfare, the

Police Department, the Fire Department, the Department of Health), in special authorities (Transit, Housing, Triborough Bridge and Tunnel, or the Port of New York Authority), or in overhead agencies (the Budget Bureau, the Personnel Department, the Law Department, the City Planning Department, for example). Each of these decision centers is surrounded by satellite groups especially concerned with its decisions—the leaders of the interests served, the interests regulated, professional societies and associations, organized bureaucracies, labor unions, suppliers of revenues and materials, and others. Usually, the groups concerned chiefly with particular functions are uninterested in decisions in other, unrelated functional areas, so that most of the decisions (about appointments as well as programs and policies) in each decision center are worked out by an interplay among the specialized core and its satellite groups.

Most officials have a dual role. They appear not merely in core groups but also as satellites of other officials. From the point of view of the general organs, for instance, the agency heads are claimants endeavoring to influence decisions in the city's central governmental institutions. From the point of view of a department head, the general organs are satellites making demands. Although the general organs' influence on agency leaders is especially strong, it is not by any measure complete domination; the agency leaders commonly preserve a region of autonomy free from invasion by the central organs as well as from other groups and institutions. Department heads also often see their own official colleagues (particularly the heads of overhead agencies), as well as the leaders of the organized bureaucracies, acting as satellite groups, as wielders of influence, and as competitors. Their counterparts in other governments tend to appear in the same light. Other officials (themselves core groups in their own respective areas) are thus likely to appear among the satellites of any particular official core group.

The leaders of the city's organized bureaucracies are, strictly speaking, never members of a core group but always a satellite group seeking to exert influence over one or more core groups. Their role is not without ambiguity in this respect, however, for many bureaucrats also occupy significant decision-making posts in the city government. As members or leaders in their organized bureaucratic groups, these bureaucrats thus occasionally play a dual part; as leaders or members of satellite groups they engage in efforts to influence the actions of a core group in which they are also members. But these are not yet typical situations. In most instances, the leaders of the organized bureaucracies are satellite groups.

The leaders of the city's nongovernmental groups never formally constitute core groups, but appear instead as satellites. Functionally specialized groups, being close to the agency officials whose decisions affect them, are not far from the center of the particular arena in which they operate. But, except when they are coopted into what amounts to a part of officialdom, they cannot do what the core groups do: issue authoritative, official, binding decisions. As satellites, some of the civic groups, and the communication media, are active and frequently highly influential in a broad range of functional spheres. In any specific functional area of governmental activity, however, it is the specialized, well-organized, persistent, professionally staffed nongovernmental organizations that continuously affect the pattern of decisions. Core groups of officials tend to estimate the reactions of other nongovernmental groups that might be galvanized to action by specific decisions, and the officials respond to the representations of such groups when these groups are sufficiently provoked to exert pressure. But the impact of these organizations is more intermittent and uncertain than that of those with sustained and specialized programs of influence. Yet even the specialized are compelled by the nature of the rules to accept roles as satellites.

DECISIONS AS ACCOMMODATIONS

No single group of participants in the city's political contest is self-sufficient in its power to make decisions or require decisions of others. Every decision of importance is consequently the product of mutual accommodation. Building temporary or lasting alliances, working out immediate or enduring settlements between allies or competitors, and bargaining for an improved position in the decision centers are the continuing preoccupations of all leaders—whether party leaders, public officials, leaders of organized bureaucracies, or leaders of nongovernmental groups.

Each core group is constantly bargaining and reaching understandings of varying comprehensiveness and stability with some of its satellite groups, seeking a coalition of forces which will enable it to issue decisions that will stand against the opposition of those outside the coalition. The satellite groups, in turn, are just as constantly bargaining with each other for alliances on specific decisions or more permanent agreements. These accommodations between core and satellite group and among satellite groups represent an infinite variety of bargains, some leaving the core group with considerable freedom of movement, others tying it into close partnership with other members of an alliance, and still others imprisoning it within a powerful coalition of satellite groups. Since almost all core groups confront a competing and often numerous field of satellite groups, bargaining is perpetual.

Bargaining and accommodation are equally characteristic of the relations between one core group plus its satellites and other core groups with their satellites. These accommodations are necessary since some core groups have supervisory authority over others, some have competing jurisdictional claims, and almost all are competitors for the scarce dollars available through the budget.

Indeed, core groups themselves do not exhibit solid internal unity; each is in many respects a microcosm of the entire system. The central organs of government, for example, are in reality mosaics: The Board of Estimate with its powerful borough representatives, the office of Mayor with its many commissioners and assistants chosen by expediency rather than preference, the Council composed of councilmen representing small districts and operating through many committees—all three are assemblages of many parts. The state legislature, the Governor, and the other elected and appointed state executives are similarly divided when they become involved in the city's government and politics. Even more so are the central institutions of the federal government dealing with the city.

In much the same way, the city's administrative agencies are not monoliths but aggregates of components enjoying varying degrees of autonomy. Each department head must learn to deal with his deputies and assistants, his bureau chiefs, sometimes his organized bureaucracies. The organized bureaucracies are likewise splintered along functional, religious, professional, trade union, rank, and other lines. Party leaders may be described as a class but, in fact, they constitute a large number of rather independent participants in city government, rivaling each other, bargaining with each other, working out more or less unstable agreements with each other. The electorate itself, the sometimes remote and nebulous presence that shapes and colors the entire contest for the stakes of politics, is composed of a multitude of subdivisions—the various geographical constituencies, the regular voters and those who appear only for spectacular electoral battles, the party-line voters and the selective nonvoters, the ticket-splitters, the ethnic and religious voters, the ideological voters of all persuasions, as well as the social and economic class voters.

The process of bargaining, in short, reaches into the core of each decision center and is not confined to relations between core groups, or between core groups and their satellites, or between satellites. If there is any single feature of the system of government and politics in New York City that may be called ubiquitous and invariant, it would seem to be the prevalence of mutual accommodation. Every program and policy represents a compromise among the interested participants.

PARTIAL SELF-CONTAINMENT OF DECISION CENTERS

The decisions that flow from each constellation of groups active in each of the city's decision centers are ordinarily formulated and carried out without much calculated consideration of the decisions emanating from the other centers. They are usually made in terms of the special perspectives and values of the groups with particular interests in the governmental functions or activities affecting them. Only occasionally are they formulated in a broader frame of reference.

This fragmentation of governmental decision-making in the city is partially offset by features of the system tending to introduce more or less common premises of decision into the centers. A major "balance wheel" has been noted by David B. Truman: the overlapping memberships of many groups in society. The same individuals turn up in many contexts and in many guises, carrying to each the viewpoints and information acquired in the others. A second balance wheel is the frequency with which the core groups of one center operate as satellite groups in other centers; no center is completely isolated from the others. Overhead agencies serve as a third unifying element, for they cut across the whole range of governmental functions and activities, introducing, within the limits of their own specialties, a common set of assumptions and goals into many of the decisions of other centers. A fourth unifying factor is represented by the civic groups and the press, which exert their influence on a wide variety of decision centers without regard to the subject-matter specialties of the centers. They are not equally effective everywhere, and they are seldom so effective in any given center as the more specialized participants in it, but they help to relate what happens in every center to what goes on in others. Finally, the central institutions of government (including the courts) operate under relatively few functional restrictions and therefore make decisions with respect to all phases of the city's government and politics. Collectively, their perspectives are broad, their interests are inclusive, their desire to rationalize and balance the actions in all decision centers is strong, and their formal authority to impose a common basis for decisions is superior to that of other groups. These five factors help to keep the system from flying apart.

Yet the autonomous nature of the core group and its satellite groups in each decision center is striking. Although the leaders may belong to many groups, they behave, when particular decisions are at issue, with a remarkable lack of ambivalence. The interests immediately at stake provide the criteria of action, and they often seem unambiguous; at any given moment, group leaders and members act as though they had only one interest, one membership, at that moment. Most participants are galvanized to action by only a relatively narrow range of issues and ignore most others no matter where they occur; as a result, most of the actors in any center share very special interests in the problems at hand, and the casual outsider or the intermittent satellite group has much less effect on the decisions made there than do the strongly motivated "regulars." As modes of integrating the decisions of the city's whole governmental system, the balance wheels have therefore not been spectacularly successful.

What is perhaps most surprising is the failure of the central organs of government to provide a high level of integration for the city's system. The

Council has been weak, the Board of Estimate inert, the Mayor handicapped. The government at Albany cannot do the job of pulling the decision centers of the city together, even if it were so inclined. This would mean running the city, a task the state is unable and unwilling to assume, a task that would not win it the thanks of the city's residents or of other residents of the state. Moreover, the state government has not been inclined to strengthen the central institutions of the city, but has enacted legislation and created agencies that intensify the independence of many local officials. State administrative supervision of city agencies has encouraged many city officers and employees to develop close links with their functional counterparts in the state capital, and to rely on these to buttress their resistance to leadership from the city's central institutions. The nature of the judicial process renders the courts incapable of performing an integrative function. Thus, despite the opportunities for integration presented by the formal powers of the city's central institutions, they have generally either officially ratified the agreements reached by the active participants in each decision center, which are offered to them as the consensus of experts and interested groups, or, on an *ad hoc* basis, have chosen one or another alternative suggested when the experts and interested groups have been divided on an issue. It is in the latter role that the city's central institutions have had their greatest significance. Seldom have they imposed, on their own initiative, a common set of objectives on all the centers of decision. The central institutions are important participants in all the decision-making in the contest for the stakes of politics in the city, but they are rarely the prime movers or the overriding forces.

As a result, most individual decisions are shaped by a small percentage of the city's population—indeed, by a small percentage of those who engage actively in its politics—because only the participants directly concerned have the time, energy, skill, and motivation to do much about them. The city government is most accurately visualized as a series of semi-autonomous little worlds, each of which brings forth official programs and policies through the interaction of its own inhabitants. There are commentators who assert that Tammany, or Wall Street, or the Cathedral, or the labor czars, or the bureaucracy, or even the underworld rules New York. Some of these, it is true, are especially influential in shaping some decisions in some specialized areas. Taking the system over-all, however, none, nor all combined, can be said to be in command; large segments of the city's government do not attract their attention at all. New York's huge and diverse system of government and politics is a loose-knit and multicentered network in which decisions are reached by ceaseless bargaining and fluctuating alliances among the major categories of participants in each center, and in which the centers are partially but strikingly isolated from one another. . . .

WHO GOVERNS?

Robert A. Dahl

Robert Dahl's study of New Haven, Connecticut (population 150,000) has been a very influential book, especially upon students of political science. In Who Governs? *Dahl attempted to develop an alternative to those research methodologies which had so often before yielded evidence that American communities were "run," directly or indirectly, by an elite whose power rested on economic resources or social standing. Even more important,* Who Governs? *was a comprehensive effort to develop an empirically based theory of democratic pluralism.*

In reviewing the following excerpts drawn from throughout the original work, the reader may wish to ask: What is Dahl's concept of power and how is it exercised in New Haven? Are the issues selected for study suited in substance and number to the author's objectives? Is it possible to build a general theory of politics from the New Haven experience or from any case study?

In general, the reader might ask how the findings in other selections in this volume fit Dahl's model of democratic pluralism.

The Definition and Measurement of Influence

During three and a half centuries from Thomas Hobbes to Max Weber little was done to make widely used notions of power or influence more precise. In the last quarter century, and particularly in the last decade, the problem of providing operational meaning and measurements for the concepts of power and influence has received a good deal of attention. Nonetheless, no entirely satisfactory solutions to the numerous problems involved have yet been set forth, and this book necessarily reflects the fact that concepts and methods in the analysis of influence are undergoing rapid changes. . . .

From Robert A. Dahl, *Who Governs?* (New Haven, Conn.: Yale University Press, 1961). Reprinted by permission of the publisher.

Operational Measures of Influence

One of the most serious problems in the study of influence arises from the fact that, no matter how precisely one defines influence and no matter how elegant the measures and methods one proposes, the data within reach even of the most assiduous researcher require the use of operational measures that are at best somewhat unsatisfactory.

One way to compensate for the unsatisfactory character of all existing operational measures of influence is to be eclectic. In this study, an eclectic approach was adopted deliberately, not only to avoid putting all our eggs in one methodological basket but also in order to take advantage of the existence of a very wide assortment of data. Six methods of assessing relative influence or changes in influence were used in this study. These were:

1. To study changes in the socioeconomic characteristics of incumbents in city offices in order to determine whether any rather large historical changes may have occurred in the sources of leadership. . . .
2. To isolate a particular socioeconomic category and then determine the nature and extent of participation in local affairs by persons in this category. . . .
3. To examine a set of "decisions" in different "issue-areas" in order to determine what kinds of persons were the most influential according to one operational measure of relative influence, and to determine patterns of influence. . . .
4. To survey random samples of participants in different issue-areas in order to determine their characteristics. This method was used to locate the socioeconomic sources of the subleaders in different issue-areas.
5. To survey random samples of registered voters in order to determine the characteristics of those who participate in varying degrees and in varying ways in local affairs. . . .
6. To study changes in patterns of voting among different strata in the community. . . .

Democracy, Leadership, and Minority Control

It is easy to see why observers have often pessimistically concluded that the internal dynamics of political associations create forces alien to popular control and hence to democratic institutions. Yet the characteristics I have described [relatively firm control of an association's direction by a small leadership stratum] are not necessarily dysfunctional to a pluralistic democracy in which there exists a considerable measure of popular control over the policies of leaders, for minority control by leaders within associations is not necessarily inconsistent with popular control over leaders through electoral processes.

For example, suppose that (1) a leader of a political association feels a strong incentive for winning an election; (2) his constituents comprise most of the adult population of the community; (3) nearly all of his constituents are expected to vote; (4) voters cast their ballots without receiving covert rewards or punishments as a direct consequence of the way they vote; (5) voters give heavy weight to the overt policies of a candidate in making their decision as to how they will vote; (6) there are rival candidates offering alternative policies; and (7) voters have a good deal of information about the policies of the candidates. In these circumstances, it is almost certain that leaders of political associations would tend to choose overt policies they believed most likely to win the support of a majority of adults in the community. Even if the policies of political associations were usually controlled by a tiny minority of leaders in each association, the policies of the leaders who won elections to the chief elective offices in local government would tend to reflect the preferences of the populace. I do not mean to suggest that any political system actually fulfills all these conditions, but to the extent that it does the leaders who directly control the decisions of political associations are themselves influenced in their own choices of policies by their assumptions as to what the voting populace wants.

Although this is an elementary point, it is critical to an understanding of the chapters that follow. We shall discover that in each of a number of key sectors of public policy, a few persons have great *direct* influence on the choices that are made; most citizens, by contrast, seem to have rather little direct influence. Yet it would be unwise to underestimate the extent to which voters may exert *indirect* influence on the decisions of leaders by means of elections.

In a political system where key offices are won by elections, where legality and constitutionality are highly valued in the political culture, and where nearly everyone in the political stratum publicly adheres to a doctrine of democracy, it is likely that the political culture, the prevailing attitudes of the political stratum, and the operation of the political system itself will be shaped by the role of elections. Leaders who in one context are enormously influential and even rather free from demands by their constituents may reveal themselves in another context to be involved in tireless efforts to adapt their policies to what they think their constituents want.

To be sure, in a pluralistic system with dispersed inequalities, the direct influence of leaders on policies extends well beyond the norms implied in the classical models of democracy developed by political philosophers. But if the leaders lead, they are also led. Thus the relations between leaders, subleaders, and constituents produce in the distribution of influence a stubborn and pervasive ambiguity that permeates the entire political system.

Some Hypotheses

Given these assumptions, one might reasonably expect to find in the political system of New Haven that the distribution of influence over important decisions requiring the formal assent of local governmental officials is consistent with the following hypotheses:

First, only a small proportion of the citizens will have much *direct* influence on decisions in the sense of directly initiating proposals for policies subsequently adopted or successfully vetoing the proposals of others.

Second, the leaders—i.e., citizens with relatively great direct influence—will have a corps of auxiliaries or subleaders to help them with their tasks.

Third, because a democratic creed is widely subscribed to throughout the political stratum, and indeed throughout the population, the public or overt relationships of influence between leaders and subleaders will often be clothed in the rituals and ceremonies of "democratic" control, according to which the leaders are only the spokesmen or agents of the subleaders, who are "representatives" of a broader constituency.

Fourth, because of the need to win elections in order to hold key elective offices, leaders will attempt to develop followings of loyal supporters among their constituents.

Fifth, because the loyalty and support of subleaders, followings, and other constituents are maintained by memories of past rewards or the expectation of future rewards, leaders will shape their policies in an attempt to insure a flow of rewards to all those elements whose support is needed. Consequently, in some circumstances, subleaders, followings, and other constituents will have significant *indirect* influence on the decisions of leaders. The existence of this indirect influence is an important source of ambiguity in understanding and interpreting the actions of leaders in a pluralistic system.

Finally, conflicts will probably occur from time to time between leaders' overt policies, which are designed to win support from constituents, and their covert policies, which are shaped to win the support of subleaders or other leaders. The keener the political competition, the more likely it is that leaders will resolve these conflicts in favor of their overt commitments.

To determine whether these propositions actually fit the political system of New Haven, I now propose to turn to three "issue-areas" where it is possible to examine decisions to see what processes of influence are at work. Decisions in two of these areas, public education and urban redevelopment, require the formal assent of local government officials at many points. The third, the process of making nominations in the two major parties for local elective offices, is only quasi-governmental, but I have chosen it on the assumption that whoever controls nominations might be presumed to occupy a critical role in any effort to gain the assent of local officials. . . .

DIRECT VERSUS INDIRECT INFLUENCE

The six hypotheses . . . seem to be consistent with the processes for making decisions in New Haven, at least in the three issue-areas examined in the preceding three chapters. If one analyzes the way in which influence in these three issue-areas is distributed among citizens of New Haven, one finds that only a small number of persons have much *direct* influence, in the sense that they successfully initiate or veto proposals for policies. These persons, the leaders, have subleaders and followers. Because of widespread belief in the democratic creed, however, overt relationships of influence are frequently accompanied by democratic ceremonials, which, though ceremonial, are not devoid of consequences for the distribution of influence. The choices made by constituents in critical elections, such as those in New Haven in 1945 and 1955, do have great *indirect* influence on the decisions of leaders, for results of elections are frequently interpreted by leaders as indicating a preference for or acquiescence in certain lines of policy.

Assuming one could measure the amount of influence each adult in New Haven exerts over decisions in a given issue-area, . . . many constituents have no direct influence at all; most people have very little. Subleaders of course have much more; the influence of the most powerful subleaders merges imperceptibly into that of leaders. Only a tiny group, the leaders, exerts great influence.

If one were to illustrate *indirect* influence, . . . a few citizens who are nonvoters, and who for some reason have no influential contact with voters, have no indirect influence. Most citizens, however, possess a moderate degree of indirect influence, for elected leaders keep the real or imagined preferences of constituents constantly in mind in deciding what policies to adopt or reject. Subleaders have greater indirect influence than most other citizens, since leaders ordinarily are concerned more about the response of an individual subleader than an individual citizen. Finally, leaders exert a great amount of indirect influence on one another, for each is guided to some extent by what he believes is acceptable to some or all of the other leaders.

Unfortunately, one cannot measure influence so precisely. . . . [There are] ambiguities in the relations of leaders and constituents which are extremely difficult and probably impossible to resolve satisfactorily at present by appeal to direct evidence. These ambiguities are created by the fact that leaders do not merely *respond* to the preferences of constituents; leaders also *shape* preferences.

Suppose the leaders in every issue-area are substantially identical and agree on the policies they want. One may even suppose that although not identical they are all drawn from a single homogeneous stratum of the community and therefore possess identical or complementary objectives—which is rather as it must have been in the days of the patrician oligarchy. The capacity of leaders to shape the preferences of citizens would surely be relatively high in either case. Ordinary citizens would depend on a single, unified body of leaders for information and cues about policies; they would have relatively little opportunity to pick up information about other alternatives. Moreover, if leaders in all issue-areas were substantially alike and agreed on objectives, they could combine their political resources to induce citizens to support their policies through many different techniques of coercion and persuasion. Leaders could, and presumably would, *aggregate their resources* to achieve common objectives.

Suppose, on the other hand, that leaders differ from area to area and disagree among themselves, and that because of their disagreements they actively seek for support from constituents. Then the capacity of leaders to shape the preferences of citizens would—other things remaining the same— be lower. Citizens would have alternative sources of information, and the techniques of coercion and persuasion employed by one group of leaders could be countered to some extent by other leaders.

Clearly, then, in order to answer the question, "Who rules in New Haven?" we need to know more than the *distribution* of influence. We need also to know something about *patterns* of influence. . . .

SPECIALIZATION OF INFLUENCE: SUBLEADERS

Probably the most striking characteristic of influence in New Haven is the extent to which it is *specialized*; that is, individuals who are influential in one sector of public activity tend not to be influential in another sector; and, what is probably more significant, the social strata from which individuals in one sector tend to come are different from the social strata from which individuals in other sectors are drawn.

This specialization shows up most clearly among the subleaders, whose characteristics will be examined in this chapter. In the next, evidence will be presented bearing on the specialization of the top leaders.

Similarities Among Subleaders

Considered as a group, the subleaders in the three issue-areas studied earlier—party nominations, urban redevelopment, and public education—

possess certain similarities that tend to distinguish them from the average registered voter.

First, subleaders stand somewhat above their fellow citizens in financial position, educational attainments, and social status. In a society where public life is still widely thought to be a man's world and where men rather than women are generally expected to occupy the positions of responsibility, it is not surprising that two-thirds of the subleaders are men. But they are distinguished by more than merely the conventional privileges of American manhood. Subleadership in New Haven is skewed toward the middling strata. Subleaders tend to live in better than average residential areas. The majority hold white-collar jobs. Even within the white-collar category itself, there are three times as many professionals, proprietors, and managers among the subleaders as among registered voters. The subleaders have received considerably more education. They earn more money. They are more likely to own their own homes.

Considering the electorate of New Haven, the working classes are numerically under-represented and the middle strata numerically overrepresented among the subleaders. . . . [Nevertheless] subleaders are much more similar to voters than to the Social and Economic Notability of New Haven.

SPECIALIZATION OF INFLUENCE: LEADERS

The specialization that characterizes the subleaders is also marked among the leaders. With few exceptions any particular individual exerts a significant amount of direct influence in no more than one of the three issue-areas studied.

Of the various decisions examined in redevelopment, twenty-six actors (persons or groups) succeeded in initiating a policy or vetoing a proposed policy. In party nominations, thirteen actors were successful—four in the Democratic party and nine in the Republican party. In public education, sixteen actors exerted direct influence. Eliminating duplications, fifty different individual actors initiated or vetoed policies in all three.

However, only three leaders initiated or vetoed policies in more than one issue-area. . . .

Of the remaining forty-seven leaders, twenty-seven, or more than half, exerted direct influence in only one instance. Seventeen exerted direct influence in two or three instances in only one issue-area. And three exerted direct influence in four or more instances in only one area. . . .

Altogether, six leaders successfully initiated or vetoed proposals four times or more in at least one issue-area. . . . Of these, only two—the two mayors—exerted direct influence in all three. . . .

Doubtless greater overlap could be found in other sectors of policy—for example, in party nominations, patronage, and city contracts. . . . Despite these qualifications, however, the extent of specialization of influence is striking. In New Haven, it would appear, only the mayor is in a position to exercise much direct influence on more than a few sectors of public policy.

Direct influence is not only specialized. To a great extent it reposes—or at any rate it has in recent years—in the hands of public officials. Of twenty-five persons with high or intermediate influence, sixteen were public officials. . . .

To what extent are the leaders drawn from a single homogeneous stratum of the community? Of the fifty different actors, fifteen were agencies, groups, or corporations; they acted in situations where it was impossible to ascribe the initiation or veto of policy to a particular person. Of these fifteen collective actors, four were business firms, three were citizen groups, and eight were federal, state, or local government agencies. Of the thirty-five individual persons, seven were Social or Economic Notables and the remaining twenty-eight were not. Sixteen of the individual persons were of Yankee, English, or Scotch-Irish stock; six were of Irish stock; four were of Italian stock; and nine were of various European origins, other than Ireland, Italy, or the British Isles. Seventeen were Protestants, thirteen were Catholics, and five were Jews.

As with the subleaders, the issue-area in which a leader's influence is specialized seems to be a function of durable interests or concerns. These interests can usually be traced initially to professional or occupational goals and strivings. Leaders in redevelopment are with a few exceptions officially, professionally, or financially involved in its fate. Most of the leaders in the public schools have a professional connection of some kind with education. The occupational ties of party leaders are more complex. Usually, however, there is reciprocal benefit: party connections advance the leader in his occupational goals, and occupation success in turn enables him to enhance his influence in the party.

Thus the answers to two of the questions set out [earlier] are furnished by the phenomenon of specialization:

TABLE 1   Sources of Leadership

Level of influence	Public Officials	Notables or Corporations	Others	Total
Low	11°	8°	8	27
Intermediate	12°	4°	3	19
High	4	1	1	6
Total	27	13	12	52°°

° An individual who was both an official and a Notable was counted in both columns.
°° Includes two individuals who were counted both as officials and Notables.

First, a leader in one issue-area is not likely to be influential in another. If he is, he is probably a public official and most likely the mayor.

Second, leaders in different issue-areas do not seem to be drawn from a single homogeneous stratum of the community.

Other questions remain. To what extent do leaders in different issue-areas agree on a common strategy? And how do they settle their conflicts? In short, how are the actions of different leaders with specialized influence over decisions in different issue-areas integrated?

FIVE PATTERNS OF LEADERSHIP

The number of theoretically possible patterns of integration is almost infinite. However, because of their familiarity and generality, five possibilities were considered in our study of New Haven. These were:

1. Covert integration by Economic Notables.
2. An executive-centered "grand coalition of coalitions."
3. A coalition of chieftains.
4. Independent sovereignties with spheres of influence.
5. Rival sovereignties fighting it out.

The first of these, covert integration by the Economic Notables, is a common answer suggested by studies of a number of other cities. In this pattern the top leaders consist of a unified group of private citizens who arrive at agreements about policies by covert negotiations and discussions carried on in the privacy of their clubs, homes, business firms, and other private meeting places. Leaders gain their influence from their wealth, high social standing, and economic dominance. . . .

I believe the evidence advanced in previous chapters is sufficient to warrant the rejection of the hypothesis that this pattern applies to New Haven. In every city where Economic Notables are alleged to rule covertly, it is important to note, evidently they do so by means sufficiently open to permit scholars and newspapermen to penetrate the veil; indeed, an inspection of the information contained in descriptions of these cities indicates that the job of probing into the clandestine structure of power has presented few barriers to the assiduous researcher. It is all the more improbable, then, that a secret cabal of Notables dominates the public life of New Haven through means so clandestine that not one of the fifty prominent citizens interviewed in the course of this study—citizens who had participated extensively in various decisions—hinted at the existence of such a cabal; so clandestine indeed, that no clues turned up in several years of investigation led to the door of such a group.

To abandon the hypothesis of covert integration by Economic Notables does not mean that the Economic Notables in New Haven are without influence on certain important decisions. . . .

A second pattern is envisioned in an alternative hypothesis: that today the top leaders are more likely to comprise a coalition of public officials and private individuals who reflect the interests and concerns of different segments of the community: In this view, a coalition is generally formed and the policies of the coalition are coordinated largely by elected leaders who draw on special skills and resources of influence that leaders without public office are not likely to have. This pattern of integration is usually associated with vigorous, even charismatic elected chief executives; presumably it was characteristic of the presidencies of FDR and Truman. . . .[1]

The third pattern is seen as integration of policies in different sectors by a coalition of chieftains. Something like it fits the various party and nonparty coalitions that control policy-making in Congress and particularly in the Senate.[2] The difference between the second pattern and this one is of course only one of degree; in marginal cases it would be impossible to say whether a particular pattern of integration should be called executive-centered or a coalition of chieftains. . . .

With some reservations as to historical accuracy, the fourth and fifth patterns might be regarded as analogous to a system of independent city-states or petty sovereignties. . . . In this system of petty sovereignties each issue-area is controlled by a different set of top leaders whose goals and strategies are adapted to the particular segments of the community that happen to be interested in that specific area. As long as the policies of the various petty sovereignties do not conflict with one another, the sovereigns go about their business without much communication or negotiation. When policies do conflict, the issue has to be settled by fighting it out; but since the sovereigns live within a common system of legal norms, constitutional practices, and political habits, "Fighting it out" means an appeal to whatever processes are prescribed, whether voting in a legislative or administrative body, decision by judges, executive approval, or elections. The practice of fighting it out increases the likelihood of appeals to the populace for support, and hence

---

[1]See Arthur M. Schlesinger, Jr., *The Coming of the New Deal* (Boston: Houghton Mifflin, 1959), Part VIII; James M. Burns, Roosevelt: *The Lion and the Fox* (New York: Harcourt, Brace, 1956); Richard Neustadt, *Presidential Power* (New York: John Wiley, 1960).

[2]Recent observers describe Congress in terms that would fit the pattern here, although each offers highly important differences of emphasis and interpretation. Cf. David B. Truman, *The Congressional Party* (New York: John Wiley, 1959), Ch. 4; William S. White, *Citadel, The Story of the U.S. Senate* (New York: Harper, 1956), Chs. 8 and 14; Roland Young, *The American Congress* (New York: Harper, 1958), Ch. 3.

the extent to which leaders shape their policies to what they think are the predominant preferences of the populace. However, since fighting it out is mutually costly and the results are highly uncertain, strong spheres of influence may develop with a relatively clear understanding as to the limits of each sphere; in this case, fighting it out is avoided, appeals to the populace are less likely, and policies are shaped more to meet the goals of leaders, subleaders, and special followings.

Thus the way in which petty sovereignties integrate their policies tends to assume one of two patterns, depending on the extent to which the policies of the one sovereign are consistent with those of the other. If the petty sovereigns perceive their policies to be strictly inconsistent, in the sense that a gain for one means an equivalent loss to the other, then conflict is unavoidable and fighting it out is likely to be the method of settlement. This is the case, for example, if the sovereignties are two highly competitive parties, both intent on winning office for their candidates.

However, if the petty sovereigns perceive their policies to be consistent or even complementary, in the sense that a gain for one entails no loss for the other and may even produce a benefit, then fighting it out is likely to be avoided. Possibility of conflict is minimized by mutually accepted spheres of influence, combined with a strong presumption that the *status quo* must be adhered to; it is also understood that if disagreements arise they are to be resolved by implicit, or occasionally explicit, bargaining among the petty sovereigns without an appeal to the populace or other external authorities.

These five patterns of coordination seemed to us most likely to cover the range of possibilities in New Haven, though the likelihood of finding still other patterns could not be excluded *a priori*. During our investigation of New Haven two possible variations on the five patterns became obvious. First, the prevailing pattern might vary with different combinations of issue-areas. For example, the pattern of integration applying to nominations and elections might not be the same as the pattern applying to education and redevolpment. Second, patterns of integration might vary over time. The variations might be long-run changes, such as the decline of the patrician oligarchy; they might be short-run changes; conceivably one might even encounter more or less regular fluctuations in integrative patterns associated with, say periodic elections.

Except for the first pattern (covert integration by Economic Notables), which it now seems safe to reject, all of these possibilities appear to be entirely consistent with the evidence so far. In the chapters that follow I shall demonstrate, from an examination of particular decisions, that all of the remaining four patterns have actually existed in New Haven in recent years. Before 1953 there existed a pattern of independent sovereignties with spheres of influence, which I shall call Pattern A. This gave way briefly to a coalition of chieftains and then, under Mayor Lee, to an executive-centered "grand coalition of coalitions," which I shall call Pattern B. Standing quite apart, the pattern of integration with respect to the political parties has been that of rival sovereignties fighting it out, which I shall call Pattern C. . . .

THE EXECUTIVE-CENTERED COALITION

During Mayor Lee's first term the political order was swiftly transformed. The pattern of petty sovereignties he had inherited soon gave way to another of the five patterns mentioned earlier, a coalition of chieftains. However, this pattern proved to be transitional, and we need not concern ourselves with it here. The executive-centered coalition that followed proved to be more durable. In this pattern, only the Mayor was a member of all the major coalitions, and in each of them he was one of the two or three men of highest influence. . . .

The mayor was not at the peak of a pyramid but rather at the center of intersecting circles. He rarely commanded. He negotiated, cajoled, exhorted, beguiled, charmed, pressed, appealed, reasoned, promised, insisted, demanded, even threatened, but he most needed support and acquiescence from other leaders who simply could not be commanded. Because the mayor could not command, he had to bargain.

The centrifugal forces in the system were, in short, persistent and powerful; the fullest and most skillful use of all the resources available to the mayor added barely enough centripetal thrust to keep the various parts from flying off in all directions. Or, to change the image again, the system was like a tire with a slow leak, and the mayor had the only air pump. Whether the executive-centered order was maintained or the system reverted to independent sovereignties depended almost entirely, then, on the relative amount of influence the mayor could succeed in extracting from his political resources. . . .

Thus, although the executive-centered order of Mayor Lee had drastically curtailed the independence of the old petty sovereignties and had whittled down the relative influence of the various chieftains, that order was no monolith. The preferences of any group that could swing its weight at election time—teachers, citizens of the Hill, Negroes on Dixwell Avenue, or Notables—would weigh heavily in the calculations of the Mayor, for the executive-centered coalition was not the *only* important pattern of influence in New Haven. The unending competition between the two political parties constituted another pattern of influence; thanks to the system of periodic elections, the Mayor and his political opponents were constantly engaged in a battle for votes at the next election, which was always just around the corner.

RIVAL SOVEREIGNTIES

. . . The leadership of the two political parties presents a pattern strikingly different from those that have prevailed in other parts of the political system in New Haven.

Within both the Republican and Democratic parties, it will be recalled, nominations for local office have for years been tightly controlled by very tiny sets of leaders. In describing control over nominations, I have also said something of the relations among the leaders *within* each of the two parties. But what of the relations between the leaders of each of the two parties?

In brief, the pattern that prevails in New Haven is one of petty sovereignties in periodic conflict in campaigns and elections. The men who control the nominations and manage campaigns in the Republican party are ordinarily a somewhat different set from those who control nominations and manage campaigns in the Democratic party. The two parties are to a great extent independent and competitive. Probably the competition between them has always been rather vigorous. Although rotation in office is not decisive proof of competition, in the past three-quarters of a century only once, during Mayor Murphy's fourteen-year span from 1931–45, has a single party held the office of mayor for more than a decade. In that same period there have been only four occasions when one party has held the mayor's office for as long as eight years; there have been two six-year periods of control by one party and two four-year stretches. In all the other elections, or almost exactly half, the incumbent party was defeated after only a single two-year term in the mayor's office. . . .

What can we conclude about the specific effects of political competition in New Haven?

First, the elected officials of New Haven have had a significant influence on many policies—on schools and redevelopment, for example. And whatever may be the relation between elections and the preferences of citizens as to local policies, elections do determine—sometimes by an exceedingly small margin of votes—*who* is elected to office. Thus even if recent elections in New Haven were interpreted only as a choice of individuals to hold elective office, the effects on some policies were considerable.

Second, political competition and elections, at a minimum, lead to the rejection of a great range of possible policies, some of which may be discussed in campaigns but many of which are never discussed at all. Thus the assumption, referred to in Chapter 8, among members of the political stratum that the essential characteristics of the socioeconomic system should remain substantially unchanged means in effect that every election is an implicit rejection of all policies that would entail sweeping changes in the social or economic structure of New Haven.

Third, the attempt of political leaders to win the votes of the various ethnic groups in New Haven has had a sizable effect on many policies that are not openly discussed in campaigns—on the ethnic and social characteristics of the men and women nominated for public office and on decisions concerning appointments, contracts, and other public expenditures. Two important side effects of these efforts to appeal to ethnic groups have probably been (1) to speed assimilation, transmit political skills, and gain acceptability among them for the American creed of democracy and equality, and (2) to inhibit the growth of distinctive working-class political identifications, ideologies, and political parties.

Finally, from time to time elections clearly have had a decisive effect on specific policies. Rightly or wrongly—but probably rightly—the election of Celantano in 1945 was interpreted throughout the political stratum as a vote in favor of spending more money on the schools. Rightly or wrongly—but probably rightly—the re-election of Lee in 1955 was taken as a sign that the voters had given overwhelming approval to urban redevelopment.

In short, New Haven is a republic of unequal citizens—but for all that a republic. . . .

The Distribution of Political Resources

. . . The resources available to political man for influencing others are limited, though not permanently fixed. For our purposes in this book, a resource is anything that can be used to sway the specific choices or the strategies of another individual. Or, to use different language, whatever may be used as an inducement is a resource.

How one classifies resources is to some extent arbitrary. It would be possible to list resources in great detail, distinguishing one from the other with the utmost subtlety or to deal in very broad categories. One could search for a comprehensive and logically exhaustive classification or simply list resources according to the dictates of common sense. One could employ elaborate psychological categories derived from theories of modern psychology, or one could use more commonplace terms to classify resources. To the extent that we can explain the patterns of influence in New Haven, it will do, I think, to use categories dictated by common sense; to do more at this stage of our knowledge would be pseudoscientific window dressing.

Some resources can be used more or less directly as inducements. Or, put another way, the kinds of effective and cognitive experiences mentioned a moment ago as peculiarly fundamental and universal depend rather directly on some kinds of resources and more indirectly on others.

A list of resources in the American political system might include an individual's own time; access to money, credit, and wealth; control over jobs; control over information; esteem or social standing; the possession of charisma, popularity, legitimacy, legality; and the rights pertaining to public office. The list might also include solidarity: the capacity of a member of one segment of society to evoke support from others who identify him as like themselves because of similarities in occupation, social standing, religion, ethnic origin, or racial stock. The list would include the right to vote, intelligence, education, and perhaps even one's energy level.

One could easily think of refinements and additions to this list; it is not intended as an exhaustive list so much as an illustration of the richness and variety of political resources. All too often, attempts to explain the distribution and patterns of influence in political systems begin with an *a priori* assumption that everything can be explained by reference to only one kind of resource. On the contrary, the various manifestations of influence in New Haven described in earlier chapters can be explained, as we shall see, only by taking into account a number of different political resources.

Although the kinds and amounts of resources available to political man are always limited and at any given moment fixed, they are not, as was pointed out a moment ago, permanently fixed as to either kind or amount. Political man can use his resources to gain influence, and he can then use his influence to gain more resources. Political resources can be pyramided in much the same way that a man who starts out in business sometimes pyramids a small investment into a large corporate empire. To the political entrepreneur who has skill and drive, the political system offers unusual opportunities for pyramiding a small amount of initial resources into a sizable political holding. This possibility will prove to be highly important, as we shall see, in accounting for changes in influence in New Haven.

Hypotheses

We saw how the monopoly over public life enjoyed by the Congregational patrician families of New Haven was destroyed, how the entrepreneurs without inherited social position and education acquired the prerogatives of office, and how these men were in their turn displaced by ex-plebes who lacked the most salient resources of influence possessed by their predecessors: hereditary social status, wealth, business prominence, professional attainments, and frequently even formal education beyond high school. The change in the New Haven political system from the election of Elizur Goodrich in 1803 to John W. Murphy in 1931—the first a descendant of a sixteenth-century Anglican Bishop, a Yale graduate, a Congregationalist, a lawyer, a judge, congressman, Federalist; the second a descendant of Irish immigrants, a Catholic, a Democrat, and a union official in Samuel Gompers old Cigar Makers International Union—represented nothing less than an extended and peaceful revolution that transformed the social, economic, and political institutions of New Haven.

This change in New Haven is fully consistent with three of the key hypotheses in this study. First, a number of old American cities, of which New Haven is one, have passed through a roughly similar transformation from a system in which resources of influence were highly concentrated to a system in which they are highly dispersed. Second the present dispersion is a consequence of certain fundamental aspects of the social, economic, and political structures of New Haven. Third, the present dispersion does not represent equality of resources but fragmentation. The revolution in New Haven might be said to constitute a change from a system of *cumulative inequalities* in political resources to a system of noncumulative or *dispersed inequalities* in political resources.

This system of dispersed inequalities is, I believe, marked by the following six characteristics.

1. Many different kinds of resources for influencing officials are available to different citizens.
2. With few exceptions, these resources are unequally distributed.
3. Individuals best off in their access to one kind of resource are often badly off with respect to many other resources.
4. No one influence resource dominates all the others in all or even in most key decisions.
5. With some exceptions, an influence resource is effective in some issue-areas or in some specific decisions but not in all.
6. Virtually no one, and certainly no group of more than a few individuals, is entirely lacking in some influence resources. . . .

STABILITY, CHANGE, AND THE PROFESSIONALS

New Haven, like most pluralistic democracies, has three characteristics of great importance to the operation of its political system: there are normally "slack" resources; a small core of professional politicians exert great influence over decisions; and the system has a built-in, self-operating limitation on the influence of all participants, including the professionals.

Slack in the System

Most of the time, as we have already seen, most citizens use their resources for purposes other than gaining influence over government decisions. There is a great gap between their actual influence and their potential influence. Their political resources are, so to speak, slack in the system. In some circumstances these resources might be converted from nonpolitical to political purposes; if so, the gap between the actual influence of the average citizen and his potential influence would narrow.

The existence of a great deal of political slack seems to be a characteristic of pluralistic political systems and the liberal societies in which these systems operate. In liberal societies, politics is a sideshow in the great circus of life. Even when citizens use their resources to gain influence, ordinarily they do not seek to influence officials or politicians but family members, friends, associates, employees, customers, business firms, and other persons engaged in nongovernmental activities. A complete study of the ways in which people use their resources to influence others would require a total examination of social life. Government, in the sense used here, is only a fragment of social life.

The Professionals

The political system of New Haven is characterized by the presence of two sharply contrasting groups of citizens. The great body of citizens use their political resources at a low level; a tiny body of professionals within the political stratum use their political resources at a high level. Most citizens acquire little skill in politics; professionals acquire a great deal. Most citizens exert little direct and immediate influence on the decisions of public officials; professionals exert much more. Most citizens have political resources they do not employ in order to gain influence over the decisions of public officials; consequently there is a great gap between their actual and potential influence. The professionals alone narrow the gap; they do so by using their political resources to the full, and by using them with a high degree of efficiency.

The existence of a small band of professionals within the political stratum is a characteristic of virtually all pluralistic systems and liberal societies. The professionals may enjoy much prestige or little, they may be rigidly honest or corrupt; they may come from aristocracies, the middle strata, or working classes. But in every liberal society they are easily distinguished by the rate and skill with which they use their resources and the resulting degree of direct influence they exert on government decisions.

Probably the most important resource of the professional is his available *labor time.* Other citizens usually have occupations that demand a large part of their labor time; they also feel a need for recreation. Measured by the alternatives he has to forego, the average citizen finds it too costly to sacrifice at most more than a few hours a week to political activities.

The professional, by contrast, organizes his life around his political activities. He usually has an occupation that leaves him freer than most citizens to engage in politics; if he does not, he is likely to change jobs until he finds one that fits easily into political routines. Celentano was an undertaker, Lee a public relations man for Yale, DiCenzo a lawyer, Golden an insurance broker—all occupations that permit innumerable opportunities for political work. As a public official, of course, the politician can work virtually full-time at the tasks of politics.

Most citizens treat politics as an avocation. To the professional, politics is a vocation, a calling. Just as the artist remains an artist even as he walks down a city street, and the scientist often consciously or unconsciously remains in his laboratory when he rides home in the evening, or the businessman on the golf course may be working out solutions to his business problems, so the successful politician is a full-time politician. The dedicated artist does not regard it as a sacrifice of precious time and leisure to paint, the dedicated scientist to work in his laboratory, nor the dedicated businessman to work at his business. On the contrary, each is likely to look for ways of avoiding all other heavy claims on his time. So, too, the dedicated politician does not consider it a sacrifice to work at politics. He is at it, awake and asleep, talking, negotiating, planning, considering strategies, building alliances, making friends, creating contacts—and increasing his influence.

It is hardly to be wondered at that the professional has much more influence on decisions than the average citizen. The professional not only has more resources at the outset than the average citizen, but he also tends to use his resources more efficiently. That is to say, he is more *skillful*.

Skill

Skill in politics is the ability to gain more influence than others, using the same resources. Why some people are more skillful than others in politics is a matter of great speculation and little knowledge. Because skills in politics is hard to measure, I shall simply assume here that professionals are in fact more skillful. However, two hypotheses help to account for the superior skill of the politician.

First, the stronger one's motivation to learn, the more one is likely to learn. Just why the professional is motivated to succeed in politics is as obscure as the motives of the artist, the scientist, or the businessman. But the whole pattern of his calling hardly leaves it open to doubt that the professional *is* more strongly motivated to acquire political skills than is the average citizen.

Second, the more time one spends in learning, the more one is likely to learn. Here the professional has an obvious advantage, as we have just seen: he organizes his life, in effect, to give him time to learn the art of politics.

I have just said the *art* of politics. Although politicians make use of information about the world around them, and hence depend on "scientific" or empirical elements, the actual practice of politics by a skilled professional is scarcely equivalent to the activities of an experimental physicist or biologist in a laboratory.

Even the professional cannot escape a high degree of uncertainty in his calculations. If the professional had perfect knowledge of his own goals, the objective situation, and the consequences of alternative strategies, then his choice of strategy would be a relatively simple and indeed a "scientific" matter. But in fact his knowledge is highly imperfect. He cannot be sure at what point rival professionals will begin to mobilize new resources against his policies. When new opposition flares up, he cannot be sure how much further the battle may spread or what forces lie in reserve. He cannot even be certain what will happen to his own resources if he pursues his policies. He may lose some of his popularity; campaign contributions may fall off in the future; the opposition may come up with a legal block, an ethnic angle, a scandal.

Because of the uncertainty surrounding his decisions, the politician, like the military leader, rarely confronts a situation in which his choice of strategies follows clearly and logically from all the information at his disposal, even when he happens to be well-informed as to his own goals. Surrounded by uncertainty, the politician himself necessarily *imputes* a structure and meaning to the situation that goes beyond empirical evidence and scientific modes of analysis. What the politician imputes to the situation depends, in sum, not only on the information at his disposal but also on his own inner predispositions. His strategy therefore reflects his predispositions for caution or boldness, impulsiveness or calculation, negotiation or toughness, stubbornness or resilience, optimism or pessimism, cynicism or faith in others. The strategies of professionals may vary depending on the forces that generate needs for approval, popularity, domination, manipulation, deception, candor, and so on. The effect of inner dispositions on a professional's strategies is by no means clear or direct. But as one works back from a given situation with all its uncertainties to the professional's interpretation of the situation and his choice of strategies, usually some element in the interpretation or the choice is difficult to account for except as a product of his own special dispositions imposing themselves on his selection of strategies.

Differences in predispositions that result in differences in strategies often reveal themselves in dramatic differences in the style of a chief executive: the differences between a Roosevelt and Eisenhower, for example, or a Wilson and a Coolidge, or the early Truman doubtful of his inherent fitness for the presidency and the later, cocky, self-confident President. Differences also show up at the local level—for example, the contrast between the cautious demeanor of Mayor Celentano and the aggressive, programmatic behavior of Mayor Lee.

Just as individuals vary, so professionals vary in the extent to which they use all the resources at their disposal. Some professionals seem driven not only to use all the resources they have but to create new resources and thus to pyramid their influence. They are a kind of political entrepreneur. In an authoritarian milieu perhaps the political entrepreneur might even be driven to dictatorship. But in a pluralistic political system, powerful self-limiting tendencies help to maintain the stability of the system.

The Art of Pyramiding

We have seen that in the pluralistic political system of New Haven, the political order that existed before 1953—the pattern of petty sovereignties—was gradually transformed into an executive-centered order. How could this change take place? There were few formal changes in the structure of government and politics. The city charter not only remained unaltered, but as we have seen a proposed charter that in effect would have conferred full legality and legitimacy on the executive-centered order was turned down decisively in the same election in which the chief of the new order was re-elected by one of the greatest popular majorities on record.

The transformation of petty sovereignties into an executive-centered order was possible only because there were slack resources available to the mayor which, used skillfully and to the full, were sufficient to shift the initiative on most questions to the chief executive. Initially, the new mayor had access to no greater resources than his predecessor, but with superb skill he exploited them to the limit. In this way, he managed to accumulate new resources; he rose to new heights of popularity, for example, and found it increasingly easy to tap the business community for campaign contributions. His new resources in turn made it easier for him to secure the compliance of officials in city agencies, enlarge his staff, appoint to office the kinds of people he wanted, obtain the cooperation of the Boards of Finance and Aldermen, and gain widespread support for his policies. Thus the resources available to the mayor grew by comparison with those available to other officials. He could now increase his influence over the various officials of local government by using these new resources fully and skillfully. An executive-centered order gradually emerged. . . .

What then stops the political enterpreneur short of dictatorship? Why doesn't the political entrepreneur in a pluralistic system go on pyramiding his resources until he overturns the system itself? The answer lies in the very same conditions that are necessary to his success. If slack resources provide the political entrepreneur with his dazzling opportunity, they are also the source of his greatest danger. For nearly every citizen in the community has access to unused political resources; it is precisely because of this that even a minor blunder can be fatal to the political entrepreneur if it provokes a sizable minority in the community into using its political resources at a markedly higher rate in opposition to his policies, for then, as with the White Queen, it takes all the running he can do just to stay in the same place. Yet almost every policy involves losses for some citizens and gains for others. Whenever the prospect of loss becomes high enough, threatened citizens begin to take up some of the slack in order to remove the threat. The more a favorable decision increases in importance to the opposition, the more resources they can withdraw from other uses and pour into the political struggle; the more resources the opposition employs, the greater the cost to the political entrepreneur if he insists on his policy. At some point, the cost becomes so high that the policy is no longer worth it. This point is almost certain to be reached whenever the opposition includes a majority of the electorate, even if no election takes place. Normally, however, far before this extreme situation is approached the expected costs will already have become so excessive that an experienced politician will capitulate or, more likely, search for a compromise that gives him some of what he wants at lower cost.

Three aspects of Mayor Lee's situation made it possible for him to avoid costly opposition. These were: the wide degree of latent support for redevelopment that already existed in New Haven and needed only to be awakened; the evident need for a high degree of coordination among city agencies if redevelopment were to be carried out; and the Mayor's unusual skill at negotiating agreement and damping down potential disagreements before they flared into opposition. These aspects of Lee's situation are not prevalent in New Haven all the time, nor, certainly, do they necessarily exist in other cities. In the absence of any one of them, opposition might have developed, and the attempt to transform the independent sovereignties into an executive-centered order might have become altogether too costly.

Thus the distribution of resources and the ways in which they are or are not used in a pluralistic political system like New Haven's constitute an important source of both political change and political stability. If the distribution and use of resources gives aspiring leaders great opportunities for gaining influence, these very features also provide a built-in throttle that makes it difficult for any leader, no matter how skillful, to run away with the system.

These features are not, however, the only source of stability. Widespread consensus on the American creed of democracy and equality, referred to many times in the previous pages, is also a stabilizing factor. The analysis in the preceding pages surely points, however, to the conclusion that the effectiveness of the creed as a constraint on political leaders depends not only on the nature of the political consensus as it exists among ordinary citizens but also as it exists among members of the political stratum, particularly the professionals themselves. . . .

THE RULERS AND THE RULED: CLASSIFYING POWER STRUCTURES AND POLITICAL REGIMES

Robert E. Agger, Daniel Goldrich and Bert E. Swanson

The volume from which this selection is drawn continues, in our judgment, to be one of the most sophisticated analyses of community power by political scientists to date. Based on their ten year study of two towns in a western state, and a four to five year study of two southern cities, the authors derive a multi-dimensional model for categorizing community systems. They focus on limited variables to develop typologies of "power structure" and "regimes" which later are combined into "political systems." Further, they place great emphasis not only on the distribution of power but on the rules by which the "game" of politics is played, and on the interrelationship between these two elements.

Agger and his co-workers also suggest additional dimensions which can modify and proliferate the simple typologies into multi-faceted models which extend their many concepts to fit a range of real-world situations. In addition, the authors' use of the time factor allows us to move from a "snapshot" to a "motion picture" of community politics.

FOUR TYPES OF POWER STRUCTURES

The conception of a community power structure as a functioning organization has led [us] to a typology of power structures based on two variables: the extent to which political power is distributed broadly or narrowly over the citizenry, and the extent to which the ideology of the political leadership is convergent and compatible or divergent and conflicting.[1] By dichotomizing each variable, four types of power structure are delineated.

From Robert E. Agger, Daniel Goldrich, and Bert E. Swanson, *The Rulers and the Ruled* (New York: John Wiley & Sons, Inc., 1964), pp. 73–112 (excerpts).

[1]The analyst must decide which of the many aspects or dimensions of political-power relations merits investigation first. Additional subcategories of these two variables, as well as additional dimensions, may be introduced to produce a more com-

The typology indicates that if only one political leadership group shared a single ideology, the power structure would be consensual, whether mass or elite.[2] There may be two or more political leadership groups, whose ideologies could be either compatible or conflicting. An example of a condition of compatible ideologies would be two sets of political leaders representing different socio-economic interests but agreeing on a compromise-bargaining-trading perspective; an example of a conflicting-ideology condition would be two sets of political leaders who had such firm emotional commitments to an overall program for the scope of government relating to all areas of life that the loss of a single decisional battle or the prospect of compromise would be almost intolerable.[3] These conditions are based on the findings in the four communities, findings we would expect in communities throughout the United States. But if communities in nations marked by more violent ideological conflict were compared with these American communities, the American communities might all have to be classified as consensual in character rather than competitive.

This simple typology of power structures raises several points. As one example, the competitive-consensual dimension is based upon the state of ideology in the groups that have attained positions of political leadership in a power structure. However, two Consensual Elite structures may differ in the extent to which there are groups of people aspiring to enter the leadership. One may face no outside challenge; another may have to face a group that has been actively aspiring to take over leadership without success. Such differences are noted if they occur.

As another example of a point suggested by this typology, the broad-narrow power dimension raises the question of the extent of overlap between the leadership and the rank and file. As has already been indicated, political leaders may comprise a small proportion of or be the entire working force in a community power structure. Power structures that are classified as mass in

---

plex set of power-structure types. We constructed the present typology by adapting and reducing much more complex, multidimensional schemes to the limited number of communities and measured variables available in this study.

[2]The terms "mass" and "elite" are used in a somewhat special sense to refer to the extent to which proportions of the citizens share in political power, that is, purposefully contribute in various ways to decisional outcomes. They do not refer to comparisons of the size of political leaderships, although it may be that elite distributions of power are associated with relatively small political leaderships—"elite" in a more traditional sense. Nor do these terms as used here have any connotation of permanence or long duration.

[3]We might point out here that the measurement of the relative degree of convergence or divergence of the political leadership's ideology rests on operations designed to establish the degree to which the opposition, if there is more than one political leadership group, is viewed as a power-monopolizing, mortal enemy which threatens the community's way of life or as a power-sharing opponent whose political success, while undesirable, will not injure the community irreparably.

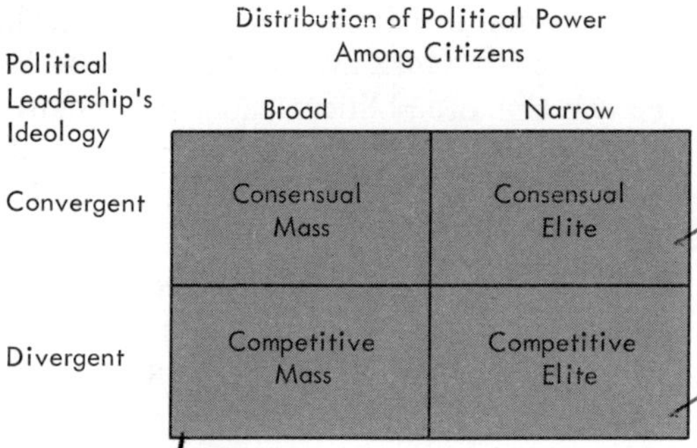

Distribution of Political Power
Among Citizens

Political Leadership's Ideology	Broad	Narrow
Convergent	Consensual Mass	Consensual Elite
Divergent	Competitive Mass	Competitive Elite

C. W. Mills

pluralists

FIGURE 1. TYPE OF POWER STRUCTURES. *Tocqueville - Democracy in America*

character might still have a minority of citizens sharing in power, although the minority would be larger than that of elite power structures. This also is an empirical question. Nor does this typology as it stands provide for classifying power structures according to the extent to which there are decisional conflicts with "winners" and "losers." A politics of personal or group interests theoretically may produce as intense a conflict as that of competing ideologies. Interest groups may be competing politically at the same time that ideological consensus exists at the leadership level of the power structure. Political participation may be high and political power broadly distributed whether there is a single ideology or convergent ideologies represented at the leadership level of the power structure. This is one reason for positing the possibility of a Consensual Mass power structure.[4]

The criteria used to classify a community power structure should be made explicit. For example, the problem of estimating and comparing distribution of political power among citizens in such a way that a community power structure can be classified as mass or elite depends directly upon the decisional processes selected for making the estimates. If one decision that has brought shares in political power to many citizens is overlooked, the distribution of power may be underestimated. We made our assessments from those decisions that a widely representative panel of officials of the communities' formally organized voluntary associations regarded as very important. These decisions will obviously differ from community to community in number and character. The specific political decisions that have emerged in each community and the sense of importance they evoke from the citizens are both relevant to the classification of power structure types. With the exceptions of school desegregation and school consolidation, decisions that

[4]A Consensual Mass power structure might exist even if there were no political-interest-group conflict within the framework of a single ideology, if some citizens feel strongly that their civic duty is to participate. It is important to understand, however, that in the absence of ideological conflict among the political leaders, the power structure is classified as consensual no matter how conflicting the interest-group politics may be.

were concerned with the functioning of the public schools were excluded from consideration, because we purposely phrased questions to elicit responses about decisions involving municipal government.[5] Otherwise the decisions in each community come from a variety of scope areas and are classified under one or more of the general categories of local government decisions: economic, social, governmental reorganization, or civic improvement. To classify power structures by type we must compare the distribution of power among citizens in each set of selected decisional processes that took place in a specific time period. The assessment of broad or narrow distribution of power is not specific to subdomains or subsets of decisions.[6]

The distribution of political power may vary from decisional process to decisional process within a community during a given time period. We classified a community power structure as mass to the extent that the distribution of power was broader in one or more decisional processes of the selected set than it was for any of the processes in another community.[7] In those communities classified as having mass power structures, there were ordinarily narrow or elite distributions of political power in most decisional processes. But the central interest here is in the gross differences in patterns of such distribution from community to community.

As with the other classificatory variables to be discussed, the categories used to define the power structure emerged from an interplay of theoretical interests and the actual comparisons of the four communities. The degree of ideological convergence or divergence of leadership and the degree to which power is distributed broadly or narrowly among the citizens are relative matters that depend on the comparison of real situations, rather than upon an arbitrary yardstick.[8] If communities vary slightly on either count the use

---

[5]For every question about participation in local government and community affairs, a corresponding question was asked about participation in school affairs. However, the data derived from the latter questions have not been included.

[6]As a result, we do not distinguish between and among common power structures even though they may differ in regard to the kinds of decisional categories under which citizens may have acquired their power.

[7]Future studies may classify types of power structures further by distributions of power by category or scope areas; they may use multiple classifications according to the distributions of power by particular decisions, or averages or other summary statistics.

[8]It should be stressed that the classification "mass" does not necessarily mean a majority—50 per cent or more—of the adults or of the eligible participant citizens. Cf. Robert A. Dahl, "The Analysis of Influence in Local Communities," in *Social Science and Community Action*, ed. by Charles R. Adrian (East Lansing, Michigan: by the Board of Trustees, 1960), p. 28; and Herbert McClosky, "Ideology and Consensus in American Politics" (unpublished paper delivered at the 1962 Annual Meeting of the American Political Science Association). McClosky defined "consensus" as a state of agreement equaling or exceeding 75 per cent, recognizing the arbitrariness of setting a specific figure for a continuous variable. Such specifications are in order when a sufficient number of readings have been taken on such variables as the distribution of power to ensure having cases on both sides of the specified figure, or when it is unimportant for a particular analysis that comparisons be made on the particular variable.

of different classificatory terms could lead a reader to focus on insignificant differences. Generally, however, the differences observed are sufficiently large to obviate this danger. For example, if we compared one of the four research communities to a power structure in still another community, our Competitive Mass power structures might be classified as Consensual Elite structures, thereby eliminating this basis of comparison among the original four. Rather than use categories with values fixed in an *a priori* fashion that would have masked important differences between and among the four research communities, we decided to use relative standards in classifying power structures. . . .

FOUR TYPES OF REGIMES

By "regime" we do not mean the structure of political power but rather the "rules of the game" in political decision-making as political leaders and other citizens in a polity conform to and interpret them.[9] Polities have both power structures and regimes; the term *democracy* is applied to regimes. By themselves, the four types of power structure reveal nothing about the state of democracy in the community. Theorists or philosophers of democracy do not insist that a single or convergent set of ideologies among political leaders is incompatible with democracy, nor that a broad distribution of political power is a necessary component of democracy.[10] In fact, a high level of satisfaction with life in a community and a low level of unsatisfied needs might be expected to produce or reinforce a Consensual Elite type of power structure in a democracy.[11]

The writings of political philosophers offer two variables for defining the extent to which a polity's regime, regardless of its type of power structure, is democratic. The first is a sense of electoral potency. This exists where citizens believe that they can attempt to obtain authorities responsive to their decisional preferences through elections without suffering illegitimate

[9]This conception is more specific and narrower than, but congruent with, David Easton's definition of a regime in "An Approach to the Analysis of Political Systems," *World Politics*, IX, Number 3 (April, 1957), 392. See also Lasswell and Kaplan's use of the term "regime" in *Power and Society* (New Haven: Yale University Press, 1950), pp. 130–31, wherein they seem to refer primarily to the sense-of-electoral-potency variable. Our usage of regime is not the customary one, which refers only to the governors rather than to both the governors and the governed.

[10]This statement holds for both political power and political influence, as defined, subject to the qualifications introduced below.

[11]This proposition, of course, is testable. In the process of operationally defining such terms as "level of satisfaction with life in a community," some definitions may yield different empirical findings. It is so frequently taken for granted that Consensual Elite power structures are "undemocratic" that the reader needs to be specially sensitized to differences between power structures and regimes.

sanctions. . . . The second variable is the probability that citizens' efforts to shift or maintain the scope of government will be blocked by the use of illegitimate sanctions. The four types of regimes that result from dichotomizing each variable are presented in Figure 2.

One of the two variables defining regimes refers to elections rather than other forms of political participation. The constitutional guarantees of freedom of speech, right of assembly, and right of petition may be considered analogous to stages of decision-making: policy deliberation, organization of political support, and authoritative consideration. If citizens are deprived of any one of these rights—the right to become involved in any one of these stages—democracy becomes an empty symbol in reference to the political decision-making process.[12] Although these rights and stages are necessary for a fullblown democratic political process, they are not sufficient to guarantee it. The right to petition or to organize political support behind decisional preferences may be useless if the electoral process is controlled by and restricted to a small set of inaccessible people. The formal structure of democracy may exist without the core electoral process; in some nation-states, the electoral process only marks tightly controlled policy-deliberation, organization-of-political-support, and authoritative-consideration stages. It is assumed that the sense of *electoral* potency will be low if citizens do not feel that they can freely and effectively speak, assemble, or petition.[13]

An optimistic feeling about the right to use elections in order to express preferences is a necessary but insufficient element in a fully developed democracy: the optimism may be unjustified. It is possible that if such optimism were to lead citizens into attempting to use elections or other methods

[12]Mass turnout at the polls is a well-known phenomenon in totalitarian countries but at variance with traditional conceptions of the democratic process, assuming that citizens have pre-electoral rights.

[13]This is a working assumption, which should be investigated in a cross-cultural study of politics where political cultures differ in the values placed on such stages.

Sense of Electoral Potency	Probability of Illegitimate Sanctions Blocking Efforts to Shift the Scope of Government	
	Low	High
High	Developed Democracy	Guided Democracy
Low	Underdeveloped Democracy	Oligarchy

FIGURE 2. TYPES OF REGIMES.

to affect the scope of government, they would be countered by illegitimate sanctions which would render their expectations invalid. Thus, it is only when electoral potency is realistically considered high, when there is a low probability of illegitimate sanctions being used effectively to block efforts to shift the scope of government, that the regime is classified as a Developed Democracy. "Sense of electoral potency," then, refers to the expectations that citizens can use elections to obtain authorities responsive to their decisional preferences regarding the appropriate scope of government. It does not mean that they must feel sanguine about their prospects of electoral victory; only that this political channel is available.

If the sense of electoral potency is high but mistaken, the regime is labeled a Guided Democracy.[14] Oligarchy is the absence of either of these attributes of a democracy.[15] An Underdeveloped Democracy is a regime in which the electorate's sense of electoral potency is lower than it realistically should be: the probability that illegitimate sanctions will be used effectively is low. The term "democracy" is thus reserved for regimes in which at least one of the two attributes of democracy is present.

It would be unrealistic and utopian to suggest that in real world politics men can interact and not sanction one another. An aspect of political maturity, as of human maturity, is the realization that it is not always possible to please everyone; loss of status or prestige is to be expected at some times in a political career. Social ostracism or economic boycotts, when applied for the first time in a polity, may effectively deactivate those who are making certain demands. Paradoxically, the more such sanctions are used, the more they may become both expected and accepted. Thus, they can lose their illegitimate character and their effectiveness. Changes may occur in the effectiveness and illegitimate character of sanctions as alternative social group satisfactions develop and alternative economic opportunities emerge from shifts in the local economy.[16] An analyst must keep these possibilities in mind when classifying regimes by type and assessing changes in regimes.

[14]Argentina might be considered an example of a Guided Democracy when Peronistas were allowed officially to run for office in 1962, following which the Frondizi administration was overthrown by the military. Both before and after that period Argentina had a more oligarchic character. The sense of electoral potency apparently was high when the ban against Peronistas was lifted; at the same time, the military was prepared to use illegitimate sanctions to prevent the shifts in the scope of government expected if those elected took office.

[15]This restricted usage of the term "Oligarchy" to denote a type of regime is not common. "Oligarchy" usually refers to what we would call a type of power structure, in which political power is restricted to a small set of citizens. See Lasswell and Kaplan, *Power and Society*, p. 218; see also Robert A. Dahl, "The Analysis of Influence in Local Communities," p. 28.

[16]The strength, flexibility, and continued growth, as well as some of the less ideal aspects, of the American constitutional system stem from the fact that the Bill of Rights does not to any great extent specify illegitimate deprivations, but broadly states that citizens may not be deprived of certain rights.

Regardless of the difficulties introduced by the notion of "illegitimate" sanctions, our position in this study is that it is possible, useful, and, indeed, necessary to the scientific analysis of "democracy" to specify the importance of such sanctions in classifying regimes.

For our purposes we regard such sanctions as loss of employment opportunities in the private sectors of the economy and extreme social ostracism as among the major illegitimate political sanctions. However, we might also include the right to a job in the government itself, particularly in the established civil service. Ordinarily, civil servants are not as free to become involved in political activities as are private citizens. Because there may be some questions about this matter, we shall assume in this study that loss of government jobs, failure to be promoted or receive salary increases that are normally expected in the bureaucracy, or failure to obtain expected positions as a consequence of political activity are legitimate sanctions. This assumption might be thought incompatible with the classificatory prerequisites we have set up for a Developed Democracy. We do not think that any regime in the present study would need to be reclassified even if the operational definition of illegitimate sanctions were broadened in this particular regard. It should be stressed again that the effectiveness of illegitimate sanctions needs to be assessed for the purposes of classifying regimes.

The conception of illegitimate sanctions in the present context has a broad two-fold referent. On the one hand, they refer to a set of procedures wherein otherwise legitimate sanctions, including incarceration, capital punishment, fines, or restrictions on economic activities are regarded as illegitimate because of their use in an arbitrary, capricious, personalized, unpredictable, unequal, or unfairly discriminatory manner. In other words, the way they are used violates accepted norms of legal and judicial procedures. They apply legitimately to an act already declared unlawful by the constitutional authorities, but their application may not meet norms of due process. . . . In its second sense, the conception of illegitimate sanctions refers to relatively severe deprivations, excluding relatively minor withdrawals or withholding, of affection, respect, or money that are considered to be wrong when used for the purpose of preventing or punishing peaceful, politically motivated behavior. Although, normally, government officials are the potential violators of legal and judicial procedures, private citizens with either the knowing assistance or the unwitting cooperation of police, judges, or other government officials may be responsible for illegitimate sanctions in either sense.

Because of what historical analyses indicate to be the development of substantially juridical regimes—in the first, procedural sense of illegitimate sanctions—in all four of our research communities following the Second World War, the major concern herein is with assessing expectations of illegitimate sanctions in the second sense. Negro citizens, particularly in one of the Southern cities, feared that police and judicial procedures would be used in a discriminatory manner, violative of the equal-protection-of-law aspect of due process. However, the most likely sources of illegitimate sanctions were groups of private citizens, particularly those with relatively large amounts of economic, social, and political power. We look to the political leaderships, whether consisting of government officials, private citizens, or both, in estimating, at various points in time, the likelihood of the use of illegitimate sanctions, primarily in the second sense. . . .

The *permeability* of the power structure is another way of viewing the "probability" dimension of a regime: permeability varies with the probability that certain political demands can be pushed to the electoral process, it need be, without having illegitimate sanctions applied to those who make the demands. . . .

Our definition of permeability does not mean that a permeable set of power strata will necessarily be permeated, and thereby altered, in a subsequent period of time. Neither does it mean that certain political demands will be pushed to the electoral stage; nor that if so pushed, the demands would constitute the decisional outcomes, for they might be defeated by political opponents. Proponents may refrain from pushing their demands because they do not feel that the demands are sufficiently appealing to others, or because they believe the power structure to be impermeable, even if such is not the case.

An Underdeveloped Democracy exists when citizens who have political demands to make feel impotent because they erroneously expect that illegitimate sanctions will be used against them. A sense of electoral impotence may lead to a self-fulfilling expectation: a citizen who fears sanctions may not make his demands because of that fear; one who does not fear sanctions may make the sanctions ineffective by disregarding them. The mistaken belief that illegitimate sanctions will be used may result from the use of such sanctions in the past, and the failure of the potentially sanctionable to recognize a subsequent decrease in the disposition to use them. Or this mistaken belief may be rooted in a myth from the past maintained as an operative belief in the present.

In a Guided Democracy, as in an Oligarchy, illegitimate sanctions may or may not be actually invoked. Occasions for their application may not occur in either regime. Such sanctions accomplish their purpose through deactivating citizens who are making demands that are opposed by political leaders. Deactivation occurs not only when the consequences of continued participation are understood but also when a participant's energies are effectively redirected toward other ends. If a person begins to lose customers as a result of a politically inspired boycott he may direct all of his efforts to his business and leave politics alone—at least for the while. He may even be unaware that the loss of customers is due to a politically inspired boycott. He may maintain his faith in democracy by treating this illegitimate sanction as an idiosyncratic event that will not be repeated. Guided Democracies may not be more stable than Oligarchies, in which the actual rules of the game are understood by the potentially sanctionable. In Oligarchies illegitimate sanctions may accomplish their purpose to greater degree by discouraging "undesirable" citizen political activity than by deactivating the desperate or the martyr.

Deviation from a Developed Democracy on either dimension of regimes constitutes a departure from the hitherto unmentioned principle "majority rules." Polities are Developed Democracies to the extent that an electoral outcome is determined by counting each citizen's ballot as equal to every other citizen's ballot, with the victory going to the man with the greatest number of votes—a majority or a plurality—and to the extent that citizens understand, correctly, that they may cast ballots without suffering illegitimate sanctions. The typology of regimes discussed here emphasizes the rights of minorities or powerless majorities to become the ruling majority; it stresses the fact that the spirit or intent of the democratic rule for weighing and counting votes can be violated in fact as well as through law. But since the compound democratic rules of one citizen, one vote, and victory to the man who gets more votes tend to be universal in modern cultures, this does not pose special classificatory problems, and certainly not in American communities. Infringement of these rules because of the use of an open rather than a secret ballot would be taken into account when one assessed the condition of the two defining variables of regimes. There is a special difficulty, however, if in some political systems such rules are not part of the political culture. . . .

RELATIONSHIPS OF REGIMES TO POWER STRUCTURES

A Developed Democracy theoretically may have any type of power structure; similarly, an oligarchic regime theoretically may have at least three, if not all four, types of power structure. Ordinarily, Oligarchies are thought of as regimes in which citizens justifiably feel that they are impotent as an electorate, and as power structures with a single, united political leadership sharing but one ideology, in which relatively few citizens share in political power. This is a Consensual Elite structure in the terms of our typology. However, a similar regime-power-structure combination where the leadership has become divided ideologically into two competing groups —a Competitive Elite structure—also is possible. It is even possible to conceive of an oligarchic regime to which citizens have become so accustomed that relatively large numbers of citizens contribute to decisional outcomes in one way or another—a Consensual Mass structure. An oligarchic regime with a Competitive Mass power structure is most difficult to imagine. Yet it is conceivable that two or more otherwise ideologically antagonistic leadership groups can agree upon who should not share in power.

Underdeveloped Democracies are theoretically and logically possible but, empirically, they may not exist as types of regimes. Similarly, although we can conceive of an Oligarchy with a Competitive Mass power structure, a regime and power-structure combination of that type may not exist in the real world. Theoretically, every one of the four types of regimes may exist with any one of the four types of power structures. The combinations and recombinations found in the four research communities over time are of central interest in the following chapters.

Actually, it is inaccurate to suggest that the writings of democratic theorists nowhere require that political power in a Democracy be distributed broadly. Because of their current prominence and appropriateness to this study, we shall re-examine the views of those modern democratic theorists referred to earlier as pluralists.[17] Although each pluralist has his own views, and ambiguity exists at a variety of crucial points, the following presentation of the pluralist position in regard to the interlocking character of a democratic regime and type of power structure seems to be an accurate summary of major tenets that they share.

As one pluralist puts it:

> A pair of competing party hierarchies, a polyarchal political structure in which many minorities participate, a pattern of interest groups and pressure politics appear as the most effective ways in which modern democracies can operate.

It would appear that in the pluralist view, regimes, or constitutional-legal orders, have primarily one dimension: a rule of law or the absence of illegitimate sanctions at one pole and rule by arbitrary fiat or the prevalence of illegitimate sanctions at the other. Types of power structures in American communities also are differentiated on the basis of one dimension: the degree to which citizens acquire political power when they oppose a political leadership, either through direct participation in decision-making or by using the ballot to replace an unresponsive set of officials. The term "democracy" is usually applied to those power structures that are inclined toward the appropriate pole on this dimension, the implicit assumption being that such democratic power structures have the appropriately "democratic" rules of law. Oligarchies are power structures in which the ruling minority is en-

---

[17]A recent criticism of pluralists and of power elitists that implies a commitment to a widespread sharing of political power as a fundamental component of democracy is to be found in Peter Bachrach, "Elite Consensus and Democracy," *The Journal of Politics*, 24, No. 3 (August, 1962), 439–52.

trenched; this minority does not lose in decision-making conflicts. Oligarchies also are assumed to be regimes that rule by the threat or use of illegitimate sanctions, rather than by law.

Pluralists assume that few American communities are Oligarchies. The only community that has been described as an Oligarchy was New Haven, Connecticut, before the middle of the nineteenth century.[18] Yet pluralists seem to distinguish Democracies according to the degree to which they have institutionalized democratic processes or the extent to which they have become what might be called (in a different sense than we define this term) "Developed" Democracies.

They assume that in Democracies, whether developed or underdeveloped, some citizens whose political interests differ to some extent will periodically make conflicting political demands. In more developed Democracies, competitive and complementary political interests are organized. Men who want to be elected to governmental positions because of personal or group interests tend to organize in parties. Usually, parties stand for somewhat different political programs. Since parties periodically must gain electoral support from the citizens at large, these programs must appeal to a relatively wide variety of political interests, thereby diluting what otherwise might tend to be an ideological politics. To gain and maintain elective office, officials must compromise conflicting demands; but they are likely to suffer decisional defeats periodically during their tenure in office or even be turned out of office on occasion, as minorities whose demands they could not meet rally to their electoral opponents.

A Developed Democracy in the pluralistic sense is more likely to exist, they suggest, in a large metropolis than in a small city or suburb. It is in the large, complex city that a heterogeneous citizenry is to be found; this citizenry is differentiated along social, economic, ethnic, and racial lines which become group interests and lead to, or facilitate, the formation of political interest groups. It is in the large metropolis that electoral competition is likely to develop. The pluralists expect to find in large cities the power structure that we call a Consensual Mass power structure. This, as we have mentioned, would have relatively broad distributions of power in elections and periodically in nonelectoral decision-making; and competitive parties and

---

[18]Robert A. Dahl, *Who Governs?*, pp. 11–24. Dahl's classification of New Haven as an Oligarchy prior to about 1840 apparently was not based on regime type. The classification seems to rest on the evidence that the political leadership was a single, unified group committed to a single ideology, with common upper-class backgrounds and interests, in whose hands rested top political, economic, and social power. This group had almost invariable success at the polls, the implication being that not only did other citizens fail to oppose them successfully but they also failed to make opposing political demands during that period. Thus the term Oligarchy seems to have been based on power structure assessments.

political interest groups would share pluralistically in the political power that accrues to those who, on occasion, successfully oppose the group in power or force the latter to compromise.

In the small city, according to the pluralists, the rule of law can be more easily undermined, so that an oligarchic regime and a Consensual Elite power structure might exist, representing a dominant interest.[19] Illegitimate social and economic sanctions are more likely to be used effectively in the "extended family" type of community, where political difference is seen by the father-leaders of the community as political deviance that threatens the whole group. Even if democracy exists in a small community, the power structure may be of the type that inhibits the expression of divergent political interests and that does not encourage the organization of opposition groups. Thus, there may be little overt opposition to the decisional preferences of the political leadership, which may itself not bother to run for elective office; electoral competition, which allows alternative programs to be offered to the voters, also may be absent. In our terminology, such polities would have democratic regimes, but such power structures would be Consensual Elite.[20]

Comparable situations presumably existed in the patrician communities of yesterday; perhaps they still exist in an occasional larger, but still homogeneous, simple city of today. The modern, metropolitan suburb is today's counterpart of yesterday's small city which had comparably "underdeveloped" democratic politics.

The present study is specifically interested in exploring the nexus assumed by the pluralists to be increasingly the norm in American communities: a democratic regime and Consensual Mass power structure. Because the present typology of regimes is based on two major dimensions, the connections presumed by pluralists between Developed Democracies and Consensual

[19]The dangers to the rule of law in small towns as a consequence of the operations of a spirit of fraternity are discussed by Robert C. Wood, *Suburbia: Its People and Their Politics* (Boston: Houghton Mifflin Co., 1959), pp. 276–80. Since the pluralists have not explored comparatively the distribution of political power among the citizens, we do not mean to imply that they have specifically indicated that a mass type of power structure is the norm in large American cities. Minority political participation has increasingly been recognized by all schools of thought as the norm in American community politics. Yet the dominant connotation seems to be that there is a wider distribution of political power over the citizens in larger than in smaller cities, in cities with a competitive party politics than in cities with one party dominance, etc. Although the extent of ideological divergence in the political leadership has rarely been studied in a conscious, systematic, comparative manner, the implication is clear that most pluralists do not think that ideology is a major variable at all. It is safer to conclude that they posit consensual-power-structure situations as the norm, but we think that it is a fair statement that they also perceive relatively mass distributions of power as the other power-structure-dimension norm.

[20]Springdale, as described by Arthur J. Vidich and Joseph Bensman, is in many ways of this character. See *Small Town in Mass Society* (Princeton, N.J.: Princeton University Press, 1958).

Mass power structures are of special interest. At the same time, we also shall explore the pluralist image of deviation from the norm: the existence of Oligarchy and a Consensual Elite power structure in small towns. One of our communities is very small; a second is much smaller than the third and fourth. Although a study of four communities can do very little in the way of assessing norms or typical patterns in the country as a whole, it is hoped that the findings will illuminate what are sometimes the hopes and values—rather than the empirical findings—of those democratic theorists who are committed to pluralism as the most desirable kind of political system for communities and nation-states. . . .

SOME CLASSIFICATORY CONSIDERATIONS: REGIMES

The assessment of the "probability" dimensions poses such special problems as how to classify sanctions as legitimate or illegitimate. Within the United States there is some degree of consensus on what constitute legitimate or illegitimate sanctions. In this cultural context, the major types of illegitimate sanctions are loss of job or economic advancement and extreme social ostracism, involving expulsion from formal or informal social organizations, because of "undesirable" political participation. . . .

The effectiveness of illegitimate sanctions must be assessed in the context of existing conditions. By "the context of existing conditions" we mean that a particular action, such as a boycott, loss of a job, or social ostracism, may not be an effective sanction if the sanctioned person has alternative sources of economic or social gratification. These acts may occur under various types of conditions and may vary in the extent to which they effectively block political participation. This also means that changing conditions may make an effective illegitimate sanction ineffective, and vice versa.

It is necessary to study prior time periods in order to assess the "probability" dimension, that is, what is likely to happen in a future time period. The state of the "probability" dimension can be assumed not to have changed if there is evidence that an effort to shift the scope of government has been blocked recently by the use of illegitimate sanctions, if the sanctioners are still able and disposed to act in the same way, and if the situation of the potentially sanctionable citizens has not changed. Given such conditions, the situation at Time M, the time of measurement, is projected and presumed to hold for the next period of time, Time M to $M + 1$. On the other hand, illegitimate sanctions may never have been used; they may never have occurred, or only in the distant past. The crucial consideration in such cases is the disposition of potential sanctioners in the event of certain political demands. . . .

Can regimes be compared and classified if, in a set of decisional questions selected for classifying purposes, one or more of the questions is of concern to people in one polity but of no concern to those in another polity? By "no concern" we mean that people never have had occasion to think or to formulate policy preferences about a question, or that they are indifferent to the matter. How can the potentially sanctionable be identified if a demand has never been deliberated?

One approach to the problem is to examine the perspectives of the people interested in the decisional question in the polity or polities in which it exists. From these perspectives it may be possible to identify the people in another polity who would be the potentially sanctionable, and then to classify regimes on the basis of the same kinds of potential political demands. However, we have rejected this approach in favor of one that classifies regimes on the basis of political demands that are extant in each polity, although these may vary by number and kind from polity to polity. A similar approach was taken in classifying power structures by type. . . .

The set of decisional processes selected as the basis for classifying regimes by type includes those that have become subjects of policy deliberation, at least of informal political discussion, in any of the four cities. It is ordinarily larger than that selected for classifying power structures, since it may include processes that have been repressed or tabled during a policy-deliberation stage, before reaching the point where political power can properly be assigned by the analyst. Although such processes are not included among those selected to classify power structures, they may differentiate one type of regime from another. Election and nomination decisions are considered but not actually used in classifying power structures. Since they are significant in the conception of regime, however, they are included in the sets of decisional processes used to classify regimes.

In selecting decisional questions in order to determine types of regimes, policy formulations not being deliberated were excluded from consideration. This was done on the assumption that the four communities were sufficiently "democratic" to allow for at least covert deliberation of intensely held political preferences. This, in turn, assumed that two or more persons with an intense preference wanted to deliberate it, and that people with such a preference had been able to find others who shared that preference so that they could at least discuss it.

Such conditions might not have existed. There is, therefore, the possibility that there may be serious repression of decisional preferences in at least one of the four research communities, so that classifying any of them as a Developed Democracy, for example, may distort reality. If decisional preferences for the establishment of a socialist city government were being repressed by some citizens because of the fear of illegitimate sanctions, but the proponents of the preference were unable to locate one another, so that a demand as we define it was not in being, a regime might still have been classified as a Developed Democracy. To the extent that people develop decisional preferences but do not let them be known for fear of being sanctioned illegitimately, the likelihood of even covert, informal deliberation may be reduced. A regime thus could be classified as a Developed Democracy when there were instances of severe repression of demands due to fears of illegitimate sanctions, either because classifications are relative to situations in other selected communities where there may be fewer such instances, or because the operational definitions used herein were insufficiently rigorous.

The estimate of permeability of the power structure is affected by assumptions about the form of political action in which the potential participants may engage. Theoretically, the effectiveness of sanctions is partly a function of the number of people participating, because this affects the alternative resources available to any one participant. The effectiveness of sanctions is also partly a function of the characteristics and relationships among these potentially sanctionable people. The effect of a given sanction may vary with the character of the political roles played by the potential participants, and with the connections and interrelationships such roles would have with each other.

The probable tactics of the potentially sanctionable thus need to be examined, as do the images held by the potential sanctioners of the tactics likely to be adopted by their opponents. These images may affect the disposition of the potential sanctioners to use illegitimate sanctions. Estimating the "probability" dimension is quite complicated because, at this stage, it involves speculation for which only further research and theoretical development can provide a firmer foundation. . . .

More Complex Regime Typologies for Future Studies

This examination of classificatory problems will conclude with suggestions for modifications that should be considered in future studies of regimes, particularly those of the Developed Democracy and Oligarchy types.

There are several ways of classifying types of Oligarchies which we shall mention. It has already been suggested that if it is probable that political participation within a polity will be met by the use of such illegitimate sanctions as death or imprisonment, the particular lines drawn for this study between an Oligarchy and other types of regimes may need to be redrawn. We shall elaborate on another way of distinguishing Oligarchies.

The traditional civil liberties are analogous to the stages of our decision-making model: free speech, free assembly, and the freedom to petition correspond in some ways to policy deliberation, organization of political support, and authoritative consideration. Free elections are the "last chance" to change the authorities who determine decisional outcomes and the scope of government. Freedom of thought is the basis of all civil liberties; policy formulation is basic to all decision-making processes. The more totalitarian the regime, the harder the rulers try to eliminate institutional mechanisms that produce uncontrolled political actions that take these forms or correspond to these stages. While control of any stage renders all prior stages futile, it is dangerous for rulers to permit any one of the stages to exist.

There seems to be a natural order of difficulty in suppressing these basic political liberties or in eliminating institutional mechanisms that facilitate uncontrolled expression of political behavior. Formal elections open to all adult citizens are the simplest to eliminate. Petitions, appeals, and demands made directly to the political leaders are fairly easily restricted to politically "eligible" segments of the citizenry. If necessary, ancestries can be checked, ghettos established, and yellow stars sewn on the garments of the ineligible. But the right to assemble is more difficult to control. Assembly does not need to take place in a public forum nor does it need to be formally organized. Political parties may be eliminated, but clandestine organizations dedicated to opposition or overthrow of the regime require more alert internal-security forces.

The formally organized opposition groups may be prevented more easily than may small informal groups which covertly deliberate policies and the possibilities of action. The most totalitarian rulers will not even stop here but will try to prevent the thinking that results in subversive policy formulations, to propagandize the younger generation and control dissident elements in the older. The family may find itself in a setting where no one may speak without fear that his mate or his child will serve as an informer. The difficulty in controlling the policy-formulation stage is attested by the tenacity of the family as an important unit of social organization in all regimes, and by the magnitude of efforts by totalitarian regimes to control it. . . .

The typology of regimes also may be elaborated and extended for Developed Democracies, as for Oligarchies. In some communities, regimes may be classified as Developed Democracies which have a highly effective propaganda system, controlled by a consensual political leadership and devoted to developing or maintaining citizen support for that leadership. In others, a Developed Democracy may be due more to political education and to a nonmanipulative political-socialization and information process. . . .

In Developed Democracies, as well as in other regimes, political values are inculcated in the young through what have been called political-socialization processes. Regimes of the same type, such as Developed Democracies, may be differentiated according to the degree to which communication from adults to children and from politicized adults to apolitical adults is propaganda or education. Estimates of the effects of intended deceit and the extent to which political manipulation is deliberate are also relevant to a classification of Developed Democracies or other types of regimes by such a dimension as political manipulation. . . .

Another dimension that might be introduced into the typology of regimes is citizen apathy. Two regimes, equally deserving to be classified as Developed Democracies, may differ considerably in the degree to which their citizens are indifferent to politics. Moreover, it is possible that Developed Democracies with mass power structures may differ sharply in the degree to which the citizens not sharing in political power are politically interested or apathetic. Even if the sense of electoral potency is high, and there is little fear of illegitimate sanctions, there may be variations among communities with Developed Democracies in citizen fear of legitimate sanctions, pessimism about the prospects of winning in an admittedly fair political fight, or cynicism about the responsiveness of officials in office or of those who might replace them. Apathy itself can be conceived as a multi-dimensional variable which necessitates further classifications, not only of Developed Democratic regimes, but also of all four types of regimes identified by the elementary fourfold classification used in this study. . . .

It is quite possible that a system of segregation by race or socio-economic class, whether maintained by law directly or indirectly, produces political conditions that constitute deviations from what we have termed Developed Democracy. On the other hand, it is conceivable that under some conditions, if not under most modern American conditions, communities with such segregation systems can have at the same time a relatively high sense of electoral potency among both segregators and segregated and a low probability that illegitimate sanctions would be used effectively by the former against the latter. Even with civil rights, a minority may be unable to convince the majority that government should do away with segregation. This is imaginable, however unlikely, if there were a very strong commitment to democratic rules of the game and a faith by the segregated that over the long run they would convince a sufficient number of segregators of the errors of their ways and that segregation would then be abolished by a majority. Since other kinds of reactions than these can easily be visualized, one might find few if any cases in the real world, but it would be useful to examine communities empirically in that connection. Given such special circumstances of the American Negro as his violent enslavement, the obliteration of any political heritage other than his new one in the New World, and his attainment of a nonslave through the deeds of men who then preached inevitable progress by hard and good work and through faith in a just God and a fundamentally benevolent, manipulatable political order, it is not entirely surprising that in one of our two Southern cities such dynamics seemed to have produced prior to the time of field work just those kinds of reactions—to the point of that regime's deserving the classification Developed Democracy when compared to the other three regimes.

A system of segregation may take its political toll in other ways than by generating or reinforcing fears of illegitimate sanctions, producing a condition of low resistance to such sanctions and a disposition by segregators to exercise them to maintain political, racial, and/or socio-economic dominance. Assuming that such are not the consequences in a particular community of a system of sharp segregation, and theoretically they may well be the consequences, there are still other important political implications of systems of segregation that bear on the concept of Developed Democracy. One might conceive of democracy as a political system that ensures not only permeability of the political leadership of the power structure in the sense of minimizing the role of illegitimate sanctions but also *maximum accessibility to top power positions.* This does not mean that democracy in that sense would require actual penetration by masses of people of the political leadership; a power structure in a democracy might still be a consensual or competitive, mass or elite type.

Some citizens' channels of access may be closed by the political actions of other citizens that, by definition, intentionally—as at least one end in view—are directed to that end. Besides such illegitimate sanctions that impair freedom of speech, assembly, petition, and electoral participation, there are a variety of extrapolitical conditions that can have the same effects. Such conditions are different in kind from illegitimate sanctions, in the sense that they can apply constantly to some categories of citizens in such a way as to make them relatively disadvantaged in exercising their political rights or in using the channels of political access to the political leadership, which rights and channels they may enjoy on an apparently equal basis with all citizens. Illegitimate sanctions, on the other hand, involve an actual or threatened or feared differential allocation of resources consequent upon someone's engaging in political activity permitted others in the polity.

In what ways does a system of segregation constitute ordinarily a set of constant political liabilities for the segregated? Assume for the moment that the segregated are not disqualified politically by formal or informal laws, such as the White primary, "grandfather" clauses, poll taxes, etc. Residential segregation makes it more difficult for the segregated, for example, to engage in personal political dialogues with the segregators. This constitutes a political impediment for minority points of view to become majority opinions over time. This is analogous to the political implications of socio-economic structures. The more sharply structured and differentiated are classes, the more likely it is that those at the bottom suffer the political disadvantages encountered by the poor—a fact of political life that has resulted in the unequal distribution of the political liabilities as well as the relative economic costs of the poll tax. Not all prisoners, whether physically in jail or in such socio-psychological prisons as ghettos, lose their civil rights, but their opportunities to participate politically in the larger community are less than perfect.

As segregation in school and society impairs personality development among its victims, their political personality may also be impaired. That is, segregation may result in the failure to develop political interest, competence, and a sense of political responsibility. The resulting political apathy means that the segregated may formulate no demands for a shift in the scope of government, and hence the regime can be, "by default," a Developed Democracy. This would be the case because, as we define it, regime type depends upon citizens' formulating demands.

If widespread political discourse and equal opportunity to obtain political influence and power are dimensions to be built into a typology of regimes, the more segregated communities are less likely to be Developed Democracies, even if the sense of electoral potency and the permeability of the power structure were both high relative to illegitimate sanctions.

The conceptual alternative adopted here was to reserve the term Developed Democracy to the more restricted sense. This means that such types of regimes are probably far from ideal not only relative to the two defining dimensions, and in the degree of citizen apathy, cynicism, or manipulation found therein, but also in terms of the distribution of such political disadvantages or liabilities as those associated with systems of segregation. By adopting that terminological convention self-consciously, and by pointing to such other options, we hope to reduce the ambiguities that ordinarily creep into discussions of democracy. By restricting the meaning of the term Developed Democracy to its narrow sense we also hope to underline the need for additional modifying objectives or alternative terms in thinking about such other dimensions of democracy as the patterns of political liabilities or disadvantages present in such regimes. Such classificatory labels as Equalitarian and Nonequalitarian Developed Democracies might be in order to enrich our vocabularies so that we could consider intelligently the riches to be mined from the various ways of conceiving political regimes. We would also hope that our use of the more restricted conception of political democracy would result in a greater realization that men may have other than political needs and values, e.g., for social or personal dignity, which may not automatically be realized by the improvement of Developed Democracy in the United States or by its establishment abroad, since in its narrow sense it could exist alongside racial, socio-economic, or cultural segregation. It is useful to be aware of the limitations of such regime constructs as they are used conventionally, but also of the possibility of elaborating and extending them to encompass specifically dimensions that are at issue in an ambiguous way and that need to be intentionally built into, or cast out of, political system concepts. . . .

PART TWO

Methodological Problems in Specifying Patterns of Community Power

If we are to develop theories of community power and its consequences, it is necessary to be certain that the key variable—the distribution of power over the allocation of community resources and values—is accurately identified and measured. As obvious as this may seem, much of the more recent research aimed at comparative analysis and theory building seems to have left the problems of assessing social power behind—and unsolved.

These problems can be summarized by four questions:

1. How do we know power when we see it and how can we measure it?
2. Given the complexity of social interaction in most communities, at what events or in what arenas do we look for evidence of who has power over important community decisions?
3. How do we assess the relative importance of different decisions and issue arenas in developing a summary picture of the distribution of power?
4. When we decide where to look for power, how do we identify important decision makers, either individuals or organizations?

Obviously these questions are interrelated—an answer to one will facilitate answers to others; but let's examine each in turn.

THE ASSESSMENT OF POWER

As noted earlier, power is one of the most important and most ubiquitous concepts with which social scientists deal. And yet, when we seek operational contact with power, it proves a most elusive phenomenon. Thus, the first general problem in the study of community power which concerns us in Part Two is the difficulty of measuring power.

As we have seen, there has been little agreement about the meaning of "power" among students of community influence, except perhaps the minimum agreement that power involves the capacity to bring about or to resist change. But this modest consensus falls far short of being a conceptualization that can facilitate the explanation and prediction of the outcome of social contests.

The articles in Chapter Three deal with two closely related questions—what is it that we are looking for when we seek to assess power, and, having found it, how can we measure its component parts? The excerpt from James March's article indicates a number of alternative concepts of social power found in the scholarly literature. Obviously, the concept employed to define power will affect the way in which we measure it. While March does not propose a single theory of power—in fact, he is rather pessimistic that such a theory is possible at this time—his models of power may bring us closer to that objective.

If we can agree on a conceptual understanding of what it is that we wish to assess, how should the assessment proceed? The second selection in Chapter Three offers some considerations in assessing the relative power of participants in the decision-making process. Refining Robert Dahl's seminal article on "The Concept of Power,"[1] economist John Harsanyi develops a framework for analyzing the components of power relations. His focus is upon the need to examine the comparative "costs" incurred by individuals or groups when they seek to use their power resources. "Costs" are a function of the situation, including the motives and resources of all actors involved.

It seems to us that these two pieces illustrate not only the creative insights produced by complex intellectual problems, but the increasingly rigorous demands of methodology and conceptualization which underlie current efforts to develop more sophisticated predictions about the results of decision making. A number of authors, including March and Harsanyi, have pro-

---

[1]Robert Dahl, "The Concept of Power," *Behavioral Science* 2 (July 1957), 210–15.

duced complex mathematical models of power relationships, highlighting the changes from early work in this field.[2]

Our emphasis on the difficulty of measuring power should not imply that such measurement can be, or needs to be, quantified with great precision before the search for community power goes on; however, with the help of ideas such as those offered below, it is conceivable that we can substantially improve our assessment of the distribution of social and political power.

The articles in Chapter Three do not solve the problem of measuring power relationships in American communities. But perhaps they serve to emphasize the need for a greater concern among researchers to specify what it is they mean when they are talking of power and to avoid the apparent temptation to develop unique conceptualizations and measurements which compound the problems of comparative research.

WHERE DO WE BEGIN THE SEARCH?

The study of community power is concerned with the sources and conditions of personal influence, but it seeks to put such political power in context. Thus, we are interested in determining *patterns* of value allocation which are reasonably persistent or patterns whose variations can be accounted for in theoretical terms.

There are a very large number of settings in which those in search of patterns of community power might begin. Thus, it is necessary to establish some criteria for deciding which political arenas are most likely to yield evidence that will, in effect, predict the outcome of future decision making across a certain range of specific issues.

We know that patterns of power will differ from issue to issue, and we need some way to distinguish between issues that are significant from those that are inconsequential. And, if we find that A is powerful in political arena X, but that B is powerful in arena Y, is their any way to predict who would prevail if the two contested in a third arena?

In other words, we know that the "simple" demonstration that any given group or individual has power on any particular matter does not tell us about patterns of *community* power. We want to know more than how we might account for the way a community's parks are landscaped or who is responsible for the scheduling of parades and Little League games. We also need to distinguish between those who make policies and those who administer them,

---

[2]See, for example, John Harsanyi, "Measurement of Social Power in N-Persons Reciprocal Power Relations," *Behavioral Science* 7 (January 1962), 81–91; William H. Riker, "Some Ambiguities in the Notion of Power, *American Political Science Review* 58 (June 1964), 341–49; and Benjamin Walter, "On the Logical Analysis of Power Attribution Procedures," *Journal of Politics* 26 (November 1964), 850–66.

recognizing that people we call administrators may—and do—make policy. And, we want to know how matters are resolved that are "significant" or "critical" to the determination of the most highly valued resources and privileges any given political arena can dispense.

It is not likely that we can gain full agreement among scholars (or anyone else) about how we might rank the importance or significance of certain issues or types of issues. But it does seem necessary that those in search of community power encounter this problem and make explicit the criteria they utilized to select the subjects of their inquiry and how they justify deriving generalizations that transcend the specific objects of their research.

In the lead article of Chapter Four, Peter Bachrach and Morton Baratz suggest that the importance of a decision is related to the degree to which it represents a challenge to the dominant values or the established "rules of the game" in a given community. The second article in Chapter Four, Frederick Frey's comprehensive consideration of most of the problems posed above, takes this idea of Bachrach and Baratz and builds on it in order to make the kinds of refinements necessary to empirical inquiry.[3]

One of the most vexing difficulties faced by the student of community power is closely related to the problem of choosing and weighing issues. Even if researchers are able to analyze carefully all of the important community decisions, there is always the possibility that other "issues" or problems are not being discussed or perceived, or in fact are being directly or indirectly suppressed, and that these other issues may be more important for an understanding of a community's power structure than those which reach relatively high levels of political visibility. The articles in this chapter, then, explore the difficulties posed for the analysis of community power by the "nonissue" or the "nondecision," and make some modest suggestions for possible approaches to this problem.

There appear to be a number of possible ways to deal with the problem of the "nonissue," although none of these possibilities is without serious methodological and conceptual difficulties. Bachrach and Baratz outline a way in which one might begin to assess the role played by individuals in the reinforcement of the values, myths, and "rules of the game" of a given situation from which these individuals benefit. Frederick Frey seeks to specify a number of different kinds of "nonissues" (or different sources thereof) and suggests various ways each might be pursued.

Generally, those who have undertaken to demonstrate empirically the na-

---

[3]Other significant efforts to prescribe ways that we might assess the relative importance of community issues are those of Linton Freeman and his associates (see the final selection in Chapter 5); Nelson Polsby, *Community Power and Political Theory* (New Haven: Yale University Press, 1963); and Andrew McFarland, *Power and Leadership in Pluralist Systems* (Stanford: Stanford University Press, 1969), Chapter 5.

ture of a community's power structure have asked, among other questions, why and how certain decisions take place. It may be that we can make headway in resolving some of the "nonissue" problems described above by asking why certain decisions and actions *do not* occur. In other words, we might formulate a series of hypotheses concerning the circumstances under which certain types of community conflict are likely to occur; where such conflict does not take place, the reason *may be* that conflict has been suppressed by the exercise of influence. Thus, if the community analyst finds an absence of conflict under conditions which, in other communities, have been associated with conflict, he or she may not have definite evidence that a "nonissue" situation involving power exists but does have some reason and guidelines for exploring that possibility.

A fundamental difficulty with this approach is that our knowledge about the structural and situational correlates of conflict is presently quite limited. Only a handful of comparative studies of community conflict are available. One of the most important of these studies in James S. Coleman's *Community Conflict.*[4] After examining the literature on community controversy, Coleman suggests that conflicts of varying intensity, dealing with various kinds of issues, seem to be associated with certain community characteristics: the community's past history, the homogeneity and stability of the population, the economic structure, the citizens' identification with the community, the organizational density, the rates of participation, and the role of the mass media. Chapter Four includes an article by William A. Gamson which draws heavily on some of Coleman's ideas and seeks to identify certain community characteristics which are associated with particularly hostile conflict. Gamson is concerned with one particular aspect of community conflict, but his research provides a model of comparative analysis which seems to be of substantial heuristic value. In the light of the suggestions by Bachrach and Baratz that community power research should focus on issues which do or could threaten the status quo, Gamson's suggestion that hostile conflict and community change appear to be related is especially important.

Still another approach to the "nonissue" problem, and particularly that aspect of the problem dealing with the possibility of the covert exercise of power, is to ask why various individuals and groups in the community are inactive although they might be expected to be active participants in decisions relating to certain issues. The first step in this approach is to identify possible sources of power. The reader might develop a list of such sources from the articles in this book, especially those by Weber, Simon, Dahl, and Clark.

The possession of power resources does not necessarily mean that an individual is or should be influential, but the nature and extent of a person's

---

[4]James S. Coleman, *Community Conflict* (New York: Free Press, 1967).

resources suggest potential influence. Power requires resources, but it also depends on the will and ability of the individual who holds the resources and on the relevance of the resources to desired objectives.

Moreover, just as the possession of power resources or the reputation for power are not in themselves evidence of influence, participation in decision-making may also be misleading. A person has influence only to the degree that his or her action (or anticipated action) affects the substance of the ultimate policy or results in its success or defeat. Moreover, if the role played by an individual is totally defined by others or could easily have been assigned to someone else, the apparent influence of that person may not be his or her own. This suggests the importance to analysts of decision making of specifying the type of role played in the decision-making process by the various participants. For example, those who legitimize a decision may have less influence on that decision than those whose role it is to initiate the idea or to bring together those who have either sufficient prestige or formal authority to secure community acceptance.

We should be aware that decision making itself is often unsystematic, and we risk error in assuming that policy outcomes always reflect the victory of one set of contending forces over another. The fact that a political or social system may produce a policy output which was not intended seems to have received inadequate attention from most community power analysts.[5] This fact is, of course, another reason to consider carefully the various roles played by presumed or potential decision makers from the inception of an idea to its implementation or dismissal.

LOCATING DECISION MAKERS

Once we decide where to look for evidence of control in patterns of community decision making, we are faced with the problem of what evidence we will accept that any given individual or group is exercising power. Contemporary researchers have tended to place primary emphasis on one or two general approaches to locating decision makers:

    (1) assessing power in terms of the positions or reputations of those described as influential, or

    (2) focusing on participation in political decision making as evidence of influence.

[5]This point is made most forcefully by Norton E. Long, "The Local Community as an Ecology of Games," *American Journal of Sociology* 63 (November 1958), 251–61.

There has been considerable debate, sometimes bitter, between the advocates of these two approaches. While this debate seems less vehement these days than it was in the mid-sixties, the issues that divide the two groups have not yet been resolved completely and cannot be dealt with by noting that each approach has its advantages.

As we have seen, Floyd Hunter, in his study of "Regional City," employed what has come to be called the "reputational" approach to reveal community power. This technique has been used most often by sociologists who have found an "elite" which dominates community policymaking. The basic question guiding this research has been, "Who has the power in the community?" or, in effect, "Who is running this town?" Such questions assume that there exists a set of power holders whose control of a broad spectrum of resources enables them to determine public policies. Operationally, the methodology involves asking "knowledgeables"—those who are in a position to have information about community affairs—for the names of those who are generally most important in getting things done or whom the "knowledgeables" would enlist if they wanted to get something done. Whether using one or two stages, this technique results in a list of the names of the "influentials" most nominated by the "knowledgeable" panel. In some studies, the members of this list of "influentials" are then interviewed to determine how they exercise power and with whom they interact in public or private affairs.[6]

A variation on this technique, often used in conjunction with other approaches as a first step, is the "positional approach," which involves the simple ascription of power to those persons in high formal positions of local public and private groups or agencies. The findings of both the "reputational" and "positional" approaches have generally been similar: American communities are run by a small group of persons, primarily business and social leaders, with the citizenry essentially uninvolved or unimportant in the development of community policies.

Herbert Kaufman and Victor Jones, both political scientists, were among the first to attack the validity of "positional" and "reputational" methods of detecting leaders when they reviewed Hunter's book.[7] They laid down the basic criticism of both Hunter's approach and findings—criticism which has been elaborated further in later studies by other political scientists. They argued that the answers to Hunter's queries about the holders of power would provide only a picture of the reputation for power, which is not the same

---

[6]See Charles Bonjeans, "Community Leadership: A Case Study and Conceptual Refinement," *American Journal of Sociology* 68 (May 1963), 672–81.

[7]Kaufman and Jones, "The Mystery of Power," *Public Administration Review* 14 (Summer 1954), 205–12.

thing as establishing that "real" power exists. It was these critics' claim that we could find power holders only by examining instances in which power was actually employed, by individuals or groups, to influence the outcome of a decision in the direction desired. This "decisional approach" was to become the hallmark of the writings of the "pluralist" school, which began to appear in print in noticeable volume after 1960. As we have seen, this school tended to conclude that power was not concentrated in the hands of one group but was dispersed among a number of groups, each of which tended to be limited to its special sphere, with only the top elected political leader providing some coordination of power resources—if then. These scholars tended to conclude that the mass of citizens have varying degrees of influence upon the outcome of events even though this influence may be indirect, in the sense that officials tend to anticipate and be guided by citizens' concerns.

Thus, there has been little consensus among social scientists on the prevailing structure of power in American cities and towns and on the way that structure should be studied. This disagreement raises an important question in the sociology of knowledge: why do different sets of analysts employ such disparate methodologies and reach such different conclusions? Some believe that the answer may lie in part in the different outlook on American society which sociologists and political scientists have adopted as a result of their professional training, but the evidence on this bit of conventional wisdom is unclear.[8]

Sociologists have been fascinated with the structure of class and status in terms of the division of labor, attitudes, life-styles, etc. This disposition may lead to a hierarchial view of society in which a few people have many resources and much status while many people have very little of either. To the sociologist, furthermore, "power" is likely to mean broad influence exercised through economic and social institutions as well as through the formal structures of government. On the other hand, political scientists, at least since World War II, have been shifting their focus from the traditional study of formal, legal, and governmental institutions to the political behavior of the

---

[8]Whether the sociology-of-knowledge position carries much weight seems to depend on which studies one looks at. John Walton, considering some thirty-three studies, argues that discipline does matter; see "Discipline, Method and Community: A Note on the Sociology of Knowledge," *American Sociological Review* 31 (October 1966), 684–89. Examining many more community studies, Terry Clark and his associates find no persuasive evidence that the scholar's training was systematically associated with the pattern of power they found; see Terry N. Clark et al., "Discipline, Method, Community Structure and Decisionmaking: The Role and Limitations of the Sociology of Knowledge, *American Sociologist* 3 (August 1968), 214–17. But the fact that Clark and his associates looked at more studies does not in itself mean they have the best of the argument; classifying the findings of other scholars, many of whom were not directly concerned with defining the structure of community-wide influence in the cities they studied, is a precarious business.

men operating within such institutions. This new orientation has been concerned with the exercise of power at many levels of government, the making of decisions, and the authoritative allocation of values. When analyzing a community in this context, political scientists tend to focus upon political actors who can be observed actually participating in the decision-making process. For them, the formal political system is the dominant institution in community decision making.

Although the professional orientation of political scientists and sociologists may introduce a subtle form of bias into the way they approach their research and analysis, it does not, of course, necessarily invalidate their conclusions. A good scholar is aware of the problem of bias, which is checked by two important controls—his personal and professional standards of scholarship, and the scrutiny of his peers. These two controls sit on his shoulders when he writes, insuring that he does not work completely alone. In community power analysis, moreover, two disciplines (at least) are scrutinizing one another.

As the debate over methodology wore on, it became increasingly clear that each method might well be striking at a different dimension of power within the same setting. A number of researchers began to examine empirically the usefulness of the reputational and decisional approaches. Such inquiry had produced, by the mid-sixties, some awareness of the strengths and limitations of these as well as other research methods. This analysis of methodology has demonstrated that no one method is the sovereign key to wisdom, that each contributes important insights into the phenomenon in which we are interested, and that the best methodology requires a judicious combination of a number of research techniques. There is no agreement, however, about what the right mix is, and practical considerations, such as the desirability and the high cost of multi-community studies, lead many scholars to adopt admitted compromises with ideal procedures.

The articles in Chapter Five guide the reader through some of this interdisciplinary debate. In their selections, Robert Dahl and Raymond Wolfinger examine what they regard to be the inadequacies of the reputational and positional approaches. On the other hand, Howard Ehrlich, while acknowledging the inherent biases of the reputational approach, suggests that this research method does provide some important insights, not only about the distribution of power, but about power holders themselves. Then, in the selection from Linton Freeman and his associates, we turn to an effort to resolve the dispute by comparing the major methods within an empirical framework.

Finally, the reader should understand that Part Two of this book represents a demonstration not only of the difficulties but of the significance of methods of research. Alternative conceptualizations and research methods may spring from different assumptions about the nature of social "reality" and may lead to different findings about that "reality." We suggest that having read the articles below, the reader may want to examine once again the contrasting findings of the selections in Chapter 2 and ask how much difference there actually is in the results of the elitists and pluralists. Indeed, is it possible that both sociologists and political scientists see the same phenomenon, but the former call it elitist and the latter call it pluralist? Or are there quite important differences between types of communities? In a very substantial sense these were the questions Aristotle was pursuing when he analyzed the constitutions of the Greek city-states.

CHAPTER THREE

*Measuring the
Relative Power of Group
and Individuals*

THE POWER OF POWER

James G. March

*This article formulates several models of power relations and explores
the problems involved in using each of these to analyze systems of social
choice. It represents an important step toward the development of empirical theories of community power.*

*Another value of these models of social power is that each suggests an
alternative pattern in the distribution of community power. When formulating study designs, researchers would do well to keep these models in
mind to ensure that their methods of inquiry do not preclude the discovery of any of these alternatives. Similarly, the models suggest what
things one may want to look for when evidence developed in the process*

Abridged from "The Power of Power" by James G. March in *Varieties of Political Theories*, David Easton, ed., © 1966. By permission of Prentice-Hall, Inc.,
Englewood Cliffs, N.J.

139

of research suggests that the dominant pattern of power in a community resembles one model more than another.

Students with a quantitative background will find their understanding of March's ideas enhanced by turning to the original article with its mathematical formulation of the models.

INTRODUCTION

Power is a major explanatory concept in the study of social choice. It is used in studies of relations among nations, of community decision making, of business behavior, and of small-group discussion. Partly because it conveys simultaneously overtones of the cynicism of *Realpolitik*, the glories of classical mechanics, the realism of elite sociology, and the comforts of anthropocentric theology, *power* provides a prime focus for disputation and exhortation in several social sciences.

Within this galaxy of nuances, I propose to consider a narrowly technical question: To what extent is one specific concept of power useful in the empirical analysis of mechanisms for social choice? The narrowness of the question is threefold. First, only theories that focus on mechanisms of choice are considered. Second, only considerations of utility for the development or testing of empirically verifiable theories are allowed. Third, only one concept of power—or one class of concepts—is treated. The question is technical in the sense that it has primary relevance for the drudgery of constructing a predictive theory; the immediate implications for general theories of society, for the layman confronted with his own complex environment, or for the casual student, are probably meager. They certainly are not developed here.

By a mechanism for social choice, I mean nothing more mysterious than a committee, jury, legislature, commission, bureaucracy, court, market, firm, family, gang, mob, and various combinations of these into economic, political, and social systems. Despite their great variety, each of these institutions can be interpreted as a mechanism for amalgamating the behavior (preferences, actions, decisions) of subunits into the behavior of the larger institution; thus, each acts as a mechanism for social choice. The considerations involved in evaluating the usefulness of power as a concept are the same for all the mechanisms cited above, although it is patently not necessarily true that the conclusions need be the same.

By an empirically verifiable theory, I mean a theory covered by the standard dicta about prediction and confirmation. We will ask under what circumstances the use of *power* contributes to the predictive power of the theory.

The specific concept of power I have in mind is the concept used in theories having the following general assumptions:

1. The choice mechanism involves certain basic components (individuals, groups, roles, behaviors, labels, etc.).
2. Some amount of power is associated with each of these components.
3. The responsiveness (as measured by some direct empirical observation) of the mechanism to each individual component is monotone, increasing with the power associated with the individual component.

There are a number of variations on this general theme, each with idiosyncratic problems; but within a well-defined (and relatively large) class of uses of the concept of power, power plays the same basic role. It is a major intervening variable between an initial condition, defined largely in terms of the individual components of the system, and a terminal state, defined largely in terms of the system as a whole. . . .

I wish to examine six different classes of models of social choice that are generally consistent with what at least one substantial group of students means by *social power*. In this examination, I will ask what empirical and technical problems there are in the use of the concept of power and in the use of alternative concepts, and under what circumstances the concept of power does, or can, contribute to the effective prediction of social choice. . . .

SIX MODELS OF SOCIAL CHOICE AND THE CONCEPT OF POWER

I wish to explore the utility of the concept of power in the analysis of systems for social choice. The utility depends first, on the true characteristics of the system under investigation. The concept of power must be embedded in a model and the validity of the model is a prerequisite to the utility of the concept. Second, the utility depends on the technical problems of observation, estimation, and validation in using the concept in an empirically reasonable model.

Consider six types of models of social choice. . . .

1. Chance models, in which we assume that choice is a chance event, quite independent of power.
2. Basic force models, in which we assume that the components of the system exert all their power on the system with choice being a direct resultant of those powers.
3. Force activation models, in which we assume that not all the power of every component is exerted at all times.
4. Force-conditioning models, in which we assume that the power of the components is modified as a result of the outcome of past choices.
5. Force depletion models, in which we assume that the power of the components is modified as a result of the exertion of power on past choices.
6. Process models, in which we assume that choice is substantially independent of power but not a chance event. . . .

Chance Models

Let us assume that there are no attributes of human beings affecting the output of a social-choice mechanism. Further, let us assume that the only factors influencing the output are chance factors, constrained perhaps by some initial conditions. . . .

What are the implications of such models? . . .

. . . All of the chance models generate power distributions. They are spurious distributions in the sense that power, as we usually mean it, had nothing to do with what happened. But we can still apply our measures of power to the systems involved. After observing such a system, one can make statements about the distribution of power in the system and describe how power was exercised. Despite these facts, I think that most students of power would agree that if a specific social-choice system is in fact a chance mechanism, the concept of power is not a valuable concept for that system.

To what extent is it possible to reject the chance models in studies of social choice? Although there are some serious problems in answering that question, I think we would probably reject a pure-chance model as a reasonable model. I say this with some trepidation because studies of power have generally not considered such alternative models, and many features of many studies are certainly consistent with a chance interpretation. The answer depends on an evaluation of four properties of the chance models that are potentially inconsistent with data either from field studies or from the laboratory.

First, we ask whether power is stable over time. With most of the chance models, knowing who won in the past or who had a reputation for winning in the past would not help us to predict who would win in the future. Hence, if we can predict the outcome of future social choices by weighting current positions with weights derived from past observations or from a priori considerations, we will have some justification for rejecting the chance model. Some efforts have been made in this direction, but with mixed results. Even conceding the clarity of the tests and the purity of the procedures and assuming that the results were all in the predicted direction, the argument for the various power models against a chance model would be meager. The "powerful" would win about half the time even under the chance hypothesis.

Second, we ask whether power is stable over subject matter. Under the chance models, persons who win in one subject-matter area would be no more likely to win in another area than would people who lost in the first area. Thus, if we find a greater-than-chance overlap from one area to another, we would be inclined to reject the chance model. The evidence on this point is conflicting. As was noted earlier, some studies suggest considerable specialization of power, while others do not. On balance, I find it difficult to reject the chance model on the basis of these results; although it is clear that there are a number of alternative explanations for the lack of stability, non-chance explanations are generally preferred by persons who have observed subject-matter instability.

Third, we ask whether power is correlated with other personal attributes. Under the chance model, power is independent of other attributes. Although it might occasionally be correlated with a specific set of attributes by chance, a consistent correlation would cast doubt on the chance hypothesis. It would have to be saved by some assumption about the inadequacy (that is, ir-relevance) of the power measure or by assuming that the covariation results from an effect of power on the correlated attribute. Without any exception of which I am aware, the studies do show a greater-than-chance relation between power and such personal attributes as economic status, political office, and ethnic group. We cannot account under the simple chance model for the consistent underrepresentation of the poor, the unelected, and the Negro.

And fourth, we ask whether power is *susceptible to experimental manipulation*. If the chance model were correct, we could not systematically pro-duce variations in who wins by manipulating power. Here the experimental evidence is fairly clear. It is possible to manipulate the results of choice mechanisms by manipulating personal attributes or personal reputations. Although we may still want to argue that the motivational or institutional setting of real-world choice systems is conspicuously different from the standard experimental situation, we cannot sustain a strictly chance inter-pretation of the experimental results.

Chance models are extremely naïve; they are the weakest test we can imagine. Yet we have had some difficulty in rejecting them, and in some situa-tions it is not clear that we can reject them. Possibly much of what happens in the world is by chance. If so, it will be a simple world to deal with. Pos-sibly, however, our difficulty is not with the amount of order in the world, but with the concept of power. Before we can render any kind of judgment on that issue, we need to consider some models that might be considered more reasonable by people working in the field.

Basic Force Models

Suppose we assume that power is real and controlling, and start with a set of models that are closely linked with classical mechanics although the de-tailed form is somewhat different from mechanics. In purest form, the sim-ple force models can be represented in terms of functions that make the

resultant social choice a weighted average of the individual initial positions
—the weights being the power attached to the various individuals. . . .
Consider the basic characteristics of the simple force models:

1. There are a fixed number of known power sources.
2. At any point in time, each of these sources can be characterized as affecting the social choice by exerting force in terms of two dimensions,
   magnitude (power) and direction (initial position or behavior).
3. Any given source has a single, exogenously determined power. That is,
   power is constant (over a reasonable time period and subject-matter
   domain of observation) and always fully exercised.
4. The result (social choice) is some sum of the individual magnitudes and
   directions.

Insofar as the determinate models are concerned, both experimental and
field observations make it clear that the models are not accurate portrayals
of social choice. In order for the models to be accepted, the total power
resources of each individual (as defined in the models) must be stable. As far
as I know, no one has ever reported data suggesting that such resources are
stable in a determinate model. The closest thing to such stability occurs in
some experimental groups where the choices consistently come close to the
mean, and in some highly formal voting schemes. In such cases, the power
indices are occasionally close to stable at a position of equal power. Nevertheless, few students of power have claimed stability of the power indices.

When we move to the probabilistic case—or if we add an error term to
the determinate models—the situation becomes more ambiguous. Since it
has already been observed that rejection of a purely chance model is not too
easy with the available data, the argument can be extended to models that
assume significant error terms, or to models in which the number of observations is small enough to introduce significant sampling variation in the estimate of underlying probabilities. . . .

The basis for rejecting the simple force models (aside from the necessity
of making them untidy with error terms) is twofold:

1. There seems to be general consensus that either potential power is differ-
   rent from actually exerted power or that actually exerted power is
   variable. . . .
2. There appears to be ample evidence that power is not strictly exogenous
   to the exercise of power and the results of that exercise. . . .

These objections to the simple force model are general; we now need to
turn to models that attempt to deal with endogenous shifts in power and with
the problem of power activation or exercise. As we shall see, such models
have been little tested and pose some serious problems for evaluation on the
basis of existing data. We will consider three classes of models, all of which

are elaborations of the simple force models. The first class can be viewed as *activation models*. They assume that power is a potential and that the exercise of power involves some mechanism of activation. The second class can be described as *conditioning models*. They assume that power is partly endogenous—specifically that apparent power leads to actual power. The third class can be classified as *depletion models*. They assume that power is a stock, and that exercise of power leads to a depletion of the stock.

Force Activation Models

The basic force models accept the postulate that all power is exerted all of the time. In fact, few observers of social-choice systems believe this to be true, either for experimental groups or for natural social systems. . . . It is frequently suggested that power must be made relative to a specific set of actions or domain of joint decisions. . . .

We often assume that the participants in the system can vary their exercised power from zero to the total of their power resource. . . .

Consider the problem of relating the activation models to observations of reality. Let us assume initially that potential power is constant over all choices. We assume that there is something called *potential power* that is associated with a component of the choice system and that this power resource does not depend on the choice. In effect, this assumes that [potential power] is also constant over time, for we will require a time series of observations in order to make our estimates. We will relax this assumption in subsequent classes of models, but the constancy assumption is characteristic of most activation models.

Given the assumption of fixed potential power we have two major alternatives. First, we can attempt to determine the degree of activation for each component and each choice and use that information to estimate the potential power for each component. If we can determine by direct observation either the level of power utilization or the distribution of power utilization (or if we can identify a procedure for fixing the extent of utilization), we can estimate the potential power by a simple modification of our basic force models. . . .

The second major alternative, given the assumption of constant potential power, is also to assume a constant utilization of power over all choices. Under such circumstances, the power exerted by any individual is a constant over all situations. If both utilization and potential power are constant, we are back to the simple force model. . . . Under such circumstances, the introduction of the concepts of power utilization and power potential is unnecessary and we can deal directly with power exercised as the core variable.

The force activation model has been compared with empirical data to a limited extent. Hanson and Miller undertook to determine independently the potential power and power utilization of community members and to predict from those measures the outcome of social choices. Potential power was determined by *a priori* theory; utilization was determined by interviews and observation. The results were consistent not only with the force activation model but also with a number of other models. . . . Dahl used a force activation model as a definition of power in his study of New Haven. That is, he assumed the constancy of the power exerted within subject-matter partitions in order to estimate power. On the basis of other observations, Dahl, Polsby, and Wolfinger seem to have concluded that it is meaningful to separate the two elements for certain special purposes (thus the classification as a force activation model rather than a simple force model). A New Haven test of the model, however, requires a subsequent observation of the stability of the indices.

It is clear from a consideration both of the formal properties of activation models and of the problems observers have had with such models that they suffer from their excessive a posteriori explanatory power. If we observe that power exists and is stable and if we observe that sometimes weak people seem to triumph over strong people, we are tempted to rely on an activation hypothesis to explain the discrepancy. But if we then try to use the activation hypothesis to predict the results of social-choice procedures, we discover that the data requirements of "plausible" activation models are quite substantial. As a result, we retreat to what are essentially degenerate forms of the activation model—retaining some of the form but little of the substance. This puts us back where we started, looking for some device to explain our failures in prediction. Unfortunately, the next two types of models simply complicate life further rather than relieve it.

Force-Conditioning Models

The conditioning models take as given either the basic force model or the force activation model. The only modification is to replace a constant power resource with a variable power resource. The basic mechanisms are simple: (1) People have power because they are believed to have power. (2) People are believed to have power because they have been observed to have power. It is possible, of course, to have models in which one or the other of these mechanisms is not present. If we assume the first but not the second, we have a standard experimental paradigm. If we assume the second but not the first, we have an assortment of prestige learning models. . . .

Models of this general class have not been explored in the power literature. Experimental studies have demonstrated the realism of each of the two mechanisms—success improves reputation, reputation improves success

As a result, conditioning models cannot be rejected out of hand. Moreover, they lead directly to some interesting and relevant predictions.

In most of the literature on the measurement of power, there are two nagging problems—the problem of the chameleon who frequently jumps in and agrees with an already decided issue and the satellite who, though he himself has little power, is highly correlated with a high-power person. Since these problems must be at least as compelling for the individual citizen as they are for the professional observer, they have served as a basis for a number of strong attacks on the reputational approach to the attribution of power. But the problem changes somewhat if we assume that reputations affect outcomes. Now the chameleon and the satellite are not measurement problems but important phenomena. The models will predict that an association with power will lead to power. Whether the association is by chance or by deliberate limitation, the results are substantially the same.

To the best of my knowledge, no formal efforts have been made to test either the satellite prediction in a real-world situation, or to test some of its corollaries, which include:

1. Informal power is unstable. Let the kingmaker beware of the king.
2. Unexercised power disappears. Peace is the enemy of victory.
3. Undifferentiated power diffuses. Beware of your allies lest they become your equals.

Moreover, it is really not possible to re-evaluate existing data to examine the plausibility of conditioning models. Virtually all of the studies are cross-sectional rather than longitudinal. The data requirements of the conditioning models are longitudinal. They are also substantially more severe than for the basic force models. . . . In order to have much chance of using the model (or variants on it), we will probably need to have data on variables in addition to simply social choice and individual attitudes or behavior. For example, we will probably need reputational data. We will need data that is subscripted with respect to time. We will probably have to make some additional simplifying assumptions, particularly if we want to allow for probabilistic elements in the model or introduce error terms. I do not think these are necessarily insuperable problems but I think we should recognize that even simple conditioning models of this type will require more and different data than we have been accustomed to gather.

Force Depletion Models

Within the conditioning models, success breeds success. But there is another class of plausible models in which success breeds failure. As in the conditioning models, we assume that power varies over time. As in the force activation models, we assume that not all power is exercised at every point in time. . . . We consider power to be a resource. The exercise of power depletes that resource. Subject to additions to the power supply, the more power a particular component in the system exercises, the less power there is available for that component to use. . . .

Under this scheme, it is quite possible for power to shift as a result of variations in the rates of power utilization. So long as additions to the power supply are independent of the exercise of power, the use of power today means that we will have less to use tomorrow. We can show various conditions for convergence and divergence of power resources or exercised power. We can also generate a set of aphorisms parallel to—but somewhat at variance with—the conditioning model aphorisms:

1. Formal power is unstable. Let the king beware of the kingmaker.
2. Exercised power is lost. Wars are won by neutrals.
3. Differentiation wastes power. Maintain the alliance as long as possible.

As far as I know, no one has attempted to apply such a model to power situations, although there are some suggestions of its reasonableness (at least as a partial model). . . .

Even if power resources are exogenous, the problems of testing a simple depletion model are more severe than the problems of testing the basic activation model. As in the case of the conditioning model, we require longitudinal data. Thus, if we can assume that power resources or increments to power resources are a function of social or economic status, skill in performing some task, or physical attributes (e.g., strength), the model probably can be made manageable if the simplifying assumptions made for force activation models are sensible. On the other hand, if we combine the depletion model with a conditioning model—as I think we probably ought to—we will have complicated the basic force model to such a point that it will be difficult indeed to be sanguine about testing.

One way of moderating the test requirements is to use experimental manipulation to control some variables, and experimental observation to measure others. If we can control the resources available and directly measure the extent to which power is exercised, we can develop depletion and depletion-conditioning models to use in experimental situations.

If, however, we want to apply any of the more elaborate force models to a natural system, or if we want to develop natural-system predictions from our experimental studies, we will need far more data than recent research provides. Perhaps a model that includes considerations of activation, conditioning, and power depletion can be made empirically manageable, but such a model (and associated observations) would be a major technical achievement. We are not within shouting distance of it now.

Once we do get such a model, we may well find that it simply does not fit and that a new elaboration is necessary. From a simple concept of power in a simple force model, we have moved to a concept of power that is further and further removed from the basic intuitive notions captured by the simple model, and to models in which simple observations of power are less and less useful. It is only a short step from this point to a set of models that are conceptually remote from the original conception of a social-choice system.

Process Models

Suppose that the choice system we are studying is not random. Suppose further than power really is a significant phenomenon in the sense that it can be manipulated systematically in the laboratory and can be used to explain choice in certain social-choice systems. I think that both those suppositions are reasonable. But let us further suppose that there is a class of social-choice systems in which power is insignificant. Unless we treat *power* as true by definition, I think that supposition is reasonable. If we treat *power* as a definition, I think it is reasonable to suppose there is a class of social-choice systems in which power measurement will be unstable and useless.

Consider the following process models of social choice as representative of this class:

> *An exchange model.* We assume that the individual components in the system prefer certain of the alternative social choices, and that the system has a formal criterion for making the final choices (e.g., majority vote, unanimity, clearing the market). We also assume that there is some medium of exchange by which individual components seek to arrange agreements (e.g., exchanges of money or votes) that are of advantage to themselves. These agreements, plus the formal criterion for choice, determine the social decision. . . .

A problem-solving model. We assume that each of the individual components in the system has certain information and skills relevant to a problem of social choice, and that the system has a criterion for solution. We postulate some kind of process by which the system calls forth and organizes the information and skills so as systematically to reduce the difference between its present position and a solution. . . .

A communication-diffusion model. We assume that the components in the system are connected by some formal or informal communication system by which information is diffused through the system. We postulate some process by which the information is sent and behavior modified, one component at a time, until a social position is reached. . . .

A decision-making model. We assume that the components in the system have preferences with respect to social choices, and that the system has a procedure for rendering choices. The system and the components operate under two limitations:

1. Overload: They have more demands on their attention than they can meet in the time available.
2. Undercomprehension: The world they face is much more complicated than they can handle. . . .

I am impressed by the extent to which models of this class seem to be generally consistent with the reports of recent (and some not so recent) students of political systems and other relatively large (in terms of number of people involved) systems of social choice. . . .

Such descriptions of social choice have two general implications. On the one hand, if a system has the properties suggested by such students as Coleman, Long, Riesman, Lindblom, and Dahl, power will be a substantially useless concept. In such systems, the measurement of power is feasible, but it is not valuable in calculating predictions. The measurement of power is useful primarily in systems that conform to some variant of the force models. In some complex process systems we may be able to identify subsystems that conform to the force model, and thus be able to interpret the larger system in terms of a force activation model for some purposes. But I think the flavor of the observations I have cited is that even such interpretations may be less common-sensible than we previously believed.

On the other hand, the process models—and particularly the decision-making process models—look technically more difficult with regard to estimation and testing than the more complex modifications of the force model. We want to include many more discrete and nominal variables, many more discontinuous functions, and many more rare combinations of events. Although some progress has been made in dealing with the problems, and some predictive power has been obtained without involving the force model, the pitfalls of process models are still substantially uncharted.

THE POWER OF POWER

. . . Although *power* and *influence* are useful concepts for many kinds of situations, they have not greatly helped us to understand many of the natural social-choice mechanisms to which they have traditionally been applied.

The extent to which we have used the concept of power fruitlessly is symptomatic of three unfortunate temptations associated with power:

Temptation No. 1: The obviousness of power. To almost anyone living in contemporary society, power is patently real. . . .

Because of this ubiquity of power, we are inclined to assume that it is real and meaningful. . . . We run the risk of treating the social validation of power as more compelling than it is simply because the social conditioning to a simple force model is so pervasive.

Temptation No. 2: The importance of measurement. The first corollary of the obviousness of power is the importance of the measurement problem. . . . Since we have a persistent problem discovering a measurement procedure that consistently yields results which are consistent with the model, we assert a measurement problem and a problem of the concept of power. We clarify and reclarify the concept, and we define and redefine the measures. . . .

We should consider whether subsuming all our problems under the rubric of conceptual and measurement problems may be too tempting. I think we too often ask *how* to measure power when we should ask *whether* to measure power. The measurement problem and the model problem have to be solved simultaneously.

Temptation No. 3: The residual variance. The second corollary of the obviousness of power is the use of *power* as a residual category for explanation. We always have some unexplained variance in our data—results that simply cannot be explained within the theory. It is always tempting to give that residual variance some name. . . . But where the unexplained variance is rather large, as it often is when we consider social-choice systems, we can easily fool ourselves into believing that we know something simply because we have a name for our errors. In general, I think we can roughly determine the index of the temptation to label errors by computing the ratio of uses of the variable for prediction to the uses for *a posteriori* explanation. On that calculation, I think power exhibits a rather low ratio, even lower than such other problem areas as personality and culture. Having been trapped in each of these cul-de-sacs at one time or another, I am both embarrassed by the inelegance of the temptations involved and impressed by their strength. We persist in using the simple force model in a variety of situations in which it is quite inconsistent with observations. As a result, we bury the examination of alternative models of social choice under a barrage of measurement questions.

I have tried to suggest that the power of power depends on the extent to which a predictive model requires and can make effective use of such a concept. Thus, it depends on the kind of system we are confronting, the amount and kinds of data we are willing or able to collect, and the kinds of estimation and validation procedures we have available to us. Given our present empirical and test technology, power is probably a useful concept for many short-run situations involving the direct confrontations of committed and activated participants. Such situations can be found in natural settings, but they are more frequent in the laboratory. Power is probably not a useful concept for many long-run situations involving problems of component-overload and undercomprehension. Such situations can be found in the laboratory but are more common in natural settings. Power may become more useful as a concept if we can develop analytic and empirical procedures for coping with the more complicated forms of force models, involving activation, conditioning, and depletion of power.

Thus, the answer to the original question is tentative and mixed. Provided some rather restrictive assumptions are met, the concept of power and a simple force model represent a reasonable approach to the study of social choice. Provided some rather substantial estimation and analysis problems can be solved, the concept of power and more elaborate force models represent a reasonable approach. On the whole, however, power is a disappointing concept. It gives us surprisingly little purchase in reasonable models of complex systems of social choice.

THE MEASUREMENT OF SOCIAL POWER
AND OPPORTUNITY COSTS

John C. Harsanyi

The central theme of this article by John Harsanyi is that the analysis of influence must contemplate the interplay of both the costs and benefits of exercising power. He further argues that the power of an individual cannot be assessed outside the context of the situation or outcome he wishes to influence. If Harsanyi is correct, it follows that the power of a group or an individual will vary from issue to issue and over time.

Harsanyi identifies a number of the components of power which it is necessary to take into account if we are to improve our capacity to assess an individual's or a group's share in the distribution of community power. In view of the often conflicting views of community power held by political scientists and sociologists, the reader may wish to give particular attention to the importance of evaluating an individual's "scope of power," i.e., the various issues on which a holder of power resources can effectively exert his influence. While, as Robert Presthus has observed, there are probably no purely private or public issues in community politics, nevertheless the way in which values in communities are allocated might be clarified if more attention were given to specifying an individual's "scope of power" and if more distinctions were made between matters which are essentially public and those which are private.

The analysis of power measurement is here set in the context of a two-person "bargaining game." Of course, community decisions invariably involve more complex interactions between individuals and groups. However, the difficulty of measuring power in simple interrelationships must be understood and dealt with before we can successfully tackle more complicated problems. Moreover, the arguments below can be extrapolated to multi-person situations, as Harsanyi has shown in another article.*

From John C. Harsanyi, "The Measurement of Social Power, Opportunity Costs, and the Theory of Two Person Bargaining Games," *Behavioral Science* VII (January, 1962), 67–75.

* John Harsanyi, "Measurement of Social Power in N-Person Reciprocal Power Situations, *Behavioral Science*, 7 (January, 1962), 81–91.

INTRODUCTION

Recent papers by Simon (1957), by March (1955, 1957), and by Dahl (1957) have suggested measuring person A's power over person B in terms of its actual or potential *effects*, that is, in terms of the changes that A causes or can cause in B's behavior.[1] As Dahl puts it, A has power over B to the extent to which "he can get B to do something that B would not otherwise do" (1957, p. 203).

As Simon and March have obtained very similar results, I shall restrict myself largely to summarizing Dahl's main conclusions. Dahl distinguishes the following constituents of the power relation:

(a) the *base* of power, i.e., the resources (economic assets, constitutional prerogatives, military forces, popular prestige, etc.) that A can use to influence B's behavior;

(b) the *means* of power, i.e., the specific actions (promises, threats, public appeals, etc.) by which A can make actual use of these resources to influence B's behavior;

(c) the *scope* of power, i.e., the set of specific actions that A, by using his means of power, can get B to perform; and finally

(d) the *amount* of power, i.e., the net increase in the probability of B's actually performing some specific action X, due to A's using his means of power against B (1957, pp. 203–205).

If A has power over several individuals, Dahl adds a fifth constituent:

(e) the set of individuals over whom A has power—this we shall call the *extension* of A's power.

Dahl points out that the power of two individuals can be compared in any of these five dimensions. Other things being equal, an individual's power is greater: (a) the greater his power base, (b) the more means of power available to him, and the greater (c) the scope, (d) the amount, and (e) the extension of his power. But Dahl proposes to use only the last three variables for the formal definition and measurement of social power. He argues that what we primarily mean by great social power is an ability to influence many people (extension) in many respects (scope) and with a high probability (amount of power). In contrast, a large power base or numerous means of power are not direct measures of the extent of the influence or power that one person can exert over other persons; they are only instruments by which great power can be achieved and maintained, and are indicators from which we can normally *infer* the likely possession of great power by an individual.

[1] I am indebted to Professor Jacob Marschak, of U.C.L.A., and to Professors Herbert A. Simon and James G. March, of Carnegie Institute of Technology, for helpful discussions on this and related topics.

Among the three variables of scope, amount, and extension, amount of power is the crucial one, in terms of which the other two can be defined. For the scope of A's power over B is simply the set of specific actions X with respect to which A has a nonzero amount of power over B, i.e., the set of those actions X for which A can achieve a nonzero increase in the probability of these actions actually being performed by B. Similarly, the extension of A's power is the set of specific individuals over whom A has power of nonzero scope and amount.

While the amount of power is a difference of two probabilities, and therefore is directly given as a *real number*[2] all other dimensions of power are directly given as lists of specific objects (e.g., a list of specific resources, a list of specific actions by A or by B, or a list of specific individuals over whom A has power). But Dahl and March suggest that at least in certain situations it will be worthwhile to develop straight numerical measures for them by appropriate aggregating procedures—essentially by counting the number of comparable items in a given list, and possibly by assigning different weights to items of unequal importance (e.g., we may give more "marks" for power over an important individual than for power over a less important one) (March, 1957, pp. 213–220). In other cases we may divide up a given list into several sublists and may assign a separate numerical measure to each of them, without necessarily aggregating all these numbers into a single figure. That is, we may characterize a given dimension of power not by a single number, but rather by a set of several numbers, i.e., a vector. (For instance, we may describe the extension of President de Gaulle's power by listing the numbers [or percentages] of deputies, of army officers of various ranks, of electors, etc., who support him, without trying to combine all these figures into one index number.)

TWO ADDITIONAL DIMENSIONS OF SOCIAL POWER

A quantitative characterization of a power relation, however, in my view must include two more variables not mentioned in Dahl's list:

(f) the opportunity costs to A of attempting to influence B's behavior, i.e., the opportunity costs of using his power over B (and of acquiring this power over B in the first place if A does not yet possess the required power), which we shall call the *costs* of A's power over B; and

(g) the opportunity costs to B of refusing to do what A wants him to do, i.e., of refusing to yield to A's attempt to influence his behavior. As

---

[2]But as the probability that B will actually perform a specific action X suggested by A will in general be different for different actions X and for different individuals B, the total amount of A's power (or even the amount of A's power over a given individual B) will also have to be described by a vector rather than by a single number, except if some sort of aggregation procedure is used.

these opportunity costs measure the strength of *B*'s incentives for yield-
ing to *A*'s influence, we shall call them the *strength* of *A*'s power
over *B*.[3]

More precisely, the *costs* of *A*'s power over *B* will be defined as the *expected value* (actuarial value) of the costs of his attempt to influence *B*. It
will be a weighted average of the net total costs that *A* would incur if his
attempt were successful (e.g., the costs of rewarding *B*), and of the net total
costs that *A* would incur if his attempt were unsuccessful (e.g., the costs of
punishing *B*).

Other things being equal, *A*'s power over *B* is greater the smaller the cost
of *A*'s power and the greater the strength of *A*'s power.

Both of these two cost variables may be expressed either in physical units
(e.g., it may cost *A* so many bottles of beer or so many working hours to get
B to adopt a given policy *X*; and again it may cost *B* so many bottles of
beer or so many years' imprisonment if he does not adopt policy *X*), in
monetary units (e.g., *A*'s or *B*'s relevant costs may amount to so many actual
dollars, or at least may be equivalent to a loss of so many dollars for him),
or in utility units. (In view of the theoretical problems connected with interpersonal comparisons of utility, and of the difficulties associated with utility
measurement even for one individual, in practice the costs and the strength
of power will usually be expressed in physical or in monetary units. But for
the purposes of theoretical analysis the use of utility costs sometimes has
important advantages, as we shall see.)

Unlike the power base and the means of power, which need not be included in the definition of the power relation, both the costs of power and
the strength of power are essential ingredients of the definition of power.
A's power over *B* should be defined not merely as an ability by *A* to get *B*
to do *X* with a certain probability *p*, but rather as an ability by *A* to achieve
this at a certain total cost *u* to himself, by convincing *B* that *B* would have
to bear the total cost *v* if he did not do *X*.

The Costs of Power

One of the main purposes for which social scientists use the concept of *A*'s power over *B* is for the description of the policy possibilities open
to *A*. If we want to know the situation (or environment) which *A* faces as a
decision-maker, we must know whether he can or cannot get *B* to perform
a certain action *X*, and more specifically how sure he can be (in a probabil-

---

[3]Of course, instead of taking the opportunity costs (i.e., the net disadvantages)
associated for *B* with noncompliance, we could just as well take the net advantages
for him with compliance—they both amount to the same thing.

ity sense) that B will actually perform this action. But a realistic description of A's policy possibilities must include not only A's ability or inability to get B to perform a certain action X, but also the *costs* that A has to bear in order to achieve this result. If two individuals are in a position to exert the same influence over other individuals, but if one can achieve this influence only at the cost of great efforts and/or financial or other sacrifices, while the other can achieve it free of any such costs, we cannot say in any useful sense that their power is equally great. Any meaningful comparison must be in terms of the influence that two individuals can achieve at comparable costs, or in terms of the costs they have to bear in order to achieve comparable degrees of influence.

For instance, it is misleading to say that two political candidates have the same power over two comparable constituencies if one needs much more electioneering effort and expenditure to achieve a given majority, even if in the end both achieve the same majorities; or that two businessmen have the same power over the city government if one can achieve favorable treatment by city officials only at the price of large donations to party funds, while the other can get the same favorable treatment just for the asking.

Of course, a power concept which disregards the costs of power is most inaccurate when the costs of using a given power become very high or even prohibitive. For instance, suppose that an army commander becomes a prisoner of enemy troops, who try to force him at gunpoint to give a radio order to his army units to withdraw from a certain area. He may very well have the power to give a contrary order, both in the sense of having the physical ability to do so and in the sense of there being a very good chance of his order being actually obeyed by his army units—but he can use his power only at the cost of his life. Though the scope, the amount, and the extension of his power over his soldiers would still be very great, it would clearly be very misleading in this situation to call him a powerful individual in the same sense as before his capture.

More generally, measurement of power merely in terms of its scope, amount, and extension tends to give counterintuitive results when the possessor of power has little or no real opportunity to actually use his power. For example, take the case of a secretary who has to compile various reports for her employer, according to very specific instructions which leave her little actual choice as to how to prepare them. Suppose that her employer then uses these reports as a basis for very important decisions.[4] Physically she could exert considerable influence on her employer's policies by omitting certain pieces of information from her reports, or including misleading information. In this sense, the scope and the amount of her power over her employer is considerable. But normally she will have little opportunity for

---

[4] I owe this example to Professor Jacob Marschak.

using this power, and social scientists would hardly wish to describe her as a powerful individual, as they would have to do if they used Dahl's power concept without modification.

In terms of our own power concept, however, the secretary in question has little real power if all dimensions of her power are taken into account. Though she does have power of great scope and great amount over her employer, this fact is normally more than offset by the very high costs of using her power. If she intentionally submits misleading reports she probably will be found out very soon and will be dismissed and/or punished in other ways. Moreover, if she is a loyal employee such flagrant violation of her instructions would in itself involve very high disutility costs to her.

To conclude, a realistic quantitative description of A's power over B must include, as an essential dimension of this power relation, the costs to A of attempting to influence B's behavior.

THE STRENGTH OF POWER

While the costs of power must be included in the definition of our power concept in order to ensure its descriptive validity, the variable of *strength* of power must be included to ensure the usefulness of our power concept for explanatory purposes.

As March (1955, pp. 431–432) has pointed out about the concept of influence, one of the main analytical tasks of such concepts as influence or power (which essentially is an ability to exert influence) is to serve as *intervening variables* in the analysis of individual or social decision-making. Therefore we need a power or influence concept which enables us in the relevant cases to explain a decision by a given private individual or by an official of a social organization, in terms of the power or influence that another individual or some social group has over him. But fundamentally, the analysis of any human decision must be in terms of the variables on the basis of which the decision-maker concerned actually makes his decision—that is, in terms of the advantages and disadvantages he associates with alternative policies available to him. In order to explain why B adopts a certain policy X in accordance with A's wishes, we must know what *difference it makes* for B whether A is his friend or his enemy—or more generally, we must know the *opportunity costs* to B of not adopting policy X. Hence, if our power concept is to serve us as an explanatory intervening variable in the analysis of B's decision to comply with A's wishes, our power concept must include as one of its essential dimensions the opportunity costs to B of non-compliance, which measure the strength of B's incentives to compliance and which we have called the strength of A's power over B.

For instance, if we want to explain the decision of Senator Knowland to support a certain bill of the Eisenhower administration we must find out, among other things, which particular individuals or social groups influenced his decision, and to what extent. Now suppose that we have strong reasons to assume that it was President Eisenhower's personal intervention which made Senator Knowland change his mind and decide to support the bill in question. Then we still have to explain *how* the variables governing the Senator's decision were actually affected by the President's intervention. Did the President make a promise to him, i.e., did he attach new *advantages*, from the Senator's point of view, to the policy of supporting the bill? Or did the President make a threat, i.e., did he attach new *disadvantages* to the policy of opposing the bill? Or did the President supply new information, pointing out certain already *existing* advantages and/or disadvantages associated with these two policies, which the Senator had been insufficiently aware of before? In any case we must explain how the President's intervention increased the opportunity costs that Senator Knowland came to associate with opposing the bill.

If we cannot supply this information, then the mere existence of an influence or power relationship between President Eisenhower and Senator Knowland will not *explain* the latter's decision to support the bill. It will only pose a *problem* concerning this decision. (Why on earth did he comply with the President's request to support the bill, when it is known that he had many reasons to oppose it, and did actually oppose it for a while?)

There seem to be four main ways by which a given actor *A* can manipulate the incentives or opportunity costs of another actor *B:*

1. *A* may provide certain *new* advantages or disadvantages for *B*, subject to *no condition.* For instance, he may provide certain facilities for *B* which make it easier or less expensive for *B* to follow certain particular policy objectives desirable to *A*. (For example, country *A* may be able to induce country *B* to attack some third country *C*, simply by supplying arms to *B*, even if *A* supplies these arms "without any strings attached"—and in particular without making it a condition of her arms deliveries that *B* will actually attack *C*.) Or *A* may withdraw from *B* certain facilities that could help *B* in attaining policy objectives undesirable to *A*. More generally, *A* may provide for *B* goods or services complementary to some particular policy goal *X*, or competitive to policy goals alternative to *X*, so as to increase for *B* the net utility of *X*, or to decrease the net utility of its alternatives; or *A* may achieve similar results by depriving *B* of goods or services either competitive to *X* or complementary to its alternatives.[5]

---

[5]Case 1 is discussed in some what greater detail because power based on providing services or disservices without any conditions attached is often overlooked in the literature. For our purposes, the distinction between unconditional advantages or disadvantages on the one hand, and conditional rewards or punishments on the other hand, is important because the latter lend themselves to *bargaining* much more easily than the former do.

2. *A* may set up *rewards* and *punishments*, i.e. *new* advantages and disadvantages subject to certain *conditions* as to *B*'s future behavior.

3. *A* may supply *information* (or misinformation) on (allegedly) already *existing* advantages and/or disadvantages connected with various alternative policies open to *B*.

4. *A* may rely on his legitimate *authority* over *B*, or on *B*'s personal *affection* for *A*, which makes *B* attach *direct disutility* to the very act of disobeying *A*.

Of course, in a situation where *A* has certain power over *B* either party can be mistaken about the true opportunity costs to him of various alternatives. Therefore both in discussing the costs of *A*'s power over *B*, and in discussing the strength of his power, we must distinguish between *objective* costs and *perceived* costs—between what these costs actually are and what the individual bearing these costs thinks them to be. For the purpose of a formal definition of the power relation, the costs of *A*'s power over *B* have to be stated as the *objective* costs that an attempt to influence *B* would actually entail upon *A*, while the *strength* of *A*'s power over *B* has to be stated in terms of the costs of noncompliance as *perceived* by *B* himself. The reason is that the costs of *A*'s power serve to describe the objective policy possibilities open to *A*, whereas the strength of *A*'s power serves to explain *B*'s subjective motivation for compliant behavior. (Of course, a full description of a given power situation would require listing both objective and perceived costs for both participants.)

THE STRENGTH OF POWER, AND THE AMOUNT OF POWER IN DAHL'S SENSE

Clearly, in general the greater the *strength* of *A*'s power over *B*, the greater will be *A*'s *amount* of power over *B* with respect to action *X*. The relationship between these two variables will take a particularly simple mathematical form if the strength of *A*'s power is measured in *utility* terms, i.e., in terms of the disutility costs to *B* of noncompliance.[6]

We shall use the following model. *A* wants *B* to perform action *X*. But *B* associates disutility *x* with doing *X*. Nevertheless *B* would perform *X* with probability p_1 (i.e., would adopt the mixed strategy $s[p_1]$ assigning probability p_1 to doing *X* and probability $[1 - p_1]$ to not doing *X*), even

---

[6]To simplify our analysis, in what follows we shall be concerned only with the case where *A* is able to influence *B* in the intended direction, i.e., has a nonnegative amount of power over him. (*A* can have a negative amount of power over *B* only if he seriously misjudges the situation, because otherwise he can always make the amount of his power at worst *zero*, by simply refraining from intervention.)

in the absence of A's intervention.[7] B would adopt this strategy because if he completely refused to do X (i.e., if he adopted the mixed strategy $s[O]$) he would obtain only the utility payoff u_0 −; while if he did X with probability p_1 (i.e., if he adopted strategy $s[p_1]$), then he would obtain the higher utility payoff u_1, making his total expected utility $u_1 - p_1 x > u_0$.

Now A intervenes and persuades B that B will obtain the still higher utility payoff u^2 if he agrees to do action X with a certain probability $p_2 > p_1$ (i.e., if he adopts strategy $s[p^2]$), making his total expected utility $u_2 - p_2 x$. In view of this, B does adopt strategy $s[p^2]$.

Under these assumptions, obviously the *amount* of A's power over B will be the difference $\triangle p = p_2 - p_1$, while the *strength* of A's power over B will be the difference $u_2 - u_1$. As $p_2 \leqslant 1$, we must have $\triangle p \leqslant 1 - p_1$. Moreover, by assumption (cf. Footnote 7): $\triangle p \geqslant 0$.

If B tries to maximize his expected utility, then he will adopt strategy $s[p_2]$ only if

$$u_2 - p_2 x \geqslant u_1 - p_1 x, \tag{1}$$

that is, if

$$\triangle p = p_2 - p_1 \geqslant \frac{u_2 - u_1}{x} = \frac{\triangle u}{x} \tag{2}$$

This gives us:

Theorem I. The maximum *amount* of power that A can achieve over B with respect to action X tends to be equal to the *strength* of A's power over B (as expressed in utility units) divided by the disutility to B of doing action X—except that this maximum amount of power cannot be more than the amount of power corresponding to B's doing action X with probability *one*.

The strength of A's power over B divided by the disutility to B of doing X may be called the *relative strength* of A's power over B. Accordingly, we obtain:

Theorem I'. The maximum *amount* of power that A can achieve over B with respect to action X tends to be equal to the *relative strength* of A's power over B with respect to action X (except that, again, this maximum amount of power cannot be more than the amount of power corresponding to B's doing action X with probability one).

Of course, in the real world we seldom observe B to use a randomized

---

[7]We follow Dahl in considering the more general case where B would do action X with some probability p_1 (which of course may be zero), even in the absence of A's intervention.

mixed strategy of form $s[p]$, in a literal sense. What we do find is that, if we watch B's behavior over a series of comparable occasions, he will comply with A's wishes in some proportion p of all occasions and will fail to comply in the remaining proportion $(1 - p)$ of the occasions. Moreover, the disutility to B of compliant behavior will vary from one occasion to another. Hence if B wants to comply with A's wishes in pn cases out of n then, other things being equal, he will tend to select those pn cases where compliance is associated with the smallest disutility to him. For example, suppose that a U.S. senator, with political attitudes rather different from the administration's, decides to vote for the president's legislative program often enough to avoid at least an open break with the administration. Then he is likely to select for his support those administration bills which are least distasteful to him and to his constituents. This means that the total disutility to B of a given strategy $s[p]$ (which now has to be defined as a strategy involving compliance in *proportion p* of all cases) will tend to increase somewhat more than proportionally as p increases, because should B decide to increase the frequency of his compliant behavior he would have to include a higher fraction of "difficult" cases.

Accordingly, if we restate our model in terms of empirical *frequencies*, rather than theoretical *probabilities*, we must expect that the maximum *amount* of power that A can achieve over B will increase somewhat less than in proportion to increments in the *strength* of A's power over B (measuring this strength now in terms of the *average* utility value of B's incentives for compliance over all occasions). But our Theorem I is likely to retain at least its approximate validity in most empirical situations.[8]

POWER IN A SCHEDULE SENSE

We have just seen that the greater the strength of a person's power over other persons the greater the amount of his power over them tends to be. But likewise, the greater the strength of a person's power over other people, the greater both the scope and the extension of his power over these people. That is, the stronger incentives he can provide for compliance, the larger the number of specific actions he can get other people to perform for him will be, and the larger the number of individuals he can get to perform these actions.

[8]More exactly, in most unilateral power situations. The distinction between unilateral and bilateral power situations will be discussed below.

Note that in empirical applications based on a *frequency* interpretation, a further complication may arise owing to the fact that the utilities to A, and the disutilities to B, of a set of several compliant actions $X_1, \ldots, X_k$ by B may *not* be simply *additive* (as they may have the nature of complementary or of competitive "goods" from A's point of view, and/or the nature of complementary or of competitive "evils" from B's point of view).

But while the scope, the amount, and the extension of his power are all functions of the *strength* of his power over all individuals, the strength of his power is itself a function of the *costs* of power he is prepared to bear. The greater efforts and sacrifices he is prepared to make, the stronger incentives for compliance he will be able to provide and the greater will be the strength of his power over them.

Therefore, a given individual's power can be described not only by stating the specific values of the five dimensions of his power (whether as single numbers, or as vectors, or as lists of specific items), but also by specifying the mathematical *functions* or *schedules* that connect the costs of his power with the other four dimensions. When power is defined in terms of the specific values of the five power variables we shall speak of power in a *point* sense, and when power is defined in terms of the functions or schedules connecting the other four power variables with the costs of power we shall speak of power in a *schedule* sense.[9]

Power in a schedule sense can be regarded as a "production function" describing how a given individual can "transform" different amounts of his resources (of his working time, his money, his political rights, his popularity, etc.) into social power of various dimensions (of various strengths, scopes, amounts, and extensions). The commonsense notion of social power makes it an *ability* to achieve certain things—an ability that the person concerned is free to use or to leave unused. It seems to me that this notion of power as an ability is better captured by our concept of power in a schedule sense than it is by the concept of power in a point sense. (The latter seems to better correspond to the commonsense notion of actually exerted *influence*, rather than to that of power as such.)

If a person's power is given in a mere schedule sense, then we can state the specific values of his five power dimensions only if we are also told how much of his different resources he is actually prepared to use in order to obtain social power of various dimensions—that is, if besides his power schedules we know also his *utility function*. Whereas his power defined in a schedule sense indicates the conditions under which his environment is ready to "supply" power to him, it is his utility function which determines his "demand" for power under various alternative conditions.

BILATERAL POWER AND THE "BLACKMAILER'S FALLACY"

So far we have tacitly assumed that, in situations where *A* has power over *B*, *A* is always in a position to determine, by his unilateral decision, the incentives he will provide for *B*'s compliance, as well as the

---

[9] In analogy to the distinction in economic theory between demand or supply in a point sense and in a schedule sense.

degree of compliance he will try to enforce. Situations in which this is actually the case may be called unilateral power situations. But it very often happens that not only can A exert pressure on B in order to get him to adopt certain specific policies, but B can do the same to A. In particular, B may be able to press A for increased rewards and/or decreased penalties, and for relaxing the standards of compliance required from him and used in administering rewards and penalties to him. Situations of this type we shall call bilateral or reciprocal power situations. In such situations, both the extent of B's compliant behavior (i.e., the scope and the amount of A's power over B) and the net incentives that A can provide for B (i.e., the net strength of A's power over B) will become matters of explicit or implicit *bargaining* between the two parties.

Of the four ways in which A can increase his strength of power discussed previously, we tend to obtain unilateral power situations in cases 1, 3, and 4, where A's power over B is based on providing *unconditional* advantages or disadvantages for B, on conveying information or misinformation to him, or on having legitimate authority over B and/or enjoying B's personal affection (though there are also exceptions where these cases give rise to bilateral power). For example, it is usually largely a matter for A's personal discretion whether he provides certain facilities for B, whether he discloses certain pieces of information to him, or whether he gives him an order as his legitimate superior. In case 2, on the other hand, when A's power over B is based on A's ability to set up rewards and/or punishments for B *conditional* upon B's behavior, normally we find bilateral power situations (though again there are important exceptions).[10] Here B can exert pressure on A by withholding his compliance, even though compliance would be much more profitable than noncompliance. He may also be able to exert pressure on A by making the costs of a conflict (including the costs of punishing B for noncompliance) very high to A.

For bilateral power situations Theorem I and Theorem I′ do not hold true. For these conclusions have been completely dependent on the assumption that if a certain strategy s_1, involving some given degree of compliance by B, is more profitable to B than any alternative strategy s_2 involving a lesser degree of compliance (or none at all), then B will always choose strategy s_1 and will never choose strategy s_2—not even as a result of dissatisfaction with the terms A offers in return for B's cooperation. While in unilateral power situations this assumption is perfectly legitimate (as it amounts to no more than assuming that B tries to maximize his utility or expected utility), in bilateral power situations this assumption would in-

---

[10]Viz. in cases when A is able to persuade B that he, A, has irrevocably committed himself in advance to not making any concessions to B.

volve what I propose to call the "blackmailer's fallacy" (Harsanyi, 1956, p. 156).

A would-be blackmailer A once argued that as he was in a position to cause damage worth \$1,000 to a certain rich man B, he should be able to extract from B *any* ransom r short of \$1,000, because after payment of $r < \$1,000$, B would still be better off than if he had to suffer the full \$1,000 damage.

But this argument is clearly fallacious. By similar reasoning, B could also have argued that A would accept *any* ransom r larger than nil, because after accepting a ransom $r < \$0$, A would still be better off than if no agreement were reached and he did not receive anything at all. What both of these arguments really show is that in any bargaining between two rational bargainers, the outcome must fall between what may be called the two parties' *concession limits*, which are defined by each party's refusal to accept any agreement that would make him actually worse off than he would be in the conflict situation. But the two arguments in themselves say nothing about where the two parties' agreement point will actually lie *between* these two limits. They certainly do not allow the inference that this agreement point will actually coincide or nearly coincide with one party's concession limit. (Only if we know the two parties' attitudes towards risk-taking, and in particular towards risking a conflict rather than accepting unfavorable terms, can we make any predictions about where their agreement point will lie between the two concession limits.)

Either party's actual behavior will be a resultant of two opposing psychological forces. On the one hand, for example, B will admittedly have some incentive for agreeing to any ransom payment less than \$1,000. But B will also know that A will likewise have some incentive for accepting any ransom payment greater than zero, and this fact will make B expect to get away with a ransom payment of much less than \$1,000. This expectation in turn will provide B with some incentive to resist any ransom payment too close to \$1,000. Any realistic theory of B's behavior must take full account of *both* of these psychological forces—both of B's motives for compliance, and of the reasons which make him expect some concessions on A's part which will render full compliance on his own part unnecessary. . . .

CHAPTER FOUR

Issues and Nonissues: Where Does One Look for Community Power?

TWO FACES OF POWER

Peter Bachrach and Morton S. Baratz

While Peter Bachrach and Morton Baratz focus their attack in this article on pluralist studies of community power, especially on the work of Robert Dahl, their central argument is applicable to almost all studies of community influence.

The thrust of their argument is that power has "two faces"—one manifest in the outcome of the overt decision-making process, the other manifest in the capacity of individuals and groups to prevent issues or contests from arising which could threaten their interests. In making their case Bachrach and Baratz point to the importance of establishing criteria with which to judge the relative importance of various decisions.

In their concluding paragraphs the authors suggest the broad outlines

From Peter Bachrach and Morton Baratz, "The Two Faces of Power," *American Political Science Review*, LVII (December, 1962), 947–952.

of an approach for resolving the difficulties they have raised. The student might critically examine these proposals with the goal of formulating some tentative ideas about problems and methods of operationalizing them in field research.

I

Against the elitist approach to power several criticisms may be, and have been, levelled.[1] One has to do with its basic premise that in every human institution there is an ordered system of power, a "power structure" which is an integral part and the mirror image of the organization's stratification. This postulate the pluralists emphatically—and, to our mind, correctly—reject, on the ground that

> nothing categorical can be assumed about power in any community. . . . If anything, there seems to be an unspoken notion among pluralist researchers that at bottom *nobody* dominates in a town, so that their first question is not likely to be, "Who runs this community?," but rather, "Does anyone at all run this community?" The first query is somewhat like, "Have you stopped beating your wife?" in that virtually any response short of total unwillingness to answer will supply the researchers with a "power elite" along the lines presupposed by the stratification theory.[2]

Equally objectionable to the pluralists—and to us—is the sociologists' hypothesis that the power structure tends to be stable over time.

> Pluralists hold that power may be tied to issues, and issues can be fleeting or persistent, provoking coalitions among interested groups and citizens, ranging in their duration from momentary to semi-permanent. . . . To presume that the set of coalitions which exists in the community at any given time is a timelessly stable aspect of social structure is to introduce systematic inaccuracies into one's description of social reality.[3]

A third criticism of the elitist model is that it wrongly equates reputed with actual power:

> If a man's major life work is banking, the pluralist presumes he will spend his time at the bank, and not in manipulating community decisions. This presumption holds until the banker's activities and participations indicate otherwise. . . . If we presume that the banker is "really" engaged in running the community, there is practically no way of disconfirming this notion, even

---

[1]See especially Nelson W. Polsby, "How to Study Community Power: The Pluralist Approach," *Journal of Politics*, 22 (August 1960), 476.

[2]*Ibid.*, pp. 478–79.

[3]*Ibid.*

if it is totally erroneous. On the other hand, it is easy to spot the banker who really *does* run community affairs when we presume he does not, because his activities will make this fact apparent.[4]

This is not an exhaustive bill of particulars; there are flaws other than these in the sociological model and methodology[5] including some which the pluralists themselves have not noticed. But to go into this would not materially serve our current purposes. Suffice it simply to observe that whatever the merits of their own approach to power, the pluralists have effectively exposed the main weaknesses of the elitist model.

As the foregoing quotations make clear, the pluralists concentrate their attention, not upon the sources of power, but its exercise. Power to them means "participation in decision-making"[6] and can be analyzed only after "careful examination of a series of concrete decisions."[7] As a result, the pluralist researcher is uninterested in the reputedly powerful. His concerns instead are to (a) select for study a number of "key" as opposed to "routine" political decisions, (b) identify the people who took an active part in the decision-making process, (c) obtain a full account of their actual behavior while the policy conflict was being resolved, and (d) determine and analyze the specific outcome of the conflict.

The advantages of this approach, relative to the elitist alternative, need no further exposition. The same may not be said, however, about its defects—two of which seem to us to be of fundamental importance. One is that the model takes no account of the fact that power may be, and often is, exercised by confining the scope of decision-making to relative "safe" issues. The other is that the model provides no *objective* criteria for distinguishing between "important" and "unimportant" issues arising in the political arena.

II

There is no gainsaying that an analysis grounded entirely upon what is specific and visible to the outside observer is more "scientific" than one based upon pure speculation. To put it another way,

[4]*Ibid.*, pp. 480–81.
[5]See especially Robert A. Dahl, "A Critique of the Ruling-Elite Model," *American Political Science Review*, 52 (June 1958), 463–69; and Lawrence J. R. Herson, "In the Footsteps of Community Power," *American Political Science Review*, 55 (December, 1961), 817–31.
[6]This definition originated with Harold D. Lasswell and Abraham Kaplan, *Power and Society* (New Haven: 1950), p. 75.
[7]Robert A. Dahl, "A Critique of the Ruling-Elite Model," *loc. cit.*, p. 466.

If we can get our social life stated in terms of activity, and of nothing else, we have not indeed succeeded in measuring it, but we have at least reached a foundation upon which a coherent system of measurements can be built up. . . . We shall cease to be blocked by the intervention of unmeasurable elements, which claim to be themselves the real causes of all that is happening, and which by their spook-like arbitrariness make impossible any progress toward dependable knowledge.[8]

The question is, however, how can one be certain in any given situation that the "unmeasurable elements" are inconsequential, are not of decisive importance? Cast in slightly different terms, can a sound concept of power be predicated on the assumption that power is totally embodied and fully reflected in "concrete decisions" or in activity bearing directly upon their making?

We think not. Of course power is exercised when A participates in the making of decisions that affect B. But power is also exercised when A devotes his energies to creating or reinforcing social and political values and institutional practices that limit the scope of the political process to public consideration of only those issues which are comparatively innocuous to A. To the extent that A succeeds in doing this, B is prevented, for all practical purposes, from bringing to the fore any issues that might in their resolution be seriously detrimental to A's set of preferences.[9]

Situations of this kind are common. Consider, for example, the case—surely not unfamiliar to this audience—of the discontented faculty member in an academic institution headed by a tradition-bound executive. Aggrieved about a long-standing policy around which a strong vested interest has developed, the professor resolves in the privacy of his office to launch an attack upon the policy at the next faculty meeting. But, when the moment ·of truth is at hand, he sits frozen in silence. Why? Among the many possible reasons, one or more of these could have been of crucial importance: (a) the professor was fearful that his intended action would be interpreted as an expression of his disloyalty to the institution; or (b) he decided that, given the beliefs and attitudes of his colleagues on the faculty, he would almost certainly constitute on this issue a minority of one; or (c) he concluded that, given the nature of the law-making process in the institu-

---

[8]Arthur Bentley, *The Process of Government* (Chicago: 1908), p. 202, quoted in Polsby, (150), p. 481 n.

[9]As is perhaps self-evident, there are similarities in both faces of power. In each, A participates in decisions and thereby adversely affects B. But there is an important difference between the two: in the one case, A openly participates; in the other, he participates only in the sense that he works to sustain those values and rules of procedure that help him keep certain issues out of the public domain. True enough, participation of the second kind may at times be overt; that is the case, for instance, in cloture fights in the Congress. But the point is that it need not be. In fact, when the maneuver is most successfully executed, it neither involves nor can be identified with decisions arrived at on specific issues.

tion, his proposed remedies would be pigeonholed permanently. But whatever the case, the central point to be made is the same: to the extent that a person or group—consciously or unconsciously—creates or reinforces barriers to the public airing of policy conflicts, that person or group has power. Or, as Professor Schattschneider has so admirably put it:

> All forms of political organization have a bias in favor of the exploitation of some kinds of conflict and the suppression of others because *organization is the mobilization of bias.* Some issues are organized into politics while others are organized out.[10]

Is such bias not relevant to the study of power? Should not the student be continuously alert to its possible existence in the human institution that he studies, and be ever prepared to examine the forces which brought it into being and sustain it? Can he safely ignore the possibility, for instance, that an individual or group in a community participates more vigorously in supporting the *nondecision-making* process than in participating in actual decisions within the process? Stated differently, can the researcher overlook the chance that some person or association could limit decision-making to relatively non-controversial matters, by influencing community values and political procedures and rituals, notwithstanding that there are in the community serious but latent power conflicts?[11] To do so is, in our judgment, to overlook the less apparent, but nonetheless extremely important, face of power.

III

In his critique of the "ruling-elite model," Professor Dahl argues that "the hypothesis of the existence of a ruling elite can be strictly tested only if . . . [t]here is a fair sample of cases involving key political decisions in which the preferences of the hypothetical ruling elite run counter to those of any other likely group that might be suggested."[12] With this assertion we

---

[10] E. E. Schattschneider, *The Semi-Sovereign People* (New York: 1960), p. 71.

[11] Dahl *partially* concedes this point when he observes ("A Critique of the Ruling-Elite Model," pp. 468–69) that "one could argue that even in a society like ours a ruling elite might be so influential over ideas, attitudes, and opinions that a kind of false consensus will exist—not the phony consensus of a terroristic totalitarian dictatorship but the manipulated and superficially self-imposed adherence to the norms and goals of the elite by broad sections of a community. . . . This objection points to the need to be circumspect in interpreting the evidence." But that he largely misses our point is clear from the succeeding sentence: "Yet here, too, it seems to me that the hypothesis cannot be satisfactorily confirmed without something equivalent to the test I have proposed," and that is "by an examination of a series of concrete cases where key decisions are made. . . ."

[12] *Ibid.,* p. 466.

have two complaints. One we have already discussed, viz., in erroneously assuming that power is solely reflected in concrete decisions, Dahl thereby excludes the possibility that in the community in question there is a group capable of preventing contests from arising on issues of importance to it. Beyond that, however, by ignoring the less apparent face of power Dahl and those who accept his pluralist approach are unable adequately to differentiate between a "key" and a "routine" political decision.

Nelson Polsby, for example, proposes that "by pre-selecting as issues for study those which are generally agreed to be significant, pluralist researchers can test stratification theory."[13] He is silent, however, on how the researcher is to determine *what* issues are "generally agreed to be significant," and on how the researcher is to appraise the reliability of the agreement. In fact, Polsby is guilty here of the same fault he himself has found with elitist methodology: by presupposing that in any community there are significant issues in the political arena, he takes for granted the very question which is in doubt. He accepts as issues what are reputed to be issues. As a result, his findings are fore-ordained. For even if there is no "truly" significant issue in the community under study, there is every likelihood that Polsby (or any like-minded researcher) will find one or some and, after careful study, reach the appropriate pluralistic conclusions.[14]

Dahl's definition of "key political issues" in his essay on the ruling-elite model is open to the same criticism. He states that it is "a necessary although possibly not a sufficient condition that the [key] issue should involve actual disagreement in preferences among two or more groups."[15] In our view, this is an inadequate characterization of a "key political issue," simply because groups can have disagreements in preferences on unimportant as well as on important issues. Elite preferences which border on the indifferent are certainly not significant in determining whether a monolithic or polylithic distribution of power prevails in a given community. Using Dahl's definition of "key political issues," the researcher would have little difficulty in finding such in practically any community; and it would not be surprising then if he ultimately concluded that power in the community was widely diffused.

The distinction between important and unimportant issues, we believe, cannot be made intelligently in the absence of an analysis of the "mobilization of bias" in the community; of the dominant values and the political myths, rituals, and institutions which tend to favor the vested interests of one or more groups, relative to others. Armed with this knowledge, one could conclude that any challenge to the predominant values or to the established "rules of the game" would constitute an "important" issue; all

---

[13]*Ibid.*, p. 478.
[14]As he points out, the expectations of the pluralist researchers "have seldom been disappointed." *Ibid.*, p. 477.
[15]*Ibid.*, p. 467.

else, unimportant. To be sure, judgments of this kind cannot be entirely objective. But to avoid making them in a study of power is both to neglect a highly significant aspect of power and thereby to undermine the only sound basis for discriminating between "key" and "routine" decisions. In effect, we contend, the pluralists have made each of these mistakes; that is to say, they have done just that for which Kaufman and Jones so severely taxed Floyd Hunter: they have begun "their structure at the mezzanine without showing us a lobby or foundation,"[16] *i.e.,* they have begun by studying the issues rather than the values and biases that are built into the political system and that, for the student of power, give real meaning to those issues which do enter the political arena.

IV

There is no better fulcrum for our critique of the pluralist model than Dahl's recent study of power in New Haven.[17]

At the outset it may be observed that Dahl does not attempt in this work to define his concept, "key political decision." In asking whether the "Notables" of New Haven are "influential overtly or covertly in the making of government decisions," he simply states that he will examine "three different 'issue-areas' in which important public decisions are made: nominations by the two political parties, urban redevelopment, and public education." These choices are justified on the grounds that "nominations determine which persons will hold public office. The New Haven redevelopment program measured by its cost—present and potential—is the largest in the country. Public education, aside from its intrinsic importance, is the costliest item in the city's budget." Therefore, Dahl concludes, "It is reasonable to expect . . . that the relative influence over public officials wielded by the . . . Notables would be revealed by an examination of their participation in these three areas of activity."[18]

The difficulty with this latter statement is that it is evident from Dahl's own account that the Notables are in fact uninterested in two of the three "key" decisions he has chosen. In regard to the public school issue, for example, Dahl points out that many of the Notables live in the suburbs and that those who do live in New Haven choose in the main to send their children to private schools. "As a consequence," he writes, "their interest in the public schools is ordinarily rather slight."[19] Nominations by the two political parties as an important "issue-area," is somewhat analogous to

---

[16]Herbert Kaufman and Victor Jones, "The Mystery of Power," *Public Administration Review*, 14 (Summer 1954), 207.

[17]Robert A. Dahl, *Who Governs?* (New Haven: 1961).

[18]*Ibid.*, p. 64.

[19]*Ibid.*, p. 70.

the public schools, in that the apparent lack of interest among the Notables in this issue is partially accounted for by their suburban residence—because of which they are disqualified from holding public office in New Haven. Indeed, Dahl himself concedes that with respect to both these issues the Notables are largely indifferent: "Business leaders might ignore the public schools or the political parties without any sharp awareness that their indifference would hurt their pocketbooks . . ." He goes on, however, to say that

> the prospect of profound changes [as a result of the urban-redevelopment program] in ownership, physical layout, and usage of property in the downtown area and the effects of these changes on the commercial and industrial prosperity of New Haven were all related in an obvious way to the daily concerns of business men.[20]

Thus, if one believes—as Professor Dahl did when he wrote his critique of the ruling-elite model—that an issue, to be considered as important, "should involve actual disagreement in preferences among two or more groups,"[21] then clearly he has now for all practical purposes written off public education and party nominations as key "issue-areas." But this point aside, it appears somewhat dubious at best that "the relative influence over public officials wielded by the Social Notables" can be revealed by an examination of their nonparticipation in areas in which they were not interested.

Furthermore, we would not rule out the possibility that even on those issues to which they appear indifferent, the Notables may have a significant degree of *indirect* influence. We would suggest, for example, that although they send their children to private schools, the Notables do recognize that public school expenditures have a direct bearing upon their own tax liabilities. This being so, and given their strong representation on the New Haven Board of Finance,[22] the expectation must be that it is in their direct interest to play an active role in fiscal policy-making, in the establishment of the educational budget in particular. But as to this, Dahl is silent: he inquires not at all into either the decisions made by the Board of Finance with respect

---

[20]*Ibid.*, p. 467.
[21]*Ibid.*, p. 467.
[22]*Who Governs?*, p. 82. Dahl points out that the main policy thrusts of the Economic Notables is to oppose tax increases; this leads them to oppose expenditures for anything more than minimal traditional city services. In this effort their two most effective weapons ordinarily are the mayor and the Board of Finance. The policies of the Notables are most easily achieved under a strong mayor if his policies coincide with theirs or under a weak mayor if they have the support of the Board of Finance. . . . New Haven mayors have continued to find it expedient to create confidence in their final policies among businessmen by appointing them to the Board." (pp. 81–2).

to education nor into their impact upon the public school.[23] Let it be understood clearly that in making these points we are not attempting to refute Dahl's contention that the Notables lack power in New Haven. What we *are* saying, however, is that this conclusion is not adequately supported by his analysis of the "issue-areas" of public education and party nominations.

The same may not be said of redevelopment. This issue is by any reasonable standard important for purposes of determining whether New Haven is ruled by "the hidden hand of an economic elite."[24] For the Economic Notables have taken an active interest in the program and, beyond that, the socio-economic implications of it are not necessarily in harmony with the basic interests and values of businesses and businessmen.

In an effort to assure that the redevelopment program would be acceptable to what he dubbed "the biggest muscles" in New Haven, Mayor Lee created the Citizens Action Commission (CAC) and appointed to it primarily representatives of the economic elite. It was given the function of overseeing the work of the mayor and other officials involved in redevelopment, and, as well, the responsibility for organizing and encouraging citizens' participation in the program through an extensive committee system.

In order to weigh the relative influence of the mayor, other key officials, and the members of the CAC, Dahl reconstructs "all the *important* decisions on redevelopment and renewal between 1950–58 . . . [to] determine which individuals most often initiated the proposals that were finally adopted or most often successfully vetoed the proposals of the others."[25] The results of his test indicate that the mayor and his development administrator were by far the most influential, and that the "muscles" on the Commission, excepting in a few trivial instances, "never directly initiated, opposed, vetoed, or altered any proposal brought before them. . . ."[26]

This finding is, in our view, unreliable, not so much because Dahl was compelled to make a subjective selection of what constituted *important* decisions without what he felt to be an *important* "issue-area," as because the finding was based upon an excessively narrow test of influence. To measure relative influence solely in terms of the ability to initiate and veto

---

[23]Dahl does discuss in general terms (pp. 79–84) changes in the level of tax rates and assessments in past years, but not actual decisions of the Board of Finance or their effects on the public school system.

[24]*Ibid.*, p. 124.

[25]*Ibid.* "A rough test of a person's overt or covert influence," Dahl states in the first section of the book, "is the frequency with which he successfully initiates an important policy over the opposition of others, or vetoes policies initiated by others, or initiates a policy where no opposition appears." *Ibid.*, p. 66.

[26]*Ibid.*, p. 121.

proposals is to ignore the possible exercise of influence or power in limiting the scope of initiation. How, that is to say, can a judgment be made as to the relative influence of Mayor Lee and the CAC without knowing (through prior study of the political and social views of all concerned) the proposals that Lee did *not* make because he anticipated that they would provoke strenuous opposition and, perhaps, sanctions on the part of the CAC?[27]

In sum, since he does not recognize *both* faces of power, Dahl is in no position to evaluate the relative influence or power of the initiator and decision-maker, on the one hand, and of those persons, on the other, who may have been indirectly instrumental in preventing potentially dangerous issues from being raised.[28] As a result, he unduly emphasizes the importance of initiating, deciding, and vetoing, and in the process casts the pluralist conclusions of his study into serious doubt.

V

We have contended in this paper that a fresh approach to the study of power is called for, an approach based upon a recognition of the two faces of power. Under this approach the researcher would begin—not, as does the sociologist who asks, "Who rules?" nor as does the pluralist who asks, "Does anyone have power?"—but by investigating the particular "mobilization of bias" in the institution under scrutiny. Then, having analyzed the dominant values, the myths and the established political procedures and rules of the game, he would make a careful inquiry into

[27]Dahl is, of course, aware of the "law of anticipated reactions." In the case of the mayor's relationship with the CAC, Dahl notes that Lee was "particularly skillful in estimating what the CAC could be expected to support or reject," (p. 137). However, Dahl was not interested in analyzing or appraising to what extent the CAC limited Lee's freedom of action. Because of his restricted concept of power, Dahl did not consider that the CAC might in this respect have exercised power. That the CAC did not initiate or veto actual proposals by the mayor was to Dahl evidence enough that the CAC was virtually powerless; it might as plausibly be evidence that the CAC was (in itself or in what it represented) so powerful that Lee ventured nothing it would find worth quarreling with.

[28]The fact that the initiator of decisions also refrains—because he anticipates adverse reactions—from initiating other proposals does not obviously lessen the power of the agent who limited his initiative powers. Dahl missed this point: "It is," he writes, "all the more improbable, then, that a secret cabal of Notables dominates the public life of New Haven through means so clandestine that not one of the fifty prominent citizens interviewed in the course of this study—citizens who had participated extensively in various decisions—hinted at the existence of such a cabal . . ." (p. 185).

In conceiving of elite domination exclusively in the form of a conscious cabal exercising the power of decision-making and vetoing, he overlooks a more subtle form of domination; one in which those who actually dominate are not conscious of it themselves, simply because their position of dominance has never seriously been challenged.

which persons or groups, if any, gain from the existing bias and which, if any, are handicapped by it. Next, he would investigate the dynamics of *nondecision-making*; that is, he would examine the extent to which and the manner in which the *status quo* oriented persons and groups influence those community values and those political institutions (as, *e.g.*, the unanimity "rule" of New York City's Board of Estimate[29]) which tend to limit the scope of actual decision-making to "safe" issues. Finally, using his knowledge of the restrictive face of power as a foundation for analysis and as a standard for distinguishing between "key" and "routine" political decisions, the researcher would, after the manner of the pluralists, analyze participation in decision-making of concrete issues.*

We reject in advance as unimpressive the possible criticism that this approach to the study of power is likely to prove fruitless because it goes beyond an investigation of what is objectively measurable. In reacting against the subjective aspect of the sociological model of power, the pluralists have, we believe, made the mistake of discarding "unmeasurable elements" as unreal. It is ironical that, by so doing, they have exposed themselves to the same fundamental criticism they have so forcefully levelled against the elitists: their approach to and assumptions about power predetermine their findings and conclusions.

[29]Sayre and Kaufman, *op. cit.*, p. 640. For perceptive study of the "mobilization of bias" in a rural American community, see Arthur Vidich and Joseph Bensman, *Small Town in Mass Society* (Princeton: 1958).

*Ed. Note: The student should not misunderstand the authors' position here to mean that determining the distribution of values or benefits in a social or political system wi.. allow one to know the distribution of power. The temptation to equate the possession of values and benefits with influence is strong, but should be resisted. The reasons for this have been cataloged by Nelson Polsby: "(1) value distributions occur without explicit decisions taking place, hence may tell us nothing about decision-making; (2) values within the community may be distributed in important ways as a by-product of decisions and "non-decisions made outside the community; (3) there are many irrationalities in decision-making, which may lead to the distribution of values in unpredictable, unintended ways; (4) the powerful may intentionally distribute values to the non-powerful."

ON ISSUES AND NONISSUES
IN THE STUDY OF POWER

Frederick W. Frey

   In the previous article, Peter Bachrach and Morton Baratz pointed out that in addition to looking at how specific decisions are made or issues resolved, it is also important to an understanding of the distribution of community power to know how the decision-making agenda is set and why issues get confronted. In other words, why and how do certain matters and not others—given the possible range of ambitions, grievances and inequities that exist in any community—secure a visible and public response by power-holders.

   There are those who argue that the empirical investigation of this "other face of power," i.e., nondecision making or nonissues, is either impossible or not worth the effort. In this article Frederick Frey argues for the importance of looking for power outside of formal, legitimized decision-making areas and he suggests some ways that this might be done.

   Professor Frey also considers the question of how one might go about selecting the issues one would study in order to most accurately identify those individuals and groups that will community power.

   Among the questions the readers will want to consider with respect to this significant article is whether the insights and direction Professor Frey provides can readily be reflected in comparative research strategies. Could we, in other words, go into the field and conduct research that would meet the criticisms of Bachrach and Baratz on the one hand (see above) and the skepticism, on the other hand, of those who argue that nondecisions and nonissues are nonevents and thus cannot reliably be studied? In addition, one might want to apply the criteria Frey suggests

Reprinted with permission of the author and the publisher. From Frederic W. Frey, "Comment: On Issues and Nonissues in the Studies of Power." *American Political Science Reviews*, 65 (December, 1971), 1081–1101. This article was written in response to Raymond E. Wolfinger's, "Nondecisions and the Study of Local Politics," *American Political Science Review*, 65 (December, 1971), 1063–1080.

for selecting the issues to the community studies presented earlier in this book and to those in succeeding chapters. Assuming that these other researchers were interested in identifying fundamental and persistent patterns of community power (though not everyone had this objective), were the events they studied likely to yield adequate evidence?

. . . Cut to the bone, the basic considerations seem to be the following: In all but the smallest and simplest social units, an extremely large variety of issues might be examined. . . . Such a situation means that the researcher must select for his study a manageable subset from the very large universe of issues or policies which might be examined. As the "pluralists" and other careful analysts of power have long noted, however, findings about power may differ according to the issue selected. For instance, the power configurations for tax matters may diverge markedly from those for civil rights. If there is much variation of this type, a researcher could knowingly or unwittingly bias his results by choosing special, limited, or inappropriate issues. Hence, the scrupulous scholar confronts the formidable task of justifying his particular selection of issues through which power is analyzed. How is he to do this?

Current approaches to issue selection. . . . those analysts who have dutifully confronted the problem of justifying their selection of issues have usually discerned two basic strategies. They maintain either that the set of issues chosen was *representative* of the larger universe of issues which might have been chosen, or else they contend that they have fastened upon the most *important* issues. Since there are further variations on these two themes, let us briefly scrutinize them more closely.

Justification through representativeness. The fundamental problem with selecting issues allegedly representative of all issues in the system has been well stated by Polsby: "There seem to be no satisfactory criteria which would identify a universe of all decisions [issues] in the community so that a sample of 'typical' or 'representative' decisions could in principle be drawn." Ordinarily, the universe of actual (let alone submerged or potential) issues is so numerous, so varied, so subjectively defined, and so uncertain in its boundaries that it eludes sufficient specification to permit meaningful sampling. Put another way, there usually appears to be no acceptable sampling frame to allow the construction and evaluation of a representative sample.

What has just been said, however, needs qualification. Much depends on the meaning given to the term "issue" or "decision." Many studies have left these crucial notions undefined, and there are also certain problems with the explicit or implicit conceptions that have been used, as we shall see later. Nevertheless some interpretations of "issue" and "decision" do ease the sampling problem noted above. For example, one can focus on the formally enunciated decisions of government, as manifested in bills, laws, regulations, hearings, and the like. Over any limited time period, this is likely to be a manageable, enumerable set whose sampling offers no great practical problems. Similarly, though slightly more broadly, one can define issues in terms of those topics that appear in community newspapers and other media over a stipulated period. Or one can rely on participant observers to list what they regard as "key issues" and decisions. If the conception of each issue or decision is quite global, so that fewer are needed to cover the set of activities involved, such listing may even be small enough to permit a complete inventory rather than a sample. . . . Many will find such approaches to the sampling problem unsatisfactory on various grounds. For instance, the development of an effective description of the universe of "issues" or "decisions" (a sampling frame) is accomplished by such restriction of the basic meaning of those terms as to render them inappropriate. The focus becomes restricted to the formal activities of one agency—government. Though that agency and its activities are significant, many researchers define their analytic interests much more broadly. Local governmental decision making is only one aspect of community power for many scholars.

Also, the question always remains whether all issues were indeed covered by the described procedures. One must probe how newspapers and other media, or how participant observers, form their interpretations of what constitute issues. Unfortunately, researchers generally fail to provide adequate information to the reader for making these judgments. Unless an extremely narrow conception of what constitutes an "issue" or "decision" is taken, any convincing support for the issue judgments made by mass media or participant observers would again require delineating the relevant universe in order to show that it had been well sampled. For these and other reasons, it is not surprising that relatively few scholars have explicitly asserted that their studies dealt with a representative sample of all issues or decisions.

Justification through importance. More common has been the effort to support the particular set of issues analyzed by contending that it includes important or key matters. Using this approach one can develop a more cogent general justification than through attempting to argue representativeness, but profound problems still remain. Right at the start we see, in my opinion, one of the less happy legacies of the "elitist-pluralist controversy." Very few analysts have asserted that they were able to examine *all* important issues. Rather, they contend that all the issues they have examined are important—i.e., the cases investigated include no trivial issues. Viewed baldly, such a strategy poses an immediately apparent problem. Because a selection includes no trivial issues, only important ones, does not mean that it is unbiased or generalizable, unless one makes the major assumption that patterns of power will be the same for the entire class of important issues.

What, then, is the appeal of such an approach? The answer is that it can be used to refute strong assertions of a dominant elite—assertions which charge that a ruling elite controls on all issues of importance in the community. Locating demonstrably important issues for which this is not true undermines such assertions. It may or may not be a very good strategy for determining what are the theoretically most instructive patterns of power in the community under scrutiny, but it is a useful strategy for answering popular though extreme "elitist" hypotheses in the literature. Once that thicket is cleared, however, the deeper problems with this approach emerge.

Probably the most basic difficulty is with the notion of importance itself. To employ this justification, one must specify the criteria by which importance is to be judged. Several suggestions have been made, a few quite sensible or ingenious. But up to now, none have been able to eliminate the basic element of subjectivity or relativism that plagues interpersonal comparisons of utility welfare, interests, and importance.

Criteria proposed for establishing the importance of issues fall largely into two categories, one subjective and the other ostensibly objective. Under the former, an attempt is made to let the participants themselves determine the importance of issues, while under the latter the researcher usually determines it according to more commonly observable data. . . .

[The subjective] procedure, which has not yet been widely used in power research, has severe limitations, however. These revolve mainly about the issue of weighting and aggregating the responses. How can interpersonal differences in the magnitude and intensity of feeling be determined and convincingly weighted? One man's "very important" is often not the same as another's. Does the fifty per cent who feel that an issue is "moderately important" equal the twenty five per cent who feel it is "very important"? Should actors be weighted not only in accordance with the degrees and directions of their feelings but also in accordance with their power positions in the community? In short, should one merely count heads and designate the issues with the greatest degrees of ascribed importance as the key issues? Or should one instead follow some more sophisticated weighting scheme—and, if so, which one and why? These long-standing questions of normative philosophy have not yet succumbed to any ready formula. It seems very unlikely that they will now surrender because a solution is needed for issue selection in community power analyses. Determining important issues through subjective ratings by participants also necessarily neglects some types of "nonissues" or "nondecisions" discussed in the following section.

Because of the comparability barrier confronting subjective definitions of importance, most plausible criteria offered by competent analysts fall into the ostensibly objective category. Nonetheless, the fundamental objection to them is that they, too, ultimately cannot escape the subjectivity which largely precludes comparison and demonstrably valid rankings. Either the researcher intrudes his own values, with which others may reasonably disagree, or else the supposedly objective criteria can be seen finally to depend on assumptions about subjective evaluations of the type just described.

The two most sophisticated and explicit attempts to grapple with the problem from this perspective have been made by Polsby and by McFarland.[1] Polsby suggests four criteria for ranking decisions according to their importance: 1) how many people are affected by the outcomes, 2) how many different kinds of community resources are distributed by the outcomes, 3) how much in amount of resources is distributed by the outcomes, and 4) how drastically present community resource distributions are altered by the outcomes.

These are thoughtful suggestions, but they depend upon implicit value judgments which many might not share. Setting as a criterion how many people are affected by the outcome weights people equally, without regard for how intensely those people feel about matters or who they are. The number of kinds of different resources affected and the total amount of resources distributed (measured in what kinds of units?) both ignore qualitative distinctions. And using the criterion of how drastically the present community resource distributions are altered ignores trends and expectations, making the status quo the preferred standard for evaluating change. Moreover, what is meant by "drastic"? Who is to say if a fifty per cent alteration in one resource is as drastic as a thirty per cent alteration in another? More profound examination of these problems would reveal that subjective evaluations must ultimately reenter the criteria, which leads to the possibility of logically irreconcilable disagreement regarding the ranking of issues in terms of their "importance."

In an interesting recent discussion, McFarland accepts Polsby's four criteria of issue importance, but finds them incomplete and adds at least four others . . . which do focus on the perceptions of the actors:

(1) the number of people actually engaged in the political issue; (2) the amount of money, time, and other resources engaged in the issue; (3) other measures of the intensity of conflict, particularly violence or near violence; (4) whether or not the issue involves possible changes in the procedural rules of the game. (p. 82)

[1]Polsby, *Community Power*, . . . pp. 95–96; Andrew S. McFarland, *Power and Leadership in Pluralist Systems* (Stanford: University Press, 1969), Chapters 5 and 6, pp. 70–124, esp. Chapter 5.

McFarland labels these additions "activity criteria." They appear to contribute a useful dimension, but they also incorporate further implicit and contestable value judgments, while still probably not doing justice to the feelings of the participants. For example, how can one infer evaluations from amounts of money, time, etc., without subjective weightings of the value placed upon these resources? How legitimate is it to assume that for all groups the resort to violence indicates more intensely important issues than do other forms of political activity? In short, the *perceptions* and *evaluations* of the actors can by no means be automatically inferred from the *activities* described.

McFarland also offers another vehicle for distinguishing important issues. Building on earlier distinctions between "critical" and "routine" decisions, he equates importance with decisional generality in the context of a hierarchical tree structure of interrelated decisions. Essentially, more important decisions are those that disproportionately determine or shape other decisions. An important issue has many more consequences for other issues than does an unimportant one. For a given decisional unit, individual or collective, it is often possible to order hierarchically nested sets of interrelated decisions, i.e., to perceive an integrated and coherent structure of choices. The most antecedent and determinative of these decisions, choices, or issues are regarded as most important.

One again, this perspective, which he calls the "behavior-tree model," has much intuitive appeal. But it ultimately confronts the same problem of subjectivity that besets the other proposed criteria. McFarland candidly notes four serious "limitations" to the scheme he suggests. One of these is that neither individuals nor organizations display the fully coherent and integrated structure of choices envisioned by the model. Numerous limited or partial structurings seem to be the rule, rather than a single, complete and fully integrated one. This fact, in turn, raises the profound problem of how to assess the relative importance or issues located in different hierarchies.

Second, the level of generality itself, and thus of importance, depends fundamentally upon the subjective values of the rater. To use McFarland's example, for one person taxation may be more important than education, so that educational choices flow from more basic choices regarding appropriate levels of taxation. But for another person, education may be more general and important than taxation, so that tax policy flows from more basic choices regarding educational objectives. Confronted with these divergent evaluations, how is one to arrive at a single assessment of importance? How can one aggregate ranking differences among actors? We are again faced with the same ineluctable problem of subjectivity and comparability previously encountered with regard to other proposed criteria. . . .

The crucial point . . . is that any such formulation of issue importance is essentially a value judgment and ultimately subjective. "Importance" is basically a normative and evaluative term. In the context in which it has been applied, it calls for a moral judgment, as opposed to a professional value judgment regarding which strategy is most likely to lead to the critical development. Everything considered, selecting issues on the basis of a completely defensible determination of their normative importance seems nearly as dubious as selecting them on the basis of their general representativeness.

An alternative approach. What, then, is the analyst of power to do? Must he give up and slink back to more traditional, narrow, non-comparable and noncumulative studies? Or can he discern some promising way out of the difficulty? . . .

At this juncture it is instructive to reexamine the basic difficulty. Empirical political analysis must have a less than global focus. In discovering through specific empirical research how policies are made, how outputs are allocated, how power is exercised, or even how government works in some social unit, one cannot cover every aspect of an enormously multidimensional reality. Selection is essential.

If all studies involve focal selections, what then is the problem? Some readers might be uninterested in the selections made—the foci chosen—but that engenders no great intellectual or research problem as long as others are interested. As McFarland observes, however, ". . . the catch-all critique of an empirical decision-making analysis of political power is the assertion: 'You have studied the wrong issues.' "

The phonology here is critical. The issues studied are not branded uninteresting, pointless, or inconsequential, but "wrong." Wrong in what sense? Wrong in the sense that they do not accurately reveal the power structure of the community under study. . . .

Much of the difficulty, therefore, seems to lie in the implicit goal that induces one to claim general representativeness or normative importance for the issues studied rather than presenting them in terms of whatever their intrinsic interest may be, arguing neither global representativeness nor undeniable importance. This implicit—and infectious—goal is generalizing to "*the* power structure" of the unit. . . .

An alternative approach, not without lingering problems but significantly more promising, would be the following: We must recognize that the notion of "*the* power structure" of a social unit is a dangerously misleading siren. There are as many power structures as there are issues fruitfully distinguished. Some of these structures, perhaps most of them, may in certain kinds of units strongly resemble one another, though in complex units at least minor differences will always be found. One of the outstanding tasks for power analysis is to discover better ways of measuring and expressing these relationships—measures of the degrees of structural isomorphism and positional stability across the various issue-based power structures of a unit. Such research should lead to intriguing theory about the kinds of units in which there is a high degree of isomorphism and positional stability and the kinds in which there is little, along with the consequences of these tendencies for other values. Harold Lasswell started this quest years ago with his conception of "agglutination."[2] Further thought and effort are now needed to move ahead.

Since generalization to *"the* power structure" of the unit is presently pointless, power analyses must state their generalizing hypotheses much more carefully than they have heretofore. "Power in Oshkosh" is, almost by definition, an insufficiently specific notion. Instead we must always indicate the issue or scope involved. Communities or other social units can then be compared only within this framework. One might, for example, study the distribution of power with regard to education in five cities, not claiming to contrast their patterns of power in any respect other than that. Of course, as competent studies of the same communities were gradually done for other issues, one could examine the cross-issue structural similarities previously mentioned, assuming the divergent time periods did not preclude comparison. But meantime, until many issues have been systematically researched, the temptation to speak globally about "power in Subject City" must be resisted.

At least two remaining and related problems, however, are bared by the preceding analysis. The first is that even the great reduction in attempted generality here proposed does not in principle completely eliminate all the difficulties previously discussed. . . . Hence, even at markedly lower levels of generalization, selection and inference are still present.

The crucial difference, however, is that at lower levels of generalization, effective conceptualization of the relevant universe of subissues or decisions becomes much more feasible, and the possibility of representativeness in selection more real. Part of the art of power analysis is to find the maximal level of generality at which this effective conceptualization is possible. That maximum is patently less than the universe of all issues for the total community, for instance. It may even be well below the level of such a broad issue-area as public education or urban redevelopment. But the trick is to find the most general level at which one can validly operate.

The other prominent problem highlighted by this analysis is common to all comparative research, even though it has not been much discussed in connection with issue selection for power studies. It is the problem of

---

[2]"Agglutination" refers to a situation in which the structural . . . positions of a person or group in different value patterns [power, wealth, prestige, etc.] and to approximate one another. The patterns of different values tend to coincide. Harold Lasswell and Abraham Kaplan, *Power and Society* (New Haven: Yale University Press, 1950), 57–58.

equivalence. One may, for instance, investigate the issue-area of public education in two communities. Ordinarily, in each community the specific issues which comprise this issue-area will overlap to some degree and diverge to some degree. In one community the hiring of a new superintendent may be a salient decision. In the other that decision may not be present at all, but the acquisition by the city of a parochial school building may be prominent. Several other similar discrepancies in the specific issue indicators which make up the issue-area may also exist. Hence, the obvious query arises: are the two issue-areas of "public education" truly equivalent in these communities? What does "equivalence" mean, conceptually and operationally, in this context? How can it be demonstrated?

It is not possible in this discussion to explore the matter more fully. Available treatments of equivalence in comparative research seem quite appropriate. However, a specific means of handling the problem will have to be developed for comparative research on patterns of power in social units.

The "Nonissue" as a Research Problem

A prime concern [in power analysis] is the "nonissue" or "nondecision," most recently brought to our attention by Bachrach and Baratz and by Anton.[3] [Raymond] Wolfinger raises a number of probing queries about the fruitfulness and feasibility of this concept for empirical political analysis, presenting at least four major contentions. The first and most important is that the very conception of a "nonissue" or "nondecision" is inadequate. The second is that many critical aspects of nonissues cannot practically be researched. The third is that the data which might be gathered on nonissues do not provide an adequate basis for conclusions about the distribution of power. And the fourth is that the concept of power structures, and perhaps even of power itself, poses insurmountable difficulties.

Though appreciating many insightful points included in these arguments, I would disagree with each of the major contentions. Rather than take them up *seriatim*, I shall attempt to present an alternative approach to the same topics. The discussion will focus first on the notions of what is an issue and a nonissue and second on the researchability of nonissues, . . . and analyses, including the kinds of conclusions.

Identifying issues and nonissues. At first blush, a nonissue or nondecision may seem to be merely the complement of whatever is defined as an issue or decision. Actually, this is not the case, suggesting yet another in-

[3]Bachrach and Baratz, "Two Faces of Power"; Thomas J. Anton, "Power, Pluralism, and Local Politics," *Administrative Science Quarterly*, 7 (March, 1963), 425–457.

stance of the poor labeling and notation nearly endemic among social scientists. "Suppressed issue" might be a more accurate expression.

Be that as it may, it is nonetheless useful to begin with a glance at the basic conceptions of an issue and a decision. Both terms, but especially "issue," are seldom defined in the community power literature. . . .

Of the two concepts, "decision" is usually the more basic. It also is more frequently defined. Almost all definitions interpret decision as a choice among alternatives. An issue can then be correspondingly defined as a matter calling for or involving a decision. Another related term is "issue-area," as used in the New Haven study. . . . In general, then, we have three related concepts in common use: decision, issue, and issue-area.

Issues and conflict. The central connotations of the term "issue" suggest contest and controversy. Although it is neither logically nor definitionally necessary, the assumption that power implies conflict and is only revealed by it is made in many power analyses oriented toward issues and decisions. Such an assumption is both venerable and understandable, although unfortunate in my opinion. . . .

The assumption that power implies conflict arises from several very legitimate concerns shared by most serious students of power. Outstanding among these are recognition of the need to distinguish *influenced* behavior from *autonomous*, self-directed behavior; the need to study power through empirically verifiable procedures and to eliminate subjective intrusions as far as possible; and the related need to avoid what Dahl aptly characterized as an "infinite regress of explanations." For successful research, the concept of power must be adequately operationalized and studied with replicable procedures. This, in turn, means that overt behavioral evidence is ultimately essential to support assertions about the nature and distribution of power.

These principles, strongly insisted upon by the New Haven group and others, seem unexceptionable. They do not imply, however, that conflict, under any ordinary definition of that term, is necessary for power to be manifested. Indeed, the very conception of power itself, as well as recollection of some of its real and imagined manifestations, indicates the error of assuming that power necessarily implies conflict.

In one of the most influential formulations, Dahl roughly defined power as one actor's ability to get another to do something he would not otherwise have done. . . . Let us define power as a relationship such that the behavior of one actor (individual or collective) alters the behavior of another actor. But neither under Dahl's potential power conception nor under this actual-exercise conception is there any stipulation that the person influenced (influencee) does not want to do what he is influenced to do. The deliberate stipulation is merely that the person influenced would not have acted as he did were it not for the action of the influencer in the given situation. The behavior of the influencer must be adduced to explain the behavior of the influencee.

There are numerous important instances in which power so defined is clearly exerted but in which conflict (regarded as visible contention, controversy, or even as opposition of interests) is absent. Among these are the cases in which: 1) the influencer induces the influencee to pursue one rather than another of several attractive and mutually exclusive alternatives: 2) the influencer's power is the result of the influencee's identification with the influencer, and his concomitant desire to be and to appear to be influenced by him; 3) the influencer has socialized the originally indifferent influencee to want to behave as the influencer wishes him to behave. . . .

In most general terms, a nonmonotonic relationship seems to exist between the distribution of power in a social unit and the appearance of visible conflict. After a very high threshold of power concentration is reached, the probability of manifest conflict revealed in public decisions is markedly reduced. Hence, the analyst cannot assume that power must be manifested by visible conflict over issues. If it exists, conflict certainly affords one of our best insights into many aspects of the power situation. But it has clear limitations as a vehicle for examining several important power processes. Any research strategy, however useful it may otherwise be, which focuses solely upon conflicts and ignores other glimpses into the phenomena of power must be regarded as incomplete. Issue analysis does not compel such a limited focus, but it often seems to foster it.

A broader approach to empirical power research might be called activity analysis. It provides an orientation which comprehends issue analysis plus other topics that are often neglected because of the conflictual overtones surrounding the concept "issue." The specificity of focus demanded by empirical research is furnished by designating activities of interest rather than issues of interest. These activities, such as joining a political organization, paying taxes, employing workers, bribing, or rioting, are regarded as the possible scopes (influenced behaviors) of significant power relations. One attempts to discover which actors in the system, if any, influence which other actors with regard to the selected activities. The term "activity" may actually be too narrow, since demonstrable attitudinal change is also included.

Of course, the activities initially designated ordinarily lead to examination of other activities which produce them, leading in turn to still other activities, etc., in a chain of influence that is terminated either by the limitations of the data or arbitrarily by the researcher.

Usually, an issue or decision in a power analysis can be construed as a set of influenced activities or power relations. It is not merely a choice among alternatives, but additionally it is an *influenced* choice among alternatives or else a choice among alternatives that *influences* the activities of others. From a power perspective, creating the Redevelopment Agency and determining the educational budget are issues which can be expressed as more or less complex sets of influenced or influential activities. An activity focus performs the same heuristic and organizational functions as an issue focus; it is more complicated, but it is less likely to become restricted to conflictual phenomena. In most cases, it seems wise to include if possible both issue analyses and activity analyses in a power research design, though the activity analysis is difficult in units larger than small organizations of a few hundred people.

The focus of power studies utilizing either an issue analysis or a decisional analysis approach has often been further limited by the particular construction placed upon "community power." Once again, while power is often defined, community power is quite commonly left vague. Unfortunately, several divergent interpretations have been given to community power. The most general minimally involves designating the community of reference and the scope of the investigation (activity, issue, or decision), which may be any well defined focus of interest regardless of how many or few actors in the community are involved and whether they include its formal authorities or not. One can thus refer to power relations in Boston concerning professional football, power processes in Berkeley regarding the use of city parks, or power patterns in Belchertown related to fair employment practices. The scopes most interesting for political analysis, however, tend to be those involving power over the allocation and distribution of power itself. In every instance, though, the initial focus is presumed to include all potentially participant actors in the community, and government is regarded as merely one actor (or set of actors) among others.

On the other hand, a great many studies explicitly or implicitly restrict community power to decision making in the name of the community, or decision making which affects all or at least a large segment of the community's population. Many studies go even further to confine community power to formal public policy making, customarily defined local "politics," or "municipal government," as Wolfinger overmodestly allows. One by no means denigrates these efforts by asserting that for many scholars community power includes much more than local governmental decision making having a wide impact.

It is sometimes claimed and frequently implied that almost all important community issues will at some point be funneled through local government, and so will be picked up by a focus on governmental decision making. This seems to me a dubious contention. Our political culture, for example, apparently renders unto business certain important types of decision making that various other societies handle through government—many production, investment, location, and employment decisions, for instance. Although aspects of these decisions may sometimes involve local government, many crucial elements ordinarily do not. And while "business" cannot be assumed to be the dominant actor in community power structures, neither can local government. A focus primarily oriented to the latter may produce fascinating and valuable findings; but for many analysts it cannot purport to cover all facets of what they mean by community power.

Finally, we should note that many inconspicuous decisions and activities may cumulate into major patterns of power. As Janowitz observed about Banfield, many studies have been ". . . interested exclusively in controversies that generate big, dramatic decisions, but in the city . . . the legal, administrative, and political structure makes hundreds of decisions daily, out of which emerge crucial patterns of social change." Everyday activities, such as certain reactions toward women or thousands of minor policies in the granting of financial credit, may almost unconsciously pervade the life of a community and be just as critical as any "momentous" controversy over urban redevelopment or welfare policy. In short, we must be wary lest a narrow interpretation of "community power" combine with a very conflict-oriented conception of an "issue" to produce a literature on community power structures that is empirically somewhat sounder, but misleadingly narrow.

The "nonissue" and "nondecision." . . . It is not surprising . . . that very few scholars deny the potential significance of nonissues, even though their researchability is doubted and the conception of the nonissue is found unclear and perhaps excessively subjective. . . .

Despite the seeming importance of the topic broached by Bachrach and Baratz, one may feel less content with their particular formulation of the idea of the nonissue. For example, they imply that the nonissue is a tool for the preservation of the status quo by vested interests. Such may usually be the case, but it is not necessarily so and should not be implied by the very definition of the nonissue. Wolfinger accurately notes the utility that nonissue considerations can have in enabling masses to influence elites. One can also conceive of situations so clearly favoring change that the mobilization of bias is against the status quo (unless one wishes to define status quo in this case as the inertia toward continued change). Similarly, a nonissue situation can exist without any clear "grievance" being present. In short, it seems possible to refine the concept of the nonissue beyond the valuable start provided by Bachrach and Baratz.

A nondecision occurs when a choice among alternatives by one actor is either not perceived by him or, if perceived, is not made, and always, in either case, because of some exercise of power by another actor. A nonissue is a matter presumably calling for a decision but which is not perceived as such or, if perceived, is suppressed, always because of some actor's use of power. These ideas can be further generalized in a more rigorously power analytic framework. *The nonissue involves the effective use of power by some actors in a political system to deter other actors in that system from even attempting to exert influence.* Thus, anything not occurring or not chosen—any alternative foregone—is not a nondecision. Acceptance of one policy when others are not even discussed does not indicate a nonissue. The nonoccurrence, nondecision, or nonissues must be the result of the exercise of power by some actors in the system.

From this perspective, then, the two critical elements of the nonissue are *expectation* and *prevention.* The analyst must first justify his expectation of attempted influence by some actor—that is, he must show good cause for us to suspect that the lack of attempted influence by some actor, or the lack of a certain issue, is not merely due to an autonomous disinterest or decision. We must have good reason to anticipate attempted influence by such an actor under the given conditions, or to anticipate the presence of such an issue in the given system and setting.

Second, once the expectation of attempted influence or issue formation is established, the analyst must proceed to demonstrate the mechanism of prevention. This mechanism must be some form of the exercise of power—conscious or unconscious—by other actors in the system. One may speak loosely of rules of the game, dominant values, biasing beliefs, and the like; but these must be disseminated through some specifiable influence process if one is to argue convincingly for a nonissue or suppression of influence attempts. Independently formed judgments of the rules of the game—beliefs not demonstrably inculcated by other actors in the system—hardly betoken a nonissue. Though decisional analysis may not always be the most appropriate research method, Dahl was quite right in insisting that there must be some point in the process of creating myths, false consciousness, biased beliefs, etc., at which the power process occurs. The nature of this process must be established for a nonissue argument to be convincing.

Such an analysis of the nonissue suggests that it has a mirror-image on the positive side which should be interesting. If the nonissue involves the use of power by some actors to *deter* others from attempting influence, its mirror-image refers to the use of power by some actors to *encourage* others to attempt influence. The mobilization of bias, for example, works both positively and negatively, deterring some actors from attempting influence or raising issues while inducing others to do those very things. The positive side, prompting some issues, may be no less important than the negative, suppressing others.

Types of nonissues. . . . Six [types of nonissues] seem meaningful:

1. The actor is aware of his interests, partially restricts his influence attempts, and is led to do this because of anticipated negative reactions.
2. The actor is aware of his interests, completely withdraws from influence attempts in the given area, and is led to do this because of anticipated negative reactions.

3. The actor is aware of his interests, partially restricts his influence attempts, and is led to do this for reasons other than anticipated negative reactions, such as confusion about how, when, and where to exert influence.
4. The actor is aware of his interests, completely withdraws from influence attempts in the given area, and is led to do this for reasons other than anticipated negative reactions.
5. The actor is unaware of his interests and thus partially limits his influence attempts. When the actor is unaware of his interests the preventive mechanism would seemingly have to be something other than anticipated negative reactions, e.g., inculcated false values, educational deprivations, etc.
6. The actor is unaware of his interests and thus completely neglects influence attempts in the given area.

While this elaboration is far from earth-shaking, types three and four (are seldom noted and) do seem significant. Their absence from the other typologies seems more generally indicative of an insufficient amplification of the mechanisms available to induce nondecisions. Such mechanisms are much more diverse than the "anticipated reactions," "foisting of values" or "false consensus" arguments seem to suggest. They lead into as yet largely unexplored areas of political socialization. Especially important are inculcated conceptions of legitimacy, learned preferences among influential behaviors, expectations of failure, and confused perceptions of power processes and structures. Such orientations are less clear perhaps than anticipated negative reactions, but possibly no less effective as deterrents of influence attempts.

The researchability of nonissues. . . . What now follows is an attempt to evaluate the main criticisms leveled against the researchability of nonissues, plus a very general indication of how such research should proceed.

As I have said, the two crucial elements of the nonissue are expectation and prevention. The analyst of the nonissue must first determine and justify his consideration of certain nonevents (failures to attempt influence) as possibly indicative of power relations. Then he must be able to show empirically that the failure of some actor (elite or nonelite) to attempt influence was significantly caused by some other actor in the system rather than being an autonomous decision. Beneath the polemics, there seems to be considerable implicit agreement on this point by both "neo-elitists" and "pluralists."

Expectations of influence. How is the analyst to develop a useful and plausible set of expectations about the probable influence attempts of the main actors in the political system being scrutinized? . . .

Foremost among the tools for determining expectations regarding influence attempts by various actors is *theory.* What is obviously needed is a psychology of power—some fairly reliable body of knowledge about power motivations and related cognitions, as they lead to attempted influence. We need to construct a reasonably general understanding of what leads various types of political actors to protest, rebel, vote, bargain, command, connive, threaten, promise, persuade, and so on, through the basic repertory of politically significant influential behaviors.

. . . I must grant that, at the individual level, it is almost amazing to me that political science as a discipline has not only done so little toward fathoming people's power orientations, but that it has *attempted* so little. Despite Harold Lasswell's early work and compelling exhortations, systematic empirical efforts to assess individuals' "power drive" (their desire for power of various sorts), "power styles" (their repertories of influential behaviors, among other things), and what I should call "power salience" (the relative degrees of attention they pay to power phenomena) have been almost nonexistent. Moreover, the few that do exist have come much more from social psychologists than political scientists.

At other levels, however, we have a good deal of fairly crude theory about the wellsprings of interest group activity or the sources of governmental action (including conscious inaction). . . . These scattered nuggets need to be reintegrated under a more comprehensive theoretical perspective, but even now it is possible in limited areas for us to present many rough but useful hypotheses about how the various actors in a community will try to exert influence. Existing theory of this type may not be sufficient to make an open-and-shut demonstration that no plausibly expected influence attempt has been neglected; hence, complete protection in advance against charges of a hidden element's influence through non-decision making may be impossible. Those making such charges, however, as Wolfinger indicates, must themselves specify the kinds of influence attempts which have presumably been overlooked. They should also give some fairly cogent, albeit hypothetical, indication of the power mechanisms by which these expected influence attempts were deterred. It is as easy to charge hidden factors as it is to sue for damages. In either instance, to avoid a prompt dismissal, the plaintiff must present clear presumptive evidence.

In addition to developing expectations of influence attempts from available theory concerning power motivations and perceptions, the researcher usually must also conduct empirical investigations to learn whether the theoretically predicted orientations were actually present in the actors involved. Reference group theory and notions of relative deprivation, for example, in conjunction with other data, might induce one to expect discontent leading to a certain type of influence attempt by a particular group. This theoretically formed expectation should then normally be buttressed by empirical evidence of such discontent and of the psychic association between it and the urge toward the expected influential behavior. The theoretical expectation provides a specific focus for the empirical investigation. It is true that unconscious phenomena are always difficult to research and may be important for nearly any political investigation, not only power analyses. But sophisticated research following clear theoretical guidelines can take us very deeply into those orientations which are psychically more available. . . .

In all these matters we cannot now operate with great elegance and precision. . . . The early stages of a science are especially hard because the theory on which to erect more theory is meager and frail. But there is no alternative. Actually, as I shall argue again in a moment, the power analyst is not so terribly ill-positioned in this respect. If the theory which permits him to identify an expected influence attempt that did not materialize wrong, then he should be unable to complete the second necessary step of his investigation into the nonissue, namely, determining how some identifiable actor forestalled the expected influence attempt—by creating anticipations of negative reactions, by inculcating values or perceptions which deterred action, and so on.

The second major tool for developing plausible expectations about influence attempts is explicit empirical *comparison*. For example, of seven communities having very similar air pollution levels and matched along several other dimensions, if six display popular protest movements about pollution while the seventh does not, one would be led to look for possible nonissue phenomena in the seventh city. If virtually all groups within a given system which have suffered a sharp decline in perceived status respond by partisan political activity but two do not, then one is led to look for latent power processes which might possibly have deterred such action. . . . Strictly controlled comparison is rarely possible for the communities of interest in the natural world. Too many factors vary simultaneously. But that also is one of the awkward facts facing most social analysis. Informative, though less than decisive, comparison is still possible and important. Political science has made such lamentably little use of experimentation that most of our knowledge has come through this less rigorous but still useful route of comparison that is only partially or grossly controlled.

Along these lines, another avenue of investigation seems promising. Most writers acknowledge some intuitively clear cases of nonissues, such as the "false consciousness" of the southern Negro, . . . women's opportunities in society, the treatment of American Indians, preservation of the environment, etc. Careful, theoretically informed study of these few presumably manifest cases of nonissues might be most useful in helping develop theories about the conditions under which various types of issues are likely to be suppressed, intentionally or otherwise.

As another tool for forming expectations about influence attempts, Bachrach and Baratz urge "inquiry into which persons or groups, if any, gain from the existing bias and which, if any, are handicapped by it." . . .

We can suspect nonissues when: 1) glaring inequalities occur in the distribution of things avowedly valued by actors in the system, and 2) these inequalities do not seem to occasion ameliorative influence attempts by those getting less of those values. Such suspicion of a nonissue may prove correct or false, depending always upon further empirical confirmation, especially through more concrete evidence that the initially inferred values are actually held and through location of the power mechanisms by which their expression has been suppressed. . . .

Preventive power mechanisms. Discovering, if possible, a set of plausibly expected influence attempts which never materialize is but the first part of researching nonissues. A perhaps easier but no less crucial phase of the process is the subsequent effort to locate for each unrealized expectation the power mechanisms of suppression which establish the existence of a nonissue rather than an autonomous determination. This second phase naturally cannot ensure that all nonissues have been unearthed; but it does constitute the main protection against spurious inclusions, ensuring that all nonissues accepted are genuine.

In general, discovery of the power mechanisms used for preventing influence attempts proceeds through the usual techniques for locating and measuring power, including attributions by participants, reconstructive decisional analysis, direct observations, and so on. . . .

One of the most basic distinctions among these various suppression mechanisms involves a key aspect of any power relation—recognition. Some of the suppression mechanisms will be recognized by both the influencers and those influenced. Blatant threats such as, "If you dare raise that matter you'll be fired," are an example. Some are recognized by only one party, either the influencer or the influencee. And, at the other pole are those suppression mechanisms recognized by neither party. These are likely to be relationships so thoroughly woven into the culture that all participants take them for granted. The last are obviously quite difficult to uncover, though the best hope lies in a cross-cultural perspective.

The most conspicuous practical research approach into nonissues suggested by Bachrach and Baratz deals mainly with the more unrecognized situations. They propose investigation of ". . . the particular 'mobilization of bias' in the institution under scrutiny." This requires analysis of the "dominant values, the myths, and the established political procedures and rules of the game." In short, they advocate analysis of the power consequences for influence attempts of the prevailing political culture and institutional framework.

Bachrach and Baratz are quite vague, however, about how this is to be done. Perhaps the essential point here is that merely showing that there are dominant values and beliefs or institutional arrangements which differentially enhance the power of some actors and hinder others (mobilize bias) does not indicate a nonissue, as previously defined. One must show further that those currently prevailing belief systems and institutional arrangements are the result of influences by specifiable actors in the system, rather than the result of largely autonomous processes. The situation often gets complicated because beliefs and institutional arrangements which foster the power of some actors over others may be perpetuated by still other actors and be unrecognized and remote from those whom they most advantage. In this last instance, a nonissue is present, but it may not be the one superficially concluded.

An educational system, for example, may teach values which aid the power of an elite stratum. The teachers and educational officials inculcating such values may not be of that stratum themselves and may not profit in any clear way from the situation. Moreover, there may not be any chain of influence through which the benefited elite can be shown to control the educational system. On deeper analysis one might find that the teachers and officials act rather independently in this respect, gaining psychic gratification from identifying with the elite rather than being subject to any apparent direct or indirect influence from the elite. Of course, one can always contend that the fabric of the social structure itself produces this tendency toward identifying with high status elements—in fact, produces the very stratification system itself. But one would then still have to show that this elite was responsible for the social structure and stratification system. This can be a very awesome task indeed.

On the other hand, there seem to be many instances in which the mobilization of bias is much more easily discovered. In these cases, the researcher would try to determine which elements of the prevailing political culture and which institutional arrangements were significantly related to the limited issue-area or activity he was investigating. . . . Such analyses refer to cultural norms like legality, the avoidance of violence, a concern for governmental economy, preferences for or dislike of certain verbal styles and physical appearances, the legitimacy of business as an essential and proper institution, the acceptability of compromise, and so on. . . . The analyst of power concerned about nonissues must examine those tacit understandings which seem to bear upon the particular scope he is investigating. He must first determine what they are, and then ascertain how they are established, at least sufficiently to know whether they can be attributed to the influence of particular actors in the political system he is analyzing.

The same kind of analysis must be applied to institutional arrangements. Particular institutional patterns, formal and informal, may advantage some actors and disadvantage others in their exercise of power. Voting schemes offer the most familiar example, but numerous others come to mind, such as access to information, time schedules, the size of decisional units, property rights, etc. The effect of such institutional factors on power in the scope being investigated must first be ascertained, and then one must determine the extent to which thost arrangements can be said to be the result of the power of identifiable actors in the system. . . .

The same type of analysis, incidentally, applies in the case of anticipated reactions. One must first discover the relevant anticipations. These may or may not be the result of some exercise of power. If they are, then it is essential to discover who created the anticipations. It may or may not be the actor whose behavior is being anticipated. The actors inducing the anticipations constitute the true influencers. Occasionally there may be an extremely complex reciprocal power relationship such that all actors are simultaneously creating and reacting to anticipations created by others. In such instances, the analyst may not be able to proceed beyond establishing the reciprocal linkages—i.e., he may not be able to decipher all the individual causal flows. In general, however, anticipations, like failures to attempt influence, may be essentially self-generated or the result of extremely diffuse processes, so that every instance of anticipated reactions altering behavior is not necessarily a power relationship.

RANCOROUS CONFLICT IN COMMUNITY POLITICS

William A. Gamson

The following article reports a study of conflict in eighteen New England communities. Nine communities in which community conflicts are often rancorous or hostile are compared with an equal number of communities in which rancorous conflict is rare. In all, William Gamson studied 54 different issues, including the fluoridation of water systems (which arose in all 18 cities), as well as education, zoning, and community development.

The author seeks to identify factors which might explain the different ways the communities handle conflict. He does not explicitly consider the relationship between the nature of conflict and the patterns of community influence, but, as we suggested in the section introduction, work of this sort may provide the groundwork upon which such relationships can be formulated.

Community issues differ in many respects. Some involve vitriolic exchanges of threats and denunciations while others run their course through routine hearings and are resolved before unfilled council chambers. The same issue—for example, fluoridation—may run its course in undramatic fashion in one town, but prove to be the trigger for an explosive confrontation in another town with seemingly similar characteristics. This paper addresses itself to the structural differences between those communities in which such outbursts occur and those in which they do not.

In particular, two ways of carrying on conflict in the local community are contrasted. In *conventional conflicts*, established means of political expression are used to influence the outcome of issues. Opponents regard each other as mistaken or as pursuing different but legitimate goals, but not as the representatives of evil forces. Such tactics as threats of punishment, personal vilification, and deliberate, conscious deceptions are not involved. In contrast to conventional conflicts, *rancorous conflicts* are characterized

From William A. Gamson, "Rancorous Conflict in Community Politics," *American Sociological Review*, XXXI (January, 1966), 71–81.

by the belief that norms about the waging of political conflict in American communities have been violated. In such conflicts, actions occur which produce a shared belief that tactics used to influence the outcome are "dirty," "underhanded," "vicious" and so forth.

Some communities are much more prone than others to rancorous conflicts. The differences between rancorous and conventional communities can be organized under three general headings: structural conduciveness, structural strain, and structural integration.[1] *Conduciveness* refers to the extent to which structural characteristics in the community permit or encourage rancorous conflicts. *Strain* refers to the extent to which structural characteristics generate discontent or dissatisfaction among the community members. *Integration* refers to the extent to which structural characteristics prevent or inhibit rancorous conflict. Although integration is just the other side of conduciveness, each refers to different structural elements. In other words, we do not consider the absence of integration as an element of conduciveness or the presence of integration as the absence of conduciveness.

The three categories of determinant are highly related to each other. High conduciveness will not produce rancorous conflict if unaccompanied by strain nor if, although accompanied by strain, structural integration is great. High strain will not produce rancorous conflict unless the social structure is conducive to conflict and structural integration is inadequate. The absence of structural integration will not produce rancorous conflict if there is little strain or conduciveness. In other words, we should expect rancorous conflicts *to occur most frequently in those communities characterized by high conduciveness, high strain, and low integration.*

Structural conduciveness. Such highly general categories as conduciveness, strain, and integration need specification if they are to be measured. With respect to conduciveness, we will focus on two aspects of community social structure: the degree to which it encourages widespread citizen participation and the degree to which it offers highly visible targets for the expression of rancor.

Participative political structure. The more the political structure permits or encourages widespread citizen participation, the greater is the conduciveness to rancorous conflict. Since it is typically argued that such conflict is encouraged by the *closing* of channels of legitimate political expres-

---

[1] I draw here on Neil J. Smelser, *Theory of Collective Behavior* (New York: The Free Press of Glencoe, 1963). He organizes his discussion of the determinants of collective behavior under six categories. Three of them are covered here with slight differences in terminology and formulation. The other three—the growth and spread of a generalized belief, precipitating factors, and mobilization of participants for action—are not included because our objective is to understand the structural differences between communities rather than the outbreak of a given episode at a particular time in a community. The discussion which follows also draws heavily on James S. Coleman, *Community Conflict* (New York: The Free Press of Glencoe, 1957).

sion, this hypothesis needs defense. The argument for the proposition may take a weak or a strong form. In the weak form, a distinction is made between the intensity and the frequency of rancorous conflict. In high participation communities, it is argued, the political system offers not only an instrumental channel but an expressive one as well. Mild discontent which might otherwise find no outlet or a non-political one is encouraged to find political expression. In finding frequent release in this fashion, such discontent does not build up an explosive potential. Although rancorous conflicts may occur less frequently in communities with a non-participative political structure, they have more intensity when they do occur.

The stronger form of the argument is a denial of the counter-proposition that the blocking of channels of political expression encourages rancorous conflict. This argument challenges the assumption that there is a reservoir of discontent which will either find controlled outlet in legitimate political expression or will accumulate until the dam bursts. Instead, it is assumed that the relief or exacerbation of discontent depends on the nature of the resultant decisions made and not on the catharsis which comes from political expression. If the political system allows for high political participation but does not deal successfully with the sources of dissatisfaction, then rancorous conflicts are *more* likely to occur because strain is combined with high conduciveness. Only when political participation is combined with the influence which can alleviate the source of discontent do rancorous conflicts become less likely. This argument does not imply that high citizen participation is necessarily conducive to rancorous conflict (and hence is bad), but merely that participation does not automatically remove strain.

Given the truth of this proposition, then it is false that such actions as civil rights demonstrations must lessen the probability of other less orderly expressions. As long as the underlying sources of strain are not dealt with, such participation simply increases structural conduciveness and thus makes other expressions more likely. Of course, if the action also helps to remove the strain, for example, by aiding the passage of remedial legislation, then the *net* effect may be to reduce the probability of other less orderly expressions.

A study of fluoridation by Crain, Katz, and Rosenthal contains some suggestive results concerning this hypothesis.[2] They find that the participative nature of the political structure affects both the degree of controversy about fluoridation and the likelihood of its adoption. "Governments which do not place 'obstacles' such as political parties between the citizen and the decision-makers experience the pattern of a large number of referenda and

[2]Robert L. Crain, Elihu Katz, and Donald B. Rosenthal, *The Fluoridation Decision: Community Structure and Innovation*, forthcoming.

high controversy [as well as high rejection]." Fluoridation is at least more likely to provoke strong controversy where participative political structures provide conduciveness.[3]

Solidary groups. The greater the clarity of solidary groups within a social structure, the greater is the conduciveness to rancorous conflict. Communities differ in the extent to which they contain sub-groups with: (1) feelings of membership or identification with a group or collectivity; (2) feelings of common interest with respect to political decisions; (3) a common style of life, norms, and values; (4) a high rate of interaction among themselves. The degree of solidarity of a sub-group is its magnitude on the above characteristics; the clarity of solidary group structure is the extent to which there exist community sub-groups of high solidarity.

Clearly identifiable solidary groups are conducive to rancorous conflict because they provide readily identifiable targets for hostility. Such subdivisions of the community do not in themselves signify cleavage. Nevertheless, any clear-cut basis of differentiation among the citizens of a town may provide a structural basis for the development of inter-group hostility if there also exist strains and low integration among solidary groups.

Structural strain. Any part of the social structure may produce strains which are relevant for rancorous conflict in the community. Many strains originate outside of the community but have ramifications for the social and political life of the town. There are undoubtedly strains deriving from fear of nuclear war, increasing bureaucratization, depersonalization, commercialism, manipulation, and so forth. Such strains may make their own contributions to rancorous conflicts in the community,[4] but they are felt by all communities, rancorous as well as conventional. Therefore, we must turn to strains which can differentiate our communities in order to explain why some are prone to rancorous conflict and others are not.

There are many possibilities. Although the specification of such strains requires detailed knowledge of the particular communities in question, it seems likely that they are connected with change. The change might include, for example, rapid economic growth or decline, heavy in-migration or out-migration, or shifts in the distribution of power in the community. For two reasons I have chosen to focus on strains emanating from a shift

---

[3]The volatile nature of California politics may be due (among other things) to the structural conduciveness stemming from a long tradition of initiative and referendum.

[4]A good deal of recent work on such strains has used the rubric of "alienation." See, for example, John E. Horton and Wayne E. Thompson, "Powerlessness and Political Negativism: A Study of Defeated Local Referendums," *American Journal of Sociology*, 68 (March, 1962), 485–93; Kenneth Kenniston, "Alienation and the Decline of Utopia," *American Scholar*, 29 (Spring, 1960), 161–200; and William A. Gamson, "The Fluoridation Dialogue: Is it an Ideological Conflict?" *Public Opinion Quarterly*, 25 (Winter, 1961), 526–37.

in political control: (1) the existence or non-existence of a shift in control sharply differentiates the communities studied here; (2) a shift in political control is likely to be a reflection of other strains as well as a creator of strains in its own right.

Shifts in political control are a source of structural strain which contribute to rancorous conflict. I have in mind here something broader than the circulation of elites. In particular, two kinds of shift will be considered. They have in common the existence of a relatively homogeneous group whose leaders find that they face competition in areas of decision-making where they did not before, or that they are competing less successfully than before. In one type of community, there are clear solidary groups with one gaining or losing political power relative to others. In a second type of community, a homogeneous native population has been, or threatens to be, supplanted by a large, heterogeneous, and politically active group of newcomers.

Structural integration. Strain and conduciveness deal with those characteristics of social structure that promote or encourage rancorous conflict. We now turn our attention to those features which tend to control or inhibit such expressions. Basically, we expect rancorous and conventional communities to differ in the extent to which potential antagonists are bound together. In particular, we examine the connections which exist between those with different opinions on community issues. Are proponents and opponents bound by associational ties, by friendship, or by shared backgrounds? If they are not, then we should expect a given amount of strain and conduciveness to be more likely to produce rancorous conflict. We will consider three kinds of tie here.

Organizational ties. The greater the degree of common organizational membership among proponents and opponents, the greater the resistance to rancorous conflict. If the organizational life of a community puts potential antagonists together in a variety of meetings over a variety of issues, they are likely to find occasions for agreement, to develop bonds of friendship, a sense of joint accomplishment, and other integrative ties. When a disagreement occurs, it should be less likely to produce the kind of break in a relationship which rancorous conflict represents.

Interpersonal ties. The greater the degree of friendship among proponents and opponents, the greater the resistance to rancorous conflict. If potential antagonists know each other well socially, such friendship bonds should help to provide that degree of trust and belief in good faith which inhibit rancorous conflicts.

Shared background. The more proponents and opponents tend to be of different length of residence, nationality background, education, and religion, the less the resistance to rancorous conflict. These four bases of differentiation were chosen because they seemed particularly likely to be correlated with partisan divisions in the set of New England communities we studied. Since these are the bases of differentiation that presumably underlie solidary groups, this hypothesis might appear to be simply another statement of the earlier one on structural conduciveness. We argued above that the existence of clear sub-groups was conducive to rancorous conflict but that they did not, in themselves, signify cleavage. It is possible to have solidary groups which cross-cut issues, thus giving proponents and opponents an important common group membership. It is also possible to find the opposite—that proponents and opponents have different background characteristics but lack any feeling of membership or identification with distinct community sub-groups. Even where clear solidary groups are not present, the absence of these integrative bonds should make such communities more vulnerable to rancorous conflict. Finally, it is possible to have full fledged cleavages in which clearly defined solidary groups exist and do correspond to divisions on issues. This condition combines conduciveness with lack of integration; when strain is added, we should particularly expect rancorous conflict.

STUDY DESIGN

The data to be presented here are drawn from a study of fifty-four issues in eighteen New England communities. The towns ranged in size from 2,000 to 100,000, with a median of approximately 10,000. Seven of the communities were essentially suburbs of Boston, three were resort towns, and the remaining eight were more or less independent cities with some industrial base of their own. All but two of the communities were in Maine or Massachusetts.

Material on these communities was gathered through interviews with 426 informants, an average of twenty-four per town, supplemented by information from a variety of documents. Interviewing was done by teams of three or four individuals who stayed in each community for several days. Three issues were studied in each town, one of which, fluoridation, was common to all eighteen. The presence of a decision on fluoridation was, in fact, the basis of selection of these communities; the eighteen comprise all those New England communities which made a fluoridation decision during an eighteen-month period of data collection.

Before any interviews began, each town was investigated through such sources as the local newspaper, formal statistical data from the state and federal censuses, city planning reports, annual town reports, and various state manuals. The persons interviewed fell into two categories: active partisans on both sides of each of the three issues; and people named by these "issue leaders" as influential in the community, i.e., as "reputational leaders." . . .

RESULTS

As Table 1 indicates, shifts in political control are clearly related to rancorous conflict in this particular set of New England communities. Only one of the nine conventional towns is undergoing political change while two-thirds of the rancorous towns are undergoing such change. Are these rancorous towns also higher on our measures of conduciveness and lower on integration than the conventional towns?

There is a limit to how far one can examine interrelationships among variables with only eighteen communities. Nevertheless, some attempt at this is necessary even at the risk of breaking these eighteen cases down into meaninglessly small cells. Eighteen may be a small number, but it is a great deal larger than the case study or comparison of two or three communities which is typical of the literature on community politics.

There is little overall relationship between the measures of conduciveness used here—participative political structure and presence of clear solidary groups—and the presence of rancorous conflict. As Table 2 indicates, communities without town meetings are about as likely to have rancorous conflicts as those with them. Solidary groups are present about as often in rancorous as in conventional ones. These results are not, in themselves, negative evidence since we would not expect higher conduciveness alone (without evidence of strain) to produce differences between the two kinds of community. However, there is little suggestion in these data that, for those seven towns with political instability, the presence of town meetings or solidary groups increases the likelihood of rancorous conflict. It is true that four out of five politically unstable communities which have town meetings are rancorous, but then both of the unstable towns without town meetings are rancorous also. Three out of four of the unstable towns with solidary groups are rancorous but all three of the unstable towns without such groups are rancorous. Put another way, the one exception among the

TABLE 1   Rancorous Conflict and Political Instability

	Rancorous	*Conventional*
Undergoing political change	6	1
Politically stable	3	8
N	9	9

P < .05 (Fisher's Exact Test).

TABLE 2   Rancorous Conflict and Structural Conduciveness

	Rancorous	Conventional
Has town meeting form of government	6	5
Does not have town meeting form of government	3	4
N	9	9
Solidary groups present	4	5
Solidary groups absent	5	4
N	9	9

seven politically unstable communities is *not* lower on our measures of conduciveness; it has both solidary groups and town meetings to accompany its political strain but still it is not rancorous. For the measures used here the evidence on the conduciveness hypotheses must be considered inconclusive at best.

There is no overall relationship between rancorous conflict and the extent to which some organization provides a central focus for those involved in community affairs. However, if we focus specifically on the seven politically unstable towns, there is some indication that this variable does have an effect. Using as our measure the ratio of the largest number of respondent memberships in any single organization to the total number of respondents in a town, we find that the six politically unstable rancorous communities have an average ratio of 0.32 as against 0.41 for the eleven towns without political strain ($p < 0.05$); the one conventional town among the politically unstable has a ratio of 0.45, well above average on this measure of integration.

The average degree of acquaintance among opponents is substantially lower in rancorous than in conventional towns—2.89 vs. 2.39 ($p < 0.05$, using a one tailed test).[5] Among the politically unstable towns, the relationship is even stronger; the average is 2.97 for the six rancorous towns and the score is 1.50 for the conventional town, ranking it first among the set of 18 in friendship among opponents.

The Coefficient of Cleavage, our last measure of integration or lack of integration, shows similar results.* As Table 3 indicates, six of eight towns

---

[5]A lower score indicates closer friendships.

*Ed. Note: The "Coefficient of Cleavage" is a function of an issue position held by those surveyed in each community compared to their length of residence, nationality background, religion and education. It is meant to reflect the total cleavage in the community on any given issue. Gamson gives this example: "If there are 10 Protestants and 10 Catholics among 12 proponents and 8 opponents on fluoridation, we would expect by chance to get six Protestant proponents. However, we could get as many as 10 or as few as 2. Thus, the denominator of the coefficient of cleavage (CC) would be: 10 (Maximum frequency) − 6 (Expected frequency) = 4. If there were ac-

TABLE 3   Rancorous Conflict and Cleavage

	Rancorous	*Conventional*
All Towns		
CC of .5 or higher on at least one issue°	6	2
CC of less than .5 on all issues	3	7
N	9	9
Politically Unstable Towns		
CC of .5 or higher	5	0
CC of less than .5	1	1
Politically Stable Towns		
CC of .5 or higher	1	2
CC of less than .5	2	6
N	9	9

°(Or, 50% or less cross-cutting on at least one issue.) CC stands for Coefficient of Cleavage.

which have at least one issue with a high degree of cleavage between proponents and opponents are rancorous. Five of the six politically unstable and rancorous towns have such sharp differences between proponents and opponents but only three of the other twelve.

Summary. In the towns studied here there were four exceptions to the relationship between political instability and the appearance of rancorous conflict. One of these, a town which is politically changing but is not rancorous, scores high on all our measures of integration. But there are also three towns without the kind of political strain measured here which are rancorous. One of these three is the only town among the eighteen which is experiencing severe economic strain. Seven years earlier, a major mill closed and the unemployment rate remained quite high. Numerous stores were empty on Main Street and many of those who were able to leave had already done so. The two other exceptions are not so easily explained. Not only are they not undergoing any political or other obvious strain but they score high on our measures of integration as well. One can, of course, always find some sort of strain in any town but in the absence of special evidence to suggest such strains, rancorous conflict in these two communities must be regarded as unexplained by the hypotheses presented here.

There are two final variables which, while they play no role in the hypotheses, might well be affecting the results. The first of these—the type of community—has no relationship to rancorous conflict for this set of towns;

---

tually nine Protestant proponents, the numerator of the CC would be: 9 (Actual frequency) − 6 (Expected frequency) = 3, and the CC would be $\frac{3}{4} = 0.75$. The direction of relationship has no significance here. To avoid artificial results due to discontinuity and to simplify calculation, the expected frequencies were always rounded to the nearest integer."

four of the nine rancorous communities and four of the nine conventional ones are independent towns rather than suburbs or resorts. Size of town, the second control variable, also has no overall relationship to rancorous conflict; five of the nine largest and four of the nine smallest towns are rancorous. Nevertheless it turns out that all of the exceptions fall among those with population under 5000. As Table 4 indicates, there is a perfect relationship between political instability and rancorous conflict for communities over 5000.

DISCUSSION

It is important to specify some content for such general classes of variable as structural strain, conduciveness, and integration. I have tried to do this here by explaining rancorous conflict in terms of the strain which political change provides or reflects, the conduciveness which a participative structure and solidary groups provide, and the integrative ties which a common organizational focus, friendships, and common bonds of nationality, religion, education and length of residence provide. . . .

This paper has a purpose more general than understanding modes of community conflict. Both the specific variables used and the general strategy of political analysis are relevant to a wide variety of political expression. The politics of fluoridation is not so far removed from battles over open-occupancy housing or school Bible readings. The present explanation of rancorous conflict in small communities is not very different in kind from the explanation we would use in contrasting countries with or without revolutionary movements. Of course, the content of such general classes of variable as structural conduciveness, strain, and integration may vary in different social-organizational settings. However, if one can establish that a participative political structure promotes conduciveness to rancorous conflict in one setting, it becomes a more plausible hypothesis for other

TABLE 4 Rancorous Conflict and Political Instability Controlled for Size of Town

	Rancorous	*Conventional*
Towns over 5000		
Undergoing political change	6	0
Politically stable	0	5
Towns under 5000		
Undergoing political change	0	1
Politically stable	3	3
N	9	9

settings. For example, this may explain why apparent improvements or efforts to remove strains may be accompanied by increases in rancorous conflict. Such changes may have their initial or most radical effects on conduciveness or on sources of structural integration or control and only secondary effects on the removal of sources of discontent. The study of such limited phenomena as rancorous conflicts in communities may teach us something more general about social movements and social change.

Because of the negative connotations of a term like "rancorous conflict," some final observations about the towns studied here are worth making. Many of the conventional communities are rather dull and stagnant, while some of the rancorous ones are among the most vital. Some of the conventional towns not only have an absence of rancorous conflict but a general absence of change; the rancorous towns have the strains that accompany change but some of them also have the advantages of stimulation and growth. The absence of rancorous conflict is no necessary sign of an "ideal" community.

CHAPTER FIVE

Locating Decisionmakers

A CRITIQUE OF THE RULING ELITE MODEL

Robert A. Dahl

This article, a prelude to the author's now classic study, Who Governs?, *opens the debate over methodology which comprises this section with a direct and incisive criticism of the elitist theory. Dahl argues that the "ruling elite model" assumes the existence of important characteristics of the community without empirical backing. Further, he offers a test of the theory implicit in the model in terms of research requirements, and he asserts that these have never really been fulfilled: "The evidence for a ruling elite, either in the United States or in any specific community, has not yet been properly examined so far as I know. . . . because the examination has not employed satisfactory criteria to determine*

From Robert A. Dahl, "A Critique of the Ruling Elite Model," *The American Political Science Review*, LII (June, 1958), 463–469.

what constitutes a fair test of the basic hypothesis." Blunt words these, and they outline the battlefield upon which the heated and continuing dialogue takes place.

A great many people seem to believe that "they" run things: the old families, the bankers, the City Hall machine, or the party boss behind the scene. This kind of view evidently has a powerful and many-sided appeal. It is simple, compelling, dramatic, "realistic." It gives one standing as an inside-dopester. For individuals with a strong strain of frustrated idealism, it has just the right touch of hard-boiled cynicism. Finally, the hypothesis has one very great advantage over many alternative explanations: It can be cast in a form that makes it virtually impossible to disprove.

Consider the last point for a moment. There is a type of quasi-metaphysical theory made up of what might be called an infinite regress of explanations. The ruling elite model *can* be interpreted in this way. If the overt leaders of a community do not appear to constitute a ruling elite, then the theory can be saved by arguing that behind the overt leaders there is a set of covert leaders who do. If subsequent evidence shows that this covert group does not make a ruling elite, then the theory can be saved by arguing that behind the first covert group there is another, and so on.

Now whatever else it may be, a theory that cannot even in principle be controverted by empirical evidence is not a scientific theory. The least that we can demand of any ruling elite theory that purports to be more than a metaphysical or polemical doctrine is, first, that the burden of proof be on the proponents of the theory and not on its critics; and, second, that there be clear criteria according to which the theory could be disproved.

With these points in mind, I shall proceed in two stages. First, I shall try to clarify the meaning of the concept "ruling elite" by describing a very simple form of what I conceive to be a ruling elite system. Second, I shall indicate what would be required in principle as a simple but satisfactory test of any hypothesis asserting that a particular political system is, in fact, a ruling elite system. Finally, I shall deal with some objections.

A Simple Ruling Elite System

If a ruling elite hypothesis says anything, surely it asserts that within some specific political system there exists a group of people who to some degree exercise power or influence over other actors in the system. I shall make the following assumptions about power:

1. In order to compare the relative influence of two actors (these may be individuals, groups, classes, parties, or what not), it is necessary to state the scope of the responses upon which the actors have an effect. The

statement, "A has more power than B," is so ambiguous as to verge on the meaningless, since it does not specify the scope.

2. One cannot compare the relative influence of two actors who always perform identical actions with respect to the group influenced. What this means as a practical matter is that ordinarily one can test for differences in influence only where there are cases of differences in initial preferences. At one extreme, the difference may mean that one group prefers alternative A and another group prefers B, A and B being mutually exclusive. At the other extreme, it may mean that one group prefers alternative A to other alternatives, and another group is indifferent. If a political system displayed complete consensus at all times, we should find it impossible to construct a satisfactory direct test of the hypothesis that it was a ruling elite system, although indirect and rather unsatisfactory tests might be devised.

Consequently, to know whether or not we have a ruling elite, we must have a political system in which there is a difference in preferences, from time to time, among the individual human beings in the system. Suppose, now, that among these individuals there is a set whose preferences regularly prevail in all cases of disagreement, or at least in all cases of disagreement over key political issues (a term I propose to leave undefined here). Let me call such a set of individuals a "controlling group." In a full-fledged democracy operating strictly according to majority rule, the majority would constitute a controlling group, even though the individual members of the majority might change from one issue to the next. But since our model is to represent a ruling elite system, we require that the set be *less than a majority in size*.

However, in any representative system with single member voting districts where more than two candidates receive votes, a candidate *could* win with less than a majority of votes; and it is possible, therefore, to imagine a truly sovereign legislature elected under the strictest "democratic" rules that was nonetheless governed by a legislative majority representing the first preferences of a minority of voters. Yet I do not think we would want to call such a political system a ruling elite system. Because of this kind of difficulty, I propose that we exclude from our definition of a ruling elite any controlling group that is a product of rules that are actually followed (that is, "real" rules) under which a majority of individuals could dominate if they took certain actions permissible under the "real" rules. In short, to constitute a ruling elite a controlling group must not be *a pure artifact of democratic rules*.

A ruling elite, then, is a controlling group less than a majority in size that is not a pure artifact of democratic rules. It is a minority of individuals whose preferences regularly prevail in cases of differences in preference on key political issues. If we are to avoid an infinite regress of explanations, the composition of the ruling elite must be more or less definitely specified.

SOME BAD TESTS

The hypothesis we are dealing with would run along these lines: "Such and such a political system (the U.S., the U.S.S.R., New Haven, or the like) is a ruling elite system in which the ruling elite has the following membership." Membership would then be specified by name, position, socio-economic class, socio-economic roles, or what not.

Let me now turn to the problem of testing a hypothesis of this sort, and begin by indicating a few tests that are sometimes mistakenly taken as adequate.

The first improper test confuses a ruling elite with a group that has a high *potential for control*. Let me explain. Suppose a set of individuals in a political system has the following property: there is a very high probability that if they agree on a key political alternative, and if they all act in some specified way, then that alternative will be chosen. We may say of such a group that it has a *high potential for control*. In a large and complex society like ours, there may be many such groups. For example, the bureaucratic triumvirate of Professor Mills would appear to have a high potential for control. In the City of New Haven, with which I have some acquaintance, I do not doubt that the leading business figures together with the leaders of both political parties have a high potential for control. But a potential for control is not, except in a peculiarly Hobbesian world, equivalent to actual control. If the military leaders of this country and their subordinates agreed that it was desirable, they could most assuredly establish a military dictatorship of the most overt sort; nor would they need the aid of leaders of business corporations or the executive branch of our government. But they have not set up such a dictatorship. For what is lacking are the premises I mentioned earlier, namely agreement on a key political alternative and some set of specific implementing actions. That is to say, a group may have a high potential for control and a *low potential for unity*. The actual *political effectiveness* of a group is a function of its potential for control *and* its potential for unity. Thus a group with a relatively low potential for control but a high potential for unity may be more politically effective than a group with a high potential for control but a low potential for unity.

The second improper test confuses a ruling elite with a group of individuals who have more influence than any others in the system. I take it for granted that in every human organization some individuals have more influence over key decisions than do others. Political equality may well be among the most Utopian of all human goals. But it is fallacious to assume that the absence of political equality proves the existence of a ruling elite.

The third improper test, which is closely related to the preceding one, is to generalize from a single scope of influence. Neither logically nor empirically does it follow that a group with a high degree of influence over one scope will necessarily have a high degree of influence over another scope within the same system. This is a matter to be determined empirically. Any investigation that does not take into account the possibility that different elite groups have different scopes is suspect. By means of sloppy questions one could easily seem to discover that there exists a unified ruling elite in New Haven; for there is no doubt that small groups of people make many key decisions. It appears to be the case, however, that the small group that runs urban redevelopment is not the same as the small group that runs public education, and neither is quite the same as the two small groups that run the two parties. Moreover the small group that runs urban redevelopment with a high degree of unity would almost certainly disintegrate if its activities were extended to either education or the two political parties.

A Proposed Test

If tests like these are not valid, what can we properly require?

Let us take the simplest possible situation. Assume that there have been some number—I will not say how many—of cases where there has been disagreement within the political system on key political choices. Assume further that the hypothetical ruling elite prefers one alternative and other actors in the system prefer other alternatives. Then unless it is true that in all or very nearly all of these cases the alternative preferred by the ruling elite is actually adopted the hypothesis (that the system is dominated by the specified ruling elite) is clearly false.

I do not want to pretend either that the research necessary to such a test is at all easy to carry out or that community life lends itself conveniently to strict interpretation according to the requirements of the test. *But I do not see how anyone can suppose that he has established the dominance of a specific group in a community or a nation without basing his analysis on the careful examination of a series of concrete decisions.* And these decisions must either consitute the universe or a fair sample from the universe of key political decisions taken in the political system.

Now it is a remarkable and indeed astounding fact that neither Professor Mills nor Professor Hunter has seriously attempted to examine an array of specific cases to test his major hypothesis. Yet I suppose these two works more than any others in the social sciences of the last few years have sought to interpret complex political systems essentially as instances of a ruling elite.

To sum up: The hypothesis of the existence of a ruling elite can be strictly tested only if:

1. The hypothetical ruling elite is a well-defined group.
2. There is a fair sample of cases involving key political decisions in which the preferences of the hypothetical ruling elite run counter to those of any other likely group that might be suggested.
3. In such cases, the preferences of the elite regularly prevail.

DIFFICULTIES AND OBJECTIONS

Several objections might be raised against the test I propose.

First, one might argue that the test is *too weak*. The argument would run as follows: If a ruling elite *doesn't* exist in a community, then the test is satisfactory; that is, if every hypothetical ruling elite is compared with alternative control groups, and in fact no ruling elite exists, then the test will indeed show that there is no minority whose preferences regularly prevail on key political alternatives. But—it might be said—suppose a ruling elite *does exist*. The test will not *necessarily* demonstrate its existence, since we may not have selected the right group as our hypothetical ruling elite. Now this objection is valid; but it suggests the point I made at the outset about the possibility of an infinite regress of explanations. Unless we use the test on every possible combination of individuals in the community, we cannot be certain that there is not some combination that constitutes a ruling elite. But since there is no more *a priori* reason to assume that a ruling elite does exist than to assume that one does not exist, the burden of proof does not rest upon the critic of the hypothesis, but upon its proponent. And a proponent must specify what group he has in mind as his ruling elite. Once the group is specified, then the test I have suggested is, at least in principle, valid.

Second, one could object that the test is *too strong*. For suppose that the members of the "ruled" group are indifferent as to the outcome of various political alternatives. Surely (one could argue) if there is another group that regularly gets its way in the face of this indifference, it is in fact the ruling group in the society. Now my reasons for wishing to discriminate this case from the other involve more than a mere question of the propriety of using the term "ruling elite," which is only a term of convenience. There is, I think, a difference of some theoretical significance between a system in which a small group dominates over another that is opposed to it, and one in which a group dominates over an indifferent mass. In the second case, the alternatives at stake can hardly be regarded as "key political issues" if we assume the point of view of the indifferent mass; whereas in the first case it is reasonable to say that the alternatives involve a key political issue from the standpoint of both groups. Earlier I refrained from defining the concept "key political issues." If we were to do so at this point, it would seem reasonable to require as a necessary although possibly not a sufficient condition that the issue should involve actual disagreement in preferences among two or more groups. In short, the case of "indifference vs. preference" would be ruled out.

However, I do not mean to dispose of the problem simply by definition. The point is to make sure that the two systems are distinguished. The test for the second, weaker system of elite rule would then be merely a modification of the test proposed for the first and more stringent case. It would again require an examination of a series of cases showing uniformly that when "the word" was authoritatively passed down from the designated elite, the hitherto indifferent majority fell into ready compliance with an alternative that had nothing else to recommend it intrinsically.

Third, one might argue that the test will not discriminate between a true ruling elite and a ruling elite together with its satellites. This objection is in one sense true and in one sense false. It is true that on a series of key political questions, an apparently unified group might prevail who would, according to our test, thereby constitute a ruling elite. Yet an inner core might actually make the decisions for the whole group.

However, one of two possibilities must be true. Either the inner core and the front men always agree at all times in the decision process, or they do not. But if they always agree, then it follows from one of our two assumptions about influence that the distinction between an "inner core" and "front men" has no operational meaning; that is, there is no conceivable way to distinguish between them. And if they do not always agree, then the test simply requires a comparison at those points in time when they disagree. Here again, the advantages of concrete cases are palpable, for these enable one to discover who initiates or vetoes and who merely complies.

Fourth, it might be said that the test is either too demanding or else it is too arbitrary. If it requires that the hypothetical elite prevails in *every single case*, then it demands too much. But if it does not require this much, then at what point can a ruling elite be said to exist? When it prevails in 7 cases out of 10? 8 out of 10? 9 out of 10? Or what? There are two answers to this objection. On the one hand, it would be quite reasonable to argue, I think, that since we are considering only key political choices and not trivial decisions, if the elite does not prevail in *every* case in which it disagrees with a contrary group, it cannot properly be called a ruling elite. But since I have not supplied an independent definition of the term "key political choices," I must admit that this answer is not wholly satisfactory. On the other hand, I would be inclined to suggest that in this instance as in many others we ought not to assume that political reality will be as discrete and discontinuous as the concepts we find convenient to employ. We can say that a system approximates a true ruling elite system, to a greater or lesser degree, without insisting that it exemplify the extreme and limiting case.

Fifth, it might be objected that the test I have proposed would not work in the most obvious of all cases of ruling elites, namely in the totalitarian dictatorships. For the control of the elite over the expression of opinion is so great that overtly there is no disagreement; hence no cases on which to base a judgment arise. This objection is a fair one. But we are not concerned here with totalitarian systems. We are concerned with the application of the techniques of modern investigation to American communities, where, except in very rare cases, terror is not so pervasive that the investigator is barred from discovering the preferences of citizens. Even in Little Rock, for example, newspaper men seemed to have had little difficulty in finding diverse opinions; and a northern political scientist of my acquaintance has managed to complete a large number of productive interviews with White and Negro Southerners on the touchy subject of integration.

Finally one could argue that even in a society like ours a ruling elite might be so influential over ideas, attitudes, and opinions that a kind of false consensus will exist—not the phony consensus of a terroristic totalitarian dictatorship but the manipulated and superficially self-imposed adherence to the norms and goals of the elite by broad sections of a community. A good deal of Professor Mills' argument can be interpreted in this way, although it is not clear to me whether this is what he means to rest his case on.

Even more than the others this objection points to the need to be circumspect in interpreting the evidence. Yet here, too, it seems to me that the hypothesis cannot be satisfactorily confirmed without something equivalent to the test I have proposed. For once again either the consensus is perpetual and unbreakable, in which case there is no conceivable way of determining who is ruler and who is ruled. Or it is not. But if it is not, then there is some point in the process of forming opinions at which the one group will be seen to initiate and veto, while the rest merely respond. And we can only discover these points by *an examination of a series of concrete cases where key decisions are made:* decisions on taxation and expenditures, subsidies, welfare programs, military policy, and so on.

It would be interesting to know, for example, whether the initiation and veto of alternatives having to do with our missile program would confirm Professor Mills' hypothesis, or indeed any reasonable hypothesis about the existence of a ruling elite. To the superficial observer it would scarcely appear that the military itself is a homogeneous group, to say nothing of their supposed coalition with corporate and political executives. If the military alone or the coalition together is a ruling elite, it is either incredibly incompetent in administering its own fundamental affairs or else it is unconcerned with the success of its policies to a degree that I find astounding.

However I do not mean to examine the evidence here. For the whole point of this paper is that the evidence for a ruling elite, either in the United States or in any specific community, has not yet been properly examined so far as I know. And the evidence has not been properly examined, I have tried to argue, because the examination has not employed satisfactory criteria to determine what constitutes a fair test of the basic hypothesis.

REPUTATION AND REALITY IN THE STUDY OF COMMUNITY POWER

Raymond E. Wolfinger

The general criticisms raised by Dahl in the previous article were subsequently explicated in great detail by two of his students, Nelson Polsby and Raymond Wolfinger. In this selection Raymond Wolfinger objects to the reputational technique as it had been applied in specific studies to that date. The major thrust of his argument is that the technique of employing persons knowledgeable about the town, in order to reveal those with a reputation for power, assumes that appearance and reality are equivalent. His position is that the researcher and the respondent use ambiguous terms such as "power," and that there is no way to validate the latter's opinions of who has influence. Thus a construct of a small elite arrived at in this imprecise fashion is an artifact of bias.

Few books in recent years have had more influence on the study of local politics than Floyd Hunter's *Community Power Structure*.[1] Based on a new research technique which promised to make the study of political influence easier and more systematic, this volume reported that power in "Regional City" (Atlanta) was concentrated in a small, cohesive elite of businessmen. Following the publication of *Community Power Structure* a number of researchers used Hunter's method in other cities and, for the most part, produced similar findings of business dominance. The basic assumption underlying this method is that reputations for influence are an index of the distribution of influence. The researcher asks respondents either to rank names

From Raymond E. Wolfinger, "Reputation and Reality in the Study of Community Power," *American Sociological Review*, XXV (October, 1960), 636–644. Reprinted by permission of the author and publisher.

[1] My thinking on the topics covered in this paper has been greatly influenced by Robert A. Dahl and Nelson W. Polsby. I am indebted to them and to Fred I. Greenstein, Charles E. Lindblom, and Barbara Kaye for their many valuable comments on an earlier draft of this paper. References to New Haven are based on intensive research on that city's politics by Robert A. Dahl, Nelson W. Polsby, and myself. This research is reported in Dahl, *Who Governs?* (New Haven: Yale University Press, 1961); and Wolfinger, *The Politics of Progress* (New Haven: Yale University Press, forthcoming).

on a list or to name individuals who would be most influential in securing the adoption of a project, or both. He assigns power to the leader-nominees according to the number of times they are named by respondents; the highest-ranking nominees are described as the community's "power structure." This technique for describing a local political system is referred to below as the *reputational* or *power-attribution* method.

Several scholars have criticized Hunter's work on various grounds, but there has been no detailed evaluation of the reputational method. Judging by the flow of research making use of this technique, it continues to be highly regarded. The purpose of this paper is to explore the utility of the reputational method for the study of local political systems. This inquiry involves two questions: (1) Are reputations for power an adequate index of the distribution of power? (2) Even if the respondents' perceptions of power relations are accurate, is it useful to describe a political system by presenting rankings of the leading participants according to their power?

It can be argued that the reputational method should be regarded as merely a systematic first step in studying a city's political system rather than a comprehensive technique for discovering the distribution of power. Under this modest construction the researcher would not rely on the method to identify and rank all decision makers but would use it as a guide to knowledgeable persons who would in turn give him leads to other informants until he had a complete picture of the political system under study. Viewed in this unambitious light, the reputational technique is little more than a methodologically elaborate variant of the older procedure of asking insiders—city hall reporters, politicians, and so on—for a quick rundown on the local big shots in order to identify potentially useful interviewees.

The reputational researchers do not make such modest claims for their method, nor do their critics take such a limited view. While I am not aware of any explicit published statement to this effect, the reputational studies give the impression that the technique is regarded as considerably more than a ritualized political introduction. The putative validation of findings yielded by this method, the assumption that a "power structure" consists of those persons most often given high rankings by panels of judges, and a tendency to limit descriptions of decision making to the activities of the top-ranked leaders all point to a belief that this method is a sufficient tool to study the distribution of political power in a community.

THE PROBLEM OF AMBIGUITY

Assuming for the moment that it is worthwhile to rank political actors with respect to their power, is the reputational method adequate for this purpose? There are two major causes of ambiguity inherent in asking respondents to name in rank order the most powerful members of their community: the variability of power from one type of issue to another; and the difficulty of making sure that researcher and respondent share the same definition of power. Each of these problems is examined in turn below, using the familiar concept of power: "A has power over B to the extent that he can get B to do something that B would not otherwise do." The term *scope* is used to refer to those actions by B which are affected by A's exercise of power; for example, the major scope of a school superintendent's power is public education.

In order to compare the power of two individuals one must either assume that power is distributed evenly for all scopes or present a different set of rankings for each scope. Otherwise, if A is judged to be the most powerful man in town on school affairs and B is named the most powerful on urban renewal there is no way to compare their power except by asserting that power in one scope is more "important" than in another. Most of the reputational researchers, by their failure to specify scopes in soliciting reputations for influence, assume that the power of their leader-nominees is equal for all issues; some researchers specifically state that they are concerned with "a general category of community leadership."[2] This is an exceedingly dubious assumption. It is improbable, for instance, that the same people who decide which houses of prostitution are to be protected in return for graft payments also plan the public school curriculum. Moreover, recent research reveals specialized leadership, for example, in studies of Bennington, Vermont, and New Haven.

An individual's political power varies with different issues. Therefore "general power" rankings are misleading. Furthermore, the researcher cannot be sure that his respondent is not tacitly basing his rankings of community leaders on an implicit scope, with the result that an individual may be given a high general power rating because he is perceived to be very influential on a particular issue which is either currently important to the community or salient to the respondent. Data presented in a paper by Robert Agger—the only case, I believe, in which respondents' rankings are presented both for specific issues and general power—suggest that this is

[2]Robert O. Schulze and Leonard U. Blumberg, "The Determination of Local Power Elites," *American Journal of Sociology*, 63 (November 1957), 292n. Miller and Hunter also express interest in a "general power structure." See Floyd Hunter et al., *Community Organization: Action and Inaction* (Chapel Hill: University of North Carolina Press, 1956), pp. xi–xii; and Delbert C. Miller, "Industry and Community Power Structure: A Comparative Study of an American and English City," *American Sociological Review*, 23 (February, 1958), 10, and Miller, "Decision-Making Cliques in Community Power Structures: A Comparative Study of an American and an English City," *American Journal of Sociology*, 64 (November 1958), 300.

more than an academic possibility.[3] Agger reports the number of nominations received by each of eight leader-nominees. Three of these reputed leaders received the bulk of the nominations for "most influential," but the distribution of nominations in the three specialized areas is quite different: "H," who was not named as generally influential by a single respondent, received 47 per cent of all nominations for most influential on "community welfare"; "G" received four per cent of the nominations for general influence and 29 per cent for influence on school affairs; the corresponding figures for "F" were five and 35 per cent. What scopes these respondents had in mind when they made their nominations of general leaders is anybody's guess.

The validity of the reputational method is weakened by the difficulty of determining whether the interviewer and his respondents have the same idea of what the former seeks. The problem of defining political power has vexed generations of social scientists, many of whom have suggested definitions which display considerable conceptual and logical ingenuity. A researcher asking questions based on this complicated concept can either inflict his definition of power on each respondent or use a simplified analogous question. It would require a "man in the street" to be cooperative to the point of masochism to stand still while an interviewer labored through the definitions and qualifications that are found in the literature on power. But the alternative embraced by many researchers has equally great disadvantages because of the ambiguity of their questions. Several researchers have used some variant of the following question: "If a project were before the community that required *decision* by a group of leaders—leaders that nearly everyone would accept—which *ten* on the list of forty would you choose?" This question could ask for popularity, malleability, or willingness to serve on committees.[4] Hunter's "Who is the 'biggest' man in town?" is also susceptible of numerous interpretations.[5]

The ambiguity of such questions is illustrated by a study in which the researchers asked 107 steel union members and officials to identify the

[3]Robert E. Agger, "Power Attributions in the Local Community: Theoretical and Research Considerations," *Social Forces*, 34 (May 1956), 322–31. A study soliciting nominations in several specialized areas produced quite different rankings of individuals in each of three scopes, with the exception of one nominee, the local newspaper editor. See A. Alexander Fanelli, "A Typology of Community Leadership Based on Influence and Interaction within the Leader Subsystem," *Social Forces*, 34 (May, 1956), 332–38.

[4]Hunter tacitly acknowledges this drawback in mentioning that one very powerful man in Regional City ranked comparatively low on responses to this question because of his reputation for refusing to serve on committees; Floyd Hunter, *Community Power Structure* (Chapel Hill: University of North Carolina Press, 1953), p. 64. This question assumes that the nature of the "project" under consideration would make no difference in one's nominations.

[5]*Ibid.*, p. 62. Polsby has pointed out the ambiguity of such questions; see "The

"big shots" in town.[6] The respondents named the banker, the Chamber of Commerce, the mayor, other city officials, the gambling syndicate, and the steel company, which dominated the town economically. No respondent mentioned the union or its officers. Hunter and others might take this as evidence of the union's political impotence. But the union obviously was an influential force in local politics. All but three of the respondents said that the police were friendly and partial to them in collective bargaining, the most important issue for most union members; the three exceptions termed the police neutral. In fact, the union leaders had made a deal with the mayor, trading union political support for police favoritism. The police were so friendly that they cooperated in periodic drives in which all non-members were forcibly prevented from entering the steel plant. Most union members did not, however, view police favoritism as a *political* phenomenon. One might also explain their listing of "big shots" as attribution of status rather than power (with the exception, perhaps, of the gambling syndicate).

The reputational method appears to be particularly susceptible to ambiguity resulting from respondents' confusion of status and power. This difficulty is amplified by the low esteem in which labor leaders, local politicians, and municipal officials are often held, as well as by their usually lower socio-economic status compared to businessmen and leaders of charitable organizations. In many cities control of political parties and municipal offices has passed from "Anglo-Saxon" businessmen to people of recent immigrant stock and generally lower social status.[7] For example, scarcely any New Haven economic or social leaders participate in party politics, an activity in which the city's populous Irish, Jewish, and Italian groups predominate. In another New England city where the outnumbered high-status Yankees have shifted their attention and aspirations to activities in which money, leisure, and social status count more heavily, "the func-

---

Sociology of Community Power: A Reassessment," *Social Forces*, 37 (March, 1959), p. 232. The influence of the wording of questions on respondents' answers has long been a serious problem for public opinion researchers and others. Some of the reputational researchers seem not to have been too careful about the phrasing of their questions. It would be interesting to use split-pair techniques to learn how responses vary with changes in the wording of the basic "Who has the power?" question. See, e.g., Hadley Cantril, *Gauging Public Opinion* (Princeton: Princeton University Press, 1947), Chapters 1 and 2.

[6]Joel Seidman, Jack London and Bernard Karsh, "Political Consciousness in Local Unions," *Public Opinion Quarterly*, 15 (Winter, 1952), pp. 692–702.

[7]James B. McKee has described this process in Lorain, Ohio in "Status and Power in the Industrial Community: A Comment on Drucker's Thesis," *American Journal of Sociology*, 58 (January), pp. 364–70. McKee reports that union leaders do not participate very much in decision making in private civic welfare activities and that politically powerful members of minority ethnic groups still tend to have rather low social status. See also Peter H. Rossi and Alice S. Rossi, "An Historical Perspective on the Functions of Local Politics." revision of a paper presented at the annual meeting of the American Sociological Society, Detroit, 1956.

tions of status allocation and recognition, which were once performed by public office-holding, have been shifted in this period to . . . the community service organization."

These differences pose a problem for reputational researchers, who often rely on voluntary organizations for initial nominations of leaders. The nominees are then ranked by panels which usually are composed largely of business and professional people. One might expect that as the wealthy become less influential in politics they value political office less highly.[8] In these circumstances, questions which do not distinguish between status and power, and between public and private scopes, are likely to lead researchers to leader-nominees whose power may be exercised chiefly on a country club's admission committee. Businessmen, when asked questions about "projects," are apt to base their answers on those types of private activity in which they are most active and influential, and which are most salient to them. This may be one reason why the reputational method tends to turn up ruling elites consisting largely of businessmen.

Ambiguity can be minimized by asking questions about specific scopes and eschewing the "Who's the local big shot?" approach. This would eliminate situations in which the interviewer assumes that he is getting reports on political power when respondents in fact are ascribing status or merely revealing who pulls the strings in the Rotary Club's program committee. Limiting the questions to specific political issues still will not impose on respondents the same criteria that might lead a social scientist to define a certain event as reflecting a power relationship, but it is probably the best than can be done with this method.

Specifying scopes minimizes ambiguity and provides a more accurate description of politics by permitting comparisons of influence in different areas. This procedure also gives the respondent a cue to reality and weakens the force of local myths about politics. A man willing to assert that Yankee bankers run "everything" might make a more cautious reply when asked specifically about the municipal welfare department.

THE PREVALENCE OF MISPERCEPTION

Assuming now that interviewer and respondent have in mind the same phenomenon, how accurate are the respondent's perceptions? There is some evidence that these are inaccurate, and to date none of the

---

[8]"Far too frequently they [businessmen] also have a strong distaste for politics and politicians—a distaste that can be particularly strong when the politicians happen to be Democrats" (The Editors of Fortune, *The Exploding Metropolis*, New York: Doubleday, Anchor Edition, 1958, p. xvii). Scoble reports that his respondents tended to nominate as leaders those individuals who agreed with them. See Harry M. Scoble,

power attribution studies has been validated on this point by other means.[9]
One of the most striking examples of inaccurate perception appears in a
footnote to a paper by Pellegrin and Coates on the influence of absentee-
owned corporations in a southern city:

> The typical interviewee [a businessman] in this study described local gov-
> ernment officials as relatively powerless figures who do not have the back-
> ing of influential groups but secured their positions through the support of
> working-class voters. Indeed, these officials were more often than not targets
> of ridicule for those who evaluated their positions in the power structure.
> . . . The relative lack of integration of Bigtown's interest groups makes it
> possible for governmental officials to sponsor civic projects which are some-
> times successful, in spite of opposition from one or another of the "crowds"
> [of big business]. Interest groups find it difficult to express publicly opposi-
> tion to projects which attract widespread support. To do so would be "bad
> public relations," perhaps unprofitable in the long run.[10]

In the text of this paper the authors emphasize the power of the absentee-
owned corporations and report that they can veto any project which they
oppose and secure the adoption of any measure they support.[11] Perhaps
Pellegrin and Coates were unaware of the implications of the quoted passage, both for their thesis about the distribution of power in "Bigtown"
and for the more general assumption that reputations are an adequate
index of the actual distribution of power. Whether the passage reveals inaccurate perceptions or an eccentric definition of power, however, it is
clear that these respondents' rankings of the community's most powerful

---

"Yankeetown: Leadership in Three Decision-Making Processes," presented at the
annual meeting of the American Political Science Association, St. Louis, 1958, p. 41.
Similarly, see Robert Agger and Daniel Goldrich, "Community Power Structures and
Partisanship," *American Sociological Review*, 23 (August 1958), 391.

[9]Blackwell maintains that studies which Hunter has conducted in other communities have verified the findings of his inquiry in Regional City; Gordon W. Blackwell,
"A Theoretical Framework for Sociological Research in Community Organization,"
Social Forces, 33 (October 1954), p. 317. But Hunter's description of the political
system in City A is not evidence for the accuracy of his description of City B; and
since he has not studied Regional City by means of an alternative procedure, his
method has not been validated. Miller reports correlations between choice as a "key
influential" and *some* forms of participation in civic groups, but none of these activities has been shown to be an index of political power. See Miller, "Industry and
Community Power Structures," pp. 12, 13. He also asserts that "A valuable test of
this technique" of power attribution was conducted by John M. Foskett and Raymond
Hohle, (p. 10). See the latter's "The Measurement of Influence in Community Affairs,"
Research Studies of the State College of Washington, 25 (June 1957), 148–154. But
Foskett and Hohle merely compared the lists of leaders chosen by a number of
variants of the reputational method and found a high association between them,
which did not test the method by comparing its results with findings produced by
another method.

[10]Roland J. Pellegrin and Charles S. Coates, "Absentee-Owned Corporations and
Community Power Structure," *American Journal of Sociology*, 61 (March, 1956),
p. 414 n.

[11]*Ibid.*, p. 414.

men are open to serious question. So many alternate interpretations of such responses are possible that relying on them to define a "power structure" is unwarranted.

If private citizens are unreliable sources of information, people who are active in public life are not much better informants, either on general or specific questions. Key observes that "Such general conclusions [about the political efficacy of various groups] by politicians and other 'informed' citizens are wrong so much of the time that one becomes skeptical of all such remarks."[12] Rossi reports a striking example of misperception in "Bay City," where Republican politicians explained that their lack of success with various ethnic groups was due to the energetic activities of the local Catholic priests on behalf of the Democratic party. Actually most of the priests were Republicans.

In New Haven a number of prominent citizens active in public affairs could not identify other decision makers in the same policy field. This was most notably revealed in interviews with members of the executive committee of the Citizens Action Commission, a group of about 20 men who direct the Commission's activities in various aspects of civic betterment. This group has been described as the "biggest muscles in town" and includes among others the President of Yale University and the Dean of the Yale Law School, the presidents of the local power and telephone companies, the President of the New York, New Haven and Hartford Railroad, leading bankers and attorneys, the heads of several nationally known industrial firms, the President and Secretary of the Connecticut Labor Council, AFL–CIO, and the Democratic National Committeeman from Connecticut. Although these men meet formally once a month and often get together at other CAC functions, many of them could not identify other committee members. For example, a regular and articulate participant spoke glowingly about the pleasures of his association with the other men on the committee and of his fond image of them all sitting together around the conference table, but except for friends he had known before the CAC was founded, he was unable to identify a single member. Another active participant, describing his fellow committee members, thought that the president of the Labor Council was a realtor employed by the New Haven Redevelopment Agency. Clearly, these respondents' replies to questions about the relative political influence of various New Haven leaders were not very informative.

New Haven politicians were not much better reporters of the distribution of power. Several of them, interviewed on a particular issue, told researchers that a local figure was the "real power" behind the scenes and always had his way; and then, discussing the same measure, added that another politician, opposed to the first, had "rammed it through the board—no one could

[12]V. O. Key, *Southern Politics* (New York: Knopf, 1950), p. 139 n.

stand up to him." An enduring item in the political folklore of New Haven is that one political figure or another is nothing but an errand boy for Yale University. As one would expect, this accusation is most credible to those individuals who are hostile either to Yale or to whichever is currently so attacked. Some experienced political figures so devoutly believe this charge that they are impervious to contrary evidence. If people who are professionally involved in community decision making cannot perceive accurately the distribution of political power, how can the rankings of less well-informed respondents be accepted as anything more than a report of public opinion on politics?

The reputational method, then, does not do what it is supposed to do: the ranking of leaders is not a valid representation of the distribution of political power in a given community. But assuming that reputations for power do in fact constitute an adequate index of power, nevertheless the resulting list of powerful individuals would not be useful without additional research which would make the method largely redundant, and even this utility would be very limited.

In compiling a list of leaders ranked according to the degree of power attributed to each of them, the researcher must have some means of limiting its size. Hunter, in selecting the arbitrary number of 40 for his leadership group, assumed what he set out to prove: that no more than 40 people were the rulers of Atlanta, possessed more power than the rest of the population, and comprised its "power structure." He assumed that political power was concentrated in a very small group and concerned himself with identifying its members. Hunter's key question might be paraphrased as follows: "What are the names and occupations of the tiny group of people who run this city?"

Any *a priori* definition of the size of a leadership group carries such an implicit assumption about the distribution of political power. The vital point is the establishment of a cut-off point, a criterion which determines the size of the group. If the criterion is placed too high, it may exclude so many significant actors that only a small part of the total amount of influence exercised in the community is included—the top 40 leaders may be outweighed by the next 200 powerwielders.[13] If too low, it may result in diluting the leadership group with many non-leaders. Clearly the important con-

---

[13]*Cf.* Robert K. Merton," Patterns of Influence: A Study of Interpersonal Influence and of Communications Behavior in a Local Community," in P. F. Lazarsfeld and F. N. Stanton, editors, *Communications Research, 1948–49* (New York: Harper, 1949), pp. 180–219. Miller defines "power structure" so that it is composed of the most frequently nominated individuals, without knowing whether the "pyramid" of power is shaped so that his *a priori* criterion of nomination will coincide with an actual cut-off point in the distribution of power. Thus he reports that there are 12 "key influentials" and 44 "top influentials" in a city of half a million people, but presents no evidence of their ability to dominate Seattle's political system. See Miller,

sideration here is the shape of the influence "pyramid": the more steeply its sides slope, the fewer people in the elite group and the higher the researcher's cut-off point can be. Yet if he knows enough about the community to envision such a pyramid, he already knows much of what the power-attribution method is supposed to tell him, and a great deal more.

There appears to be no way out of this dilemma without making an assumption crucial to the problem. If the researcher's questions do not specify the number of leaders the respondent can nominate and only a few actors are mentioned, he is in effect passing this problem along to his respondents. For while each of the respondents may believe that the person (or persons) he names is the most powerful single individual, nominations of the most influential man in town do not include information about how much power he has compared to other actors. If the researcher decides to establish the cut-off point by a "break" in number of nominations, or by including the nominees who account for a majority of nominations, he is passing the buck to a statistical artifact, for he still has no way of knowing that his criterion corresponds to political reality.

The identification of leaders which the reputational method is supposed to achieve has very limited utility for another reason. A demographic classification of such leaders is not a description of a city's political system because it does not indicate whether they are allies or enemies. To establish the existence of a ruling elite, one must show not only that influence is distributed unequally but also that those who' have the most influence are united so as to act in concert rather than in opposition. One cannot conclude that the highest-ranked individuals comprise a ruling group rather than merely an aggregate of leaders without establishing their cohesiveness as well as their power.

Most of the reputational researchers consider this point, but then go on to draw conclusions about the probable decisions of their putative elites by assuming that political preferences can be inferred from socioeconomic status. This inference is questionable on a number of grounds. It assumes that the members of the body politic can be divided into two groups on the basis of a dichotomizing principle (such as relationship to the means of production) which determines all their policy preferences. Thus there will be a "class position" on every issue, with the same people on the same side on all issues. This in turn assumes that economic status is the only variable that determines political preferences. But associations between socioeconomic status and positions on various issues represent correlations,

---

"Industry and Community . . . ," p. 10, and "Decision-making Cliques . . . ," pp. 302–303. Other reputational researchers are less explicit about this assumption. In his later article, Miller expresses some doubt about the extent of business dominance in Seattle. These uncertainties are based on interviews with a few participants, however, not on the reputational method; the latter technique turned up a business ruling elite.

not categoric divisions; there are always sizeable numbers of people on the minority side. Furthermore, persons of different economic status may have similar attitudes on the basis of shared vocational or sectional interests: both the United Mine Workers and coal mine owners worry about competition from other fuels; New England workers and merchants alike are concerned about departing industries. For people in official positions the "norms of the office" represent role demands which often predict behavior more consistently than status. Finally, politicians want to win, to the point at times where they are ideologically indifferent. Even "issue-oriented" politicians accept the need to compromise.

While most political leaders in Bennington were business or professional men, they were split into several durable and bitterly opposed factions on the issues which Scoble studied. In New Haven the six most prominent politicians have the following occupations (or occupational background, in the case of the mayor, a full-time official): attorney (two), undertaker, bond and insurance broker, realtor, and public relations director. The first three are Republicans, the others, Democrats. The two parties are quite differentiated; a change in regime seven years ago brought marked changes in municipal policies. The policies followed by these six men cannot be predicted by reference to their occupations. It should be noted that few of the power-attribution researchers even mention the party identifications of their leader-nominees.

Another weakness of the reputational method is that it assumes and reports a static distribution of power. The three New Haven Democrats mentioned in the preceding paragraph are currently much more powerful than the three Republicans, in large measure because the Democrats are in office. The outcome of elections may be relevant to the distribution of power, a consideration which apparently has escaped the power-attribution researchers and for which their method is illsuited. Changes in the nature and distribution of the sources of power are assumed to occur very slowly, so that the only strategy for a group engaged in political action is to persuade the real elite to go along with it. The model of the political process resulting from the reputational method assumes an equation of potential for power with the realization of that potential. (It may be a misnomer to refer to this as a "process"; actually the reputational researchers appear to assume a kind of equilibrium.) This in turn assumes that all resources will be used to an equal extent and thus that political skill is unimportant. Either elections are of no consequence or one side will win all of them.

It would be interesting to replicate some of the power attribution studies at five-year intervals to learn how persistently the same individuals are nominated as leaders. A study by Donald Olmsted suggests that quite different lists might result.[14] His panel of "knowledgeable citizens" named

---

[14]"Organizational Leadership and Social Structure in a Small City," *American Sociological Review*, 19 (May, 1954), pp. 273–281.

30 community leaders in 1943 and again in 1949; the names of only nine people were on both lists. One would expect some attrition by death, moving, and so on, but the locale of Olmsted's study did not have an unusually unstable population.

Shifting distribution of power, whether the result of elections or of other factors, presents a problem in political analysis which appears to be unsolvable by the power-attribution method. While some individuals might maintain some or all of their power after a change in regime, others would not, and some relatively powerless persons would be placed high in the "power structure." The inclusion of all political actors within a supposed power elite would be neither surprising nor discriminating. The interesting questions about politics are concerned with the dynamics of policy making and are badly warped in static, reified rankings of individuals whose demographic classification is a poor substitute for analysis of goals, strategies, power bases, outcomes, recruitment patterns, and similar questions. When energetic political organization can affect elections and issue outcomes and thus "make new power,"[15] description of a dynamic process by a static concept appears to be a mismatch of method and subject matter. The gifts and energies of social scientists can be better used than in this pursuit.

[15]See, e.g., Francis Carney, *The Rise of the Democratic Clubs in California* (New York: Holt), 1959.

THE SOCIAL PSYCHOLOGY OF REPUTATIONS FOR COMMUNITY LEADERSHIP

Howard J. Ehrlich

In the following article Howard J. Ehrlich notes that a reputation for power is a phenomenon that is relevant to the study of community power, even if it is not always an accurate indicator of power itself. He compares the nominations of "influentials," made by a random sample of the adult citizens of Prince George County, Maryland (population 425,000 in 1960) with the background of the individuals making the nominations and suggests the nature of the biases that are likely to be reflected in assessments of power based on attributed influence. He concludes with a summary of the major propositions that may be derived from the literature on the social psychology of leadership.

This article clarifies some of the problems involved with the reputational approach to community power, and implies some of the factors which one must consider when evaluating the validity of power attributions. Furthermore, it should be recognized that almost all the various ways of studying community power—even those which focus on the disposition of specific issues—rely to some extent on the judgments of the observers (other than the researchers themselves) about the role played by alleged leaders. Ehrlich's contributions may allow us to make more judicious use of such information.

Abridged from "The Social Psychology of Reputations for Community Leadership," *The Sociological Quarterly*, VIII (Summer, 1967), pp. 415–530. Reprinted by permission of the author and publisher. The author adds: The materials reported here are derived from a program of research supported by the Community Projects Section of the Mental Health Study Center, National Institute of Mental Health. I am grateful to Mary Lou Bauer for her assistance, and to Patricia M. Schwier, Susan D. Spalter, and David Graeven who served as research assistants. I wish to thank Professor William V. D'Antonio, Carol Ehrlich, and my former colleagues, Dr. Sheila Feld and Dr. Harold F. Goldsmith, for their encouragement and critical aid in preparing this report. An earlier version was presented to the Midwest Sociological Society, April, 1966.

Three procedures are generally used for the identification of community leaders. Leaders may be assessed by criteria of position, by criteria of participation, and by criteria of reputation. Most researchers have relied on the latter two procedures and have made assessments exclusively on the basis of participation or on the basis of reputation. In the few studies in which both procedures have been used together, they have appeared to yield listings of community leaders of varying degrees of similarity. D'Antonio and Form, for example, report in their El Paso study that 71 to 93 per cent of the key decision-makers in one or more of the six issues they studied were also reputed leaders. In contrast, Freeman and his associates in their Syracuse study report only a 39 per cent overlap in two independently derived lists of the leading participants and the most frequently nominated leaders.[1] To be sure, the methodologies of the El Paso and Syracuse reports are not directly comparable. However, this is equally true of all of the leadership study comparisons.[2] The problem of establishing empirically meaningful criteria for such comparisons is unresolved.

If the discrepancy between these operations were only in the roster of names produced, the matter, though still challenging, might be relatively unimportant. These leadership rosters, however, form the basis for a network of subsequent research operations that typically lead to statements about the structure of power and decision-making in the local community. Where such statements are based on a single method of research, they appear to lead to systematically biased results. Walton, in a recent review of 41 community studies, found that researchers who use a one-step reputational procedure report observing factional, coalitional, and amorphous power structures with significantly less frequency than do researchers using any other procedure or combination of procedures. Of 27 communities studied by reputational procedures only, 13 were reported as having monolithic power structures. In contrast, only 2 of the 14 communities studied by other and combined techniques displayed monolithic structures. Perhaps

[1]Cf. William V. D'Antonio and William H. Form, *Influentials in Two Border Cities* (Notre Dame, Ind.: Univ. of Notre Dame Press, 1965); Linton C. Freeman, Thomas J. Fararo, Warner Bloomberg, Jr., and Morris H. Sunshine, "Locating Leaders in Local Communities." *American Sociological Review*, 28 (1963), 791–98.

[2]See for example, Robert E. Agger, Daniel Goldrich, and Bert E. Swanson, *The Rulers and the Ruled: Political Power and Impotence in American Communities* (New York: Wiley, 1964); L. Vaughn Blankenship, "Community Power and Decision-Making: A Comparative Evaluation of Measurement Techniques," *Social Forces*, 43 (1964) 207–16; M. Kent Jennings, *Community Influentials: The Elites of Atlanta* (New York: Free Press, 1964); Richard Laskin and Serena Phillett, "An Integrative Analysis of Voluntary Associational Leadership and Reputational Influence," *Sociological Inquiry*, 35 (1965) 176–85; Robert Presthus, *Men at the Top: A Study in Community Power* (New York: Oxford Univ. Press, 1964); Harry Scoble, "Leadership Hierarchies and Political Issues in a New England Town," in Morris Janowitz (ed.), *Community Political Systems* (Glencoe, Ill.: Free Press, 1961).

more surprising is Walton's finding that a two-step reputational procedure is even more likely to yield observations of monolithic structures of community power than is the (presumably less careful) one-step procedure.[3]

The assessment of community leadership reputations has been almost exclusively used as a procedure for making statements about community power structures, while the more social-psychological dimensions of the reputational procedure have been largely ignored. Rather than look at who gets nominated, we could consider those who make the nominations. Rather than look at the structural implications, we could consider individual attitudinal or behavioral implications. I have said earlier.

> Certainly, we can say that reputations for power are indeed an adequate index of the *perceived* distribution of power in the local community. To ask, then, if this is useful to describe a political system, depends intimately on the purposes at hand. Thus, for example, if we can ascertain that the way in which people perceive the power structure of the local political system affects the way in which they behave towards and in that system, then surely we are dealing with very meaningful and indeed very useful considerations.[4]

In this report I shall examine, first, the socioeconomic characteristics, community involvement, and participation behaviors of persons who can or cannot, with varying degrees of proficiency, nominate community leaders in a mass sociometric survey. Second, I shall explore the sociometric structure of these leader nominations and shall test the post factum hypothesis that demonstrably knowledgeable informants can produce systematically biased leader nominations. Finally, in a substantive appendix, I shall present a codification of the major statements in the research literature on the social psychology of leader reputations. . . .

Reputations for community leadership were assessed through a series of questions in a larger interview dealing with style of life and mental-health-related concerns of county residents. The survey, conducted by the National Opinion Research Center, was based on a multistage, household probability sample of 1,277 county residents, 18 to 59 years of age, who were interviewed in the winter of 1962–63. The leadership questions asked in the survey are reproduced here.

> We'd like to know who the important people in Prince George's County are—the people who are community leaders. You may not know many of their names—many people don't—but one of the things we want to know is how well known they are.

> A. Which persons do you think speak for or are the leaders of the *business interests* in the County—people like *bankers, manufacturers* and *real estate men?*

[3]John Walton, "Substance and Artifact: The Current Status of Research on Community Power Structure," *American Journal of Sociology*, 71 (1966), 430–38.

[4]Howard J. Ehrlich, "The Reputational Approach to the Study of Community Power," *American Sociological Review*, 26 (1961), 926–27.

B. Which persons speak for or are the leaders of the *labor unions* in the County?

C. Which persons do you think speak for or are the leaders of the *professional people* in the County—people like *doctors, lawyers, clergymen* and *teachers?*

D. Which persons do you think speak for or are the leaders of the political groups in the County—groups like the *Republican* and *Democratic* parties?

E. Are there any other important people in the County who you think ought to go on a list of community leaders?

The indicators of socioeconomic background selected were age, education, occupational prestige (NORC), family income, and length of residence.[5] Two indicators of community involvement were selected. The first, an index of membership and participation in voluntary associations, is based on a weighting of the cross-tabulation of the number of formal and active memberships reported and coded in the survey. The index ranges from 0 to 8, and the index value for this county sample is 2.92. The index has been demonstrated to yield results directly comparable with the voluntary associations research literature.[6] The second indicator of community involvement consists of responses to questions about four community issues of varying degrees of salience.

THE FINDINGS

The majority of persons in the survey, approximately 51 per cent, could not respond to any of 5 open-ended questions with the name of any person whom they could identify as a community leader. Only 18 per cent were sufficiently knowledgeable to provide 4 or more leader nominations. Among those voting, their leader nominations displayed a relatively high degree of concentration: the survey produced only 705 different names from a roster of 2,299 nominees; and 80 of the leaders cited accounted for a majority of the nominations. The number of leader nominations given by respondents displayed a strong, direct, monotonic relationship to indicators of the level of the respondents' socioeconomic background and community involvements.

Three dominant voting orientations appeared to account parsimoniously for the distribution of voting patterns. Half of those voting were able to

---

[5] The coding units for these variables were primarily prestructured by the survey agent and permitted little manipulation. Related indicators, as well as alternative cutting points where possible, were explored. They displayed few departures from the patterns reported.

[6] Howard J. Ehrlich, "Membership and Participation in Adult Voluntary Associations in Prince George's County, Maryland" (Mental Health Study Center, National Institute of Mental Health, 1966), Part One.

name a business leader or a political leader but not both. The business-oriented and the politics-oriented respondents each accounted for one-fourth of those voting. Those with a business-political orientation, those who could name both a business and a political leader, comprised 35 per cent of the voters. As in the case of leader nominations, voting orientation displayed a strong, direct, monotonic relationship to indicators of the level of the respondents' socioeconomic background and community involvements. The business-politics-oriented voters ranked first on the criterion variables followed in order by the politics-oriented, the business-oriented, the "other" voter, and the nonvoter. The joint consideration of voting and voting orientation indicated that when voting level was controlled, voting orientations were distributed in a discontinuous relation to the socioeconomic and involvement dimensions. Only for the low voters did voting orientation follow the same relationship with socioeconomic background and community involvement as without the control for voting level. . . .

Those who are knowledgeable about community leaders are not only narrowly distributed in the upper levels of education, occupation, and income; they are older, residentially more stable, and more involved in community affairs. Within this restricted range, voting orientation appears relatively independent of the socioeconomic level and involvement variables. On the other hand, for the less knowledgeable voters, who are distributed in a restricted—but lower—socioeconomic and involvement level, voting orientation does appear to be significantly related to the criterion variables.

Presumably, at a high level of knowledge about community leadership, and despite the fact that high voters are more likely to manifest a business-political orientation, voting orientation is relatively independent of socioeconomic status, stability, and community involvement. At a lower level of knowledge of community leadership voting orientation appears to be distributed by status, stability, and involvement.

Reputational Bias

Mass sociometry, unlike elite sociometry, cannot be criticized on the basis of a probable or possible bias in the selection of informants. There can be no doubt that the mass sociometric study of community leadership provides a list of names which nominally and operationally comprise a roster of reputed community leaders.[7] In contrast, the validity claims for leader-

---

[7]The assessment of research operations in a mass sociometric survey appears to be relatively straightforward: (1) Is the sample representative? (2) Is the sociometric question clear and appropriate? (3) Did the respondent understand the question? (4) Was the question answered truthfully? (5) Was the answer registered adequately?

ship rosters derived from elite sociometric studies are more problematic, particularly where researchers attempt to use these rosters as a basis for subsequent community analysis. The bias that frequently—though not always or exclusively—emerges in elite reputational studies may in fact derive from the invalid use of leadership rosters. The findings of this report may help us understand this bias. Particularly, they may help us to understand how the more extensive two-step reputational procedure leads to depictions of monolithic community power structures.

To begin with, we need to note that most reputational studies start with a nonsystematic and casual selection of some knowledgeable elite. This is true in all but 2 of the 27 community studies reviewed by Walton. Typically, I assume, these are informants of relatively high socioeconomic status who are willing to and can spontaneously identify a large number of leaders. If the informant selection were biased, i.e., if the aggregate selection over-represented the business- or the politics-oriented, then it would tend to generate a one-sided list of names.

If we move to the second stage of the reputational procedure, soliciting nominations based on this new (now more biased) listing of reputed leaders, it seems plausible to expect that we should increase the degree of bias in this listing. Thus, our mass sociometric data lead us to the post factum hypothesis that the two-stage reputational study should even more often than the one-stage study produce a monolithic depiction of the community power structure. The confirmation of this hypothesis, independent of retrospectively demonstrating bias in past informant selection, requires two tests. First, we must show that some persons who are "knowledgeables" and hence eligible as informants have, nonetheless, only a segmental knowledge of community leaders. We have accomplished that test here: approximately 28 per cent of the high voters exhibited only segmental knowledge of the county leaders.

The second test requires the demonstration that leaders reputedly influential in a single sector are more likely to nominate persons within their own sector as leaders than they are to nominate persons outside their sector. While this cannot be tested with the data of this report, D'Antonio and Form provide supporting evidence from their border cities study, "We found in general that influentials received proportionately more votes from judges within their institutional sector."[8] Presumably, at the first stage of leader nominations, a biased selection of informants could generate a list that would lead the researcher to misidentify the community leadership structure. At the second stage of leader nominations, a biased set of elite informants could result in the further misrepresentation of leaders from

[8]William V. D'Antonio and William H. Form, *Influentials in Two Border Cities* (Notre Dame, Ind.: Univ. of Notre Dame Press, 1965), p. 66.

those sectors already overrepresented and underrepresented. Thus if bias exists at stage one, it is quite probable that it will be magnified at stage two.

THE SOCIAL PSYCHOLOGY OF LEADER REPTUATIONS

Although the research on leader reputations is relatively limited, a considerable amount of information has been accumulated. The organization of these findings is of methodological importance to the political sociologist and of substantive importance to the social psychologist concerned with social perception. In this appendix I shall try to present these findings in a codified fashion that will emphasize their consistency and interrelatedness as well as their more general implications for political sociology and social psychology.

The Basic Assumptions

1. *The awareness assumption.* An awareness of a community political system, positions of community power, and the existence of community leaders develops previous to a community resident's ability to identify particular leaders.
2. *The power assumption.* All communities are perceived to be controlled through some set of formal and informal arrangements by persons of legal authority, personal influence, or technical competence.
    a) Some formal positions within the community power structure are perceived to hold more power than others.
    b) Some organized arrangements of formal positions within the community power structure are perceived to be more powerful than other arrangements.
    c) Some individuals are perceived to be more powerful than others in the community power structure.
    d) Some organized associations of individuals are perceived to be more powerful than other associations in the community power structure.
3. *The knowledgeability assumption.* Community residents vary in their perception of community leaders, from residents who perceive a high number of leaders to those who perceive none.
4. *The veridicality assumption.* Leader reputations are based in part on past leader performance and in part on a presumed potential for future performance.

Characteristics of Perceivers

5. *The mass diffusion hypothesis.* Knowledge (the perception) of community leaders is not widely diffused among community residents.
6. *The mass consensus hypothesis.* Among knowledgeable residents (those

able to identify community leaders) there is a generally high order of agreement in identifying community leaders.

7. *The mass elite hypothesis.* A resident's socioeconomic position (education, income, occupation, and family cycle) is directly correlated with knowledgeability (the number of leaders he can identify). Residents of high socioeconomic position and those in the middle years of the family cycle are most likely to be knowledgeable about community leaders.

8. *The mass participation hypothesis.* A resident's memberships and participation in voluntary and informal associations are directly correlated with knowledgeability. Residents highly engaged in formal associational and interpersonal networks are most likely to be knowledgeable about community leaders.

9. *The mass stability hypothesis.* Knowledgeability develops with length of community residence (to some limit).

10. *The mass specialization hypothesis.* Knowledgeability tends to be specialized—i.e., confined to a limited set of leaders and leadership sectors (organized arrangements or associations) in the community.

11. *The mass knowledgeability hypothesis.* In their knowledge of leaders and leadership sectors, residents of high knowledgeability are less likely to be specialized, while residents of low knowledgeability are more likely to be specialized.

Characteristics of Reputed Leaders

12. *The leader pool hypothesis.* The greater the potential leader pool, the greater the number of reputed leaders. The size of the potential leader pool will be a direct function of (1) the size of the community, (2) the number of political positions in the community, (3) the economic diversity of the community, (4) the ethnic diversity of the community, and (5) the number of voluntary associations in the community.

13. *The leader elite hypothesis.* Reputed leaders are most likely to possess the social characteristics most valued in the community. (Current studies show that reputed leaders are most likely to be native born, male, white, Protestant, middle-aged, and relatively highly educated.)

14. *The congruency hypothesis.* Reputed leaders and highly knowledgeable residents display a similar profile of socioeconomic characteristics.

15. *The leader specialization hypothesis.* Knowledge of community leaders tends to be specialized among reputed leaders.

16. *The leader consensus hypothesis.* Among reputed leaders there is relatively high agreement in identifying community leaders.

17. *The consensus congruency hypothesis.* Reputed leaders and highly knowledgeable residents tend to agree in identifying community leaders.

The Mechanisms of Leader Visibility

18. *The elite visibility hypothesis.* The ascription or achievement of those characteristics which describe perceived leaders and highly knowl-

edgeable residents should operate to increase a resident's visibility in the community. Thus, visibility should increase (to some limit) with age, residence, socioeconomic position, and membership and participation in informal and voluntary associations—particularly those related to community politics.

19. *The power hypothesis.* The greater the political resources controlled by leaders and leadership sectors, the greater the visibility of leaders in the community.

20. *The specialization hypothesis.* The less the specialization of leaders and leadership sectors, the greater the visibility of leaders in the community.

21. *The stability hypothesis.* The greater the stability of leaders and leadership sectors, the greater the visibility of leaders in the community.

22. *The legitimacy hypothesis.* The past or present occupancy of political office or the assumption of major civic responsibilities increases leader visibility.

23. *The participation hypothesis.* Leader visibility increases the greater the leader participation in community issues which (a) involve the reorganization of traditional community arrangements, or (b) elicit a high degree of controversy, or (c) entail wide community participation.

LOCATING LEADERS IN LOCAL COMMUNITIES: A COMPARISON OF SOME ALTERNATIVE APPROACHES

Linton C. Freeman, Thomas J. Fararo,
Warner Bloomberg, Jr., and Morris H. Sunshine

Defense and criticism of research methods must at some point move beyond exhortation and logical exegesis to a comparative analysis of such methods. In the following selection that step is taken in a study of Rochester by Linton Freeman and his associates. The authors directly tested four techniques designed to reveal community leaders and found that each method discovered a different set of "leaders"; no one method furnished the complete picture of the decision-making process in Rochester. Thus in effect, Freeman and his colleagues held constant all factors except the methods for finding leaders, and these varying methods achieved varying results attributable more to the method, it would seem, than to intervening variables.

Most investigators would probably agree that leadership refers to a complex process whereby a relatively small number of individuals in a collectivity behave in such a way that they effect (or effectively prevent) a change in the lives of a relatively large number. But agreement on theoretical details of the leadership process or on how it is to be studied is another matter. Much of the recent literature on community leadership has been critical. Gibb has suggested that there are a great many *kinds* of leadership—many different ways in which changes may be effected. He has proposed that leaders be assigned to various types including "the initiator, energizer, harmonizer, expediter, and the like." Banfield has stressed the importance of the distinction between intended and unintended leadership. And both Dahl and Polsby have called attention to the desirability of considering the *extent* of the effect a given leader has in expediting a particular change and the *range* of changes over which his effect holds. It seems evident, then,

From Linton C. Freeman, Thomas J. Fararo, Warner Bloomberg, Jr. and Morris H. Sunshine, "Locating Leaders in Local Communities: A Comparison of Some Alternative Approaches," *American Sociological Review*, XXVIII (October, 1963) pp. 791–798.

that although these critics might agree with the minimum definition presented above, they would all like to see some additional factors included within its scope.

Polsby has translated the comments of the critics into a set of operational guides for research. He has suggested that a satisfactory study of community leadership must involve a detailed examination of the whole decision-making process as it is exhibited over a range of issues. Here we should have to specify each issue, the persons involved, their intentions, and the extent and nature of their influence if any. Such a program represents an ideal that might be used to think about the process of community leadership. But as a research strategy, this plan raises many problems.

In the first place, both influence and intention are concepts presenting great difficulty in empirical application. Both require that elaborate observational and interviewing procedures be developed, and both raise reliability problems. May we, for example, take a person's word concerning his intentions, or must they be inferred from his behavior? And even when two persons interact and one subsequently changes his stated position in the direction of the views of the other, it is difficult to *prove* that influence has taken place. But even if these questions were eliminated, a practical problem would still remain. To follow the prescriptions listed above would be prohibitively expensive, requiring detailed observation of hundreds (or thousands) of individuals over an extended period. To record all interaction relevant to the decisions under study, it would be necessary to observe each person in a large number of varied situations, many of them quite private. Even then it would be difficult to evaluate the impact of the process of observation itself. Given these considerations, Polsby's ideal has never been reached. All existing studies of community leadership represent some compromise.

Most authors of community leadership studies would probably agree that the critics are on the right track. But most have been willing (or perhaps forced by circumstances) to make one or more basic assumptions in order to achieve a workable research design. Four types of compromise have been common. They will be discussed below.

Perhaps the most realistic of the compromise studies are those based on the assumption that active participation in decision making *is* leadership. Typically, in such studies, one or a series of community decisions are either observed or reconstructed. In so doing, an attempt is made to identify the active participants in the decision-making process. These decision-making studies frequently are restricted to a small number of decisions, and they usually fail to present convincing evidence on the questions of intent and amount of impact. But they do provide a more or less direct index of participation. If they err it is by including individuals who, though present, had little or no impact on the decision. On the face of it this seems preferable to the likelihood of excluding important influentials.

A second compromise approach is to assume that formal authority *is* leadership. Aside from arbitrarily defining which positions are "on top," these studies underestimate the impact of those not in official positions on the outcomes of the decision-making process.

The third approach assumes that leadership is a necessary consequence of social activity. This assumption leads to studies of social participation. Such studies have used everything from rough indexes of memberships in voluntary associations to carefully constructed scales of activity in such associations. In each case it is reasoned that community leadership results from a high degree of voluntary activity in community affairs. The social participation approach is thus the converse of the study of position. While the former stresses activity, the latter is concerned only with formal authority. But to the extent that activity in voluntary associations leads to having an impact upon community change, activists are leaders.

The final approach assumes that leadership is too complex to be indexed directly. Instead of examining leadership as such, proponents of this approach assess reputation for leadership. Their reasoning suggests that all of the more direct approaches neglect one or another key dimension of the leadership process. They turn, therefore, to informants from the community itself. Often rather elaborate steps have been taken to insure that the informants are indeed informed. For example, positional leaders may be questioned in order to develop a list of reputed leaders or influentials; then the reported influentials are polled to determine the top influentials. In such cases it is reasonable to suppose that the grossly uninformed are ruled out.

Various critics have condemned the indeterminacy and subjectivity of this procedure. But its defenders reason that the reputational approach is the only way to uncover the subtleties of intent, extent of impact, and the like in the leadership process. What, they ask, but a life-long involvement in the activities of a community could possibly yield sophisticated answers to the question "Who are the leaders?" The reputational approach, then, assumes the possibility of locating some individuals who unquestionably meet the criteria of community leadership, and who in turn will be able to name others not so visible to the outside observer.

Currently, the controversy continues. Proponents of one or another of these competing points of view argue for its inherent superiority and the obvious validity of its assumptions. Others take the view that all of these approaches get at leadership. But these are empirical questions; they can be answered only on the basis of comparison, not by faith or by rhetoric. A number of partial contrasts have been published, but so far no systematic overall comparison of these procedures has been reported. The present report represents such an attempt. An effort is made to determine the degree to which these several procedures agree or disagree in locating community leaders.

The data presented here represent a part of a larger study of leadership in the Syracuse, N.Y., metropolitan area. . . .

DECISION MAKING

The study of participation in the decision-making process was of central concern in the Syracuse study. The first major task of the project team was to select a set of community problems or issues which would provide a point of entry into a pool (or pools) of participants in the decision-making process. Interviews were conducted with 20 local specialists in community study and with 50 informants representing diverse segments of the city's population. Care was taken to include representatives of each group along the total range of interest and institutional commitment. These 70 interviews provided a list of about 250 community issues. The list was reduced to a set of 39 issues according to the following criteria:

1. Each issue must have been at least temporarily resolved by a decision.
2. The decision must be perceived as important by informants representing diverse segments of the community.
3. The decision must pertain to the development, distribution, and utilization of resources and facilities which have an impact on a large segment of the metropolitan population.
4. The decision must involve alternative lines of action. It must entail a certain degree of choice on the part of participants; and the outcome must not be predetermined.
5. The decision must be administered rather than made by individuals in "the market." For the purpose of this study, an administered decision was defined as one made by individuals holding top positions in organizational structures which empower them to make decisions affecting many people.
6. The decision must involve individuals and groups resident in the Syracuse Metropolitan Area. Decisions made outside the Metropolitan Area (e.g., by the state government), were excluded even though they might affect residents of the Metropolitan Area.
7. The decision must fall within the time period 1955–1960.
8. The set of decisions as a whole must affect the entire range of important institutional sectors, such as governmental, economic, political, educational, religious, ethnic, and the like.

The next step in the research process required the determination of positional leaders or formal authorities for each of the set of 39 issues. The study began with those individuals who were formally responsible for the decisions. The element of arbitrary judgment usually involved in the positional approach was thus avoided. Here, the importance of a position was derived from its role in determining a choice among alternative lines of action rather than of being the consequence of an arbitrary assumption.

The responsible formal authorities were determined on the basis of documents pertinent to the 39 decisions. In addition, several attorneys were consulted to insure that correct determinations were made. The number of authorities responsible for making each of these decisions ranged from two to 57.

The interviews started with authoritative persons. Respondents were presented with a set of 39 cards, each of which identified a decision. They were asked to sort the cards into two piles: (1) "Those in which you participated; that is, where others involved in this decision would recognize you as being involved," and (2) "Those in which you were not a participant." For those issues in which they claimed participation, individuals were then asked to name all the others who were also involved. Here they were instructed to report on the basis of first-hand knowledge of participation rather than on hearsay. Respondents were also given a questionnaire covering their social backgrounds.

When the interviews with authorities were completed, their responses for those decisions on which they possessed authority were tabulated. Then, any person who had been nominated as a participant by two authorities for the same issue was designated as a first zone influential. Two nominations were deemed necessary in order to avoid bias due to accidental contacts, mistakes of memory, or a tendency to mention personal friends. In the final tabulations this same rule of two nominations was applied to authorities also. Therefore, no person is counted as a participant unless he has two nominations by qualified nominators.

As the next step, all first zone influentials were interviewed using exactly the same procedures as those used for authorities. Their responses were tabulated for the decisions in which they had been involved, and any person nominated by one authority and one first zone influential was also classified as a first zone influential and interviewed. Then any person nominated by two first zone influentials was designated a second zone influential—two steps removed from formal authority but still involved. We did not interview beyond these second zone influentials. We might have continued with third and fourth zones and so on; but on the basis of qualitative data gathered during the interviews, we suspected we were moving well into the periphery of impact on the outcome of decision making.

In all, 628 interviews were completed. Of these, 550 qualified as participants. These participants, then, are the leaders as determined by the decision-making phase of the Syracuse study. They were ranked in terms of the number of decisions in which they were involved. For the present analysis the 32 most active participants are considered.

SOCIAL ACTIVITY

Each of the 550 participants uncovered by the decision-making study was asked to complete a questionnaire covering his social background and current activities. These questionnaires were returned by 506 informants. The answers included responses to a set of questions designed to elicit as much information as possible about voluntary association memberships. Specific questions were included to determine memberships in the following areas:

1. Committees formed to deal with community problems.
2. Community service organizations.
3. Business organizations.
4. Professional organizations.
5. Union organizations.
6. Clubs and social organizations.
7. Cultural organizations.
8. Religious organizations.
9. Political parties, organizations and clubs.
10. Veterans' and patriotic organizations.
11. Other clubs and organizations.

Memberships in these organizations were tabulated, and a rough overall index to voluntary activity was calculated by simply summing the number of memberships for each person. The respondents were ranked in terms of number of memberships, and the 32 most active organizational members were included in the present analysis.

REPUTATION

Each questionnaire also invited the respondent to list the most influential leaders in the community. Eight spaces were provided for answers. Nominations were tabulated and, following traditional procedures, the top 41 reputed leaders were listed. The responses of those 41 respondents were then tabulated separately. The top 32 were derived from their rankings. This was done in order to maximize the chances that our nominators would be informed. As it turned out, however, the top 32 nominations of the whole group and the top 32 provided by the top 41 were exactly the same persons and in the same order. For Syracuse these nominations showed remarkable consistency all along the line.

POSITION

In determining the top positional leaders it seemed desirable to avoid as much as possible making the usual arbitrary assumptions. Traditional usage of the positional approach dictated the determination of the titular heads of the major organizations in business, government, the professions, and the like. Within each of these institutional areas choice could be made in terms of size, but it was difficult to determine how many organizations should be selected in each area.

An empirical resolution for this problem was provided in a recent report by D'Antonio *et al.* These authors provided data on the proportions of reputed leaders representing each of the seven relevant institutional areas in ten previous studies. Since agreement on these relative proportions was reasonably close for the six middle-sized American communities reported, they were used to assign proportions in each institutional area in the present study. The proportions derived from D'Antonio and those used in the present study are reported in Table 1. In this case positional leaders are the titular heads of the largest organizations in each of the institutional areas, and each area is represented according to the proportion listed in Table 1. Thirty-two organizations were chosen in all. As a check on its validity, the list of organizations was shown to several local experts in community affairs. They were in substantial agreement that the organizations listed seemed consistent with their perceptions of the "top" organizations in Syracuse. The heads of these organizations might be expected to have formal control over much of the institutional system of the community.

These, then, are the raw materials of the current study. An attempt was made to determine the degree to which these several procedures would allocate the same persons to the top leadership category.

TABLE 1   Percentage of Leaders in Each Institutional Area

Institution	Six Cities	Syracuse
Business	57	59
Government	8	9
Professions	12	13
Education	5	6
Communications	8	6
Labor	4	3
Religion	5	3
Total	99	99

RESULTS

The several procedures for determining leaders did not converge on a single set of individuals. Top leaders according to one procedure were not necessarily the same as those indicated by another. An index of agreement for each pair was constructed by calculating the ratio of the actual number of agreements to their total possible number. Results are listed in Table 2.

It is possible that any of the methods used, if modified enough would have yielded significantly different results.[1] The procedures we followed seem in their essentials to be like those followed in most of the studies so far published. (Those who believe they have altered the use of positions, nominations, memberships, or other indexes in such a way as to obtain a major difference in the output of the technique have only to demonstrate this by empirical comparisons.) Our impression is that most versions of each approach represent only vernier adjustments of the same device and thus can have only marginally differing results.

Table 2 suggests that there is far from perfect agreement in determining leaders by means of these four methods. In only one case do two of these methods concur in more than 50 per cent of their nominations. Reputation and position seem to be in substantial agreement in locating leaders. To a large degree, therefore, reputed leaders are the titular heads of major community organizations. They are not, however, themselves active as participants in decision making to any great extent.

Reputation for leadership seems to derive primarily from position, not from participation. But it appears unlikely that position itself constitutes a sufficient basis for reputation. The reputations however, might belong to the organizations and not the individuals. In such a case, when an informant named John Smith as a leader what might have been intended was the fact that the Smith Snippel Company (of which John Smith was president) is influential in community decisions. Smith would thus have been

[1]The choice of the top 32 leaders in each category, is, for example, somewhat arbitrary. When another number is used, the *absolute* percentages of agreement vary, but their standings *relative* to one another remain stable.

TABLE 2   Percentage of Agreement in Determining Leaders by Four Traditional Procedures

Participation	Social activity	Reputation	Position
25			
33	25		
39	22	74	

named only because we had asked for a person's name. Our hypothesis, then, is that reputation should correspond with the participation rate of organizations rather than the participation rates of individuals.

On the basis of this hypothesis, the data on participation were retabulated. Each participant was classified according to his organization or place of employment. Then the head of each organization was credited not only with his own participation, but with the sum of the participation of his employees. In this manner an index of organizational participation was constructed and the top 30 organizational leaders were determined. Individuals so nominated were compared with those introduced by the earlier procedures. The results are shown in Table 3.

The proportions shown in Table 3 support our hypothesis. Organizational participation seems to uncover substantially the same leaders as reputation and position. The top reputed leaders, therefore, though not active participants themselves, head up the largest organizations, and the personnel of these organizations have the highest participation rates.

This result accounts for a great deal of participation in community decision making. Since organizational participation provides a workable index, many participants must be employees of large community organizations. But this does not explain the most active class of individual participants—those who were picked up by the individual participation index. These people seem to be virtually full-time participants in community affairs. We know that they are not organizational heads, but we have not determined who they are.

In view of the sheer amount of their participation, the top participants must be professional participants of some sort. And, as a class, professional participants in community affairs should be government officials and employees of full-time professional executives of non-governmental agencies formally and primarily committed to intervention in community affairs. With this as our hypothesis, the individuals nominated as leaders by the four traditional indexes were all classified into either government and professional or non-professional categories. Then percentages of government personnel and professionals were calculated for all four indexes. The results are shown in Table 4.

TABLE 3   Percentage of Agreement Between Organizational Participation and Four Traditional Procedures

Traditional Procedure	*Percentage of Agreement*
Participation	33
Social activity	25
Reputation	67
Position	80

TABLE 4   Percentage of Leaders According to Four Traditional Procedures Who Are Government Officials or Employees or Profession Participants

Traditional Procedure	Percentage of Government Personnel or Professional Participants
Participation	66
Social activity	20
Reputation	20
Position	28

Again the results support our hypothesis. The most active individual participants are typically government personnel.

The participation index thus gets at personnel quite different from those selected by reputational or positional indexes, or by social activity. These differing cadres of people seem to represent *different kinds* of leadership behavior with respect to the local community.

SUMMARY AND DISCUSSION OF RESULTS

These results indicate that at least in Syracuse "leadership" is not a homogeneous category. Which "leaders" are uncovered seems in large part to be a function of the ·mode of study. The several traditional indexes allow us to locate one or another of three basic types of "leaders."

First, there are those who enjoy the reputation for top leadership. These are very frequently the same individuals who are the heads of the largest and most active participating business, industrial, governmental, political, professional, educational, labor and religious organizations in Syracuse. They are uncovered by studies of reputation, position, or organizational participation. In view of their formal command over the institutional structure and the symbolic value of their status as indexed by reputation, these individuals may be called the Institutional Leaders of Syracuse.

These Institutional Leaders, however, are for the most part not active participants in community affairs. There is no evidence that they have any direct impact on most decisions which take place. Their activity may be limited to that of lending prestige to or legitimizing the solutions provided by others. They might conceivably be participating decision makers in secret, but more likely they serve chiefly to provide access to the decision-making structure for their underlings: the Effectors.

The Effectors are located by studying participation. They are the active workers in the actual process of community decision making. Many of the most active Effectors are government personnel and professional participants, and the others are the employees of the large private corporations directed by the Institutional Leaders. In some cases, the Effectors are in touch with their employers, and it seems likely that their activities are frequently guided by what they view as company policy; but, judging from our data, they are often pretty much on their own. At any rate, these men carry most of the burden of effecting community change.

The third type of leader might be called the Activists. There people are active—and often hold office—in voluntary organizations, community service organizations, and clubs. Although they are not involved as often as the Effectors, the Activists do participate in decision making. For the most part they seem to lack the positional stature to be Institutional Leaders. Furthermore, they often work for or direct smaller organizations in the community. They lack the power base provided by association with government or one of the major industrial or business firms. Yet, seemingly by sheer commitment of time and effort to community affairs, these Activists do help shape the future of the community.

In conclusion, the various differing approaches to the study of community leadership seem to uncover different types of leaders. The study of reputation, position or organizational participation seems to get at the Institutional Leaders. Studies of participation in decision making, on the other hand, tap the Effectors of community action. And studies of social activity seem to seek out the Activists who gain entry by dint of sheer commitment, time, and energy.

In part, our results are dependent upon the Syracuse situation. It is likely that 25 years ago, when Syracuse was smaller and less diversified, the Institutional Leaders and the Effectors were the same people. And 25 years from now this description will probably no longer hold. Other communities, in other stages of development and diversification will probably show different patterns. But until more comparative studies are done, conclusions of this kind are virtually guesses.

PART THREE

Toward
a Theory
of
Community Power

As the preceding chapters amply demonstrate, the progress of ideas in intellectual discourse is not an orderly affair. The development of a complex concept and its empirical support proceeds disjointedly because many insights and much evidence are influenced by the different perspectives of the scholars involved. Scattered case studies or limited experiments which flow from different conceptual bases flood the field in the early stages of the search for a generalizing theory. This disorder tends to coalesce slowly into a limited number of approaches or to form "schools of thought." From the conflict arising among these schools, a dialectic process leads to modification of the original, simpler ideas of "truth" which had increasingly failed to meet more rigorous canons of logic and evidence. The resulting new perspectives contain some of the old views, of course. In time, continued research and rethinking operate to create even further revision of what was once thought by many (or even most) to be the ultimate answer. Thus, the intellectual process never yields final truths—such absolutes are for the world of dogma—but only more and more proximate understandings.

The student newly come to the intellectual discourse of a field may initially experience disillusionment and frustration, especially in the social sciences. Everywhere he sees interpretive schools in conflict, and men whose names are held in respect by some are the objects of trenchant criticism by others. Yet in such seeming confusion there is often an underlying, if ill-defined, order which contains an opportunity. For when people differ and "truths" are in the process of becoming, there is opportunity to contribute new insights of concept and method.

In this book we have arranged the selections to emphasize both the evolution of ideas in the search for community power and to suggest that there is much that is not known. The preceding section focused upon some methodological problems still to be solved; in this section, we offer some of the work which suggests promising new directions for research in community power.

An important step in the evolution of ideas from the simple to the sophisticated is the collection of available data and conclusions within the context of a comparative framework. While no one disagrees about the importance of comparative analysis to future developments in community studies, John Walton's observation, reported in the first edition of this book, has lost little of its relevance, "To come to grips with the diverse social and political facets of community life in a comparative design remains the chief problem in the field."[1] To put the matter somewhat differently, it seem likely that a central reason why community power research has thus far yielded less than we might have hoped for is that the inquiry, in general, has proceeded without a widely accepted paradigm which might have ordered and facilitated the comparability of the numerous studies. As Thomas Kuhn has noted, "In the absence of a paradigm, or some candidate for a paradigm, all the facts that could possibly pertain to the development of a given science [here, a branch of science] are likely to seem equally relevant. As a result, early fact gathering is a far more nearly random activity than the one that subsequent scientific development makes familiar."[2]

We are, however, beginning to see the emergence of an analytical framework for understanding the factors that account for different patterns of decision-making power. This schema resembles the systematic model of politics set forth by David Easton.

A set of variables representing socioeconomic, demographic, and political structures of communities are identified and (apparently) conceptualized as determinants of the distribution of political resources and demands. These factors are, in turn, seen as key variables in shaping patterns of power distribution measured by control over decision making in various

[1]John Walton, "Substance and Artifact: The Current Status of Research on Community Power Structure," *American Journal of Sociology*, 71 (January 1966), 430–38.
[2]Thomas Kuhn, *The Structure of Scientific Revolutions* (Chicago: University of Chicago Press, 1962), p. 15.

issue arenas. Various statistical techniques are employed to ascertain the most significant "explanations" of the variations in decision-making structures. Much of the recent research of this genre also examines the linkage between community power distributions and the substance of policy decisions. This systems approach to community power and public policy analysis, as exemplified by the work presented here of Aiken and Alford, Clark, and Morlock, has substantial promise and moves us closer to a theoretical understanding of political decision making. Nevertheless, many important problems of community power research still await resolution and we will use this section's introduction to review these difficulties.

Assessing Power

There is a continuing need to develop some concensus about how power will be defined and operationally measured. While efforts to resolve this problem are being made, it may suffice for students of community power to be explicit about the definition of power which guided their research and the way they operationalized their concept. It seems quite clear, however, that notions of power which focus attention solely, or even primarily, on the resolution of issues that are dealt with by the formal institutions of government are inadequate.

Classifying Patterns of Community Decision Making

Related to the problem of defining political power is the difficulty of specifying a quantity that reliably differentiates the patterns of community decision making in several communities. Not only is "power" difficult to assess, but power structures are composed of several characteristics which may or may not be highly correlated. If these dimensions are not closely related, how can the individual components be weighted so as to derive a single index that reflects different patterns of decision making? The complexity of the task we are pointing to is suggested by Table 1, which outlines criteria developed by Roe L. Johns and Ralph B. Kimbrough for classifying power structures.

Improving Methodologies for Locating Decision Makers

The often tiresome but important debate about appropriate research strategies requires resolution beyond the present agreement that no one technique will suffice. It is not clear, for example, what the reputa-

TABLE 1   Criteria for Power Structure Continuum

Monopolistic Elite	Multigroup Noncompetitive	Competitive Elite	Segmented Pluralism
Singular structure	Considerable overlapping of structural groups	Limited overlapping of groups	Segmented structure
80–100% overlap on projects	70–80% overlap on issues	50–70% overlap on issues	50% or less overlap on issues
Issues contained	Minor issue competition	Competitive on issues	Segmented or specialized competition on issues
One dominant group over period of more than one election	Incomplete separation of two or more groups; consensus at times	Two or more well-defined power groups over time	Many competing groups separated due to different interests
Communication line upward and downward within group	Communication between groups allows consensus on major issues	Communication is with satellites; little with competing groups	Communication through political office-holders; little otherwise
Voting participation is low; 40–50% or less of registered voters	Voting participation approximates 55% over time	Voting participation approximates 60% over time	Voting participation approximates 65% or higher over time
Membership in groups is general	Much overlap in membership between two or more competing groups	Overlap in membership between groups	Little overlap in group membership
Few, if any, regime conflicts	Little regime conflict	Regime conflicts between two or more groups	Regime conflicts involving many groups

Source: Roe L. Johns and Ralph Kimbrough; see footnote 3.

tional approach (the identification of influentials by "knowledgeable" people in the community), which continues to be the most widely employed methodology, really tells us. Since reputation is a power resource, the reputational approach tells us something about the potential power individuals or groups might mobilize. It is less certain whether this approach allows us to specify the scope of potential power (even within issue areas) or the probabilities that such "power" will be utilized. Earlier studies employing both reputational and decision-making methods showed poor correlations between the patterns of influence that emerged from each research strategy. What is needed is a multidimensional methodology for identifying political influentials that specifies the relative validity to be placed on the data derived from different techniques.

SPECIFYING THE ELEMENTS OF COMMUNITY STRUCTURE

There is a need to specify a minimum set of variables whose consequences for the distribution of power researchers must consider. Such variables would include situational, cultural, structural, and environmental factors that might hypothetically affect the distribution of power. The articles by Aiken and Alford, Clark, and Morlock contribute to the solution of this task.

Among the factors that comparative research on community power has been least successful in dealing with is the role of political culture—e.g., norms concerning participation, corruption, local autonomy, the role of business and social elites in politics, the legitimacy of political demands by different groups (such as minorities) and the desired scope of government. The articles following by Rabinovitz and by Kesselman and Rosenthal, as well as the work of Vidich and Bensman, and of Agger, Goldrich and Swanson in Chapter Two, consider political cultures, but the multicommunity studies in these final chapters, as significant as they are, do not.[3]

Another substantial gap in the literature on community power is research on the impact that extra-community forces—especially county, state and federal governments—have on local patterns of decision making. There

---

[3]Other research which the reader may find particularly appropriate to the analysis of community power might include Roe L. Johns and Ralph Kimbrough, *The Relationship of Socioeconomic Factors, Educational Leadership Patterns and Elements of Community Power Structure to Local School Fiscal Policy* (Washington, D.C.: U.S. Department of Health, Education and Welfare, 1968); Oliver P. Williams and Charles Adrian, *Four Cities* (Philadelphia: University of Pennsylvania Press, 1963); Edward C. Banfield and James Q. Wilson, *City Politics* (Cambridge: Harvard and MIT Press, 1963); and Delbert C. Miller, "Industry and Community Power Structure—A Comparative Study of An English and An American City," *American Sociological Review*, 23 (February 1958), 9–15.

have been a number of efforts to specify the role that external economic factors play in community politics,[4] but systematic research on the linkages between what have been called the "vertical and horizontal axes" of community power has yet to be reported.[5]

The articles by Walton and by Kesselman and Rosenthal emphasize the importance of factors external to the community in understanding local politics. Vidich and Bensman's *Small Town in a Mass Society*, an excerpt of which is presented in Chapter Two above, is one of the most comprehensive efforts to identify these relationships.

A problem that must be dealt with if comparative community research is to be productive is that the measures that represent community institutions and structures must, in general, be more sensitive than those now used to the richness and variation that exist in such community characteristics. We do not, for example, have measures that very effectively tap such notions as ethnic and socioeconomic heterogeneity. Similarly, measures of the fiscal resources of communities used in most studies fail to capture the various sources of local revenue, whose proportional contribution to total resources may vary greatly. Moreover, researchers need to be clear about the community characteristics they are trying to tap. For example, measures of community wealth in terms of private wealth, (e.g., family income) may be related only loosely to resources available to local government.

Among the variables whose complexity seems most difficult to operationalize are characteristics of the political system. Party competition, for example, a variable often used in comparative political analysis, is invariably measured in terms of the division of the popular vote or party registration. These measures, however, reflect cleavages in popular opinion or party preference, but do not speak to the question of whether political party organizations are active and competitive.

In general, analysts of community decision making who employ the systems framework have tended to stress the relative importance of socioeconomic and demographic factors, vis-à-vis political ones. One reason for this may be that the measures of political variables do not tap the richness of the political process. Even such an easily identified factor as form of government is a multidimensional variable. Not only do formal institutions (such as the council-manager plan) encompass many variations, but we

---

[4]See, for example, Robert O. Shulze, "The Role of Economic Dominants in Community Power Structure" *American Sociological Review* 23 (February 1958), 3–9; Donald A. Clelland and William H. Form, "Economic Dominants and Community Power: A Comparative Analysis," *American Journal of Sociology* 69 (March 1964), 511–21; and William H. Form and Delbert C. Miller, *Industry, Labor and Community* (New York: Harper & Row, 1960).

[5]*Cf.* Roland L. Warren, *The Community in America* (Chicago: Rand McNally, 1963). See also, Robert Agger et al., *The Rulers and the Ruled* (New York: John Wiley, 1964).

know so little about the interactive effects of different political institutions that we have little basis for developing multifactor indices of political structures, such as the common typology of "reformed" and "unreformed" cities. For example, to talk about reformed government as a variable whose weight depends on the presence of one to three of the major components of municipal reform (the manager plan, nonpartisanship, and at-large elections), is to implicitly assign the same relative weight to each component and to mask the rather strong possibility that there is an interactive effect among the components that varies with the mix. For example, strong parties may tend to centralize decision-making power while wards elections may decentralize power. Another probable reason that systems analyses of community decision making have deemphasized the significance of political institutions is that the measures of output used are so closely related to fiscal resources. We shall return to this point later. Of the articles in this section, those by Rabinovitz and by Hawley, neither of which utilizes the systems framework in their analyses nor expenditures as their measures of policy, argue most strongly that political institutions matter in shaping patterns of community influence and their consequences.

Finally, our ability to develop more telling, multicommunity, comparative research is impeded by the fact that data are not readily available on many of the matters that we would like to consider. For example, in his article, Clark finds that religion is an important factor in explaining community decision making, but he is forced' to utilize data for the county in which his communities are located rather than data on the communities themselves.

CLARIFYING THE RELATIONSHIPS BETWEEN VARIABLES

Comparative community power research, despite its growing sophistication, still lacks the paradigm we spoke of earlier. A list of variables is not enough. We must begin to be clearer about the theoretical linkages between these variables so that our statistical tools can be utilized more efficiently.

Diagram 1 is an effort to spell out, within the system framework, the broad outlines of community decision making which could be the basis for further theoretical development. This analytical framework is not, of course, for some of the reasons noted above, easily operationalized. The model proposed here seeks to suggest the sequential relationships between different types of variables although we do not make explicit the relative weight of the implied associations. The schema here hypothesizes alternative paths through which different elements of community *structure* have impact on the allocation of values and resources.

Community decision making (and "non-decision making") is seen as vulnerable to extra-community factors in every dimension of the analytical scheme. It is important that students of local politics begin to try to determine the impact on communities of forces external to them. Of course, our model does not move us very far toward the achievement of that difficult task.

There are many interrelationships in our conceptualization and, even so, we have understated the complexity of the processes by which power and values are allocated. In the real world, almost every thing is related to everything else; all political interactions are reciprocal in some degree or another.[6]

We do not propose to discuss all the implications of Diagram 1. We would draw attention to one major difference between this model and many others one will find in the recent literature on the sources of public policy. We argue that community policies are not the direct result of social and economic structures, though such community characteristics shape demands and limits options. At the same time, policies—or the implementation of policies for that matter—are not the only way that values and resources, affecting the quality of life people experience, are allocated.

Obviously absent from this analytical model is what many students of politics and history consider the critical determinant of social action—leadership. While case studies of political decision making invariably stress the importance of the skill, motivation, and personal characteristics of individuals in shaping the outcome of decision-making processes, we seem to have no theories that facilitate parsimonious conceptualization of the leadership factor. Perhaps because of these problems of description students of comparative community power have not incorporated the variable of leadership into their analyses in ways which allow us to discriminate between the importance of structure and the importance of individual or group "discretionary" activity in the determination of patterns of power and of public policy. Indeed, since we can to some extent measure structures and give them a place in our analyses, it is not surprising that our analyses lead us to descriptions of decision making that are so lacking in dynamism, or to the conclusion, despite the limited power of structural explanations, that politics may not count for much.[7]

[6]See especially John Harsanyi's analysis of power in Chapter Three.

[7]This is the implicit or explicit conclusion of a substantial body of recent research on public policy. A prototype example of this work is Thomas Dye's "Governmental Structure, Urban Environment, and Educational Policy," *Midwest Journal of Political Science*, 11 (August 1967), 353–80. For a listing of this literature and a critical discussion of it, see Herbert Jacob and Michael Lipsky, "Outputs, Structure and Power: An Assessment of Changes in the Study of State and Local Politics," *Journal of Politics*, 30 (May 1968), 511–19; Phillip B. Coulter, "Comparative Community and Public Policy: Problems in Theory and Research," *Polity*, 3 (Fall, 1970), 22–43; and Ira Katznelson, in Willis D. Hawley, Michael Lipsky et al., *Theoretical Perspectives on Urban Politics* (Englewood Cliffs, N.J.: Prentice-Hall, 1974).

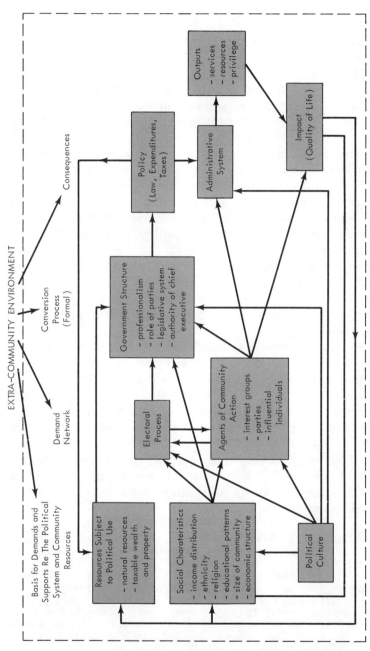

EXTRA-COMMUNITY ENVIRONMENT

Basis for Demands and
Supports Re The Political
System and Community
Resources

Demand
Network

Conversion
Process
(Formal)

Consequences

EXTRA-COMMUNITY ENVIRONMENT
Inputs from State and Federal, perhaps County, Governments
Ties of Local Political Groups to "Parent" or "Sister" Organizations
Economic Dependencies

DIAGRAM 1 THE STRUCTURE OF COMMUNITY DECISIONMAKING

Outputs
– services
– resources
– privilege

Policy
(Law, Expenditures,
Taxes)

Administrative
System

Impact
(Quality of Life)

Government Structure
– professionalism
– role of parties
– legislative system
– authority of chief
  executive

Electoral
Process

Agents of Community
Action
– interest groups
– parties
– influential
  individuals

Resources Subject
to Political Use
– natural resources
– taxable wealth
  and property

Social Charateristics
– income distribution
– ethnicity
– religion
– educational patterns
– size of community
– economic structure

Political
Culture

COMMUNITY POWER AND PUBLIC POLICY

Until the late 1960s, few studies of community power had devoted much attention to the policy consequence of different patterns of decision making.[8] Despite the paucity of past attempts to link the study of community power to policy analysis, it seems unlikely that much future research on community power will proceed without a strong emphasis on the policy consequences of different patterns of decision making. In the first place, the normative concerns of persons interested in urban research seem to have shifted from primarily philosophical or institutional analysis to policy studies. James Q. Wilson forecasted this development when he observed: " 'Who Governs?' is an interesting and important question; an even more interesting and more important question, . . . is 'what *difference* does it make who governs?' "[9]

A second and more pragmatic reason why future research on community power is likely to have a policy emphasis is that such inquiry is very costly and the sources of financial support for urban research are primarily concerned with social change rather than with issues of democratic theory or social science methodology.

Finally, the study of community power and policy analysis need to be linked not only because it is normatively important to do so or because research resources may be contingent on such a merger. The linkage is important to the development of the descriptive theory since policy outcomes may provide clues to the distribution of influence and may sometimes redefine the rules of the game that constrain the use of power resources.[10]

However, if we are going to profitably employ the systems framework for the study of public policy, we need to: (1) broaden our definition of policy and (2) distinguish, as Ira Sharkansky argues, between policies, outcomes, and impacts.[11]

---

[8]One of the best-known exceptions to this generalization is Amos Hawley, "Community Power and Urban Renewal Success," *American Journal of Sociology,* 68 (June, 1963), 422–31.

[9]James Q. Wilson, "We Need to Shift Focus," in Edward H. Buchrig, ed., *Essays in Political Science* (Bloomington: Indiana University Press, 1966), p. 331.

[10]See Andrew McFarland, *Power and Leadership in Pluralist Systems* (Stanford: Stanford University Press, 1969), Chap. 5. However, power cannot be determined by resting our analysis solely on the discovery of who benefits in a political system. Some of the reasons for this are outlined by Nelson Polsby, *Community Power and Political Theory* (New Haven: Yale University Press, 1963).

[11]Ira Sharkansky has urged that policy analysts distinguish between "policies" (formal acts of legislatures or administrative directives), "outputs" (benefits received per client, the rate of program performance, etc.), and "impacts" (effects on the popula-

As suggested earlier, most studies of the impact of community power on public policy have utilized budgetary expenditures as measures of policy. Such measures, however, have serious limitations as vehicles through which to understand politics.

First, to know how much a city taxes or how much it spends on certain types of functions is not enough. That one city spends more on parks than another is interesting, but less so than the type of facilities provided and the location of the parks thoughout the city. Similarly, the quantity of expenditures for planning seems less important, in terms of differentiating policy directions, than whether the funds are spent in developing plans to deal with social problems or with downtown traffic circulation, or whether funds are invested in long range master plans or in housing code enforcement.

Related to this point is Robert Salisbury's argument that while system resources may account for the amount of money being spent (as most systems analyses of policy conclude), "the active political system continues to be the decisive factor in determining the kind of policy, including the groups that benefit or suffer, the extent of conflict, the ability to innovate or adapt, and other questions. ..."[12] Thus, a second problem with efforts to link the characteristics of communities with fiscal policies is that such analyses will inevitably understate the importance of politics, leadership, and the like vis-à-vis social and economic structures, since the former place substantial constraints on the discretion of political leaders that they do not experience when dealing with matters not so closely tied to resources. Similarly, some issues which may be quite important to a community, such as controversy over a freeway route, zoning decisions, or a human relations program, may not show up in the budget because little or no local money is expended or because the expenditures are small and are absorbed in other accounts.

Moreover, few students of public policy have failed to note that the intent of legislation (including budgetary allocations) is frequently altered in the process of implementation by politically powerful chief executives and administrations. We might expect, therefore, that the correlations between patterns of power distribution and policy would differ depending on whether we looked at laws and budgets or at the consequences of policy for community residents. Of course, measuring the impact of policy statements is often quite difficult, but that does not mean that we can neglect the dimension of the power structure such explorations may illuminate.

---

tion). Sharkansky, "Environment, Policy, Output and Impact: Problems of Theory and Method in the Analysis of Public Policy," in Sharkansky, ed., *Policy Analysis in Political Science* (Chicago: Markham, 1970), pp. 61–79.

[12]Robert Salisbury, "The Analysis of Public Policy: A Search for Theories and Roles," in Austin Ranney, ed., *Political Science and Public Policy* (Chicago: Markham, 1968), p. 165.

THE ISSUE SPECIFIC NATURE OF POWER STRUCTURES

Finally, it seems that our analysis of community decision making should proceed, at least for the time being, one issue—or one issue arena—at a time.

Existing research makes it quite clear that we may find very different patterns of decision making from issue to issue within the same community. What we need to do is to understand whether there are some underlying characteristics of issues which would allow us to develop a typology of social issues that could help explain variations in patterns of political decision making within and across communities. The sole article in Chapter Six by E. A. T. Barth and Stuart Johnson is one of the few community-oriented commentaries that focuses on this matter.[13] Terry Clark's article in Chapter Seven also deals with distinctions among issues, in this case, by differentiating types of expenditures. As we begin then to consider this question, we should keep in mind the points made in Chapter Four that the "issues" we need to investigate should not be limited to those which have reached the political agenda. Thus, the "non-decision making" or "non-issues" described by Bachrach and Baratz and by Frederick Frey may tell us more about the use of power than a study of legitimated public policy.

THE CROSS-NATIONAL STUDY OF COMMUNITY POWER

As we have noted, during the 1960s the search for community power moved increasingly into analysis of larger subsets of communities—within the American system. By the late 1960s, though, the search had moved out of even this national environment into cross-national domains. Some of this involved application of standard methods to communities within another nation, sometimes case studies and sometimes sets of com-

---

[13]Another classification effort is Froman's distinction between areal policies—single acts which affect whole populations more or less simultaneously—and segmental policies. "The former," he says, "are more likely in homogeneous communities." See Lewis A. Froman, "An Analysis of Public Policies in Cities," *Journal of Politics*, 29 (February, 1967), 94–108. Two significant studies that explore the importance of issues in shaping the nature of political processes warrant careful study though neither deals centrally with community politics. See Theodore Lowi, "American Business, Public Policy, Case-Studies, and Political Theory," *World Politics*, 16 (July, 1964), 685–715; and Robert Salisbury and John Heinz. "A Theory of Policy Analysis and Some Preliminary Applications," in Sharkansky, *Policy Analysis*, pp. 39–60.

munities.[14] There have been, however, some studies of communities across national boundaries.[15]

It is this future direction and its attendant problems and opportunities which are analyzed in Chapter Eight. There, Mark Kesselman and Donald Rosenthal reflect not merely upon cross-national community power studies but upon the place of this research in developing a grounded theory of comparative local politics. More fully than any particular study, their treatment tells the student about where we stand now; it also suggests future concepts and problems in the comparative study of politics of which community power analysis is a part. As the recent studies edited by Terry Clark demonstrate, it is this direction that the search for community power will most likely take in the decade ahead.[16]

CONCLUSION

It is unclear how far the study of community power can take us toward a fuller understanding of, and prescription for, a truly democratic polity. In any event, it is time, it seems to us, to broaden the scope of our efforts to comprehend the nature and uses of political influence. It is time, too, to abandon those community studies whose aim is to strengthen an ideological conception of the current health or infirmity of American society. The search for community power has the potential to provide new insights which can help us with the many problems of our increasingly urban society; it is this potential above all other attractions which justifies further inquiry.

[14]For example, Robert E. Frykenberg, "Traditional Processes of Power in South India: An Historical Analysis of Local Influence," in Reinhard Bendix, ed., *State and Society* (Boston: Little, Brown, 1968), 107–25; William J. Hanna and Judith L. Hanna, "Influence and Influentials in Two Urban-Centered African Communities," *Comparative Politics*, 2 (October, 1969), 17–40; Frederick Hicks, "Politics, Power, and the Role of the Village Priest in Paraguay," *Journal of Inter-American Studies*, 9 (1967), 273–82; Gary Hoskin, "Power Structure in a Venezuelan Town: The Case of San Cristobal," *International Journal of Comparative Sociology*, 9 (1968), 188–207; T. K. Oommen, "Rural Community Power Structure in India," *Social Forces*, 49 (1970), 226–39; and Edward O. Laumann and Franz Urban Pappi, "New Directions in the Study of Elites," *American Sociological Review*, 38 (April, 1973), 212–29.

[15]John Walton, "Development Decision-Making: A Comparative Study in Latin America," *American Journal of Sociology*, 75 (1970), 828–51; William V. D'Antonio and William H. Form, *Influentials in Two Border Cities* (Notre Dame, Ind.: Univ. of Notre Dame Press, 1965); and Delbert C. Miller, *International Community Power Structures: Comparative Studies of Four World Cities* (Bloomington, Ind.: Indiana University Press, 1970).

[16]Terry N. Clark, ed., *Community Structure and Decision Making: Comparative Analyses* (San Francisco: Chandler, 1968).

CHAPTER SIX

Community Power
and Different
Issue Arenas

COMMUNITY POWER AND A TYPOLOGY
OF SOCIAL ISSUES

Ernest A. T. Barth and Stuart D. Johnson

The authors of this article seek to formulate a multi-dimensional scheme for classifying social issues which will be related to alternative patterns of community power. As we have seen throughout this book, the issues one studies may shape one's perspective of the distribution of influence. Barth and Johnson speculate on the relationship between different types of issues, different kinds of leaders, and different patterns of decision making. They readily acknowledge that their typology is only a tentative framework, and they make some useful suggestions about steps to be taken to improve their outline. One step which they do not mention is to specify the relationships among their five dimensions.

From Ernest A. T. Barth and Stuart D. Johnson, "Community Power and a Typology of Social Issues," *Social Forces*, XXXVIII (October, 1959) 29–32. Reprinted by permission of the authors and publisher.

In a recent critical analysis of the research approaches to the study of community decision making, Peter Rossi identified three major research gaps.[1] The first of these pertained to the fact that "none of the studies reviewed have considered the full range of issues which come before a particular decision maker."[2] The second is concerned with the fact that, "the issues which have been subjected to study have been on the more dramatic side, perhaps more properly labeled 'controversies.' " This constitutes a research gap in the thinking of Rossi because "by and large we can expect that most issues up for decision are settled without becoming controversies."[3] The third major gap in present research involves Rossi's belief that, "Research on decision making should be extensive rather than intensive and comparative rather than the case study technique." He amplifies this point by saying, "three levels of comparison would be made: decision makers of different types, operating within different community and institutional settings, should be compared as they come to the settlement of a *range of issues*. This approach implies a sampling of decision makers, of issues, and of communities."[4]

It is the purpose of this paper to point out the importance of concern with the *type of issue* under consideration by decision makers and to suggest the basis for a typology of issues.[5]

The primary focus of recent research on community decision making has been on the identification of decision makers and the description of their background characteristics and interpersonal relations within a given community context. Relatively little attention has been given to the systematic analysis of the conditions under which influencing behavior occurs.[6] As Rossi has indicated, one set of such conditions involves issue content, and, in the thinking of the present authors, this condition has been greatly neglected.

Failure to consider the impact of issue content on the selection of influentials has led to problems in building models adequate to describe structures of community influence. For example, Hunter, in his study of power in "Regional City," allowed his sample of community leaders to designate the issues which they thought were of major concern to the community.[7] He

[1]The authors wish to thank the Research Fund of the Graduate School of the University of Washington for the financial support which has made it possible for them to carry on research in this area.
[2]Peter H. Rossi, "Community Decision Making," *Administrative Science Quarterly*, I (March, 1957), 438–39.
[3]*Ibid.*, p. 441.
[4]*Ibid.*, pp. 438–39.
[5]For a further discussion of this point see Nelson W. Polsby, "The Sociology of Community Power: A Reassessment," *Social Forces*, 37 (March, 1959), 232–36.
[6]Rossi, *op. cit.*, p. 438.
[7]Floyd Hunter, *Community Power Structure: A Study of Decision Makers* (Chapel Hill: The University of North Carolina Press, 1954).

then discovered that these leaders held a central place in the decision-making processes centering on issues which they had described. One might ask whether the almost monolithic structure of leadership which he found in that community was not, in fact, an artifact resulting from his methodology. Might not it be argued that, had he set out to discover the patterns of power organization operating around a *range* of issues, he might have found a somewhat different and less solidary power structure? It might be further argued that if different types of issues in a community tend to be selective of different types of leaders, then the task which Hunter set before his respondents (i.e., that of choosing "the biggest man in the community," or of selecting the "ten leaders who nearly everyone would accept"), is an almost impossible task. His respondents might legitimately have asked, "Biggest man with respect to what type of activities?"

A second problem which is central to the understanding of the influencing process relates to observations that not all issues come to the attention of the most influential decision makers. If one distinguishes between the "top level" leadership and the "understructure" leadership, as did Hunter,[8] it becomes evident that some issues never come before the former group, while other issues achieve major importance to them.

A third consideration in the study of influence systems derives from attempts to compare influence systems, along with the processes which characterize them, in different community settings. For example, in attempting to characterize the structure of relations among the top leaders of "Pacific City," Miller developed the concepts of "top influentials" and "key influentials" who were viewed as interacting in accordance with what he termed a "fluid coalition" model.[9] This model is distinct from the "monolithic power structure" model which Hunter felt described the structure of power relations in "Regional City."

Since the present authors find little reason to question the major findings and conclusions of either Miller or Hunter, aside from the methodological perspective mentioned above, it seems reasonable to assume that the structure of the influence system and the kinds of participants in decision-making processes vary with the types of issues facing a community at any given time. For example, the range of issues will be very different for a metropolitan center as compared to an open-country community; for a southern as compared with a northern or western community; and for a college town as compared to an industrial center. For the reasons cited above, it appears then, that there is a pressing need for research leading to the development of a typology of issues.

[8]*Ibid.*, p. 57.
[9]Delbert C. Miller, "The Prediction of Issue Outcome in Community Decision Making," *Research Studies of the State College of Washington*, XXV, No. 2 (June, 1957).

Basis for an Empirical Typology of Issues

In a pilot project the authors attempted to derive a typology of community issues based upon industrial categories. In analyzing questionnaire data from a sample of community residents, issues were classed together when they appeared to deal with subject matter falling into given institutional sectors of community life such as economic issues, political issues, and educational issues. It quickly became apparent that classification was arbitrary, some issues falling under two or more headings, and similar patterns of influencing behavior appeared in different institutional settings. Therefore, on the basis of this experience, it was concluded that such a classification of issue content would not produce a fruitful typology.

The pilot study did provide us with the following conclusions. In developing a typology of issues it is of primary importance to view the dimensions along which community issues are to be typed in terms of two major requirements. First, to be of maximum value, the dimensions must be generic to all issues. Second, variations in each dimension must be theoretically relatable to variations in patterns of influencing behavior. Thus, they must not only meet the test of logical inclusiveness, but they must also meet the empirical test of being "tied" to observable leadership behavior. Our concern in the present analysis is with the following three aspects of influencing behavior:

(1) the types of community structures involved in the flow of influence with respect to a range of issues;
(2) the direction of the flow of influence on any issue;
(3) the direction of the flow of communications around a range of issues.

Reanalysis of the pilot study data led to the development of the following five dimensions. Each meets the specifications mentioned above in that each is generic to all community issues, and each is relatable to the structure of influencing behavior. For these reasons it is suggested that they will profitably serve as a basis for the development of a typology of community issues. It should be noted, however, that each dimension is treated from the point of view of the actors in the community—in this case from the point of view of community leaders. It is their perception of community issues that modifies the type of action which they attempt to undertake with respect to the different kinds of issues.

Unique—Recurrent Dimension

It may be predicted that differentiated social organizations tend to evolve out of a community's recurrent experiences with a given type of community issue. Thus, the problem of dealing with recurrent issues, when they arise in a community, would in all likelihood be handled by constituted community agencies having access to regularly allocated resources. On the other hand, in the case of a unique issue (one which community leaders feel has not been previously experienced), no such structure or procedure would necessarily be available to members of the community. Therefore, when decisions must be made on such issues, leadership tends to be emergent, and resources would have to be developed. Such leadership would probably be less subject to formal community social controls. In addition, such leaders would also be more likely to have less restricted access to the *means* of power, such as money and the control of jobs, than in the case of a regularly organized community agency dealing administratively with a recurrent issue.

Salient—Nonsalient to Leadership

Community issues vary along a continuum from some that are central to the interests of community leaders and the organizational structures in which they hold positions, to some that are peripheral to their interests and of little concern to them. When an issue is of great importance to community leaders, but perceived to be of little importance to the general public of a community, action taken on that issue may be unpublicized and directed through informal influence structures. If, however, leaders feel that a "public relations program" is required, communications regarding the issue will generally flow from leaders to community members, frequently through the mass media. On the other hand, community leaders may be "forced to act" on some issues that are of little relevance to their personal interests when public pressures are brought to bear upon them. Under such circumstances, they may be *reacting* to the upward flow of communications exercised through formal mechanisms of the community such as political parties or the hierarchies of public offices.

Salient—Nonsalient to Community Publics

This dimension refers to the degree of prominence, or importance, which leaders feel the various community publics attach to specific issues. Issues of low salience to community leaders, which are perceived as being of low salience to the general public, are likely to be handled by professional community organizers or lower echelon power figures. In such cases, the flow of influence and communications would be predominantly from decision makers to followers. When an issue is thought to be highly salient to the public, the potential decision makers are likely to be concerned with the "public relations" of any decision. Under such conditions one might expect that the flow of communications and influence would be generally upward, from public to "decision makers."[10]

Effective Action Possible—Effective Action Impossible

Some issues might be highly salient to the members of a community, or a segment thereof, and at the same time be perceived as necessitating impossible decisions or requiring inaccessible resources. For example, many southern communities have felt a strong need to improve the level of education offered to the local children. However, often they have had to face the fact that money was not available for new buildings, libraries, and other facilities. In addition, they realized that it was difficult to attract well qualified teachers with the low salaries which could be offered. For this type of issue, the only type of action which is undertaken involves the development of "tension-reducing mechanisms," or, perhaps, merely the manipulation of symbols.

Local—Cosmopolitan Dimension

When the leaders of a local community perceive an issue as concerning programs and problems dealt with by other organizations in the state or nation, they tend to look, in many cases, to higher levels of organization for guides and direction in program development. If, however, an issue is perceived as purely local in its implications, then it is probable that the range of alternative courses of action will be seen as less limited, and the need for recourse to "experts" from outside the community will be lessened.

[10]There appear to be two polar views of the community leadership or influencing process. In one, the leader, or decision maker, is seen as making decisions in a rather arbitrary fashion and then implementing them by manipulating the means of power at his command. The other view sees the decision maker in the *process* of decision making. It views him from the time he discovers the need for action on any particular issue until he takes action on that issue. This latter view focuses on the communications behavior of leaders. It stresses the fact that leaders are in constant communication with relevant (or interested) publics for any issue. Such an approach makes it problematic as to whether the leader is exercising individual initiative in announcing a decision, or whether he is simply expressing an already formed, but latent (uncrystallized) community consensus on that issue. It appears to the authors that both types of processes operate. The problem at present is to discover the conditions under which one takes precedence over the other.

DIRECTIONS FOR FUTURE RESEARCH

If this five-dimensional basis for a typology of community issues is to be fruitfully applied to the study of community power and influence, then the following steps will seemingly have to be undertaken.

1. An instrument will have to be developed for the purpose of measuring and locating specific issues along these dimensions.
2. A set of issues, representative of the variety of issues facing a given community will have to be obtained from community leaders, and the leaders will have to describe each issue in terms of the instrument referred to in step 1. Information will also be required regarding the patterns of influence and communications associated with each issue.
3. An empirical typology of community issues will have to be developed from the data on community issues.
4. Finally, the resulting typology of issues will have to be related to the patterns of influence and communications behavior. At this point one would expect to find identifiable patterns of influence and communications flow associated with each type of issue. It would also be expected that specific types of community structures would be regularly involved in the decision-making process for the different types of issues.

At the present stage of our thinking, it has appeared meaningful to conceive of issues as flowing through a life cycle approximating the public opinion life cycle suggested by Foote and Hart.[11] Thus, an issue would be visualized as "living through" five phases: (a) the phase of emergence of the problem; (b) the proposal phase; (c) the policy-making phase; (d) the program phase; and finally, (e) the appraisal phase. It is expected that different types of issues will exhibit varying patterns of influence and communications flow for the several stages of issue life cycle. Therefore, this factor would have to be controlled in selecting a sample of issues for study.

A classification of community issues based on the dimensions proposed in this paper will make it possible to control one of the major variables in the study of influence systems. In this manner it should be possible to clarify some of the problems characteristic of attempts to identify the structure of influence systems. In addition, it should clear the way for comparative research on influence systems in different community contexts.

---

[11] Nelson N. Foote and Clyde W. Hart, "Public Opinion and Collective Behavior," *Group Relations at the Crossroads*, Sherif and Wilson, eds. (New York: Harper and Brothers, 1953), pp. 308–31.

CHAPTER SEVEN

The Impact of Community
Structure on the Distribution
and Consequences of
Community Power

COMPARATIVE URBAN RESEARCH
AND COMMUNITY DECISION-MAKING

Michael Aiken and Robert R. Alford

In this article, two sociologists examine the relationship between various community characteristics and public policy in several hundred American cities. Professors Aiken and Alford seek to suggest the extent to which various social and economic contexts and the political institutions of communities shape the delivery of public services. They do not speak directly of how, but their data do give credence to the notion that patterns of community power are determined to some (unspecified) extent by the structural aspects of the decision-making environment. The methodology employed does not tell us very much about the relative importance of different community structures in shaping public policy.

From *The New Atlantis*, Vol. 1, No. 2 (Winter, 1970). Publisher, Marsilio Editori, Piazza De Gasperi 41, 35100 Padova, Italy.

Multivariate analysis done by the authors is not presented here, that is, the interrelationships among the independent-structural variables are not specified. Nevertheless, this study is the most comprehensive one of its type.

The reader might attempt to make explicit Aiken and Alford's implicit model of community decision-making. How fruitful do you find this analytical approach in advancing us toward a theory of community power? And, in what ways might the analysis be strengthened? For example, one might wish to examine the measures of community structure they employ to ask if they actually tap the phenomena they are meant to reflect.

Research on urban politics, community power structure, and local decision-making exhibits a diverse and checkered pattern of development in the literature in political science and sociology in the United States in the past two decades. . . .

There are at least two critical questions from this literature . . . that remain to be answered. The first is that of *consequences*. That is, what difference does it make for community outputs if many actors or few actors, if only business elites or if multiple elites, are actively involved in formulating policies for local government? Second, what are the *intervening processes* of community decision-making that account for variations in such outputs? The dominant values in a local community, the degree to which power is concentrated, the centralization and efficiency of the formal structure of government, and the degree of community integration have each been proposed as explanations of the variations in the capacity of local communities. Given the state of knowledge about these topics as of the mid-1960s, there are at least three ways that logically one could attempt to address the questions posed above.

First, one could take the studies on community power, conduct a content analysis of them in order to categorize the type of decision-making structure, and then relate the resulting typology both to structural attributes of communities . . . and to community performance or outputs. While such studies may be helpful and suggestive of alternative approaches, they are plagued by a sufficient number of methodological problems to vitiate the possibility of any definitive conclusions. Chief among these are the problem of taking studies that employed a variety of methodologies and research approaches at face value and classifying them into a set of decision-making categories, the problem of grouping together studies spanning as many as forty years, and the problem of representativeness of these case studies.

A second approach is to gather data on community performance in a variety of decision-areas for all American communities, relate these to various structural attributes of communities, and conceive of the intervening process as a «black box» which can be inferred from the results. . . .

While this comparative approach has the advantage of avoiding the problems of sampling inherent in the case-study approach, it is plagued by its own problems. Chief among these is the meaning of the indicators, which may be quite distant from the realities of the intervening process in the black box. But also there is the question, although not unique to this approach, of comparability among various decision outputs. That is, school bond referenda, school board elections, and fluoridation decisions more often involve widespread citizen participation, while decisions about urban renewal, public housing, or Model Cities are usually made by organizations —community decision organizations, the municipal government, the council, and others—that represent the interest of citizens. The decision dynamics are likely to be different for these various types of policy outputs. . . .

The third approach is to take a sizeable sample of communities and to use comparable techniques to study the intervening decision-making process in each community, using data from the second approach to define a sampling frame. Ultimately, the understanding of urban politics and decision-making will advance only with studies of this kind. . . . Aside from the problems of the enormous number of resources that are required to do such a study, there are also two additional problems: the question of what sampling frame to use to maximize knowledge about decision-making and community performance in different subsets of communities and the question of the theoretical concepts and constructs to be tested by the research design. Derivation of the theoretical strategy and concepts from the previous literature on community power runs the danger of too early a closure on the most appropriate theoretical perspective.

Concerned with a desire to increase our understanding of urban politics and decision-making and constrained by some of the dilemmas and problems inherent in the third approach, we opted, at least as a beginning step, for the second strategy outlined above. We have gathered a considerable amount of data from a variety of sources on each of the 1,654 incorporated urban places of size 10,000 or more in the United States in 1960, although most of our analysis on community decision-making, innovation, and policy outputs has been limited to the subset of 676 cities that had a population size of 25,000 or more in 1960. . . .

In this paper we shall summarize our findings about three types of policy outputs: public housing, urban renewal, and the War on Poverty. . . . In earlier discussions of these findings we have characterized such policy outputs as various aspects of community innovation: 1) the incidence of innovation in these policy areas, 2) the speed of innovation in each of these policy areas, and 3) the level of output or performance of the innovative activity. In each of the three papers examining these decision-outcomes, we found that there were extremely high interrelationships among these three indicators of innovation within each policy area, and various community attributes were similarly related to each of the three aspects of innovation. Therefore, in this summary of our findings, we shall only include one measure of output in public housing, urban renewal, and the War on Poverty. The reader should bear in mind, however, that if either of the other two aspects of community innovation in public housing, urban renewal, or the War on Poverty were substituted, the results and conclusions would be the same as those included here. These measures are described below.

The strategy employed here has also been used by a number of researchers in sociology and political science to study such community decisions . . . as fluoridation. . . . In each case the researchers used some community attributes, or set of attributes, to infer the intervening process. Nowhere have these various explanations of community decision-making dynamics been brought together and critically compared with respect to a common body of data. These five theories are:

1) *Political Culture:* Cities dominated by groups with public regarding values are hypothesized to be more innovative with respect to policies benefitting the community as a whole than cities dominated by groups with private-regarding values.

2) *Concentration or Diffusion of Community Power:* There are three aspects of this argument: concentration of systemic power, . . . diffusion of power through mass citizen participation . . . and centralization of elite power. . . . In each case the hypothesis is the same, namely, the greater the concentration of power, the greater the degree of innovation. Conversely, the greater the diffusion of power, the lower the degree of innovation.

3) *Centralization of Formal Political Structure:* Cities with centralized administrative arrangements and a strong mayor, that is, cities with city manager or partisan mayor-council governmental structures are hypothesized to be more innovative. . . .

4) *Community Differentiation and Continuity:* Older and larger cities have been hypothesized to be more bureaucratic, and consequently less receptive to policy innovations, suggesting that younger and smaller cities should exhibit higher policy innovation. . . .

5) *Community Integration:* Cities in which community integration breaks down or is extremely low have a lower probability of innovation or other collective actions. Consequently, community innovation should be highest in integrated communities. . . .

We have listed these five explanations separately and shall discuss them in greater detail below because it is possible to conceive of them as five independent theories of community innovation and policy outputs. We turn now to a description of the three output measures, some discussion of sources of data used in this paper, and a description of the methodology employed here.

DATA AND METHODS

. . . The policy outputs included here have certain characteristics in common. First, each requires some degree of initiative by the local community. . . . Only two of the programs discussed here—public housing and urban renewal—required approval by the local governing body, however. A second characteristic of these policy outputs is that there is an organization in the local community—a community decision organization—that has been specifically created to coordinate and oversee the program. Third, most funds involved come from outside the community, from the federal government, although in each case some local money has to be provided. Fourth, none of these decisions typically involved mass participation by citizens. The decisions are made, in almost all cases, by representative organizations—the community decisions organization, the municipal government, and the city council—although community citizens and groups may be utilized at critical junctures to support or perhaps oppose a decision. The decision-making dynamics of these policy areas may not be found in other types of decision such as school bonds or other referenda.

A. Public Housing

. . . The *level of output* in public housing included in this paper is the number of low-rent public housing units constructed since 1933 per 100,000 population. . . .

B. Urban Renewal

. . . The *level of output* measure in urban renewal is the number of urban renewal dollars reserved per capita as of June 30, 1966. . . .

C. The War on Poverty

. . . The *level of output* measure is the number of poverty dollars per capita allocated to each community. . . .

D. Relationships Among the Output Measures

. . . The correlation coefficients among the three output measures range from .41 (for poverty and public housing) to .53 (for urban renewal and public housing). The correlation coefficient between the War on Poverty and the urban renewal measures is .42. Thus, if a community has a high degree of outputs in one of these programs, there is a propensity (although not a certainty) for it to have high outputs in another. Since these various programs were started in 1933 (public housing), 1949 (urban renewal), and 1964 (the War on Poverty), we can also take these results to suggest that having participated actively in a program at one point in time undoubtedly contributes to the capacity (in terms of expertise, experience, and resources) to participate in a subsequent program.

Other Methodological Considerations

. . . We included in our analysis cities which both have innovated in these programs and those which have not because we are concerned with the conditions under which innovations take place, not primarily with the conditions affecting the intensity and scope of outputs after innovation of a new program has occurred. If the cities without any of these programs are excluded, the relationships between the independent variables and policy outputs are attenuated, but remain in the same direction or are significant in the same manner as the data presented.

Findings

The data testing the various theories of community policy outputs as they are related to community innovation in public housing, urban renewal, and the War on Poverty are found in Table 1. Although there is some overlap in the indicators of the different theoretical variables, a given indicator has only been classified under one theoretical concept, usually the first time it is discussed.

First, *political culture.* Cities dominated by groups with public-regarding values are hypothesized by Banfield and Wilson to be more innovative with respect to policies benefitting the community as a whole than cities dominated by groups with private-regarding values. . . .

Therefore, cities having a low proportion of foreign stock, a small proportion of Catholics . . . (the proportion of elementary school children in

TABLE 1   Relationships between Various Structural Attributes of Communities and Level of Outputs in Public Housing, Urban Renewal and the War on Poverty

Theoretical Categories and Empirical Indicators	Public Housing Number of housing units constructed per 100,000 population since 1933 (natural logarithm)	Urban Renewal Number of urban renewal dollars reserved per capita (natural logarithm)	War on Poverty Number of poverty dollars per capita (natural logarithm)
	N = 646	N = 582	N = 676
Political Culture			
Percent of native population of foreign or mixed parentage	−.08*	.02	−.02
Percent of elementary school children in private schools	−.05	.08*	.02
Median family income	−.47***	−.29***	−.39***
Percent voting Democratic, 1964	.22***	.08*	.07
Political Structure			
Presence of a city-manager form of government	−.18***	−.14***	−.12**
Presence of nonpartisan elections	−.18***	−.18***	−.12**
Percent of city council elected at-large	−.01	−.02	−.06
Number of members of the city council	.09*	.14***	.19***
Centralization of Community Power			
MPO Ratio	−.30***	−.32***	−.24***
Citizen Participation			
Percent of adult population with four years of high school education	−.51***	−.38***	−.26***
Percent of registrants voting	.17***	.18***	.20***

TABLE 1   (Cont.)

Theoretical Catego-ries and Empirical Indicators	Public Housing Number of housing units constructed per 100,000 popu-lation since 1933 (natural logarithm)	Urban Renewal Number of urban renewal dollars reserved per capita (natural logarithm)	War on Poverty Number of poverty dollars per capita (natural logarithm)
	N = 646	N = 582	N = 676
Community Differen-tiation and Continuity			
Age of the city (census year city reached 10,000 popu-lation)	−.40***	−.48***	−.48***
Size of the city (natural logarithm)	.30***	.33***	.37***
Community Integration			
Percent unemployed	.36***	.25***	.24***
Percent migrant	−.24***	−.24***	−.08*
Poverty			
Percent of housing dilapidated, 1950	.36***	.13***	.19***
Percent of families with less than $3,000 income per year, 1959	.45***	.21***	.30***
Percent adults with less than five years education (natural logarithm)	.55***	.34***	.33***
Percent 14–17 year olds in school	−.44***	−.30***	−.31***
Percent of popu-lation that is non-white (natural logarithm)	.48***	.39***	.35***

*P .05
**P .01
***P .001

private schools), and a high proportion of the population that is middle-class . . . (median family income) should be more influenced by public-regarding values, and, hence, should have higher level of performance on policies which do not directly benefit the persons voting. Such cities should thus exhibit higher outputs.

Democratic presidential voting in the county in 1964 is an additional indicator of private-regarding values. Democratic dominance of a city is seemingly a more direct measure of political culture than any of these demographic characteristics. Thus, if the political culture theory works, we should find that Democratic communities exhibit lower outputs.

In Table 1 are shown the relationships between the indicators of political culture and policy outputs. Of the twelve tests of the political culture hypothesis, seven are significant, three barely so. But, the relationships are uniformly in the opposite direction from that predicted. High income cities are *less* likely to have high outputs in all three policy areas, not more likely. Democratic cities are more likely to have high outputs in all three areas. The political culture hypothesis is thus either not supported at all, or the data are in the reverse direction.

Second, *concentration or diffusion of community power*. We refer here to three related but independent theories of community structure and consequences for the distribution of power: 1) the ecological or systemic theory which sees power as a property of dominant institutions, 2) a mass participation theory which argues that those structural features which reduce mass participation will as a consequence concentrate power, and 3) an elite participation theory which argues that the smaller the number of elite participants and the more homogeneous their interests, the more concentrated the power structure. We can test all but the last theory with quantitative data parallel to those already presented. While they differ in the feature of community organization which they single out as the critical cause of concentration of power, they share the general assumption that the fewer the actors, whether mass or elite, and the more those actors represent dominant institutions, the more concentrated the power. The further inference that concentrated power leads to greater policy outputs is not always explicitly stated, but we believe that it is a justified extension of the theories to be discussed.

In his study of urban renewal, [Amos] Hawley argued an *ecological* or *systemic* theory that communities with a greater concentration of power will have a high probability of success in any collective action affecting the welfare of the whole. He postulated two types of power: 1) functional power which is required to execute functions, and 2) derivate power which spills over into external relationships and regulates interactions between parts (units) of the system. In relatively routine issues, he suggested that power is exercised through established and well-worn channels. But for non-routine decisions affecting the entire system (such as urban renewal), the way in which derivative power is distributed is critical.

Hawley used participation in urban renewal programs as his measure of a collective community success, and he used the MPO Ratio (the proportion of the employed civilian labor force that are managers, proprietors, or officials) as his measure of the degree of concentration of community. He reasoned that the higher the MPO Ratio, the greater is the dispersion of community power; concomitantly, the lower the MPO Ratio, the more the concentration of community power.

Table 1 would seem to confirm Hawley's hypothesis. The higher the MPO Ratio (low concentration of power for Hawley), the lower the level of output in all three policy areas. Cities with high MPO Ratios are less likely to innovate than cities with low MPO Ratios.

Other data drawn from case studies contradict this interpretation of the meaning of the MPO Ratio, however. Aiken classified 31 case studies of community power (which are from among the 646 cities studied here) on a four-point scale of concentration of power ranging from «pyramidal» to «dispersed power» arrangements. Qualitative judgments of the number of groups involved in major issues in the community as reported by the original author, were used to estimate the degree of dispersion of power. The results show, first, that communities with diffused power have higher levels of innovation and outputs, and that cities having high MPO Ratios are more concentrated, not diffused as Hawley suggested.

We thus conclude that Hawley's empirical prediction is verified—cities with low MPO Ratios are indeed more innovative—but we question the meaning of the indicator of concentration of power that he used. To the extent to which the MPO Ratio measures concentration, it evidently reflects just the opposite of what he argued.

The second theory associated with the hypothesis that concentration of community power leads to greater innovation deals mainly with *citizen participation*. It has been argued by Crain and Rosenthal that the higher the level of education in a community, the higher the political participation, which in turn leads to higher conflict, producing stalemate and immobilization, and finally reduces innovation. The hypothesized relationship between the per cent of adults with a high school education and the three policy outputs (see Table 1) give strong support to this hypothesis.

While the empirical relationship between these variables is thus not in question, we question the interpretation of the meaning of this educational variable. Does a high level of educational attainment in a community reflect the presence of many well-educated, relatively affluent persons? Or does it reflect merely the absence of a poor and needy population? The correlation coefficients between per cent of adults with high school education and the upper extremes on the educational and income distribution—per cent of adults who have completed college and per cent of families with incomes of $10,000 or more per year—are .71 and .63, respectively. The correlation coefficients between the per cent of adults with four years of high school education and the lower extremes in these distributions—per cent of adults who have completed less than five years of education and the per cent of families with incomes of less than $3,000 per year—are .76

and .45, respectively. The interpretation of this variable thus depends on which end of the scale one wants to emphasize. Educational level can be used to measure either the level of poverty in a community or the size of an articulate and active middle-class.

In the analysis of 31 case studies of community power . . . it was found that cities with high educational levels were more centralized than those with low educational levels, although the relationship, it should be noted, was not a strong one. The same argument that has been made about the meaning of the MPO Ratio can be made about the meaning of the education variable, not only because of this finding, but also because of the extremely high relationship between the four year high school variable and the MPO Ratio ($r = .66$). Both of these are also strongly related to per cent white collar ($r = .87$ and .78, respectively). These are obviously measures of the degree of middle-class domination of a city, and in each case we find that middle-class cities have more centralized power arrangements than working-class cities. Clark's finding of a positive relationship between median educational level of a city and the degree of centralization of decision-making provides additional confirmation of our interpretation.

As we noted above, Crain and Rosenthal assume, without giving evidence, that a highly educated population participates more in local politics. If voting turnout can be regarded as a crude indicator of political participation, a recent study has shown that better educated cities have *lower* voting turnout than less well-educated cities. . . . We find, as shown in Table 1, that, among the 428 cities in our study for which data on voting turnout are available, *higher* voting turnout is associated with greater policy outputs in all three areas. At the very least, the hypothesis that greater participation reduces outputs is not supported. Thus, while our empirical relationships between level of education in a community and innovation and output are quite comparable to Crain and Rosenthal's findings, we have offered evidence that seriously questions their theoretical interpretation of this variable.

The third aspect of the concentration of power thesis is *elite participation*. The hypothesis here is that the fewer the number of influential persons in a community (and, by definition, the more concentrated power is in the political system), the easier it is to innovate. Although the community power literature has not dealt directly and systematically with innovation or policy outputs, the implied hypothesis by defenders of *both* the pluralist and the reputational schools is that the more centralized the political system, the greater its capacity to act. . . .

Few systematic comparative studies have been done of the concentration of community power which examined the number of actors in different issues and the consequences for community innovation. One study of 51 cities found that the greater the decentralization of community power as measured by the number of persons involved in decision-making in four issues (urban renewal, air pollution, poverty programs, and the selection of the mayor), the greater the number of urban renewal dollars per capita secured from the federal government. Clark concluded, contrary to his original hypothesis, that more decentralized communities had higher policy outputs, and advanced the new hypothesis that fragile decisions were more susceptible to blockage. The point that is relevant here is that decentralization led to higher outputs. And, as we have already seen, Aiken's coding of 31 case studies of community power into four levels of centralization came to the same conclusion.

In summary, . . . cities in which power is decentralized—whether from the systemic, citizen participation, or elite participation perspective—have greater policy outputs in public housing, urban renewal, and the War on Poverty.

Third, *centralization of formal political structure.* This argument has two aspects—one based on centralization of formal power and the second related to the political culture argument. In the first case, the thesis in the literature is that the more centralized the formal political structure, the more capable it is of policy outputs. There is some disagreement on what indicators of centralization should be used, since the usual conception of «reform» government is that its structural devices—the city manager form, nonpartisan elections, at-large elections, small city councils—were intended to centralize power in the hands of a small executive and a professional manager at the same time that potential power in the hands of citizen groups was fragmented and dispersed by removing the instruments of the political party and the ward organization. On the other hand, some have argued that strong political parties were the most effective device for centralizing power. But in either case, there was agreement that administrative or political centralization, regardless of its form, should lead to greater policy outputs. . . .

The second aspect of political structure is related to the political culture argument, because it has been argued that reform political institutions were part of the array of policies favored by groups with public-regarding values, and presumably the political instruments of such values should produce consequences similar to that of sheer demographic composition.

In most respects, the predictions which would be made by either the administrative centralization or political cultural interpretation of differences of formal structure would be the same. That is, the presence of a city manager, nonpartisan elections, at-large elections, and a small council should lead to greater policy outputs. The prediction is ambiguous only in the case of the form of election. If nonpartisan elections are regarded as decentralized, then, according to this line of reasoning, they should be associated with low outputs. But if they are regarded as instruments of groups with public-regarding values, then nonpartisan elections should be associated with high innovation and output.

Table 1 displays the correlations between four aspects of the formal political structure of American cities and three measures of policy outputs. The centralization argument is supported by none of these indicators, unless one wishes to accept the argument that partisan elections lead to administrative centralization and therefore higher levels of policy ouputs. The data support the latter proposition, but only that one. Manager cities with nonpartisan and at-large elections and small city councils either exhibit *lower* policy outputs than mayor-council cities with partisan and ward elections and large city councils, or there is no relationship.

As a corollary, the political culture argument which uses structural variation in form of government as indicators of the operation of dominant values also fails since the reform institutions are not more productive of outputs than the nonreform institutions.

Fourth, *community differentiation and continuity*. Larger and older cities have both greater structural differentiation and greater continuity. In the literature on community decision-making, it has been argued that larger and older cities are both more innovative and less innovative in two different studies. Each of these studies has focused on innovations in different issues and provided differing and contradictory theoretical explanations. Thomas Dye, . . . studying desegregation in 55 northern and southern cities . . . argued that larger cities were likely to be more bureaucratic and that . . . large bureaucracies have many built-in mechanisms to resist policy innovations. Older cities were immobilized because . . . over time persons and organizations adjust themselves to circumstances as they find them. And he did find greater segregation in older and larger cities, at least in the North, as the hypothesis would suggest.

On the other hand, a recent article dealing with public health organizations in 93 cities located in four Midwestern states and Ontario by Lawrence Mohr found that public health organizations in larger cities, which are usually older, were more innovative. (The relationship among the 676 cities included here is .54. Older cities are larger cities.) He explained this by arguing that a community decision organization such as a public health organization was larger in big cities, had more resources available, and, in such circumstances, innovative leadership was more likely to be effective. There are a number of studies of innovation in organizations that support the finding that larger organizations are more innovative.

The interpretations of the meaning of the age and size of cities are thus contradictory. On the one hand, it had been argued that older and larger cities are more rigid, more set in their ways, more complex and differentiated and, therefore, more incapable of action. On the other, such cities should be more adaptable, more experienced, and more flexible. The data in Table 1 show that older and larger cities have built more housing and obtained more urban renewal and poverty funds than have younger and smaller cities. The hypothesis that older and larger cities are less capable of adopting new programs is contradicted by these data.

Fifth, *community integration.* The argument here is that more highly integrated communities, i.e., those with highly developed networks of communication and contact among social groups, should suffer less from paralyzing conflict in the case of a new issue requiring decision, because on the one hand, channels of communication to work out compromises exist, and, on the other hand, isolated factions standing fast on their own position would not be present.

The indicators of community integration used by Pinard are quite diverse, and include several already mentioned here under other headings. . . . Low ethnicity, middle-class composition, low turnout, and small size are associated with *less* policy outputs, not more as would be predicted by the integration theory. In the case of unemployment and immigration, the thesis is that high unemployment levels will produce disintegration of community life by reducing attachments to community institutions, high conflict levels, and consequently low policy outputs. High levels of immigration will reduce integration by disrupting long-standing networks of communication and interchange among groups and organizations in a community. Contrary to expectation, low unemployment is associated with lower policy outputs, not higher (Table 1). The only indicator among these six that works in the predicted direction is immigration. Cities with high levels of immigration (which are hypothesized to be less well-integrated) do have lower outputs.

To summarize, few of the hypothesized relationships drawn from the literature discussed here are borne out completely, and we have argued that the theoretical interpretation of even most of these is questionable. The only exceptions are the hypothesized relationships with degree of immigraion and partisan elections (if the latter is interpreted to mean centralization of the formal political structure).

The main findings thus far are that older and larger cities, those with lower levels of education and income, fewer managers and officials, higher voting turnout and Democratic voting, a lower degree of inmigration, and higher unemployment levels have higher performance levels in all three policy areas.

The factor of community need must be taken into account at this point. Does the need of the community—as measured by unemployment, poverty, low education, poor housing—account for most of the statistical variation between communities in the degree and level of a particular type of output?

If so, this would be an extremely important finding indicating that need, whether manifest in political demands by the needy or in autonomous responses to need by political leaders regardless of demands, was the major source of policy outputs, regardless of the values of key groups, the concentration of power, or the integration of the community.

Table 1 thus includes some additional measures of the poverty and housing conditions among these 676 cities. Cities with more dilapidated housing in 1950, many poor families, many poorly educated adults, more high school dropouts, and many nonwhites were indeed more likely to have higher performance levels as reflected by the number of housing units per 100,000 population and urban renewal or War on Poverty dollars per capita.

But to point out these empirical relationships does not solve the problem of understanding why and how some communities secure these Federal resources and others do not. The mind is not set at rest by discovering that poorer, more needy cities have greater participation in these Federal programs. In the first place the relationships are not unusually strong. In the second place, the condition of housing or the number of poor families or per cent nonwhites alone does not tell us anything about the intervening processes which enabled some cities to mobilize local resources sufficiently to obtain Federal funds while others did not. We shall suggest an alternative interpretation of these data later.

We do not have space here to include the results of a wide variety of multivariate analyses which have been performed on the data in an attempt to isolate the variables which independently explain the most variance. . . .

From the analysis of these data, we have found that the same community characteristics—age of city, city size, per cent foreign stock, nonwhite composition, one or more community characteristics reflecting a high concentration of needy persons—are similarly and consistently related to the level of performance or output in each of three areas of community innovation—public housing, urban renewal, and the War on Poverty. Even though the mechanics of participating in each of these three Federal self-help programs is different, even though each requires different organizational arrangements in the local community, and even though they were started at different points in time—1933, 1949, 1964—the configuration of characteristics of communities innovating these programs is the same. At the outset of this paper we indicated that the level of performance or output was only one aspect of innovation. In the more detailed analysis of these data, we included two additional measures of innovation in each of these programs: the presence or absence of an innovation in each program and the speed of innovation in each program, i.e., the amount of time it took the community to enter the program, if it ever did, after it was possible to enter the program. The conclusions we reach from analysis of these data, but substituting these other measures, is the same as we have described above, with minor exceptions.

Thus, none of the theories discussed above seems to be appropriate for explaining community innovation in various federal self-help programs. . . . But if none of these are, what explanation can be offered for these results? We turn now to an alternative explanation of these data.

An Alternative Explanation

Let us start negatively by reviewing the rejected explanations. The global properties of political ethos, decentralization, and integration seemed to fare most poorly. That is, characterizations of the city as a whole, those which cannot be reduced to properties of groups and organizations, seem both to use concepts most removed from the available data and be supported most inadequately by them. If anything, the data seem to point in the direction of communities with high outputs having characteristics exactly opposite of centralization and integration. . . . An alternative theory of community policy outputs—at least for such programs as urban renewal, low-rent housing, the War on Poverty, and model cities—must begin with the proposition that successful performance in such programs is more frequently attained in decentralized, heterogeneous, and probably fragmented community systems.

Our tentative alternative explanation is that community outputs of the kind examined here must involve a two-level analysis. First, an explication of the kinds of community attributes which create the conditions for the development of certain types, number, and qualities of organizations that are critical for innovations of the type under discussion here, and, second, the kinds of attributes of organizations and their environments—or organization sets to use the term of William Evan—that facilitate the speed of implementation and subsequent performances of the innovation. To some extent these levels are the same thing examined from two points of view.

With respect to the first, . . . three properties of communities—structural differentiation, the accumulation of experience and information, and the stability and extensiveness of interorganizational networks—may contribute to the capacity of a community to generate policy outputs. While we have no direct measures of these properties and while these suggestions are only inferential, such imagery about the factors involved does appear to be consistent with our findings about the characteristics of communities that exhibit the greatest quantity of policy outputs.

Let us turn to concepts and hypotheses suitable for the second perspective, that of characteristics of organizational structures and their interorganizational field. . . .

One could hypothesize that the greater the number of centers of power in a community and the pervasive and encompassing are the interfaces in the community system, the higher the probability that a community innovation in a given issue arena will occur. The reasoning has been partially alluded to before. The more choice among units in the system—centers of power—and the greater the state of information about organizational actors, the higher the probability that a coalition sufficient to make a decision will take place.

In addition, the extent to which the interorganizational field is «turbulent» may also influence policy outputs. Where many people are moving out of a community, the existing historically developed network of organizational relationships may be relatively undisturbed, except insofar as the fact of migration out indicates an economic or perhaps political crisis which existing institutions cannot handle. Conversely, where many people are moving in, bringing with them different ideas about the appropriate functions of local government, and perhaps creating demands for new services, newly established organizations may be severely limited since they are less likely to have established organizational networks available to them which can aid in achieving an adequate level of coordination.

One aspect of this increased capacity to coordinate over time will be the emergence of specialized centers of power—community decision organizations—whose function it is to initiate special types of innovation, mobilize support for them, and either carry out the activities required by the decision or else organize and supervise those agencies charged with such activities. And, of course, the characteristics of these organizations such as extensive interorganizational ties, professionalism of staff, degree of internal differentiation, or number of resources available, to name only a few, will also be critical to understand the quality and quantity of policy outputs. Community action agencies, housing authorities, welfare councils, and health departments are examples of such organizations.

The community decision organization, then, becomes a special type of center of power whose mission it is to supervise the planning, coordination, and delivery of a community function or activity. There is a very high likelihood that the professional staffs of such organizations will generate future innovations. . . .

CONCLUSIONS

What these disparate findings suggest is that the independent variables explaining community innovation must be disaggregated. The concepts normally used to explain community behavior may reify the diversity of community structures which sponsor and carry through actions. Global concepts such as centralization, integration, or ethos may hinder the comparative analysis of urban political and governmental processes. Concepts recognizing the fundamental diversity and differentiation of cities should be incorporated into the basic analytic framework.

The utility of the data and findings reported here is that ultimately they can be used as a basis of sampling for the third type of study discussed at the outset of this paper, that is, a comparative community study in which the intervening process of community decision-making is the key focus of the research. In such a research enterprise, the data and findings in the present study could be used to select a sample that is not only characteristic of given region or size categories, but also a sample of cities having high and low potential for outputs in these various policy areas as well as high and low performance. . . .

Another procedure that could be used in sampling would be based on the calculation of residuals in regression analysis. Within a given size or region category, for example, at least three types of cities could be identified: a) over-performers, b) under-performers, and c) normal-performers, at least as predicted by a set of key independent variables in a regression analysis. These are only two possible ways of establishing a sampling frame. The data and findings reported here as well as other data about American cities that are currently in the community data bank of the Social Science Data and Program Library Service of the University of Wisconsin could be used in designing comparative research projects on American communities. This approach, of course, might also be fruitfully applied to research on communities in other societies.

But, of course, these comments leave open the question of the most appropriate theoretical perspective for research on community decision-making. We are of the opinion that the understanding of community decisions of the kind included in this report are best approached with two level of analysis. The aggregated properties of community system—structural differentiation, historical continuity, communication networks—can explain the emergence of different types of organizational forms and inter-organizational systems. The properties of organizations and their environments help explain the specific character and level of community policy outputs. Our data do not permit us to test the validity of our tentative explanations, which are essentially attempts to theorize about the nature of the processes intervening between gross attributes of community structure about which comparative data are readily available and public policy outputs. At minimum, this particular theoretical sketch explains policy outputs (at least in these three Federal programs) better than any of other theories we have examined.

COMMUNITY STRUCTURE, DECISION-MAKING, BUDGET EXPENDITURES, AND URBAN RENEWAL IN 51 AMERICAN COMMUNITIES

Terry N. Clark

In the following article, one of the most ambitious community power studies published to date, Terry N. Clark seeks to identify patterns of decision making in fifty-one American cities and to determine (1) what community characteristics explain the variations he finds in the distribution of influence and (2) whether certain public policies can be accounted for by variations in community structures and in patterns of decision making.

As Chapter Five of this book indicates, a key problem in the study of community power has been the problem of identifying the wielders of community influence and their interrelationships. In his research, Clark has utilized a blend of the reputational and decisional approaches to locating leadership patterns. Recognizing that multi-community studies are very expensive and very exhausting, the reader will want to ask whether Clark's technique provides a reasonably accurate picture of community decision-making patterns.

Two other problems of large-scale comparative research are met by Clark, and his success in dealing with them warrant evaluation. First, is Clark's selection of community characteristics and his operational measure of them satisfactory? Second, does Clark's selection of issues (or outputs) allow one to generalize his findings to the community in general?

Reprinted from Frederick M. Wirt, ed., *Future Directions in Community Power Research: A Colloquium* (Berkeley: Institute of Governmental Studies, University of California, 1971), with permission of the author and the publisher. Other reports by the author, deriving from the project upon which this article is based, include "Urban Typologies and Political Outputs," in Brian J. L. Berry, ed., *City Classification Handbook* (New York: John Wiley-Interscience, 1972), pp. 152–178; Clark, "The Structure of Community Influence," in Harlan Hahn, ed., *People and Politics in Urban Society, Urban Affairs Annual Reviews*, 6 (Beverly Hills: Sage, 1972), 283–313; Clark, "Structural Functionalism, Exchange Theory, and the New Political Economy," *Sociological Inquiry*, 42 (Summer, 1973).

. . . To determine "Who Governs," it [is] necessary also to ascertain "Where," "When," and "With What Effects."[1] This series of questions focused attention on those structural characteristics of a community that predispose it toward one or another pattern of decisionmaking. The new questions also disposed of an apt criticism of the earlier studies, that they failed to portray the impact of one or another pattern of decisionmaking on concrete community outputs. That is, a community's influence structure is best understood by examining what caused it to develop as well as the consequences of its activity.

. . . The [procedure] most satisfactory for testing comparative propositions is the quantitative study of large numbers of communities, with the collection of identical data in each case, and the use of directly comparable research methods. While the value of this procedure has been recognized for some time, only recently has it been possible to mobilize the necessary human and financial resources for its application.

. . .

This paper reports on such an undertaking, one in which 51 American communities were investigated by the field staff of the National Opinion Research Center at the University of Chicago, in the largest study of its kind to date. . . .

The 51 communities were sampled on the basis of region and population size. . . . Representing 22 different states, cities in the population range of 50,000–750,000 were selected in order to eliminate the somewhat unique metropolises and the smaller communities for which basic census-type statistics were not readily available. . . . They varied also in selected measures of socioeconomic levels, governmental policy, and organizational life. . . .

In addition to these data from central sources, other material was drawn from a series of interviews on matters such as political organization and decision making. In earlier studies, and on the basis of preliminary field-work in several communities, we had found about a dozen persons from different sectors particularly well informed about local affairs. These were not necessarily the most active participants, but were generally knowledgeable informants. To collect as much information as possible, so as to maximize reliability and validity while minimizing costs, we decided to interview 11 strategically placed informants in each community. These were: the mayor, the chairmen of the Democratic and Republican parties, the president of the largest bank, the editor of the newspaper with the largest circulation, the president of the Chamber of Commerce, the presi-

---

[1] Cf. Terry N. Clark, "Power and Community Structure: Who Governs, Where, and When?" *The Sociological Quarterly*, 8(3): 291–316 (1967), and the works cited there.

dent of the bar association, the head of the largest labor union, the health commissioner, the urban renewal director and the director of the last major hospital fund drive. . . .

To maintain comparability, informants in each community were interviewed about the same four issues: urban renewal, the election of the mayor, air pollution and the antipoverty program. These four were selected because they tended to involve different types of community actors in differing relationships with one another. . . .

All four issue areas need the support of local government to implement basic decisions. And, of course, insofar as any decision-making structure exists within a community, it will channel and redirect the activities within these various areas.[2] But it is just this decision-making structure that is illuminated by comparison of the patterns of influence in the four different issue areas.

. . .

We attempted to measure the community decision-making structure by using what we termed "the ersatz decisional method." We examined the number of major actors involved in each issue area, and the degree to which decision makers overlapped from one issue area to the next. For each issue area, we posed a series of questions that focused on these points:

(1) Who initiated action on the issue?
(2) Who supported this action?
(3) Who opposed this action?[3]
(4) What was the nature of the bargaining process? Who negotiated with whom?
(5) What was the outcome? Whose views tended to prevail?

The cross classification of the five decisional stages with the four issue areas generated for each community a 20-cell matrix, which furnished the basis for our index of centralization.

Most theoretical discussions of centralization of authority, pluralism (here understood as decentralization), and related concepts have isolated the two basic dimensions included in our index. The first is *participation:* the larger the number of actors involved in community decision-making, the greater the decentralization. Second is *overlap:* the less similar the cluster of actors in one issue area are to those in adjoining issue areas, the greater the decentralization.

To combine these conceptual dimensions in a single index, we counted

[2]We understand by *decision-making structure* the patterned distribution of *influence* exercised in a community, in contrast to the patterned distribution of *resources*, which is better referred to as a *power-structure*.

[3]If there were more than two "sides" to an issue, the third (or fourth) side was treated as a second (or third) distinct "opponent."

the number of actors named by our informants, but we counted each actor only once even if he was named in more than one issue area. Then, because a particular issue area did not exist in a few communities, . . . after we had obtained the number of actors by summing as described above, we divided by the number of issue areas present in the community. . . .

Consider first a situation regarded as that of a highly centralized or monolithic community: the mayor initiated action on a decision, was supported by the downtown businessmen and opposed by the labor unions and the newspaper. The mayor was the major entrepreneur in bargaining among the various groups, and the mayor-businessmen coalition prevailed. Under such circumstances, the total number of actors in the issue would be four: mayor, businessmen, labor unions and newspaper. If these same four actors, again playing the same roles, were the only ones involved in three other issues, there would still only be a total of four actors in all issue areas. Dividing the number of actors by the number of issue areas, would yield a final score for the community of one. This centralized community would thus rank near the bottom of our scale of decentralization.

On the other hand, if we consider a situation generally regarded as more decentralized, where, for example, five different actors were involved in each of four issue areas, the total number of actors would be 20, and, dividing by the number of issue areas, the community score would come to five. Applying this same procedure, we computed a decentralization score for each of the 51 communities. These scores are presented in Table 1.

There were a number of ambiguities and problems in dealing with the centralization of decision-making. One was the problem of identifying distinct actors. For example, in one community three labor leaders might be named as actors, while in another only "the labor unions" would be specified. We reasoned that different individuals closely similar in status should not be counted the same as three individuals from three differing sectors of the community. Therefore we devised a code of some 73 community statuses and considered that a separate actor would be counted for each status named. But two persons occupying the same status were counted only once. A single individual could thus be counted as two actors if he were named in two different issues as the occupant of two distinct statuses, e.g., county judge and chairman of a neighborhood organization. Some might disagree with this interpretation, but we reasoned that it was more logical to weight by the involvement of community institutions, rather than by the involvement of individuals.

Another ambiguity arose from conflicting or missing information from different informants. Our solution was to count each new status mentioned by any informant as nominating a new actor. But if a status were mentioned several times by different informants, it was counted only once. There were, however, slight but systematic differences in the number of

TABLE 1   Index Scores of Decentralized Decision-Making Structures for the 51 Communities

0.	Akron, Ohio	7.50	26.	Milwaukee, Wis.	7.75
1.	Albany, N.Y.	6.63	27.	Minneapolis, Minn.	8.00
2.	Amarillo, Texas	3.33	28.	Newark, N.J.	9.13
3.	Atlanta, Ga.	6.50	29.	Palo Alto, Calif.	6.50
4.	Berkeley, Calif.	5.92	30.	Pasadena, Calif.	5.50
5.	Birmingham, Ala.	5.88	31.	Phoenix, Ariz.	7.75
6.	Bloomington, Minn.	4.45	32.	Pittsburgh, Penn.	7.75
7.	Boston, Mass.	7.25	33.	St. Louis, Mo.	8.00
8.	Buffalo, N.Y.	8.67	34.	St. Paul, Minn.	8.50
9.	Cambridge, Mass.	8.67	35.	St. Petersburg, Fla.	6.75
10.	Charlotte, N.C.	6.25	36.	Salt Lake City, Utah	7.13
11.	Clifton, N.J.	5.90	37.	San Francisco, Calif.	7.75
12.	Duluth, Minn.	5.25	38.	Santa Ana, Calif.	6.50
13.	Euclid, Ohio	6.93	39.	San Jose, Calif.	5.63
14.	Fort Worth, Texas	6.75	40.	Santa Monica, Calif.	6.33
15.	Fullerton, Calif.	6.45	41.	Schenectady, N.Y.	5.75
16.	Gary, Ind.	6.75	42.	Seattle, Wash.	7.50
17.	Hamilton, Ohio	6.00	43.	South Bend, Ind.	7.00
18.	Hammond, Ind.	7.75	44.	Tampa, Fla.	8.25
19.	Indianapolis, Ind.	9.00	45.	Tyler, Texas	7.67
20.	Irvington, N.J.	7.67	46.	Utica, N.Y.	9.38
21.	Jacksonville, Fla.	6.25	47.	Waco, Texas	3.25
22.	Long Beach, Calif.	4.75	48.	Warren, Mich.	5.50
23.	Malden, Mass.	8.50	49.	Waterbury, Conn.	8.75
24.	Manchester, N.H.	4.97	50.	Waukegan, Ill.	7.67
25.	Memphis, Tenn.	6.38			

Note: Mean score for the 51 communities = 6.792.

actors named by different informants. For this reason, we constructed weights for the different informants, based on the mean number of actors they named who were not mentioned by any other informant. The weights were constructed for informants in the 36 communities where no informants were missing. Then, in the 15 communities where one or more informants were unavailable for an interview, the centralization index score for that community was increased by the amount of the weight for the missing informant(s).

Still other questions arose from what might be termed the dynamics of the decision-making process: within a given issue area, how should one perceive the relationships between the various stages of a decision? Is initiating action more important than supporting it? Does a heavy involvement of actors at the opposition stage imply greater conflict and a more decentralized decision-making process? If the answers to these two questions were clear affirmatives, they would imply, methodologically, a disproportionate weighting of the actors involved at the initiation and opposition stages. But given the absence in this area of any theory sufficiently rigorous to permit the researcher to assign specific weights, we made the conservative choice of assigning equal value to each actor in the issue area, regardless of the stage at which he became involved.

COMMUNITY STRUCTURE, DECISIONMAKING AND OUTPUTS

An earlier article formulated a series of 34 propositions relating community structural characteristics (including the demographic, economic, legal–political, cultural) to centralized and decentralized patterns of decision making. Subsequently refining certain of these propositions, we added several others relating decision-making patterns to outputs, and subsumed a number of the discrete propositions under a more general formulation:

> The greater the horizontal and vertical differentiation in a social system and the greater the differentiation between potential elites, the more decentralized the decision-making structure. Without the establishment of integrative mechanisms, this condition leads to less coordination between sectors and a lower level of outputs.

The empirical analysis reported here was primarily oriented toward testing the earlier propositions and the general formulation. We therefore focused on variables for which some theoretical proposition had already been developed, although we were prepared to include others that might account for significant differences in any of the dependent variables.

. . .

We inspected a large zero order correlation matrix and isolated variables about which we had specific hypotheses or which correlated highly with the measure of centralization of decisionmaking. Because there was a high intercorrelation of many variables, we performed a series of factor analyses to isolate clusters of variables; then from each cluster, we selected one or two with high factor loadings. Performance of regression analyses reduced the number of independent variables still further. We ended with eight, which together generated multiple correlation coefficients of .475 to .840 with centralization of decisionmaking and the two policy output variables. Before proceeding, let us briefly review each of the variables and output measures utilized.

$X_1 = $ *Population size.*

$X_2 = $ *Community poverty:* percent of population with incomes under $3,000, percent with fewer than five years of education, percent unemployed, and percent nonwhite. Since all four measures were highly intercorrelated, we simplified the analysis by using percent with income under $3,000 as an indicator for this cluster.

$X_3 = $ *Industrial activity:* percent of manufacturing establishments in the community with more than 20 employees.

X_4 = *Economic diversification:* classification of communities ranked by Nelson as diversified or financial as distinct from all other communities.[4]

X_5 = *Highly educated population:* median years of schooling completed by the community residents.

X_6 = *Catholic population:* number of members of the Roman Catholic Church in the county, standardized by county population size.

V = *Civic voluntary organization activity:* number of community members in the League of Women Voters, standardized by community population size.

W = *Index of governmental reformism:* constructed from the three governmental characteristics traditionally associated in the United States with "reform" government: professional city manager, nonpartisan elections, and at-large electoral constituencies. Communities with varying combinations of these characteristics were scored as follows:
    3 = manager government, nonpartisan elections, at-large electoral constituencies
    2 = any two of these characteristics
    1 = any one of these characteristics
    0 = none of these characteristics

Y = *Decentralized decision-making structure:* the number and overlap of decisionmakers.

Z_1 = *General budget expenditures:* total budget expenditures of the local community government, standardized by population size.

Z_2 = *Urban renewal expenditures:* total expenditures from federal and local sources on urban renewal projects in the community, up to 1965, standardized by population size.

To test our propositions and evaluate the relative importance of each variable in the model, we computed the relationships among all variables, utilizing a graphic variation of multiple regression analysis: path analysis. The reader is referred to the works cited for a more general consideration of the method. We note here only that path analysis is a procedure for representing a causal model of the relationships among a number of different variables. Arrows pointing in the direction of assumed causation connect the variables to one another. Straight arrows represent lines of causation, while double-headed bowed arrows indicate simple intercorrelations not implying dependency relationships. The numerical figure above each arrow leading away from a variable represents the separate contribution made by that variable in each of the directions indicated. Path coefficients may vary from + 1 to − 1, a negative sign indicating a negative contribution. In addition to these arrows connecting interrelated variables, there is an arrow for a residual error term for each variable dependent on others in the model. Residual error terms may vary from 1 to 0. The larger the error

---

[4]A dummy variable format was used when correlating qualitative with quantitative variables.

term, the smaller the amount of variance in the dependent variable that is explained by the model.[5]

Although over a long enough period none of the variables is without some influence on the others, at any given time we can without undue difficulty order most of the variables in a causal sequence.[6] Six variables relate to the demographic composition and economic base of the community and, for the present analysis, may be conceived as generally constant: (a) population size, (b) community poverty, (c) industrial activity, (d) economic diversification, (e) educational level of the population, and (f) per cent of the population that is Catholic. We shall examine in turn the impact of each of these independent variables on five dependent variables: (1) the level of civic voluntary organization activity, (2) the form of government, (3) patterns of community decision-making, (4) general budget expenditures, and (5) urban renewal expenditures.

Civic Voluntary Organization Activity

As one would fully expect from the literature on voluntary organizations, the educational level of the population strongly influences the level of civic voluntary organization activity. The second most influential variable was not so predictable: the size of the Catholic population. While the per cent of the community residents who were Roman Catholics shows no zero order correlation with voluntary organization activity, the influence becomes quite sizeable when other variables in the model are controlled. The impact of the extent of poverty changed even more radically from the zero order relation: from a − .269 correlation (Table 2) to a + .311 path coefficient (Figure 1). We might interpret this finding as suggesting that potential members of the League of Women Voters generally do not reside in areas with extensive poverty; but when there is poverty in their communities, they tend to become active in civic affairs.

[5]Figures I through V, when superimposed upon one another, constitute a complete path analysis diagram with all traditional elements included. The difficulties of reading such a complex diagram led us to break it down into five separate parts, each of which corresponds to a single dependent variable.

Each of the five tables also contains the corresponding regression equation, including the intercept, the unstandardized regression coefficients for each variable, and (in parentheses) the standard error of each regression cofficient. Linear least squares regression was used in every case except for ethnicity, for only a few variables were sufficiently skewed to justify transformation.

[6]There are one or two cases that follow in which the causal sequence is not as clear-cut as indicated by the path analysis diagrams. While fully recognizing this point, we felt that it was valuable to attempt causal statements wherever possible, instead of speaking merely in terms of associations. Our interpretations may then be more directly validated or revised by future studies.

TABLE 2   Correlations and Path Coefficients for Civic Voluntary Organization Activity

Dependent Variable: Civic Voluntary Organization Activity: V

Independent Variable	Zero Order Correlation	Path Coefficient
Highly educated population: X_5	.490	.744
Catholic population: X_6	.083	.369
Community poverty: X_2	−.269	.311
Economic diversification: X_4	−.335	−.232
Industrial activity: X_3	.049	.213
Population size: X_1	−.427	−.208

$R = .699$ Variance explained = 43%[a]

$$V^b = -1031.8581 - 0.000122\, X_1 + 5.8659\, X_2 + 3.5166\, X_3$$
$$\quad\quad (0.000079)\quad (2.9738)\quad (2.0055)$$

$$-58.3283\, X_4 + 85.2983\, X_5 + 3.0859\, X_6$$
$$(33.8527)\quad (17.6693)\quad (1.2286)$$

[a]In the subsequent tables, Variance explained refers to the R^2 corrected for the number of independent variables, not the simple R^2.

[b]Regression coefficients unstandardized; standard errors in parentheses.

Reform Government

Our findings about the socioeconomic correlates of reform government characteristics are generally similar to those reported by earlier students of the subject. The most influential variable by far is the educational level of the population: more highly educated populations tend to have reform governments. As Wolfinger and Field point out, this is most characteristic of western communities: our index correlated .645 with a dummy variable representing communities in the western states.

We should call attention, however, to the relationships between reformism and two variables not utilized by earlier authors. The correlation (zero order) with reformism of per cent Catholic is − .425, and that of civic activity is .276. Both of these relationships would seem to offer support for the traditional "public regardingness" thesis. However, when the other variables (other than region) in the model are introduced, the relationships between these two variables and reformism virtually disappear.

This should presumably be interpreted as implying that when Catholics move into communities (in the West or elsewhere) with highly educated populations, they assimilate a political culture of reformism. Correspondingly, potential League members in such communities may become less active, because they are reasonably content that the victory for reform has already been won. Still, the present data force these interpretations to remain highly tentative.

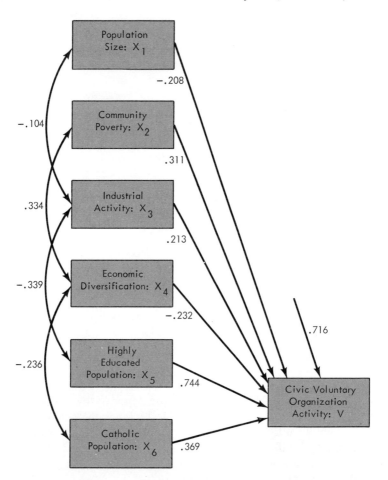

FIGURE 1 PATH COEFFICIENTS FOR CIVIC VOLUNTARY ORGAN-
IZATION ACTIVITY

Decentralization of Decision-Making Structure

As indicated above, the present study was oriented principally toward investigating the causes and consequences of community decision-making
patterns. Correspondingly, a larger number of specific propositions had
been formulated in this area than in others. Because the more general theoretical considerations concerning each proposition have been treated in
detail elsewhere, the presentation here is limited to the propositions and to
a discussion of whether the data, shown in Table 3 and Figure 2, supported them.

An hypothesis that has been advanced on several occasions is that *the larger the number of inhabitants in the community, the more decentralized the decision-making structure.*[7] But when it was subjected to empirical test, the proposition was not substantiated—to the great dismay, generally, of those forced to present the results. We found that the earlier hypothesis, while showing some support in zero order correlation between the variables of size and decentralization, loses all support in path analysis.

But for most of us who have theorized about population size, the crucial variable is not size alone, but various associated phenomena, with structural differentiation perhaps foremost. With increasing size, more differentiation appears in more community institutions—economic, political and cultural. Differentiation in the economic sphere has led to the following proposition: *The more diverse the economic structures within a community, the more decentralized the decision-making structure.* Here too, however, empirical support has often been lacking. But once again our findings support the theorized relationship: the more economically diversified communities definitely have more decentralized decision-making structures.

Although differentiation of governmental institutions is less clear than differentiation in the economic sector, reform government could be interpreted as tending toward a less differentiated pattern than the "unreformed" alternatives of our index. That is, reform government is less differentiated when political institutions are considered as a distinct subsystem of the total community. Further, we must recognize that the political subsystem generally, and reform government institutions more specifically, are im-

[7]For documentation, see Clark, "Power and Community Structure" (note 1 above).

TABLE 3 Correlations and Path Coefficients for Decentralized Decision-Making Structure

Dependent Variable: Decentralized Decision-Making Structure: Y

Independent Variable	*Zero Order Correlation*	*Path Coefficient*
Index of reform government: W	−.548	−.586
Economic diversification: X_4	.347	.477
Industrial activity: X_3	−.008	−.213
Community poverty: X_2	−.031	−.220
Highly educated population: X_5	−.332	−.061
Civic voluntary organization activity: V	−.275	.105
Population size: X_1	.384	.066
Catholic population: X_6	.254	.000

R = .738   Variance explained = 47%

$$Y^a = 11.5429 + .0000 X_1 - .0462 X_2 - .0393 X_3$$
$$\quad\quad (.000001)\quad (.0273)\quad\quad (.0219)$$

$$+ 1.3340 X_4 - .2062 X_5 + .0012 V - .6959 W$$
$$(.3751)\quad\quad (.2254)\quad\quad (.0015)\quad (.1748)$$

[a]Regression coefficients unstandardized; standard errors in parentheses.

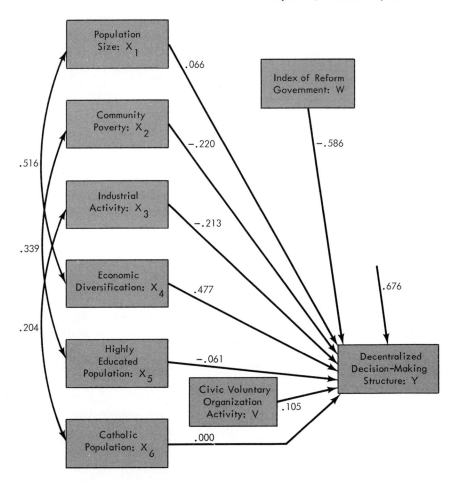

FIGURE 2 PATH COEFFICIENTS FOR DECENTRALIZED DECISION-
MAKING STRUCTURE

portant mechanisms of integration for the community system. These considerations suggest that reform governmental characteristics should lead to
more centralized patterns of decision-making, as indeed they do. Reform
government has the strongest relationship with centralization of any variable in the model.

Reform government, in turn, is strongly correlated with a highly educated population. But the zero correlation of education with decentralization is negative. This would seem, at first, to contradict our proposition that
*the higher the educational level of community residents, the more pluralistic
the decision-making structure.* When the other variables in the model are
introduced the negative association disappears, but the proposition is still
not supported.

Another variable closely related to a highly educated population is the level of civic voluntary activity. We had postulated that *the greater the density of voluntary organizations in the community, the more decentralized the decision-making structure.* The negative zero order correlation between civic activity and decentralization implies rejection of the proposition, but in the causal model, the relationship—although quite weak—was positive. Highly educated populations thus tend to lead to both reform governments and higher levels of civic activity. But while the first tends toward centralization of decision-making, the second may tend toward decentralization. Correspondingly, the general proposition about higher education leading to decentralization is not supported by the present evidence. But the intermediate links in the causal chain need to be specified more precisely before the proposition can be verified or rejected.

A final proposition that we were able to test suggested that *the higher the degree of industrialization in a community, the more decentralized the decision-making structure.* The path coefficient in our model, while not very strong, suggests the opposite relationship. Even if strongly negative, however, the substantive meaning of such a finding would not be self-evident. By international standards, the United States is obviously a highly industrialized country. But the effects of industrialization implied by the proposition do not necessarily make themselves felt in the geographic areas immediately surrounding large industrial installations. The more indirect consequences of industrialization—wealth, leisure time, education, more harmonious social relations—are apparently more important in effecting a decentralized pattern of decision-making than industrial activity per se. When these indirect benefits are separated ecologically from industrial establishments, the relationship stated in the proposition will no longer hold.

. . .

Policy Outputs: General Budget and Urban Renewal Expenditures

Until quite recently, neither theoretical nor empirical work on community decision-making was concerned with systematically relating decision-making patterns to policy outputs. Consequently, the number of propositions in this area was smaller than those predicting patterns of decision-making from community structural characteristics.

One basic proposition mentioned in the general formulation above, is that *the more centralized the decision-making structure, the higher the level of outputs.* But our findings in Table 4 . . . , with regard to both general budget and urban renewal expenditures, were precisely the opposite of those predicted by this proposition. The fact that certain studies have supported the proposition suggests that while it is not necessarily wrong, it is probably incomplete and may apply only to certain types of decisions.

TABLE 4   Correlations and Path Coefficients for the Dependent
Variable: Urban Renewal Expenditures

Dependent Variable: Urban Renewal Expenditures: Z_2

Independent Variable	Zero Order Correlation	Path Coefficient
Catholic population: X_6	.454	.620
Community poverty: X_2	.136	.527
Population size: X_1	.392	.341
Decentralized decision-making structure: Y	.350	.291
Highly educated population: X_5	−.297	.282
Economic diversification: X_4	.050	−.235
Industrial activity: X_3	.119	.181
Index of reform government: W	−.308	.052
Civic voluntary organization activity: V	−.051	.025
Residual		.708

R   = .705   Variance explained = 40%

$$Z_2{}^a = -581.9180 + .001\ X_1 + 6.7657\ X_2 + 2.0347\ X_3 - 40.1232\ X_4$$
$$\phantom{Z_2{}^a = -581.9180 + }(.00006)\quad (2.2836)\quad (1.5096)\quad (28.0434)$$

$$+ 22.0305\ X_5 + 3.5293\ X_6 + .0169\ V + \ 3.8038\ W + 17.7491\ Y$$
$$(17.2175)\quad (.9209)\quad (.1061)\quad (13.4547)\quad (10.0208)$$

[a]Regression coefficients unstandardized; standard errors in parentheses.

The concept of fragility. Earlier studies supporting the proposition have examined such decisions as fluoridation, school desegregation and urban renewal. These types of decisions have one characteristic that apparently differentiates them from our two policy outputs: their *fragility.* Fluoridation studies have continually stressed the difficulty of implementing fluoridation programs after they have come under attack by outspoken local community groups. The same is true of school desegregation. And, if we are to judge from the earlier case studies of urban renewal programs, and the quantitative data for the 1950's presented by Hawley, this would seem to have been the case for urban renewal as well, at least until recently.

Since an important component of fragility is a program's newness to a community, all things being equal, fragility should decrease over time. For with time, community residents become increasingly accustomed to the presence of an activity; the people associated with the program establish continuing relationships with other community sectors; initial projects are completed, and later projects improved. In effect, the program activities become legitimatized. The issues of school desegregation and urban renewal both seem to have become less fragile than they were a decade ago.

A small but discontented group is much more likely to be able to find a sympathetic ear among the leadership in a decentralized community than in a more centralized community, where the leadership is strong enough to ignore mild opposition. In the case of a sufficiently fragile issue, the active opposition of even a small discontented group may delay or halt action. A weak government, or one that requires the participation and active consent of many supporting groups, is more likely to have difficulty in carrying out fragile decisions than would a stronger one. Or, slightly restated, *for fragile decisions, the more centralized the decision-making structure, the higher the level of outputs.*

Insofar as budget construction and more established urban renewal programs may be classified as less fragile decisions, their size should increase with decentralization of the decision-making structure. This we found to be the case.

The influence of Catholicism. Decentralization of decision-making, however, is not the only factor behind budget and urban renewal expenditures in American communities. By far the most influential variable affecting community budget expenditures has been virtually ignored by every major study of which we are aware. This variable is the percent of the community residents who are members of the Roman Catholic Church. The zero order correlation of percent Catholic and budget expenditures was high—.610— but instead of declining in importance when the other variables in the model were introduced, as might be expected, a phenomenally strong path coefficient of .922 was generated. This was the strongest single path coefficient in our entire analysis. The path coefficient from per cent Catholic to urban renewal expenditures (Table 5) was not quite so impressive, but for budgets it was easily the strongest single path. As suggested above, the figures used for religious affiliation have remained unknown to most social

TABLE 5   Correlations and Path Coefficients for General Budget Expenditures

Dependent Variable: General Budget Expenditures: Z_1

Independent Variable	Zero Order Correlation	Path Coefficient
Catholic population: X_6	.610	.922
Index of reform government: W	−.015	.521
Community poverty: X_2	−.100	.422
Economic diversification: X_4	−.045	−.408
Decentralized decision-making structure: Y	.237	.394
Highly educated population: X_5	−.057	.382
Population size: X_1	.310	.369
Civic voluntary organization activity: V	.042	−.126
Industrial activity: X_3	−.062	.097

R   = .840   Variance explained = 66%

$Z_1{}^a$ = −459.3432 + .0001 X_1 + 3.8870 X_2 + .7850 X_3 − 50.0548 X_4
        (.00003)   (1.2558)   (.8301)   (15.4211)

    + 21.4175 X_5 + 3.7679 X_6 − .0618 V + 27.1004 W + 17.2776 Y
     (9.4679)   (.5064)   (.0584)   (7.3988)   (5.5105)

[a]Regression coefficients unstandardized; standard errors in parentheses.

scientists although they are not new. That they are somewhat outdated, and necessarily somewhat inexact, should simply lower their correlations with other variables. But that such strong relationships persist even with a crude measure seems remarkable testimony to the importance of a hitherto neglected variable.

How are we to explain these findings? Our first reaction was that there may have been errors in the data, but all figures were checked twice and found to be correct. Our second concern was multicollinearity. . . .

Searching for factors that might be more significant than Catholicism alone in explaining high community expenditures, we introduced into our standard regression model, one or two at a time, variables of region, population density, various measures of industrial activity, percent of Protestants and Jews in the population, the party of the mayor, and percent Democratic vote in the SMSA in 1960. But none of these factors, to our surprise, seriously decreased the impact of percent Catholic membership. The path coefficient from percent Catholic to budget expenditures never dropped below .680.

Per cent Catholic was also quite consistently influential when expenditures on separate budget items were analyzed, instead of the general budget figure. . . .

We then tried to specify what kinds of Catholics were most likely to spend public funds. Much of the literature on ethnic politics suggests that, among Catholics, it is the Irish who have been most consistently involved in politics. . . .

. . . With Irish as a percentage of the total community population included in our model, the path coefficient for percent Catholic dropped to .362; the path coefficient for Irish was .501. No other national group or combination of national groups significantly decreased the percent of Catholic relationship. The distinctiveness of Irish Catholics, at least with regard to this issue, suggests that the practice, currently widespread in discussions of city politics, of lumping together persons under such categories as "ethnics," "immigrants," or even "private-regarding" groups, may be highly misleading.

It has been abundantly documented in public opinion studies that Catholics prefer the Democratic over the Republican party, are favorably disposed toward increased governmental activities, and support more extensive welfare state activities. However, the special importance of *Irish* Catholicism in influencing actual policy outcomes has, to our knowledge, not been demonstrated in such striking fashion previously. It is to be hoped that future studies will more often include religious and national background variables in their analysis.

Other variables. But let us compare our findings somewhat more systematically with those reported by earlier research on community budget expenditures. Probably the most frequently analyzed variables are those associated with wealth. That association is invariably high and positive, whether the expenditures are linked to measures of personal income or to assessed property valuations of communities. These results concur with our .382 path coefficient from education (which is highly associated with measures of wealth) to budget expenditures; the coefficient was .337 from education to urban renewal expenditures. (The path coefficient for median income, when substituted in the model for median education, was lower than for education.)

Most of the rest of our findings, however, differ from earlier research. Studies of suburbs around New York and Philadelphia, for example, showed that measures of the industrial activity of the community were extremely important in explaining governmental expenditure levels. Our findings suggest that the tendency of one community to spend more than others nearby (by taxing its industries) is more a specifically suburban phenomenon. Various measures of industrial activity—the per capita number of manufacturing establishments with more than 20 employees, per capita value added by manufacturing, per cent of industrial establishments with 20 or more employees—were introduced one at a time into our model, but all were of minimal importance.

Hawley observed several years ago that the proportion of the SMSA population residing in the central city was more important in predicting budget expenditures than the actual city population, and Brazer reported the same relationship for large American cities. This proportion was not important for our sample, however, presumably because we included more small and independent communities.

The other variables that exercised some influence on budget expenditures were reform government (positively), economic diversification (negatively), the size of the poverty sector (positively), and the total population size (positively). Voluntary organization activity, however, showed no impact on budget or urban renewal expenditures. Apropos of the explanatory importance of many of our noneconomic variables, some of the recent studies by economists and economics-oriented political scientists would be more useful if they considered such noneconomic variables more systematically.

CONCLUSION

   . . . These findings, on the whole, supported our general formulation: *The greater the horizontal and vertical differentiation in a social system, the greater the differentiation between potential elites and the more decentralized the decision-making structure. Without the establishment of integrative mechanisms, this leads to less coordination between sectors and a lower level of outputs.*

Horizontal differentiation of basic community structures was best reflected in the economic sphere in *economic diversification* and to some extent in the political sphere in the *index of reform government.*

Differentiation between potential elites, although not measured directly, was to some extent indicated by active *civic voluntary associations.* These in turn reflected the degree of development of a potential elite group outside of and in addition to others formally involved in community decision-making.

Decentralized decision-making was positively associated with *economic diversification* and (very slightly) active *civic voluntary associations,* and negatively associated with the *index of reform government.* All of these relationships were consistent with our reasoning that the greater the structural support for a plurality of potential elites, the more decentralized the decision-making structure.

Our best indicator of the strength of *community integrative mechanisms* was the *index of reform government,* which tended to lead to higher outputs.

Specification and revision of the general formulation seemed most necessary in the relationship of the antecedent variables to the *level of outputs.* In contrast to our expectations, *decentralization of decision-making* was positively associated with both *budget expenditures* and *urban renewal expenditures.* We suggested one alternative interpretation of this finding, but further study of community outputs is needed before we can formulate more precise propositions relating community characteristics to various types of community outputs. It is necessary here, as with the other causal mechanisms suggested, to specify the actual content and structure of the processes involved, using all kinds of procedures.

At this point we may return to the highly detailed case study, which can once more perform an indispensable function. Content analysis and attitude questionnaires can also be profitably employed to relate political cultural variables to the largely structural variables used in our model. In this regard, analysis of social and cultural characteristics of community leaders should be especially profitable. Finally, replication of these findings is needed, both in smaller and larger American communities, and in foreign societies marked by differing structural and cultural patterns of local community decision-making. Only in this way will it be possible to generate and verify a more general theory of decision-making.

BUSINESS INTERESTS, COUNTERVAILING GROUPS AND THE BALANCE OF INFLUENCE IN 91 CITIES

Laura L. Morlock

Over the last decade, the attention of many researchers interested in community decision-making has shifted from the study of influence patterns within one particular community to the examination of correlates and consequences of variations in influence structures within a comparative community framework. But in spite of these alterations in emphasis, for the most part researchers have continued to focus their interest on one dimension of community influence: the extent to which it is widely or narrowly distributed. In many studies within the community decision-making tradition this variable has been operationalized by determining the number of individuals or the number of competing leadership groups who are reputed to have influence and/or who have participated in important community decisions.

Less attention has been paid to a systematic investigation of the degree to which influence is distributed among different, and often opposing, community interests. Yet we may hypothesize that the style and content of community decision-making is dependent not only on the number of individuals or groups or "power centers" who are influential, but also on the type of community interests that play major roles in civic affairs.

This study then is an analysis of differences among American cities in the way influence is distributed across various community interest groups. It will explore the demographic and structural city characteristics associated with different influence patterns and the consequences of variations in influence distributions for the types of issues which become subject to public debate and the level of policy outputs in several areas of social welfare.

The data analysis included in this chapter was completed under grant number 5 RO1 MH18060-04, awarded to Robert L. Crain by the Center for Studies of Metropolitan Problems, National Institute of Mental Health. For critical comments and numerous helpful suggestions I would like to thank Henry Becker, Christine Bose, Robert Crain, Wen Kuo, Michael Ornstein, Peter Rossi, and James Vanecko.
This chapter was prepared for this volume.

THE SAMPLE OF CITIES

The data for this analysis are drawn from a study of school de-segregation in the North conducted by researchers at the National Opinion Research Center and The Johns Hopkins University. The communities chosen for investigation were those ninety-five cities in NORC's Permanent Community Sample which are "non-southern," and which in 1960 had a black population of at least 3,000.[1]

Interviews were conducted in each city with a panel of nineteen informants including local politicians, government officials, civic leaders, school system personnel, and leaders in the black community. The data included in the present analysis are drawn from interviews with four of these informants: the city editor of a major local newspaper; the mayor or city manager, or his administrative assistant; an important political leader of the party in opposition to the mayor; and a major civic leader in the community whose name was obtained by a modified reputational technique.[2]

Patterns of influence Among Community Sectors: A Factor Analysis

Of central importance in an investigation of the relationships among community groups are the concepts of power, resources and influence. For the purposes of this analysis, power is conceived theoretically as the potential ability of an actor within a system to attain desired goals, or to maintain or change elements of the system in the direction of preferred values.

[1]Two cities were dropped from the sample due to difficulties in data collection. Two additional cities were omitted from this analysis due to missing data problems. The remaining 91 communities represent 37 per cent of all cities in the continental United States outside the South with a population over 50,000 in 1960. They represent the universe of all such cities with a population of 250,000 or more, and they are a fairly representative sample of all such cities between 50,000 and 250,000 with at least 3,000 black residents. Because of the desire to include only those cities with a substant black community, suburban communities are slightly under-represented in the sample. In all other respects, these cities appear to be a representative stratified sample of "big cities" in the northern United States.

[2]This "modified reputational technique" involved asking the city editor, mayor, leading politician in opposition to the mayor and a former school board member to name the most important civic leaders in their community. Civic leaders were defined as those people, other than local government officials, who have been active in supporting various community programs and in bringing new programs to the city; or, on the other hand, people who have been active in opposing or trying to significantly alter such programs. The individual named most often by these informants was interviewed.

This conception of power as a "system-relevant property" focuses on the potential abilities of different actors to regulate inputs and outputs and the flow of decisions within a system. Within this schema of power as potential, determined by a given resource base, influence is conceived theoretically as the exercise of power, as the activation of resources, for the purpose of effecting change or preventing change within a social system.

A major concern in this study was an analysis across communities of the relative importance of a variety of community sectors with potential for influence because of their access to various resource bases. Included in the investigation were: labor unions; the Democratic party organization; the Republican party organization; insurgent, independent, or reform political groups; downtown merchants; industrialists; bankers, and executives of financial institutions; the black population; Mexicans, Puerto Ricans, Indians, and Orientals; other nationality groups; neighborhood groups other than black organizations; newspapers; college students and teachers; citizens' civic organizations such as the PTA, League of Women Voters, Taxpayers' Associations, etc.; and clubs and associations such as the American Legion, lodges, church groups and athletic clubs.

The influence of each of these sectors within the decision-making system was determined by measuring each group's reputation for success in influencing issue outcomes of central concern to the community. In order to ascertain which issue areas were most important in each community the city editor of the largest newspaper was asked to name the most important problem area in this city since 1960. Then each editor was asked what he considered to be the most important program the city had adopted in order to help deal with this problem. Next he was asked to describe a program which could have made the most significant contribution toward the alleviation of this problem but which was never adopted by the city, either because it was rejected by some portion of the community, or because it never reached the point of being widely discussed.[3]

In order to assess the relative influence of community groups over the outcomes of important issues, in each city a major political leader of the party in opposition to the mayor was asked whether each community sector under study had supported, remained neutral or divided, or had opposed the major program adopted in each city and the major program which had been considered, but had failed to gain acceptance.

In addition to the major adopted and major rejected programs, mayoral elections were studied in each community as a third important issue.

---

[3]If education was named as the city's most important problem, the city editor was asked to name a second most important problem area and to think of an important adopted and rejected program within this second area. A majority of the entire study was concerned with programs in education, and the purpose of these questions was to investigate other areas of community decision-making.

First, both the mayor or mayor's assistant, and the major political leader in opposition were asked for each community sector whether its support in most mayoral elections since 1960 had been essential for the winner, important but not essential, not too important, or not important at all. Then for each group judged essential or important, the informant was asked whether that group supported or opposed the winner of a recent mayoral campaign.

We do not believe that only the "winners" in community contests have influence. However, if we examine several issues within a community, it seems reasonable to conclude that groups consistently on the winning side probably have a greater degree of influence than groups who usually lose.

Accordingly, influence scores were developed for community sectors in each issue area. High scores of two points were awarded to those community interests who had supported the city's major adopted program, opposed the major rejected program, and supported the winner of a recent mayoral campaign according to both the present mayor and the mayor's leading political opponent. Lowest scores of 0 points were given in each area to those groups who opposed the major adopted program, supported the rejected program and supported the losing candidate in the mayoral campaign. Groups who remained neutral or were divided over an issue were assigned intermediate scores of 1 point. In order to determine if similar patterns exist from city to city in the distribution of influence among community sectors, and to see if patterns persist across issue areas, intercorrelations were obtained among the influence scores for each of the three issues. Next each correlation matrix was factor analyzed, using an "eigenvalue-eigenvector method" of factor extraction and a varimax rotation procedure. (See Table 1.)

We reason on the basis of the factor analyses of community influence scores in three areas that in general two main influence dimensions exist at the city level which cut across different issues. Although the kinds of community groups which are aligned with each dimension may shift somewhat from issue to issue, a core of community interests remains the same. One group almost always consists of business interests—including downtown merchants, industrialists, bankers and executives of financial institutions, newspapers, the Republican party organization, and civic clubs. The other dimension usually consists of the Democratic party organization; insurgent, independent or reform political groups; the black community; and to the extent they are present in the city—college students and teachers; and nonwhite ethnic groups such as Mexicans, Puerto Ricans, Indians, and Orientals.

To conclude that in many cities these two congeries of influence exist does not imply that formal coalitions or even frequent informal cooperation necessarily govern the. interrelations among groups in the same influence

TABLE 1   Factor Loadings and Communalities for Thirteen Interest Groups on Three Community Issues

Community Interest Group	Major Adopted Program			Major Rejected Program			Mayoral Campaign		
	Factors			Factors			Factors		
	I*	II*	h^2	I*	II*	h^2	I	II*	h^2
Business interests	.86	-.09	.75	.60	-.13	.38	.60	.05	.36
Major newspaper	.59	-.08	.36	.43	.08	.19	.46	.03	.22
Republican party organ.	.37	.15	.16	.63	.04	.40	.63	-.51	.65
Clubs and associations (lodges, church groups, etc.)	.65	.41	.60	.68	.16	.49	.50	.46	.46
Labor unions	.29	.22	.13	.41	.24	.23	-.36	.62	.52
Other nationality groups	.44	.24	.25	.43	.09	.19	.15	.55	.32
Neighborhood groups (other than black organizations)	.47	.47	.44	.22	.05	.05	.12	.47	.24
Citizens' organizations (PTA, League of Women Voters, etc.)	.26	.32	.17	.54	.31	.39	.50	.39	.40
College students and teachers	.06	.52	.27	.10	.48	.24	.35	.45	.32
Independent parties	.13	.49	.25	.06	.35	.13	.18	.20	.07
Democratic party organ.	.29	.30	.18	.22	.44	.24	-.54	.73	.83
Mexicans, Puerto Ricans, Indians and Orientals	.16	.60	.39	.12	.66	.45	.22	.71	.55
Blacks	-.04	.77	.59	-.06	.78	.61	-.03	.56	.31

*Factor has been reflected.

dimension. On the basis of the present evidence we can infer only that groups in the same influence dimension tend to fall on the same side of a variety of community issues.

Several questions logically follow: Why do community groups align themselves in this way? What do groups in the same influence dimension have in common that differentiates them from opposing groups? We reason that groups in the same influence alignment depend on the same resource bases, have similar economic or social interests and/or share a common ideology concerning local community affairs.

THE INFLUENCE OF BUSINESS AND CIVIC INTERESTS

Undoubtedly the greatest area of consensus among researchers concerned with community decision-making in the United States is that a large proportion of influential actors in the community are businessmen. In fact, such studies generally have found a high percentage of businessmen among community influentials irrespective of the type of power structure discovered. We may hypothesize that downtown merchants, bankers, newspapers, industrialists, the Republican party organization and members of civic associations form a common influence dimension at least partly because they share similar economic interests, especially a concern with the community's economic growth. They also have access to similar resources —money and credit, high social status, and legitimacy in the eyes of other community actors such as the local government. These are all resources which are high in their liquidity, scope, and stability over time.

However, the groups in this business-oriented dimension share not only common economic interests and resources, but also many of the same values, particularly with respect to conceptions of the community interest and the proper role of government. In their view, politicians should function as representatives of the public at large, or the common welfare, not as advocates of "special interest." However, business concerns often are equated with the community good, and are rarely perceived as one of a series of special interest themselves. The proper role of the local government is seen basically as non-political and administrative in character, with emphasis on promoting economic growth, providing amenities, maintaining traditional services, or some combination of the three. In this perspective many civic matters are handled best by a "non-political," consensual process within the civic associational network.[4]

---

[4]This set of beliefs is similar in most respects to what Agger, Goldrich and Swanson have described as the Community Conservationist ideology. See Agger et al., *The Rulers and The Ruled* (New York: John Wiley & Sons, 1964), 1–32. It also resembles

THE INFLUENCE OF NON-BUSINESS INTERESTS

It is somewhat more difficult to determine what interests are held in common by the black community, other nonwhite ethnic groups, the Democratic party organization, insurgent, independent or reform political groups, and college students and teachers. Clearly these interests are more diverse than those included in the business-oriented dimension. But we may reason that they are similar, both in their opposition to many policies and programs promoted by the business community and their advocacy of programs and policies which business groups either fail to support or actively oppose. Such programs often involve the redistribution or reallocation of individual or community resources.

Certainly the unequal distribution of resources has always been one basis of cleavage in the community, separating propertied interests on one side from economically deprived groups, such as blacks and nonwhite ethnic groups, on the other. The professional politicians in control of most Democratic party organizations, regardless of their personal interests or ideologies, must depend on the support of economically and racially underprivileged groups in the central city. Insurgent, independent and reform political groups in the metropolis may also look for some support here.

College students and teachers and usually the members of independent, insurgent and reform political groups are likely to be middle class. We may suggest that they are often allied with nonwhite groups and the Democratic party organization not out of economic or political self-interest, but for ideological reasons. For we may speculate that groups in this influence dimension, like the business-oriented interests, are similar in their conceptions of the community and the proper role of local government. In their view local governments should give highest priority to the needs of disadvantaged groups, or at the very least, should serve as an arbiter among conflicting interests. According to this perspective, civic matters should be decided not by the business-dominated civic associations, but rather by elected or properly appointed public officials or by the citizens themselves in referenda.

Groups in this influence dimension have little access to the types of resources on which business-oriented groups depend. Primarily their influence is contingent, not on access to wealth or high status, but rather on

the "middle class ethos" described by Banfield and Wilson, *City Politics* (Cambridge: Harvard & MIT Presses, 1963). The different functions of local governments advocated by various community groups are discussed extensively in Williams and Adrian (1964). Oliver P. Williams and Charles R. Adrian, *Four Cities* (Philadelphia: University of Pennsylvania Press, 1963).

mass-based organizations and voting blocs. Unlike the business-oriented groups they are not associated together in the civic organization network. However, because their influence is dependent basically on voting strength, in each city they have had to build grass-roots organizations to ensure high election turnouts among minorities and other lower class groups.

Such an organizational base has two inherent disadvantages. First, it is manifestly political and therefore may have less legitimacy in the eyes of public officials and other decision-makers than the more traditional and superficially apolitical civic associations who often claim to act not on behalf of business as a special interest but rather on behalf of the welfare of the community in general. Second, as Agger, Goldrich, and Swanson have pointed out, such an organizational base is not particularly effective in decisional processes that do not involve elections. Therefore, groups in this influence dimension tend to be less well represented in the initial and intermediate stages of decision-making, which often occur within the civic association network. For these reasons, the resources available to these groups tend to be lower in their liquidity, scope and stability over time than resources accessible to groups with a business orientation.

BUSINESS, COUNTERVAILING GROUPS, AND THE BALANCE OF INFLUENCE

The analysis has focused up to this point on describing patterns in the distribution of influence among various community interests. We have found that many community groups fall into two broad influence alignments, one comprised of business-oriented interests, and the other made up of sectors often opposed to the business community. Next we might ask how cities compare with respect to the relative strengths of these two influence dimensions.

In order to answer this question three separate summary scores were created for each city. First, the average influence score was found for each group across the three issue areas. Next these scores were averaged for business interests, the Republican party organization, newspapers, and civic clubs to produce a summary score measuring the amount of influence of business-oriented interests in community affairs. A second index was created by averaging the influence scores in each city for the Democratic party organization; insurgent, independent or reform political groups; the black community; Mexicans, Puerto Ricans, Indians, and Orientals; and college students and teachers. Because these groups often fall on the opposite side of community issues from the business sector, this index was labeled countervailing influence. Next, in order to measure the relative strength of the two dimensions in each city, the business influence index was subtracted from the index of countervailing influence to form a score measuring the balance of influence in each community.

It is interesting to note that 60 cities, or almost two-thirds of the sample have higher influence scores for the business sector than for countervailing groups.[5] A number of researchers have agreed with Munger's . . . conclusion that "The only distinction that can in fact be observed among community power structures is that between systems in which only the business community exercises significant power and systems in which the business community shares power with other groups." While this statement is an exaggeration for this sample of cities taken as a whole, certainly the distribution of influence scores indicates that for a majority of communities business-oriented interests are a powerful force in civic affairs.

Our measure of the balance of influence in a community is similar theoretically to the concept of pluralism, when that term has been used to describe an influence structure in which different sectors compete with one another for control of community resources in various issue arenas. Operationally, however, researchers often have assumed that pluralism exists "if specialization and competition characterize groups of leaders who constitute some one-half of 1 per cent of the community."[6] Our measure differs then from many operational indicators of pluralism in that it is based not on the number of individuals or even on the number of competing cliques of leaders involved in decision-making, but rather on the extent to which both business and opposing interests are represented in the resolution of community issues.

The Structure of Influence: Demographic, Economic and Political Correlates

Under what demographic and structural conditions will the influence of business-oriented groups be greater or less than the strength of countervailing interests?

According to Banfield and Wilson, a high degree of business influence is dependent on at least three conditions: 1) a relatively homogeneous, mid-

---

[5]The business influence scores for each city range from a low of 0.70 to a high of 2.00 with a mean score of 1.26 and a standard deviation of 0.27. Countervailing indices range from 0.00 to 2.00 with a mean of 1.21 and a standard deviation of 0.33. Since the balance of influence score is formed for each city by subtracting its business index from its index of countervailing influence, negative scores indicate an imbalance in the direction of business-oriented interests, and positive scores the reverse. The balance of influence scores range from -0.99 to $+0.53$ with a mean of -0.01 and a standard deviation of 0.03.

[6]Robert Presthus, *Men at the Top* (New York: Oxford University Press, 1964), p. 434.

dle-class population with minimal class cleavages; 2) a "reformed" political structure; and 3) a relatively small and cohesive business sector.

We may test portions of Banfield and Wilson's argument, as well as some conclusions from other studies, by correlating the degree of business and countervailing influence and the influence balance with various city characteristics.

In order to compare research findings here with other results in the literature, the balance of influence index will be treated as similar theoretically to concepts such as pluralism, dispersed power structure, diffusion of power, and decentralized community decision-making system. We believe this procedure is justified because the theoretical constructs underlying these concepts are somewhat similar, although in most cases the operational indicators vary greatly.

TABLE 2   Correlations Among Business Influence, Countervailing Influence, the Balance of Influence and City Characteristics[a]

City Characteristic	Business Influence	Counter-vailing Influence	Balance Influence
Population characteristics:			
Total population size	−.24*	.06	.26*
Population (natural logarithm)	−.18	.16	.32**
Percent nonwhite	−.16	.22*	.34**
Percent black	−.15	.16	.29**
Number of black adults over 25	−.26*	.08	.30**
Taeuber's Segregation Index[b]	.06	−.05	−.12
Percent foreign born	.04	.01	−.00
Percent foreign stock	−.02	.11	.13
Percent migrant	.08	−.04	−.12
City variables:			
Age of city[c]	.11	−.13	−.24*
Percent of housing dilapidated, 1950	.11	.24*	.11
Educational indicators:			
Median education	.02	−.10	−.12
Percent adults with five years of education or less	−.11	.14	.25*
Percent adults with at least a high school education	.02	−.13	−.15
Educational Center Score[d]	.01	−.08	−.09
Median education of black population	−.09	−.07	.01
Economic indicators:			
Percent employed in manufacturing	.05	−.01	−.05
Percent employed in retail or wholesale trade	.03	−.01	−.04
Percent employed in white collar occupations	−.06	−.17	−.10
MPO ratio (natural logarithm)[e]	.07	−.10	−.16
Median income	.01	−.12	−.12
Median income of black population	.03	−.06	−.06
Percent earning less than $3000 yearly	−.02	.09	.10
Percent earning more than $10,000 yearly	.01	−.12	−.12
Suburbanization of High Income Population Score[f]	−.13	.04	.17

CITY SIZE, AGE OF CITY, AND POPULATION COMPOSITION

A number of researchers have hypothesized that the greater the size of a city, the more likely it is to have a decentralized, or pluralistic, decision-making structure. Increasing size, it is reasoned, is associated with a heterogeneous population, structural differentiation, and a multiplication of resource bases—all conducive to pluralist systems. The results in Table 2 lend support to this argument. Population size, whether introduced into the correlations without transformation or as a natural logarithm, appears negatively related to business influence, positively related to countervailing strength, and positively and significantly related to the balance of influence.

TABLE 2   (Cont.)

City Characteristic	Business Influence	Counter-vailing Influence	Balance Influence
Participation Indicators:			
Percent adults voting[g]	−.10	.21*	.29**
Percent registrants voting in local elections[g]	−.17	.21*	.37**
Political Structure:			
Reform government[h]	.26*	−.10	−.30**
Number of councilmen	−.06*	.04	.10
Partisan elections	.05	.06	.01
Percentage of councilmen elected at-large	.04	−.01	−.03

[a]All indicators, unless otherwise noted, are from the *County and City Data Book* 1967, Table 4, or from the U.S. Census of Population 1960, Volume 1, *Characteristics of the Population*.

[b]Source: Karl E. Taeuber and Alma F. Taeuber, *Negroes in Cities*.

[c]Census year city reached 25,000 population.

[d]Source: Jeffrey K. Hadden and Edgar F. Borgatta, *American Cities*.

[e]Proportion of the employed civilian labor force who are managers, proprietors, or officials.

[f]The score is a ratio comparing the suburbanization of families with incomes over $25,000 to the suburbanization of the city population as a whole. Suburbs are defined as within the SMSA but outside the central city.

[g]Data are from a survey taken by Eugene C. Lee, Director, Institute of Governmental Studies, University of California at Berkeley. For data collection methods see Alford and Lee (1968). The data were made available by Robert R. Alford through the Data and Program Library Service, University of Wisconsin, Madison.

[h]Highest scores are awarded to cities with city managers; lowest scores to cities with mayor–council governments.

*Significant at the .05 level.

**Significant at the .01 level.

Aiken has found that the older the city, the more diffuse power arrangements tend to be. The correlations in Table 2 support this conclusion: Business is somewhat more likely to be influential in younger cities, while older cities are more likely to have influential countervailing groups and a greater balance of influence between these groups and business.

A heterogeneous population multiplies the number of potential resource bases in a community, and most studies, as we would expect, have found a relationship between indicators of heterogeneity and pluralism. The balance of influence is strongly correlated to several measures of heterogeneity, including the size of the adult black community and the percentage of the population who are nonwhite and black. It is also correlated, although weakly, to the per cent foreign stock in a city. Communities with countervailing influence levels approaching or surpassing the level of business influence are somewhat more likely to have a smaller degree of residential segregation, as measured by scores on Taeuber's Segregation Index.

Although Banfield and Wilson predict that businessmen are more likely to exert control in middle-class, and therefore more educated, communities, other research has reported contradictory evidence. Crain *et al.* and Crain and Rosenthal found that high levels of education in a community contribute to the decentralization of decision-making. Gilbert found no relationship between pluralism and a community's educational level. Both Clark and Aiken, however, report a positive correlation between level of education and *concentration* of community influence. Their findings receive some support here: the balance of influence index is inversely related to the educational attainment of the community in general. It is correlated at the .05 level with the percentage of adults in the population with five years of education or less.

Correlations between the class composition of a community, as measured by income variables, and the influence indices are all in the expected direction, but none are statistically significant. Business influence tends to correlate positively, but very weakly, with indicators of high income populations while the reverse is true for countervailing influence. In addition, there is a negative, although weak, correlation between the strength of business interests and the extent of the "suburban flight" of families with high incomes.

Economic Structure

A number of researchers have argued that increased industrialization, economic diversification and a general dispersion of power in the whole economy should lead to the decentralization of community decision-making. They reason that economic resources are often converted into political resources and therefore a monopoly in the economy contributes toward a monolith of political power.

However, comparative research using a number of different economic indicators has failed to provide these arguments with strong empirical underpinings. Therefore it is not surprising to find no relationship in our data between either the balance of influence and the degree of industrialization as measured — per cent employed in manufacturing, . . . or the degree of economic diversity as measured indirectly by per cent of workers in wholesale and retail trade. Only per cent of the labor force employed in white collar occupations, which we may interpret as another indicator of the size of the middle class, is related to our influence measures; it shows a negative, but fairly weak correlation with the strength of countervailing interests.

Citizen Participation

The balance of influence, as we have seen, is inversely correlated with all indicators of the level of education in a community. Because several studies have shown that highly educated individuals are more likely to be involved in civic and political activities, we might reason that the level of citizen participation is higher in middle class, business dominated cities. Our thesis would be the lower the balance of influence in a city, the higher the level of citizen participation.

But as Aiken and Alford have suggested, we might also define citizen participation as activity at the polls. The balance of influence index is strongly correlated both with the percentage of adults registered to vote in a community, and the percentage of registrants who actually vote in local elections.

We may only conclude, on the basis of fragmentary evidence, that the balance of influence is associated with high levels of citizen participation in the electoral process, and probably low levels of citizen participation in the intermediate stages of decision-making which often occur in associations and public meetings.

Political Structure

Both the historical circumstances under which reformed political structures were instituted, and subsequent research on the consequences of municipal reform would lead us to expect that reformed institutions serve to enhance the strength of business over countervailing interests. In fact, only one measure of reformed government is correlated with the influence measures,

but that relationship is a strong one. Business influence is associated at the
.06 level with the presence of city managers as opposed to mayor–council
governments.

Region

Several studies have noted that community power structures are less likely
to be pluralistic in southern cities, but have discovered no significant differences in power arrangements outside the South.

In order to test the impact of region on influence patterns a one-way
analysis of variance was performed on the mean scores for cities in each
region across the three influence indices. In every region business strength
is greater than countervailing influence. The difference between the two
indices is greater in the Pacific states, although differences among regions
are not statistically significant.

Summary

In summary, Banfield and Wilson's thesis seems at least partially supported
by the evidence. Business influence is highest in relatively homogeneous,
middle class communities where it is possible for businessmen to control a
majority of resources.

In contrast, businessmen are less likely to control all the resources in
more heterogeneous cities with strong social and economic cleavages in
the population, or in cities with an unreformed, and more decentralized,
form of government. In these cities countervailing interests are strong
enough to elect politicians who are then independent of the business community. A weakened business sector, together with strong countervailing
interests, creates a greater balance of influence within the community.

ISSUES AND OUTPUTS: CONSEQUENCES OF THE COMMUNITY INFLUENCE STRUCTURE

We have been concerned in the analysis up to this point with
how communities differ in the way influence is divided among opposing
groups. But we are interested in the way community influence is distributed
because we suspect that variations in influence arrangements have differing
impacts on the quality of community life—or, more specifically, on the
style and content of community decision-making.

The Level of Controversy

Differences in styles of decision-making between cities dominated by business interests and cities in which countervailing groups exert strong influence in civic affairs have been discussed in previous sections. To summarize the theoretical argument: business-oriented groups tend to use the network of civic associations to initiate and carry out civic activities in which they are interested. The community at large is often unaware of issues raised and decisions made within this framework until these decisions have reached the status of a *fait accompli*. In this way possible opposition to projects favored by the business sector is rarely mobilized, and community decision-making in general seems a consensual process with few public conflicts.

However, we may hypothesize that the more the balance of influence shifts from business-oriented interests to countervailing groups, the more difficult it becomes to confine community decision-making to the relatively private sphere of civic associations. Strong opposing interests increase the probability of all kinds of controversy, and these conflicts are likely to be played out in the public arena.

In short, we would expect the level of controversy in a community to be directly correlated to the balance of influence between business and countervailing groups. Moreover, the balance of influence undoubtedly is related not only to the amount of community controversy, but also to the substantive content of the issues under public debate.

Issues and Non-issues

An important consequence of the balance of influence in a city may be the kind of issues which find a place on the community agenda. For as Schattschneider . . . explained a decade ago:

> . . . *The definition of the alternatives is the supreme instrument of power;* the antagonists can rarely agree on what the issues are because power is involved in the definition . . . All forms of political organization have a bias in favor of the exploitation of some kinds of conflict and the suppression of others *because organization is the mobilization of bias.* Some issues are organized into politics while others are organized out.

In any community there is a limited amount of resources and an infinite variety of ways in which these resources may be allocated. Debate in the public forum usually involves, in the last analysis, questions of resource allocation. But the important point is that we may determine which groups in a community have influence, not only by observing who wins in community conflicts, but also by noticing what kinds of issues become the focus of community debate.[7]

We may test these arguments on the amount and nature of community controversy with data from our sample. In each of the 91 cities the city editor of the largest newspaper in the city, an important political leader of the party in opposition to the mayor, and a major civic leader in the community were asked how much controversy has arisen in their city during the years since 1960 over each of the following issues: industry and economic development, housing and building, education, public improvements, culture and recreation, race and ethnic relations, social improvement and welfare, air and water pollution, corruption, local taxes and crime. The responses of all three informants were combined to create a controversy score for each issue. In addition, for each city the scores for all issues were combined to form an index measuring the total amount of controversy.[8] As we predicted, business influence is related to the *absence* of controversy in the public arena for almost every issue. There is a small positive relationship (.11) with controversy in only one area: industrial and economic development. Correlations with the absence of controversy are significant at the .05 level in the areas of public improvements ($-$.23), social improvements and welfare ($-$.23), and the combined controversy index ($-$.22).

In contrast, countervailing influence is correlated positively with controversy levels in seven out of eleven possible conflict arenas. In the four areas where countervailing influence shows slight negative correlations

---

[7]This idea is developed fully in E. E. Schattschneider, *The Semi-Sovereign People: A Realist's View of Democracy in America* (New York: Holt, Rinehart & Winston, 1960); and Peter Bachrach and Morton Baratz, "Two Faces of Power," *American Political Science Review*, 57 (December, 1962), 947–952, and "Decisions and Nondecisions: An Analytical Framework," *Ibid.*, 57 (September, 1963), 632–642; and criticized in R. M. Merelman, "On the Neoelitist Critique of Community Power," *Ibid.*, 62 (June, 1968), 451–460. For empirical studies testing this approach, see Peter Bachrach and Morton Baratz, *Power and Poverty: Theory and Practice* (New York: Oxford University Press, 1970); and Matthew Crenson, *The Un-politics of Air Pollution: A Study of Non-Decision-making in the Cities* (Baltimore: The Johns-Hopkins Press, 1971).

[8]Controversy scores were created for each of 11 issues by first assigning scores to the responses of the city editor, politician and major civic leader for each issue according to the following system:

No controversy	0 point
Little controversy	1 point
A moderate amount of controversy	2 points
A great deal of controversy	3 points

The three responses were added together for each issue to create a total controversy score for each issue with a range of 0–9. The controversy scores for all 11 issues were added together to form a total controversy index for each city with a theoretical range of 0–99.

with controversy levels, business influence shows even stronger negative relationships.

The greatest differences between the two influence indices are in the controversial areas of social improvement and welfare, air and water pollution and crime. The correlations of levels of controversy for those three areas and the balance of influence index are all statistically significant. One relationship—the correlation between balance of influence and controversy over social improvement and welfare (.32)—is significant at the .01 level.

It seems reasonable to argue, however, that these correlations may be an indication not of the tendency for public issues in cities where countervailing groups are strong to reflect the concerns of these groups, but rather an indication of the greater severity of problems in social welfare, pollution and crime in cities where these groups have influence. In other words we might well argue that our controversy measures are not reflections of priorities on the public agenda of those with influence, but instead are community concerns over problem severity. In order to test this hypothesis, the correlations for controversy over social improvements and welfare, pollution and crime were run with controls for the severity of the problem in each area. Controls on the extent of the problem, or on problem severity and city size, do not affect the correlations between the influence measures and controversy over social improvements and welfare or air and water pollution. Controlling on the severity of the crime problem and city size increases slightly the negative correlation between business influence and controversy over crime, reduces to almost zero the correlation with countervailing influence, and reduces the correlation with the balance of influence to a level where it is no longer significant. On the basis of this evidence we may conclude that controversy over welfare and pollution reflect the importance of these issues to countervailing groups, and are not simply an indication of the problem level in cities where these groups are strong.

Policy Outputs

The balance of influence, we have argued, has important consequences for both styles of community decision-making, and types of issues which become open to public debate. But are community concerns—as evidenced by the kinds of issues raised—translated into policies and programs? Does the balance of influence have an impact, not only on the content of public discussion, but on its outcome—decisions and their implementation? For example, we have observed that the higher the balance of influence in a community, the greater the degree of controversy over social improvements and welfare. Does it follow that cities with influence structures strongly balanced toward countervailing interests, with resulting high degrees of

TABLE 3 Correlations and Partial Correlations Among Influence Indices and the Level of Community Controversy over Social Improvements and Welfare, Air and Water Pollution, and Crime

Area of Controversy	Business Influence		Countervailing Influence		Balance of Influence	
	r	Partial r	r	Partial r	r	Partial r
Social improvements and welfare	-.23*		.14		.32**	
Controlling on severity of problem[a]		-.24		.16		.34**
Controlling on problem severity and city size		-.18		.15		.29*
Air and water pollution	-.02		.26*		.24*	
Controlling on severity of problem[b]		-.01		.26*		.23
Controlling on problem severity and city size		.02		.25		.20
Crime	-.13		.11		.22*	
Controlling on severity of problem[c]		-.13		.01		.15
Controlling on problem severity and city size		-.17		.02		.14

[a]Severity of the problem is measured by the percentage of families with incomes under $3000. (Source: City and County Data Book, 1967.)

[b]Severity of the problem is measured by an index of air pollution for the SMSA which includes the following: arithmetic average concentration of suspended particulates; standard geometric deviation of the suspended particulate concentrations; arithmetic average concentration of the benzene-soluble organic fraction of the suspended particulate matter; total consumption of gasoline; density of automobile emissions; arithmetic average concentration of sulfur dioxide as measured in the center city or as derived from sulfate measurements; total emissions of sulfur dioxide in the SMSA; and the density of sulfur dioxide emissions in the area. (Source: press release dated August 4, 1967, from the Public Health Service's National Center for Air Pollution Control)

[c]Severity of the problem is measured by the following crime statistics for 1967: Numbers of murders and nonnegligent manslaughters, forcible rapes, robberies, aggravated assaults, burglaries (breaking and entering), larcenies (thefts under $50), and auto thefts. (Data were made available by Robert Alford through the Data and Program Library Service, University of Wisconsin, Madison. The original data source is Uniform Crime Reports for the United States, 1967, Table 57, pp. 177–93.)

*Significant at the .05 level.

**Significant at the .01 level.

controversy over issues of social reform, will also show strong commitments to programs aimed at alleviating social problems?

We have rather strong evidence that the structure of influence is associated with policy outputs in the area of social reform. The level of business influence shows a small negative correlation (−.04) with dollars per capita spent by a city on poverty programs, while countervailing influence and the balance of influence are both positively correlated (.30 and .32) at the .01 level with poverty program expenditures.

When variables measuring the level of need in a city are introduced, the correlations are reduced, but the partial for countervailing influence (.21) is still statistically significant at the .05 level. We may conclude that even after controlling on four measures of a city's possible need for social programs (percentage of families with incomes under $3000, city age, percentage of dilapidated housing, and population size), the stronger the influence of countervailing groups, the more money is spent per capita by the city on poverty programs.

The influence structure is also associated with a city's commitment to providing low-rent housing. The degree of business influence has a zero correlation, and countervailing strength and the balance of influence strong positive correlations (.28 and .23) to the number of low-rent housing units constructed by the city under federally sponsored programs since 1933. When the same control variables measuring the extent of a city's need for social programs are introduced, the correlations remain fairly strong (.18 and .18), although they are no longer statistically significant.

In summary, the correlations we found provide fairly strong evidence that cities with influential countervailing interests are likely to have high levels of program outputs in at least one area of major concern to them— social improvements and welfare. Furthermore, this relationship is not solely a function of differing levels of need between cities with a dominant business sector and cities with strong countervailing groups. After controls for need are introduced, the correlations remain fairly high, and in the case of poverty programs, statistically significant.

The Debate over Decentralization

Our conclusions concerning the impact of differing influence structures are relevant in certain respects to the current debate over the consequences of differing degrees of decentralization of community decision-making on levels of policy outputs. Of course, conceptions and operational measures of centralization vary widely in the literature. Researchers in the Hunter-Dahl tradition are concerned with elite participation, and tend to equate centralization of decision-making with a small number of elite participants and decentralization with a broader or more fragmented group of elites. [Amos] Hawley, on the other hand, is more concerned with power as a system property than a personal resource, and reasons that power is centralized if the managerial functions through which system power is exercised are few in number. Others, like Crain and Rosenthal, are more concerned with a broad base of participation among the citizenry at-large, and conclude that power is concentrated to the extent that mass participation is limited.

Several researchers have found that the more centralized the community decision-making structure, the more successful the community will be in carrying out collective actions. In spite of differences in the way centralization is defined, the rationales are similar: concentration of power simplifies coordination, allowing for a more efficient mobilization of community resources, and/or centralized decision-making systems are less likely to be immobilized by controversy over programs and policies.

Other researchers, however, have found that the more *decentralized* the decision-making structure, whether measured in terms of elite participation or the relative number of centers of power, the greater the success of the community in carrying out collective actions. These researchers argue that for many community actions, only a limited number of influentials or power centers must participate in order to effect a given change in the community. Increases in the number of influential individuals or power centers increase the degree of issue specialization, and the likelihood that at least some individuals or power centers will be activated on any given issue. It also increases the possibility that for any issue a "moving coalition" composed of some part of the broad influence network will be formed.

The data in this study seem to support that position which holds that decentralization of community influence is associated with an increase in the level of policy outputs, although the findings may be, in part, a function of the types of programs which were examined. Certainly Clark and Aiken and Alford have supplied some of the reasons why decentralization, or in our case, a highly balanced influence structure, should be associated with increases in policy outputs. But perhaps the nature of our data sheds further light on this relationship. In this analysis we have examined in detail the differences between two broad groupings in American cities. The nature of the influence dimensions we have found suggests that high levels of innovative activity, at least in the area of social welfare, may be a function, not only of an increase in the sheer number of power centers, but of a change in the nature of the dominant ideology that accompanies systems in which the influence of business groups is balanced or exceeded by the strength of countervailing forces.

ELECTION SYSTEMS, COMMUNITY POWER, AND PUBLIC POLICY: THE PARTISAN BIAS OF NONPARTISANSHIP

Willis D. Hawley

There are many ways to approach the questions of how community characteristics affect the distribution of power and what policy differences, if any, result. The following article[1] differs from the preceding three in that it focuses attention on one aspect of community structure— the electoral system. It seeks to demonstrate that political institutions are not value free and that they are, in effect, policies themselves. The independent impact of the type of electoral system on the distribution of power is estimated by examining the consequences of actual nonpartisan elections and simulated partisan contests within the same cities. This procedure has the effect of holding constant other community characteristics that might affect the electoral success of various community interests. Rather than looking at actual policies or expenditures to determine the policy consequences of different electoral systems, this study looks at the preferences of those elected and assumes that policies of a given political system will be related to the intentions of those who govern it. The strength of this assumption deserves the reader's critical attention and the circumstances that might weaken it should be considered.

The reader may also wish to consider whether the articles in this chapter are based on similar conceptual models of how political systems work and how policy is formulated. For example, do the various authors of these articles see political institutions as primary inputs to the policy process or as intervening variables that serve to process demands for governmental action that emanate from the social and economic structure of the community? Moreover, do differences in the ways the authors conceptualize the political process account for differences in their conclusions?

Of the hundreds of studies of community power, only a handful have given more than passing attention to the impact of variations in local

---

[1]This article was prepared for this volume. Portions of it appeared as "The Partisan Consequences of Nonpartisan Elections," Vol. 12, No. 3 (June, 1971) *Public Affairs Reports* (Berkeley: Institute of Governmental Studies).

political institutions on the distribution of power and the direction of public policy. The balance of evidence from these few studies suggests that the central problem in achieving new policies, especially those that would redistribute resources and privilege, is extensive fragmentation of political influence which inhibits the aggregation of sufficient power to bring about substantial change. While this research was making its way into print, other studies seeking to explain variations in city expenditure policies raised considerable questions as to just how important the institutions of government are in giving shape and direction to community decision-making.[2] Because of the prominence of the latter studies and because most of the research which does attest to the importance of political institutions does not provide a theoretical understanding of the interaction between the social and economic characteristics of communities on the one hand and their formal political structures on the other, there is considerable doubt whether the restructuring of local governments would have much consequence.

This article focuses on the importance, within a given community, of different election systems in determining which groups control elective offices and what the consequences of their control are. Of course, political decision-making is not the exclusive prerogative of elected officials; much "authoritative allocation of values" takes place in the private sector and public administrators often significantly alter the policies they are charged with implementing. Nevertheless, elected officials do play important political roles. Moreover, the scope of the roles elected officials adopt may be related, as will be suggested below, to the type of election system which brought them to office.

The theme advanced here is that electoral institutions are not neutral. Either directly or indirectly, they tend to shape the outcome of public decisions.[3] For example, such electoral procedures as at-large or district elections, the presence or absence of a mayor on the ballot, the existence of runoff elections in contrast to a system permitting plurality victories—all influence the outcome of public voting. Consequently, they affect different groups in a community in different ways, with resulting policy implications.

The nonpartisan ballot, and all it implies for the character of elections, is a major factor in community politics. Almost two-thirds of American

[2]A number of these studies are cited in Willis D. Hawley, *Nonpartisan Elections & The Case for Party Politics* (New York: John Wiley & Sons, 1973), Chapter 6.

[3]While this assertion is probably not surprising to most readers, I am aware of no study which clearly links political institutions to variations in the *impact* of public decisions on the citizenry. See the other articles in this section for some evidence on this point. Perhaps the most important study of the impact of election systems on the distribution of political power (though policy is not considered) is Douglas Rae, *The Political Consequences of Electoral Law* (New Haven: Yale University Press, 1967).

cities—large and small, suburban and central city—elect their local leaders using ballots that have no indication of the candidates' party affiliation. If we can demonstrate the importance of nonpartisanship in shaping the distribution of power and community resources, perhaps we can encourage renewed concern for research on other political institutions. Thus, this article focuses on the question of whether nonpartisan elections systematically enhance the "electability" of Democrats or Republicans. The focus here on Democrats and Republicans provides a shorthand way of classifying common cleavages among community groups. Party is not the only referent group for community influentials or for the average citizen; indeed, it is—at least at a conscious level—unimportant for many. Nevertheless, the vast majority of people—and this is especially true for those active in political affairs—are likely to consider themselves a member of one of the two major parties and both the composition of the parties and the policy preferences of party identifiers can be linked to persistent sources of political cleavage such as ethnicity, religion and, particularly, social class.

METHODS OF RESEARCH

To assess the consequences of nonpartisanship, it is necessary to examine the success of Democrats and Republicans in specific nonpartisan elections and then compare the results with estimates of how Democratic and Republican candidates would have fared if these local elections had been partisan. For this study, a local "partisan success ratio" was devised for each party in eighty-eight California cities, based on the outcomes of all elections for state and national offices, except U.S. President, during the ten-year period from 1957 to 1966. The contest for each of several partisan offices—United States Senator and Congressman, governor, lieutenant governor, secretary of state, controller, treasurer, attorney general, state senator and state assemblyman—is treated as though its winner had been determined by the vote in a given city.[4] If, for example, Democratic candidates received a majority vote for three state and three federal offices in a given city, and Republicans had a majority of the votes cast in that city for only two state offices, Democrats are considered to have won seventy-five percent of the partisan races that year.

The "nonpartisan success ratio" for each party in a city is simply the percentage of the total mayoral and councilmanic election races which were won by persons registered in that party. The difference, if any, between the success of a given party in partisan and nonpartisan elections indicates

---

[4]The presidential race was not considered because of the volatility of the vote for that office in the cities studied.

the degree of advantage which candidates of that party enjoy from non-partisan elections. This difference is defined as the Republican or the Democratic *partisan bias of nonpartisanship*.

The eighty-eight cities in which this research was undertaken employ nonpartisan ballots in local election. Moreover, with one exception, parties are, at most, marginally active in city politics. The cities range in population from 300 to almost 400,000 and possess a variety of socioeconomic characteristics. All are located in the nine counties conventionally referred to as the San Francisco Bay Area, and represent all but three of the municipalities in the region at the time of the study. Two very small cities, where local data were unavailable, and the city of San Francisco, where recent elections have been overtly partisan, were not included in the statistical analysis.

Almost all of the councilmen and mayors in the cities studied are elected for four-year terms. All but one city elects its councilmen at-large, although in four additional cases, candidates represent districts in which they must reside. The one city utilizing district elections instituted that system in 1965.

Certain assumptions underlie the methods used in this research. Space limitations preclude discussion of these assumptions here, although they have been justified at length elsewhere.[5]

1. Over a period of years, the disposition of a city's electorate toward state and national candidates in partisan elections (excluding presidential aspirants) will approximate its partisan disposition toward *local* candidates if local elections are partisan.
2. Whatever differences there are in voter turnout rates in local partisan elections, as compared to state and national elections, will not significantly affect the relative success of Democrats or Republicans in local offices as compared with other offices.
3. If partisan elections were held in a given city, the relative activity of the two political parties would be approximately the same in local elections on the one hand and state and national elections on the other.
4. The differential success of Republicans in local elections cannot be accounted for by the fact that candidates elected in nonpartisan local elections need only a plurality vote in most of the cities studied, while it requires a majority vote to win elections in nonlocal partisan races (since only two parties seriously contest each office).

FINDINGS

Comparisons of partisan and nonpartisan elections in the San Francisco Bay Area cities indicate that if partisan local elections had been

[5]Hawley, *Nonpartisan Elections* . . . , Appendix to Ch. 3.

held during the period studied, all but eight of the cities would have had a different mix of Democrats and Republicans holding mayoral and councilmanic positions. The specific number of seats that would have changed party in individual cities depends on the size of the partisan bias and the number of local offices that were contested. . . .

Thirty-five cities would have had more Republicans on their councils over the ten-year period, with the average change in these cities being the addition of two Republicans over the decade. In forty-five cities, an average of three more Democrats would have won local office.

Whether one considers the net partisan bias of nonpartisanship for the area as a whole to be significant depends to a certain extent on one's perspectives and predispositions. In 36 per cent of the cities, to be sure, partisan elections *would not* have changed as many as two council seats from one party to the other over the ten-year period. However, in some cities the change in the distribution of seats between the two paries would have been much greater than others. In most of these cities, Democrats would have won substantially more elected positions than they did in nonpartisan elections. In other words, to the extent that the partisan makeup of governing boards would have been *substantially* changed in individual cases, that change would have much more likely resulted in the election of more Democrats. For example, in the 26 cities where more than 25 per cent of the council seats would have changed hands, nonpartisanship resulted in a Republican bias (favored Republicans) in nineteen and a Democratic bias in seven. Thus, the policy consequences of the partisan bias of nonpartisanship may be quite important if the issues dividing Republicans and Democrats are raised more often in cities where nonpartisanship has a Republican bias, than in cities in which partisan elections have a Democratic bias. This possibility is discussed below.

Toward a Theoretical Explanation of the Partisan Bias of Nonpartisanship

By eliminating the candidates' party affiliations from the ballot and reducing the likelihood of party activity, nonpartisan elections (1) often make it more difficult for the voter to identify candidates who reflect his interests, and (2) require higher levels of motivation to participate in local politics. While these "burdens" are distributed equally throughout the population, Republican voters are more likely than Democratic voters to overcome them. In other words, nonpartisan elections tend to increase the advantages Republicans enjoy with respect to organizational resources, experience and interest in political activity, and influence in politically relevant channels of communication. At the same time, nonpartisanship increases the difficulties that Democrats—who are generally less well educated and less familiar with politics than Republicans—have in linking their interests with their political behavor.

As Philip Converse has observed: ". . . the elites of leftist parties enjoy a 'natural' numerical superiority, yet they are cursed with a clientele that is less dependable or solidary in its support. The rightist elite has a natural clientele that is more limited but more dependable."

The importance of parties is highest in cities where successful candidates for public office must possess more substantial political resources and mobilize greater numbers of voters. Therefore, in these same cities, the Republicans will derive greater advantage from nonpartisanship.

Thus, we might expect that the probability that Republicans will be advantaged under nonpartisanship increases:

1. As the proportion of low income, less well educated persons increases.
2. As the size of the city increases.

Statistical evidence from this study shows that both city size and the overall socioeconomic status (SES) of a city are highly related to the partisan bias of nonpartisanship in the cities studied.[6] The data indicate quite clearly that the likelihood of Republican candidates being advantaged by nonpartisanship increases as the average SES of the community's population decreases. (The product moment correlation coefficient between a city's SES and the extent and direction of the partisan bias found in its local elections is −.52).

With respect to city size, it seems reasonable that there is some threshold beyond which the role of parties in mobilizing voters, financing campaigns and recruiting candidates becomes especially important to Democratic candidates. The findings of this study suggest strongly that this is the case. The partisan bias of nonpartisanship was not significantly related to size in cities under 50,000. In smaller cities the median Republican bias was only 2 per cent. But, in cities over 50,000 the median Republican bias of nonpartisanship was 18 per cent.[7]

In short, in the 16 largest cities in the Bay Area (San Francisco excluded), size has a substantial relationship with the Republican bias of nonpartisanship, but in smaller cities it has little systematic effect.

[6]For purposes here, city size is defined as the average population of a given city during 1957–1966. Socioeconomic status (SES) of a community is defined in terms of a factor which incorporates measures of education achieved, occupation, family income, and employment status. Another way of making the same point is to note that the product moment correlation coefficient between population and Republican bias is an insignificant .04 in the 72 cities under 50,000 and .62 in the 16 cities over 50,000. (For all cities the correlation coefficient was .33).

[7]This means that had partisan local elections been held in these cities, about one out of five elections won by a Republican would have been won by a Democrat.

Since SES and population size are statistically independent in the cities (r=.11), it is possible to examine the relative and combined impact of these two variables on the Republican bias of nonpartisanship through the use of multiple-partial correlation techniques. Looking first at all cities, SES and size together account for about 35 per cent of the variance in the Republican bias of nonpartisanship among the cities. SES alone accounts for 28 percent of such variance and thus is a better predictor than city size of the degree to which Republicans are advantaged by nonpartisanship. In the sixteen largest Bay Area cities, SES and population together account for almost 58 per cent of the variance in the partisan bias of nonpartisanship, and size and SES contribute equally to this explanation.

In summary, the data support the hypotheses that nonpartisan elections generally enhance the electability of Republicans, and that this advantage enjoyed by Republicans increases as the size of the city and the proportion of low SES citizens increases.

There are, however, a number of factors which theoretically might reduce the Republican partisan bias in given cities. It seems reasonable to theorize that party activity, a high proportion of citizens with ethnic backgrounds, a very heavily Democratic registration, district election procedures, or a local media policy of endorsing Democrats, could reduce the Republican partisan bias of nonpartisanship one might expect if only a city's SES and population size were considered. The data developed in the Bay Area cities do not allow an adequate test of these hypotheses. However, the evidence suggests the tentative conclusion that party activity and ethnicity have the predicted consequences of improving the electability of Democrats in nonpartisan contests.[8]

SOME POLICY CONSEQUENCES OF NONPARTISAN ELECTIONS

While there is substantial evidence that the policies public officials seek to implement are consistent with their own policy preferences[9] the advocates of nonpartisanship have argued that parties make no sense in city politics because local issues are not partisan in character. But this belief, based partly on the idea that municipal affairs are largely apolitical, is a myth.

For example, while there may be "no Republican or Democratic way to pave a street," party differences related to class bias may well be reflected

[8]See Hawley, *Nonpartisan Elections . . .* , Chapter 5.
[9]See especially Heinz Eulau and Robert Eyestone, "City Councils and Policy Outcomes: Developmental Profiles," in James Q. Wilson, ed., *City Politics and Public Policy* (New York: John Wiley and Sons, 1968), 37–68; Hawley, *Nonpartisan Elections . . .* , Ch. 6, for a full discussion of this proposition.

in decisions on which streets should be paved, or in the priorities to be placed on street maintenance as compared with other needs. Many city policies involve choices among values that are similar to values underlying differences in attitudes considered to be partisan at the national level and in many states. Such issues include those involving the use of governmental power in promoting racial equality, the use of state and federal aid to solve local problems, limitations on free expression (especially where public morality or alleged political subversiveness is involved), government regulation of business and public utilities, and those policies which involve a distribution of resources and privilege among socioeconomic strata—such as those affecting taxation and social welfare.[10]

Analysis of the policy preferences of about 60 per cent of the Bay Area councilmen in 1968,[11] indicates that, compared to their Republican colleagues, Democratic councilmen manifested a greater willingness to use governmental power, especially the resources of state and federal governments, in attempting to solve urban problems. Local Democrats also placed higher priorities on the solution of social problems than did Republican councilmen.

However, if local elections were partisan, it is possible that the types of Democrats and Republicans elected to local office would be different from those elected in nonpartisan elections. Thus, political party officials in the San Francisco Bay Area were surveyed on the assumption that their views would approximate the views of councilmen elected on a partisan ballot. One hundred and twelve party leaders were surveyed, 70 Republicans and 42 Democrats.[12]

The differences between the attitudes of Democratic and Republican party leaders were similar in substance, but much greater in intensity, than the attitude differences between Democratic and Republican councilmen. The differences between the policy preferences of Democratic party leaders and Democratic councilmen were substantially greater than the differences

---

[10]A number of studies demonstrate that Republican and Democratic party elites differ in their policy preferences on the types of issues cited here. With respect to California, see Edmond Costantini and Kenneth H. Craik, "The Parties ARE Different," in Eugene C. Lee and Willis D. Hawley, eds., *The Challenge of California* (Boston: Little, Brown and Co., 1970), 62–73. Cf. Gerald Pomper, *Elections in America: Control and Influence in Democratic Politics* (New York: Dodd, Mead, and Co., 1969), Chs. 7–8; and Herbert McClosky, et al., "Issue Conflict and Consensus Among Party Leaders and Followers," *American Political Science Review*, 54 (June, 1960), 406–427.

[11]The sixty percent who returned the mailed questionnaire used in this study were quite similar to all Bay Area councilmen with respect to party registration, occupation, and the size of the city governed.

[12]Sixty percent of the Republican party leaders and 50 per cent of the Democratic party leaders surveyed returned the questionnaire.

in the attitudes between their Republican counterparts. Further, on some issues, there were greater differences between the attitudes of Democratic party leaders and Democratic councilmen, than between Republican councilmen and Democratic councilmen. In short, it appears not only that nonpartisan elections favor the choice of Republicans, but also that the Democrats who are elected in nonpartisan contests may be more conservative politically than the Democrats who would come to office if the elections had been partisan.

The data suggest that a primary reason why Democratic councilmen hold views relatively similar to the views expressed by Republicans is that the agents of leadership recruitment in nonpartisan political settings are civic groups commonly dominated by persons of upper-middle class and business backgrounds.

SUMMARY

The importance of the differences just noted in the policy preferences of Democratic and Republican councilmen increases in significance when it is remembered that the nonpartisanship advantages accruing to Republicans vary with community characteristics. Thus, while Democrats have better chances of being elected in nonpartisan elections in some cities than they would in partisan elections, the policy consequences of such advantages seem minor. The issues which face smaller, relatively homogeneous middle-class cities—the communities in which Democrats are most likely to benefit from *non*partisanship—tend to be those which engender relatively little conflict. These issues often do not get to those questions on which Democrats and Republicans are most likely to differ. Indeed, one of the reasons Democrats may win elections in some middle- and upper-middle class communities may be that no one wants the job.[13]

On the other hand, cities of large size and low socioeconomic characteristics, where the greatest Republican bias of nonpartisanship is found, are much more likely to be characterized by problems of poverty and ethnic discrimination which require positive governmental involvement for solution. Indeed, given the conditions associated with substantial Republican bias, it is a political paradox that the more Republican candidates are advantaged by nonpartisanship, the greater the need, and the lower the probability, that policies calling for governmentally fostered social change will be enacted.

[13]As the social rank of the community increases, competition for city councils tends to decline in the 88 cities studied.

CONCLUSION

I have argued that nonpartisan elections affect access to positions of political power so as to systematically advantage some interests over others depending on the character of the community. A number of studies have pointed to different ways that nonpartisanship may affect community power and policy and it is appropriate to briefly review this evidence.

PARTISANSHIP MAY FACILITATE ACTION

Partisan and nonpartisan cities may differ in their policy outputs because power is more easily organized and concentrated in partisan cities. Some recent studies have concluded that an effectively functioning party system allows a city government to take action in the face of levels of controversy which tend to immobilize nonpartisan city governments.[14]

This generalization seems to be particularly applicable to larger, socially heterogeneous, cities. Given the critical character of many urban problems, it seems not unreasonable to conclude that if the impotence which many ascribe to local governments is at all traceable to nonpartisanship, it can be said that nonpartisanship affects the direction of public policy by facilitating maintenance of the *status quo*. Some evidence on the point is furnished by Robert Alford and Michael Aiken's study of policy innovation in American cities of 25,000 or more people. They found *negative* relationships between the presence of nonpartisan elections and (1) the number of housing units constructed per 100,000 population since 1933, (2) per capita expenditures on urban renewal and, (3) per capita expenditures within the city on War on Poverty programs.[15]

Further, by masking differences in non-economic values, parties may facilitate the development of formal, or electoral, coalitions among the poor and the working class. If the Democratic party serves such a function, this presumably increases the probabilities of successful efforts at income redistribution and social change.

[14]Cf. Donald B. Rosenthal and Robert L. Crain, "Structure and Values in Local Political Systems: The Case of Fluoridation Decisions," in James Q. Wilson, ed., *City Politics and Public Policy* (New York: John Wiley and Sons, 1968), pp. 217–242; J. David Greenstone and Paul E. Peterson, "Reformers, Machines, and the War on Poverty," in Wilson, *Ibid.*, pp. 267–292; and Robert Crain and James Vanecko, "Elite Influence in School Desegregation," in Wilson, *Ibid.*, pp. 125–148.

[15]Robert Alford and Michael Aiken, "Comparative Urban Research and Community Decision-making," *The New Atlantis*, 1 (Winter, 1970), 94.

NONPARTISANSHIP, DEMOGOGUERY, AND RACIAL MINORITIES

If demagoguery is defined as the search for power through the arousal of the emotions and prejudices of people, a voter's sense of party identification may be, in effect, a constraint on the appeals of demagoguery. As V. O. Key concluded in his gentle way:

> Perhaps a clue to the picturesque quality of southern political leaders lies in the fact that attention-getting antics function as a substitute for party . . . in the organization of support.[16]

The notion that nonpartisanship increases the opportunities for successful demagoguery in local elections finds support in the recent research of Dean Jaros and Gene L. Mason. On the basis of a controlled experiment examining the reaction of a large sample of voters to demagogic appeals in both the presence and absence of partisan referents, they conclude, "It is clear that the existence of party symbols decreases the likelihood of voters choosing demagogic candidates."[17]

If appeals to fear and prejudice are likely to have greater consequence in nonpartisan than in partisan elections, it may be that the probability that blacks or other racial minorities will win local elections, especially if they are city-wide, is enhanced by partisanship. And, of course, because racial minorities are disproportionally of lower socioeconomic status, the party's role as an agent of mobilization is important in maximizing electoral participation among those minorities that will most likely identify with nonwhite candidates. It may also be that parties are a form of state-sponsored, organizational subsidy to blacks and other low income minorities that facilitates electoral success.

NONPARTISANSHIP AND THE DEPOLITICIZATION
OF LOCAL ISSUES

It may be that nonpartisan and partisan cities can be differentiated in terms of the range of issues which are considered the appropriate

---

[16]V. O. Key, *Southern Politics* (New York: Knopf, 1949), 46.

[17]Dean Jaros and Gene L. Mason, "Party Choice and Support for Demagogues: An Experimental Examination," *American Political Science Review*, 63 (March, 1969), p. 108. This conclusion finds support in another experimental study in which Daniel Fleitas found that ". . . when party information was available [to "voters"] as an anchor for ballot preferences, bandwagon and underdog influences were weakened." See Fleitas, "Bandwagon and Underdog Effects in Minimal Information Elections," *American Political Science Review*, 65 (June, 1971), 438.

responsibility of government. Robert Wood argues that this occurs because the citizen, lacking any political institutions intermediate between himself and government to which responsibilites for defining issues and exploring issues might be assigned, tends to adopt a passive and narrow view of the uses of politics. Moreover, this form of depoliticization of issues is often accompanied by a propensity on the part of officials to redefine political questions as administrative questions and thus to give city bureaucrats relatively free reign.[18] The consequence of this, it is argued, is a city government that avoids issues about which there is likely to be dissensus, i.e., those which involve economic and social inequality and discrimination.

One consequence of defining local issues as either administrative or outside the scope of government is that issues are not resolved in public view, whether they are dealt with by city government or by private groups. For example, one recent study systematically comparing decision-making in six council–manager cities that employ either partisan or nonpartisan elections concludes that decisions in partisan cities are more likely to be made publicly and by those who hold elected positions.[19] Terry Clerk has examined policymaking in fifty-one cities over 50,000 and concluded that reformed political institutions, including nonpartisanship, tend to be associated with highly centralized decision-making—as measured by the number and diversity of participants.[20] By encouraging the allocation of decision-making leadership to public bureaucrats, rather than elected officials, nonpartisanship may transfer policy initiatives to those whose personal values are relatively conservative and who have little self-interest in engaging issues that are likely to create conflict or otherwise challenge the status quo.[21]

The depoliticization of community issues tends not only to increase the decision-making power of public bureaucrats, but to allow private groups to resolve, or to avoid the resolution of, such issues. Working classes and the

[18]For example, in the mid-1960s, the city manager of Oakland, California, persuaded his nonpartisan city council that minority demands for legislative control of police use of firearms was inappropriate by arguing that while the decision on whether police should carry guns was political, once their right to bear arms was established, how these weapons were used was an administrative matter.

[19]Clyde D. McKee, *The Politics of Council–Manager Forms Having and Not Having the Partisan Election* (Unpublished Ph.D. Dissertation, Univ. of Conn., 1968).

[20]Terry N. Clark, "Community Structure, Decision-making . . . ," *op. cit.*, and Terry N. Clark, "The Structure of Community Influence," in Harlan Hahn, ed., *People and Politics in Urban Society* (Beverly Hills, Calif.: Sage Publications, 1972), pp. 293–312.

[21]There appears to be no research that compares the values of city bureaucrats in nonpartisan and partisan cities, or the values of bureaucrats with those of elected officials in the same cities. However, there is some reason to believe that city managers, who play a dominant role in decision-making in most nonpartisan cities, are relatively conservative with respect to priorities placed on social change and the use of federal resources to achieve such change. See Lloyd M. Wells, "Social Values and Political Orientations of City Managers: A Survey Report," *Southwestern Social Science Quarterly*, 48 (December, 1967), 443–450; and Banfield and Wilson, Ch. 13.

poor seldom control private organizations, other than unions, that are in a position to make or enforce policies that involve the distribution or equalization of wealth or privilege. Lacking such inputs, community decision-making in nonpublic organizations is usually conservative in consequence.[22]

In other words, the political resource which those of lower status most often possess in approximate equity with those of higher status is access to public officials through the electoral process. When issues are bureaucratized or privatized, the value that such access to elected officials has in shaping policy is diminished and, thus, control over the disposition of community issues by those of lower socioeconomic status declines accordingly.

If the depoliticization of community issues is more likely in nonpartisan than in partisan cities, does it make any difference in the direction of public policies? In their analysis of taxation and expenditure policies in American cities with more than 50,000 people, Lineberry and Fowler conclude that nonpartisanship, as well as other reform institutions, tends to reduce responsiveness of city governments to social cleavages. In effect, they argue, the apparent depoliticization of public decision-making that takes place in nonpartisan cities reduces the access of minority and lower class groups to decision-makers.[23]

NONPARTISANSHIP AND THE RELATIVE IMPORTANCE OF INTEREST GROUPS IN THE LEGISLATIVE PROCESS

In partisan political arenas, the party usually serves as a vehicle for structuring the legislative process. While the extent of party cohesion in legislative policymaking may vary, with the strength of party organizations accounting for much of this variation, legislative partisanship often serves as a countervailing influence in the face of pressures by non-party interest groups. It is relevant to note that lobbyists have consistently opposed the introduction of party labels in Nebraska's *state* elections, in apparent recognition of the threat that partisanship poses to their current power.

SUMMARY

This chapter has suggested that in addition to its impact on the relative electability of Republicans and Democrats, partisanship contributes to less conservative policies than nonpartisanship because it (1) facilitates

---

[22]Terry Clark has found that the influence of business groups in decision-making is greater in "reformed" cities. Clark, "The Structure of Community Influence," *op. cit.*, p. 297.

[23]Robert L. Lineberry and Edmund P. Fowler, "Reformism and Public Policies in American Cities," *American Political Science Review*, 61 (September, 1967), 701–716.

political action in the face of conflict; (2) reduces the voters' vulnerability to demagoguery and enhances the political opportunities of ethnic minorities; and (3) encourages the resolution of community issues in the political arena by elected public officials. This is a great deal to claim for a political institution, and it must be acknowledged that the evidence upon which these inferences are drawn is not definitive. However, the possibility that any or all of these is true would seem to be sufficiently strong, and of sufficient consequence for public policy, to merit serious consideration.

TYPES OF LOCAL POLITICAL SYSTEMS AND PLANNING POLICY

Francine F. Rabinovitz

In this selection taken from Professor Rabinovitz's book, The Politics of City Planning, *the questions being asked are very similar to those posed by Clark and Aiken and Alford earlier in this chapter. However, this exploration of the relationships between characteristics of community, local politics and public policy—in this case, planning—gives much more weight to explicitly political aspects of community structure. Rabinovitz's study also differs from the previous two articles in its consideration of how historical and cultural factors have shaped the distribution and exercise of power.*

The reader may wish to weigh the relative advantages of the analytical approach employed in this study and those utilized by Clark and by Aiken and Alford. For example, what would Rabinovitz's findings have been had she considered only those factors that were readily quantifiable? And which approach—or what combination of approaches—holds the greatest payoff for the development of theories that might account for different patterns of decision-making and how such differences affect the quality of community life?

Of course, the reader will also want to consider the substantive conclusions reached in this study in light of the results of other inquiries. The comparative case study offers many advantages but it provides a limited base on which to develop generalizations or test propositions. When the results of case studies seem to conflict with the findings of other analyses, they must depend on the power of the theory which underlies them. Consider, for example, Professor Rabinovitz's proposition that political competition tends to reduce innovation—at least with respect to planning.

Reprinted from Francine F. Rabinovitz, *City Politics and Planning* (New York: Atherton Press, Inc., 1969). Copyright © 1969 Atherton Press, Inc. Reprinted by permission of the author and Aldine Publishing Co.

The variations in political systems in American cities have long been debated by students of urban affairs. The forms or patterns taken by political cal systems in different cities can probably be ranged along a continuum according to manifest differences in distribution of power, political culture, and the level of output from the system. It seems likely that in some cities influence is concentrated while in others it is more dispersed. Even within the pluralist group, differences exist in the sources of strength on which coalitions are built, the prevailing ethos of the city, the frequency of non-elite participation in decision-making, and ability of the particular city to act. Accordingly, we may ask what are the manifest characteristics of political cal systems in which effective planning has occurred according to such a classificatory scheme?*

MAJOR BANDS ON THE CONTINUUM

The Cohesive System

Montclair, the community nominated as having the most effective planning, must be placed toward the elitist extreme on the continuum. The major characteristics of this city, whose pattern of decision-making can be typed "cohesive," have already been outlined in Chapter II. While decision-making in Montclair is not a carbon copy of the power pyramid derived, for example, from the theoretical conceptions Hunter has of Regional City, it approximates monopolistic decision-making in several ways.

A primary characteristic of Montclair's political system is the tendency for policy—be it on the renewal issue, commission nominations, or the settlement of the integration problem—to be decided by a small number of recurring participants. It is unclear to what degree activists work within a framework established by less visible participants, but there is a strong indication that a covert group stands behind the overt leadership. Although Montclair has a visible group of powerful generalists who act on a wide range of issues and occupy key public positions, the approval of a few other prestigious men is one critical element in a project's initiation. Residents active in community affairs note that there are several "old families" with a tradition of service whose approval is necessary to go ahead with a project. One observer compared their attitude to that of the British ruling class, in that they are benevolent and influential but normally inactive and

---

*Editors' Note: Effective planning is defined here as the capacity of planners to affect the course of a city's development by modifying the system of people and space in ways consistent with planners' preferences. The effectiveness of planning can be determined in three situations: (1) when the expert initiates a planning policy that meets with no opposition, and it is enacted; (2) when the planner prevents a policy he opposes from being enacted; and (3) when the planner initiates a policy that meets opposition, but that is nevertheless enacted.

345 of Local Political Systems and Planning Policy

invisible in decision-making. In 1961, for example, the Community Commission went through the process of arriving at a slate for the formation of a charter-study commission. As candidates were selected for the bracketed slate, they were introduced privately to two of Montclair's "old families." It is not clear that these introductions were in any way decisive, but the need to make them suggests that projects originated by the policy-determining group proceed within limits not set by the activists.

In 1963, there was no countervailing power in Montclair to the small group of active decision-makers and covert elite, who had the ability to set limits; but the elite had increasingly to take into account various subgroupings. The most significant were the Negro subcommunity and the representatives of the radical right. The growing power of the Negro subcommunity is indicated by the number of issues, suggested to the field investigator as significant, that involved Negro-white relations.

Despite the existence of these different centers of influence, Montclair tends toward the elitist end of the continuum because of the type and impact of its political culture. What is striking is that the community operates on the basis of a high degree of normative and procedural agreement that binds both the few decision-makers whose names recur in different substantive areas and the subgroups that participate in only some of those areas. Different centers of power do exist, but, strictly speaking, they are not in competition.

A closer look at Montclair's planning policies indicates some of the points of normative agreement. There has been over the years a striking continuity in the aims of planning policy, indicating basic agreement on what the town should look like and where it should go. Even current and seemingly novel projects like the extension of an apartment zone, the creation of a cultural center in residential Upper Montclair, and the easing of zoning in the "villa zone," have all been justified to property owners as tactics to prevent further erosion likely to change the face and character of the town. The planning staff is itself an instrument used to insure that new officials understand this code. New members of the City Commission are, according to the planner, appointed to the planning board in order that they may learn how Montclair normally evaluates things. Such a control mechanism, by socializing newcomers, assures a reasonable conformity to community norms.

More striking even than the substantive consensus is the conformity to the existing "rules of the game." A community more monolithic than Montclair would probably have a bias in favor of the suppression of a very large number of conflicts. Sanctions could exist that would allow the elite to limit the scope of all decision-making to issues that presented no challenges to predominating values. In Montclair, a permissive area of legitimate conflict exists on substantive issues. But, even when the *status quo* is challenged, differences are settled without disrupting the over-all procedural accord. New interests learn to live within the common system of norms and habits, and consensus on the need to avoid extended public clashes has been achieved. Thus, even when policy conflict exists, issues are adjusted without resort to open conflict. The Negro community, instead of pushing its claims to the point where established relations are threatened, has chosen to seek a foothold within the system. Because it accepts the basic precepts of the political culture, the Negro community has negotiated to gain access and has not tried to replace the existing configuration with a new order. Thus, in most substantive areas conflict is largely avoided. Bargaining takes place but within a highly structured and relatively stable system.

Although the explanation for the presence of this kind of consensus is too broad a question to be considered here, it is interesting to juxtapose its presence with social composition factors. In terms of changes in population size; percentage of foreign born; and percentage of white-collar workers, managers, and professionals, Montclair confirms the theories indicating that stable, upper-middle class, relatively homogeneous populations are associated with greater concentrations of power. However, Montclair has a higher percentage of nonwhites than any of the other cities studied, and this suggests that there is a racial basis for conflicting power centers. It has been noted, however, that the Negro community, while an important subgroup, is not a countervailing force in the usual sense even in an era when Negro activity is high on the national level. This may be explained by the fact that Montclair's Negro population has learned to share in the political culture of the rest of the community. This learning process would seem to be associated with the fact that the Negro population is not made up of newcomers to the community but of relatively long-term residents. Among the communities identified by the New York Metropolitan Region study as having very large Negro populations, only Montclair had a nonwhite population figure of over 20 per cent in 1950; only Montclair had a nonwhite population of under 25 per cent in 1960.

More directly relevant to planning and the roles of the planner is the relation of the Montclair pattern of decision-making to output. Although, in Montclair, both planning and power operate to maintain the *status quo,* the high level of cohesion is related to a marked capability of the system to solve those difficulties accepted as problems. Montclair has proved capable of altering its physical environment—it was nominated in the previously cited North Carolina national survey as well as in New Jersey, as a community exhibiting successful planning efforts. For the present, it has coped with existing social problems. The existing system appears to decrease the reluctance of community leaders to face decisions on development. On the one hand, most decision-makers, especially those holding elected offices, wish to avoid substantive problems for fear of involving themselves in community-wide conflicts. Montclair's commissioners, on the other hand, having little basis for expecting overt conflict to occur, are less afraid of facing far-reaching problems.

The Executive Centered System

A second pattern of decision-making is associated with two cities, Paterson and Jersey City, which were nominated as having had effective planning programs during limited time periods. Here the leadership group is larger and comprised mainly of public officials and prominent private individuals representing major interests in the city. The chief executive stands at the center and is highly influential over many sectors of public policy, but he does not send orders through an absolute hierarchy of influence. The executive's power "pyramid" is disordered by uncertainty as to who holds influence, and subject to substantial negotiation and bargaining. Jersey City and Paterson fit within this pattern of the executive centered coalition. At the same time, dissimilar as Montclair and Jersey City may be in social, economic, and historical circumstances, the stamping ground of Boss Hague is a much shorter distance down the continuum from the home of company presidents than is either New Haven or Paterson.

The tradition of executive domination in Jersey City is a long one. As Hudson County's largest city, it was ruled by a succession of famous political bosses. . . . Instead of a clandestine or covert exercise of influence, Jersey City had an overt political elite. Unlike economic elites and most city bosses, both of whom prefer to operate behind the scenes, Hague held an elective office in his own community for more than a quarter of a century, transacting business through the City Hall. John V. Kenny, a former Hague ward leader, picked up the reins in 1949, leading an anti-Hague Freedom Ticket to victory.

Kenny's leadership partook more of the qualities of the executive centered coalition than had Hague's more monolithic rule. Hague's power was exercised overtly. Under his rule there was, however, an almost total internalization of conflict; and many sanctions existed to socialize actors to the norms of the Hague-run system. Kenny, while not totally eschewing the maintenance of power through the management of patronage, maintained power primarily by a process of internal negotiation. The divisive tendencies inherent in Jersey City's ethnic structure, accentuated by the city's nonpartisan commission form of government, were overcome by the control exercised by the Kenny organization in part through ballot balancing in municipal elections.

Kenny made strides in abolishing employee assessments, preventing intervention in judicial processes, and in discontinuing New Year's bonuses to city employees. However, once the solid wall of Irish executive rule had cracked, business groups, which had abdicated from the political scene by establishing a *modus vivendi* with professional politicians at the local level, became more active. The change in the holders of influence allowed the numerically inferior groups to reassert themselves. A committee of clergymen organized to ask for better housing conditions; and louder grumblings were heard over high taxes, high assessments, and the inability of public agencies to meet their financial needs because of the number of their full-time employees. Finally, in 1959, as a result of business pressure, Jersey City elected a charter revision commission; in 1960, the mayor-council form was adopted.

An executive centered system also existed in Paterson, a city organized 172 years ago by Alexander Hamilton. The original charter made his founding corporation an omnipotent enterprise, acting as the local government of the area, complete with the power of eminent domain and exemption from Federal taxation. Today, too, Paterson is unique in that it is governed by what is in some ways the strongest mayoral form of government in the nation. The city's only elected officials, in addition to the mayor, are aldermen, who represent the people of eleven wards. They, like the Board of Public Works, are limited largely to issuing licenses—for taverns, bingo, raffles, and junk. The mayor wields an unchecked power of appointment over some 250 city offices. However, since board members serve for overlapping terms and have some independent powers, mayors can be countermanded by them on some decisions, particularly at the beginning of the administration.

This extraordinary charter has never been sufficient to place Paterson's mayor at the top of a monolithic power pyramid. Successive iron, steel, locomotive, and textile industries have given the city a residue of influential business leaders and old families. While Republican mayors remained in power, the business community was content to act covertly, limiting its political activity to the specific issues it believed affected its interests. By the 1950s, however, it was estimated that there were more Democrats than Republicans among the city's 45,000 voters; in 1955, after two consecutive terms under a Republican, Paterson elected a Democrat, defeating the incumbent for office.

As the pendulum swung, the head of one of the city's old families, the publisher of the leading newspaper and an executive of a large utility, sponsored a meeting at which 75 prominent businessmen agreed to keep economic groups in the forefront of public activity in the future. They formed an association of business, financial, and community leaders that they called Forward Paterson and dedicated it to reversing the decline that characterized America's "first industrial city." As in Jersey City, the most active participants were those with major investments in the community, investments that depended on Paterson's growth. The emergence of these businessmen into overt participation is a relatively recent phenomenon, common in other cities in the 1950s and coincidental with a broader perception of the possible decline of downtown economic values because of decay in the urban core. Their entry is linked to some weakening of the traditionally dominant group in the city. The activation of the business community in Peterson coincided with the beginning of a transition toward increased Democratic influence. The new mayor was County Democratic leader as well as Mayor of Paterson. The County Freeholders and the legislative representatives of the county at Trenton were Republicans when he took office. Yet it was clear from the defeat of the Republicans in the city that a change was occurring, and the downtown business interests were spurred to the formation of new alliances to articulate their concerns more forcefully.

In Jersey City, coalition building occurred with the weakening of political rather than of economic power, but its outlines followed the same path. The business interests were strong enough to gain a charter change but were unable to capture the electoral reins under the new system. The man elected mayor in 1961 was the candidate of the party organization. Nevertheless, he chose to cast himself as a compromise figure. He stressed before business groups that he had opposed Kenny's ticket in 1953, despite reconciliation in 1957 and his election as Hudson County Supervisor. With the backing of the Kenny organization, which meant the support of ethnic leaders, already in hand, the new mayor's image was that of a business executive in the campaign. Once in office, the need for development that had caused the first breaks in the old executive-centered ethnic coalition became a tool for the consolidation of power. The consensus on the need for physical changes as the goal of the community legitimated executive leadership. The Jersey City business community was not eager to throw its support behind a machine-connected candidate, but the consensus over goals forced them to acquiesce. The mayor persuaded, insisted, and threatened until the businessmen formed an advisory committee of merchants, corporation presidents, and bankers, which publicly advertised their backing of the mayor and the plans for renewal.

In Paterson, the new mayor also hitched his administration to problem-solving programs, such as redevelopment and traffic revision, favored by the business group organized as Forward Paterson. By doing so, he linked the numerical backing of the Democrats with the merchants, leaving the Republican party with no issues and relegating to it the role of minor critic of the programs implemented by the Democrats. Voting patterns for the subsequent 10 years (to 1965) show just how effective this strategy was.

In Jersey City, and to a lesser degree in Paterson, the executive controlled. As one participant in Jersey City affairs stated: "Everyone came around to working with the mayor but he didn't have total confidence in any of them. He really made all the decisions." In Paterson, the men who made up Forward Paterson had the trappings of a power elite but could not lead. As a city reporter noted: "Forward Paterson never seems to take a firm stand on any controversial issues because of the divergent views of the membership." Subject to intramural clashes of ties and values that brought the interests and commitments of members into conflict, the business group could raise issues and promote the provision of information, but it was often paralyzed. Its inadequacy came to light as Forward Paterson split over the question of downtown renewal; a new organization, Paterson Looks Ahead Now (PLAN), was formed. When action was taken, the mayor dominated the scene.

Clearly, this system is not the perfect monolith with a hierarchical arrangement in which the mayor at the top operates through subordinates in a chain of command; and it is dissimilar to the cohesive system in which dissident groups make claims that do not change the face of the system. Jersty City's charter reform, resulting from the pressure of aggregated dissident groups, is a good example of the effect of outsiders in cities not perfectly monolithic. Mayors situated more or less as Lee in New Haven, Gangemi in Jersey City, O'Byrne and his successor, Frank Graves in Paterson have been, do not stand at the head of even a loose pyramid but rather at the center of intersecting circles. While Montclair's leaders are bargained with, the leaders of these communities are perpetually bargaining. They negotiate and cajole because they need support from ethnic leaders and business groups who are too powerful to be commanded. Yet in all three cases—in New Haven, in Jersey City, and in Paterson—similarities to the more monopolistic pattern seem to remain. Overt conflict is rare because of the efforts of the executive to settle existing differences within the system in a continuous process of bargaining. It is symptomatic that the most prominent overt conflicts in Jersey City surround the changing of the executive leader himself. Internal bargaining and the avoidance of overt conflict succeed in producing high outputs of projects, largely because the degree of consensus on goals forces and legitimates acceptance of executive leadership.

The Competitive System

A fourth city, Clifton, nominated as having effective planning for a fourteen-year period, must be placed further down the continuum in the direction of increasing pluralism, within the category of "competitive" decision-making. In contrast to the executive-centered system where one leader is dominant because of his ability to knit together existing groups, the competitive form occurs when more than one leadership clique exists in competition with others on a continuing basis. Political control of the community does not necessarily alternate; coalescence under an executive has declined to the point where the clique in power is consistently challenged and an alternative is clearly visible.

Clifton has never been a true city in the usual physical sense of the word —it lacks a center, forming a doughnut-shaped ring around the city of Passaic. Its diffuse pattern of physical development correlated with a diffusion of political influence. While other American cities were dominated by merchants from the Civil War until 1900, Clifton had neither a mercantile nor a patrician elite. The scions of the textile industry lived and worked in the Passaic core; they showed no interest in running the affairs of the hinterland, settled by the Dutch as a farming area. As Clifton began to lose its rural character, an autonomous political elite emerged. Governing the city became a game engaged in by a group led by an Irish ward boss. Although Clifton had a monopolistic political system, power remained concentrated in the governing group because the Dutch farmers were unaffected by the government. They were too far from Clifton's center of government to care what occurred there.

From 1910 on, Clifton experienced a number of building booms. Multifamily housing began to appear. The population jumped 77 per cent from 1920 to 1930 alone. The burghers, Protestant and Republican, showed their concern. In 1934, in a quiet revolution, Clifton adopted the nonpartisan council-manager form, installing a local politician, who had been the city clerk and was also Protestant and Republican, as manager. The style of politics from 1934 to the 1950s is characterized by the long tenure of the manager, who held office for seventeen years. In Florida cities and in Winnetka, Illinois, others have observed that such long tenure is normally associated with lack of cleavage in a city. Small communities with prosperous homogeneous populations most often fit this type. Their managers come to occupy positions of some strength because they are in charge of routine matters, and most matters are routine.

In the aftermath of World War II, Clifton's physical face changed again and with it the pattern of decision-making. In 1949, two new roads opened, giving developers access to abundant vacant land. The single-family housing boom was on. A surge of population growth followed, bringing in people different from the old local families. The new Cape Cod colonials were occupied by craftsmen and foremen, different not only in income and class but in expectations, from the pre-existing majority.

Since nonpartisanship is an advantage to incumbents by virtue of its recruitment and endorsement practices and because the organization of Clifton Democrats, long out of power, was outdated, the changes in Clifton's composition were not immediately reflected in shifts in the composition of the city council. Nevertheless, outside the electoral sphere, there were signs that a group divergent from the prevailing political leadership aspired to a place in political decision-making. Incipient party competition influenced other policies, since such competition was a function of differences among important values of the citizenry. . . .

Unlike the more integrated executive-centered and cohesive systems where open conflict is rare, Clifton's pattern of decision-making [has] stressed open conflict over offices in electoral campaigns. In this area, the interests of the rival groups were formed as a zero sum game—a payoff for one party meant an equivalent loss to the other. Overt conflict over the issues of development was less frequent. Both groups preferred to talk of personalities rather than policy. For the Big Four [long-term Republican councilmen], this posture rested on the belief that it was likely to be costly to have to defend current policies against the charges of economic waste and inefficiency. For the Little Three [the minority faction of the 7-member council], campaigns on the basis of personalities were proving relatively useful and did not necessitate that participants arrive at a satisfactory policy stance among themselves. In addition, policy decisions that required rapid action could always be stymied by the Big Four if it came to a showdown.

Because of the ambivalence of both groups about actually attacking Clifton's problems, many issues remained in a twilight zone of incomplete debate. . . . Routine or unavoidable decisions were placed in the hands of persons not politically responsible and pressure was applied to work out the conflicts internally. In Clifton, such decisions were aimed toward the manager, despite the disagreements over him, since he was both the instrument of the majority faction and a more neutral figure than either the Big Four of the Little Three.

When disagreements arise in the competitive system, where some cooperation is possible, the attempt is to resolve them internally. When the policies of the cliques are directly in conflict, as in the case of election to offices, leaders compete publicly. Many issues are neutralized, however. Unavoidable policy issues are shifted to non-political officials. The competitive pattern can be distinguished from the executive-centered coalitions in that the chief executive, mayor or manager, is the symbol of a unity he cannot create. Thus, while the competitive system does provide adequate services, its built-in resistance to innovation reduces the chances for the community to alter its environment.

The Fragmented System

Farthest from the cohesive community on the continuum is the city in which no visible leadership group or groups exist. Although formal holders of authority (mayors, councillors, city administrators) are thrust into the decision-making position by the vacuum in informal power, no one *leads*. Such a situation is illustrated by the pattern of decision-making in the city of Passaic, also nominated as having had effective planning.

Like New Haven in the course of the past century, Passaic has moved from oligarchy to pluralism. Leadership has passed from the hands of dominant industrialists, through those of the middle class, to politicians from working-class backgrounds who operate essentially as middle-class entrepreneurs. This transfer of power reflects alterations in the community in the course of which resources for obtaining influence have been fragmented, and a concomitant change in the decision-making pattern has occurred. In the 1800s, water power made Passaic the home of a thriving woolen and worsteds industry. Wealth and social position were the prerogatives of the owners of the leading mills who dominated the affairs of the city. Immigrants poured in and more than doubled the existing population during every decade from 1880 to 1910. When, however, the rates of population and industrial expansion slowed after World War I, families that had been prominent in civic affairs emigrated to more patrician communities. Despite the decline in industrial activity, retailers found their prosperity enhanced by suburban development along new transportation lines. The new rich occupied the seats of power vacated by the industrialists, as well as their "houses on the hill." The economic and social advancement of the immigrants gradually allowed them to produce new leaders in the community. In the first struggle for status, members of ethnic groups had depended for leadership on politicians from previously assimilated groups. Their gradual ascension into the middle strata led to an overthrowing of the incumbents. Candidates began to seek office by activating the sentiments of ethnic solidarity not only among the largely Jewish merchant group but also among the 23,000 production workers residing in Passaic. The successful sons of Slavic, Russian, and Italian laborers joined the merchants, on the "hill" and in politics. The general significance of these ethnic factors can be grasped from recent census figures. In 1960, fully 55 percent of the population was of foreign stock, either foreign born or children of immigrants. An additional 8.8 per cent was Negro and Puerto Rican; even among the remaining native white, ethnic identification retains some significance. The grandchildren of Italian immigrants, for example, might still consider themselves members of a distinct cultural group.

Passaic's nonpartisanship accentuated the tendency toward ethnic division. This type of system removes the possibility that social cleavages may cross party divisions and hence moderate conflict. Unlike Jersey City, where ethnic division was overcome by Hague's tactics despite formal nonpartisanship, the dominance of ethnic politics in Passaic affected the ability of the city to face development problems. Ethnic candidates sought to avoid divisive socioeconomic issues so that they could activate strong feelings of ethnicity in all strata of their group. Some problems were avoided because they stressed the class heterogeneity in the cultural group. Other issues, such as transportation and taxes, were less likely to create class factions but became impossible to solve because of the fragmented nature of a politics based on ethnicity. These development issues place less stress on the divisible benefits and costs and more on the advantages diffused across different groups. Development issues therefore depended on the possibility of the formation of a coalition. Ethnic politics does, however, create incentives for division. It is to the advantage of the candidate for office to differentiate himself personally in a system where each candidate seeks support individually among members of his own group, and where election organizations are *ad hoc* and therefore not responsible for policies. There is no gain in subordinating and reconciling difference as there would be if a candidate ran as a member of a balanced ticket, as in Jersey City. In Passaic, disunity does not mean defeat.

This fragmentation was further expanded by Passaic's commission government. There is often little leadership in a system where equal heads of government must contest for power and prestige. The coordination and cooperation essential to long-range planning and project development cannot be obtained. While Jersey City was able to subordinate ethnicity and nonpartisanship through the continuation of a bosslike informal apparatus and the resources provided at the county level to subdue ethnic forces in the city, no such coalescence occurred in Passaic.

Such a decision-making system has distinctive qualities of style and output. Almost all proposals for change tend to become either "issues" or the subject of controversy. This is because the system is wide open, admitting all comers. As the number of autonomous actors increases, control tends to become less structured; there are few established channels for taking action or for the suppression of conflict over unimportant decisions. Proposals existed in Passaic for firehouse renovation, but a $50,000 repair job involved a dispute and was not implemented. Attempts to eliminate a grade crossing stirred conflict. The commissioners issued ordinances in a campaign to clear vacant lots. Landlords complained and months later acrimonious debate arose as citizens complained about ragweed and poison ivy. To some extent the promotion of seemingly small decisions into issues is a function of scale. A $50,000 firehouse is objectively more important to a city the size of Passaic than it would be to Jersey City. But the tendency to make all decisions into "issues" is a product of the fact that the community has no binding view and no structure capable of imposing sanctions against controversy. It is the opposite of the cohesive community in which power is exercised in a restrictive fashion to limit the conflict potential of decision-making.

Consequently, it is difficult to obtain a real commitment to any policy course in the fragmented system. Many suggestions for changes arise through civic groups. Passaic has been in the forefront of movements toward civic reform, especially in zoning, vocational education, and urban renewal; few of these major projects make any more headway than the programs of firehouse renovation and campaigns against ragweed. This difficulty in achieving civic reform is due not so much to people with influence who would prevent anything from happening in order to protect their interests, as it is to the many parties who come in when they perceive that they may be injured by a new measure. These latter groups use their resources to block the action, and projects receiving even nominal approval bog down in the implementation stage.

Considerations of political style and output indicate that not only Passaic, where planning is said to have been effective, but also New Brunswick, where planning is said to have been ineffective, fit within the framework of the fragmented decision-making pattern. While the number of participants in New Brunswick is smaller than that in Passaic, the limitless opportunities for obstruction inherent in the system place it within this class. No decision seems to go unchallenged so innovation is attempted by political officials only when clear benefits from change are visible, as in the incorporation of the commercial zone in a new code for the city. New Brunswick's zoning difficulties illustrate how the frenzied activities of the injured can dominate policy-making.

In Passaic the fragmentation had gone further. It required an enormous expenditure of resources to overcome the disintegration and, consequently, politicians were unlikely to make formative decisions. Like Chicago's Mayor Daley, when forced to make a decision, these politicians did so as narrowly as was possible; and they avoided dealing with broad issues or principles. This attitude stands in sharp contrast to that of the mayors in New Haven or Jersey City. These mayors are able to manage other interests without waiting for the divers groups to reach their own compromise.

There have been very different judgments as to the desirability of this system. Some argue that from such diversity at the local level a truly open society results, and the system is based on built-in protections against consequences that violate values held by any one part of the community. All are able to organize and use their resources to gain access to decision-making processes for the protection of their interests. Thus, even when all consequences of action are not considered by the formal decision-makers, others will be aware of them and will use their influence to redress the damage or alter the conditions or even stop the decision from being made.

Even accepting this judgment, as opposed to the opinion that in the fragmented system there can be no correlation between the needs of the constituency and the outcomes, it does not necessarily follow that the best possible policy or planning always emerges from this process. And whether the policy derived is good or bad, it is undeniable that the system has a negative bias. The fragmented decision process takes a longer time to produce an outcome than other systems do; that outcome, when reached, is likely to be a stalemate.

THE RESULTS OF COMPARATIVE ANALYSIS

Convinced of the validity of the pluralist model of decision-making, many political scientists have concluded that comprehensive planning is impossible. They argue that while planning requires a centralization of influence, extreme decentralization is the typical pattern of influence distribution in American cities. In such a system, the output is bound to be low; in order for anything to be done under public auspices, the diffusion of legal authority and the inability to act must be overcome. The amount of influence needed to implement a comprehensive plan is so great that it overloads the capacity of the existing hierarchy. A comparative approach to the studies of single cities, however, suggests that the decision-making pattern of American communities is varied; the forms can be ranged along a continuum from integration to fragmentation, according to differences manifested in the number of persons who hold power, the norms for the style of its exercise, and the normal output of the system.

Although both the initial contrast here between a city with effective planning and one with ineffective planning and the traditional theories of plan implementation would lead us to expect that cities having effective planning will cluster at the monopolistic end of the continuum, this theory does not conform to the evidence. Instead, cities nominated as having effective planning fall all along the continuum. At the fragmented extreme, it does indeed appear that the capacity to cope with the recognized problems of the environment is normally less than adequate to keep these problems within tolerable limits; even in such a community, some people do attain their ends.

THE VERTICAL AXIS
OF COMMUNITY ORGANIZATION
AND THE STRUCTURE OF POWER

John Walton

In view of the many case studies of community power which have been carried out, it is surprising that so little systematic use has been made of the data they provide for comparative analysis of the factors associated with the distribution of influence. In the selection below John Walton examines the characteristics of a large number of communities and relates these characteristics to the structure of power which had been imputed to each community by the original researcher. David Rogers has noted the difficulties in accepting the validity of such conclusions.*

On the bases of these secondary data, Walton finds that to the extent that the local community becomes increasingly interdependent with "extra-community institutions," the structure of power becomes more competitive, i.e., more pluralistic. This "vertical axis" of extra-community influence is a factor which many earlier studies allude to as being of possible significance, but here Walton not only focuses upon estimates of its significance but places it within a broader theoretical framework.

In the relatively brief period since its inception, the study of community power structure has attracted a wide range of enthusiasts. Researchers of diverse backgrounds have found their particular interests coalesce around the assumption that local leadership processes are of central importance to the explanation of community action. . . .

In addition to fertile substantive applications, much has been done to develop the research methods of power-structure studies. . . .

[H]owever, there has been almost no progress in one vital respect; the

From *Community Structure, Power, and Decision-Making: Comparative Analysis*, ed., Terry N. Clark published by Chandler Publishing Company, San Francisco. Copyright 1968 by Chandler Publishing Company. Reprinted by permission.

*David Rogers, "Community Political Systems: A Framework and Hypothesis for Comparative Studies," in *Current Trends in Comparative Studies*, Bert E. Swanson, ed.,(Kansas City: Community Studies, Inc., 1962), 31–48.

development of theoretical explanation of the reported findings. Elaborate documentation of the atheoretical character of the field hardly seems necessary. One has only to peruse a portion of the literature to discover that the principal issues are almost entirely concerned with method and conflicting interpretations of how broadly power is distributed. Only rarely do we find some of the initial steps in theorizing represented by conceptual considerations and the development of propositional inventories.

The purpose of this paper is to develop a theoretical explanation of how power is distributed in local communities, and to consider briefly how various power arrangements may account for different forms of community action. The analysis incorporates earlier theoretical discussions of the community and a systematic review of the power-structure literature. Anticipating the conclusions for a moment, it will be argued that as communities become increasingly interdependent with extracommunity institutions, changes in the local normative order ensue producing more competitive power arrangements. . . .

FINDINGS OF PREVIOUS RESEARCH

[A] screening of the [published] literature [on community power resulted in a] list of studies [which] was checked against several lengthy bibliographies to insure its inclusiveness. Thus the studies are regarded as a universe, defined by the above criteria, rather than a sample.

Each study was reviewed and, when sufficient information was available, coded in terms of a number of self-explanatory independent variables (*e.g.,* region, population size, industrialization, economic diversity, *etc.*). Similarly, the type of power structure identified in each report was coded in terms of four categories: 1) Pyramidal—a monolithic monopolistic, or single cohesive leadership group; 2) Factional—at least two durable factions that compete for advantage; 3) Coalitional—leadership varies with issues and is made up of fluid coalitions of interested persons and groups; 4) Amorphous—the absence of any persistent pattern of leadership or power exercised on the local level. Table 1 indicates those few associations which were found to be significant or meaningful.[1]

In contrast to these positive findings, a large number of variables, including region, population size, population composition, industrialization, economic diversity and type of local government, were *not* found to be related to type of power structure.

---

[1]The cell entries in the table represent communities, rather than studies, since a single study often dealt with two or more towns.

Taking these results as a summary of the present status of research, it appears that no firm generalizations are suggested. The findings fail to con-

TABLE 1   Community Characteristics and Community Power Structure[1]

	Pyramidal	Factional, Coalitional and Amorphous	Total
Absentee Ownership[2]			
Present	2	18	20
Absent	12	9	21
Total	14	27	41
	$Q = -.85$ $.01 > p > .001$		
Economic Resources			
Adequate	9	17	26
Inadequate	6	5	11
Total	15	22	37
	$Q = -.39$ $.30 > p > .20$		
Type of City			
Independent	14	22	36
Satellite	2	10	12
Total	16	32	48
	$Q = -.52$ $.20 > p > .10$		
Party Competition			
Competitive	0	10	10
Noncompetitive	10	12	22
Total	10	22	32
	$Q = -1.0$ $.02 > p > .01$		
Change in Power Structure			
Dispersion	2	17	19
Concentration	0	0	0
No Change	3	4	7
Oscillation	2	1	3
Decline Locally	1	2	3
Total	8	24	32

[1]The variable power structure was originally coded in terms of four categories. The categories are collapsed here to avoid small N's and to provide a contrast between more and less concentrated power arrangements.
The N's in each of these subtables vary because the studies coded do not provide uniform data on each variable.

[2]Operational definitions of the following three variables are indicated by the type of information coded under such category. Adequate economic resources – includes towns with reportedly prosperous business communities and low rates of poverty and unemployment; inadequate economically – underdeveloped with high rates of poverty and unemployment. Independent city – includes central cities of metropolitan areas and independent manufacturing, commercial or agricultural centers; satellite city – suburb or town dominated by a nearby city. Party competition – the existence of two or more local parties (or affiliates in formally nonpartisan cities) which regularly contend for public office; noncompetitive – a one-party town.

form to any neat pattern such as an association between competitive power structures and greater complexity of local social and economic organization. The inadequacies of such an explanation are underscored by the negative findings. The evidence may, however, be suggestive of some less obvious explanation. In order to explore that possibility we shall look at some implicitly theoretical positions in the area of community power and a major theoretical work on American communities, asking, in both cases, how they square with the above findings and how they might inform the present analysis.

THEORETICAL APPROACHES

In one of the first attempts to bring some order out of the confusion of results, David Rogers developed a series of propositions concerning community political systems. His dependent variable, type of political system, was made up of the categories monolithic and pluralistic. In stating the relationship between these and a number of characteristics of community social structure, Rogers hypothesized that the following would be associated with a pluralistic system: a high degree of industrialization, a large population, a socially heterogeneous population, a policy differentiated from the kinship and economic systems, a local government of extensive scope, two or more political parties and the unionization, or other political and economic organization, of working-class groups. The underlying theme in this series of propositions, what has been referred to as the implicit theory, centers on the effects of industrialization, and attendant processes of urbanization and bureaucratization, the outcome of these being structural differentiation which contributes to a pluralistic power situation. The approach is, of course, central to contemporary social science whether stated in terms of *gemeinschaft* and *gesellschaft* or any other of a variety of polar types.

Amos Hawley has presented a somewhat more specific approach. Here power is defined as a system property whose distribution can be measured by the ability to mobilize resources and personnel. In any total system, such as a community, this ability lies in the various component subsystems and is exercised through their managerial functions. Hence, operationally, the greater the number of managerial personnel, the greater the concentration of power. If we grant that success in a collective action requires the mobilization of resources and personnel, and that this ability is greatest where power is most highly concentrated, then it follows that the greater the concentration of power in a community the greater the *probability* of success in any collective action. In a recent paper, inspired in part by the Hawley piece, Edgar Butler and Hallowell Pope have suggested another measure of power concentration, the number of profile or key industries and the concentration of managerial functions within these.[2]

It should be noted that the Hawley and Butler and Pope papers are concerned chiefly with community action; for each the premise is that more concentrated power situations are conducive to concerted action. Unlike Rogers they are not trying to explain patterns of power distribution but, rather, employ these to explain community action. Nevertheless, they are pertinent here because they imply a theoretical position involving the saliency of managerial functions in the determination of community power structures.

How do these explanatory schemes square with the findings culled from the existing literature? Considering first the hypotheses formulated by Rogers, the evidence runs counter to his notions of the effects of industrialization, population size and population heterogeneity. On the positive side, his proposition about political parties, though not entirely equivalent to party competition, is supported. Unfortunately, no data are available on the remaining three propositions. What evidence we have, however, indicates that Rogers' propositions do not fare very well within the present context, though they may have greater predictive power in a cross cultural or historical perspective. For our purposes the implication is that the theoretical approach implicit in these propositions is in need of revision. Perhaps it will be necessary to abandon the simplified notion of a unilinear relationship between the growing complexity of industrial society and more pluralistic local power arrangements, in favor of a more limited, yet more discriminating explanation.[3]

The evidence presented previously is not directly relevant to the Hawley and Butler and Pope approaches since these attempt to explain community action. If, however, we assume with these authors that concentrated power structures are associated with community action, and then examine the antecedent link in their chain of reasoning, we find that those community characteristics allegedly conducive to power concentration (*i.e.*, ones engendering a large number of managerial functions)—industrialization, economic diversity, proportion of absentee ownership, and economic resources —are either unrelated or associated with the less concentrated power structures in our data. This fact can hardly be taken as a refutation of the positions presented. What it does indicate is that the number of managerial

---

[2]Edgar W. Butler and Hallowell Pope, "Community Power Structures, Industrialization and Public Welfare Programs," paper read at the 61st annual meeting of the American Sociological Association, Miami Beach, Florida, August, 1966.

[3]This conclusion applies to similar propositional inventories based on the "evolutionary" or "continuum" notion. See, for example, Delbert C. Miller and William H. Form, *Industry, Labor and Community* (New York: Harper Bros, 1960).

functions appears to be a poor indicator of type of power structure (though it may indicate the number of potentially powerful people in community action).

In short, the analysis thus far demonstrates the need for theoretical statements which are both more explicit and account better for the available data.

As we shall see, Roland Warren's analysis of *The Community in America*[4] provides a pertinent general framework for dealing theoretically with the specific questions of power structure. Warren's central thesis is that American communities are undergoing a drastic transformation of their entire structure and function; "[this] 'great change' in community living includes the increasing orientation of local community units toward extra-community systems of which they are a part, with a decline in community cohesion and autonomy." Although Warren analyzes these changes along seven fundamental dimensions of community life, a summary statement indicates their relevance for present purposes:

> In the first place, they signalize the increasing and strengthening of the external ties which bind the local community to the large society. In the process, various parts of the community—its educational system, its recreation, its economic units, its governmental functions, its religious units, its health and welfare agencies, and its voluntary associations—have become increasingly oriented toward district, state, regional, or national offices and less and less oriented toward each other.
>
> In the second place, as local community units have become more closely tied in with state and national systems, much of the decision-making prerogative concerning the structure and function of these units has been transferred to the headquarters or district offices of the systems themselves, thus leaving a narrower and narrower scope of functions over which local units, responsible to the local community, exercise autonomous power.

On the basis of these observations concerning the "great change" and with the simultaneous recognition that communities (*i.e.,* "combinations of social units and systems which perform the major functions having locality reference") do persist as meaningful units, Warren finds useful a distinction between the *horizontal* and *vertical axes* of community organization. The vertical axis refers to connections between community organizations and extracommunity centers, and the horizontal axis refers to connections between community organizations. The "great change" involves an increase in the former type of connections often at the cost of the latter.

In what follows several propositions will be developed which relate Warren's approach specifically to the question of how power is distributed

---

[4]Roland L. Warren, *The Community in America* (Chicago: Rand McNally, 1963), and "Toward a Reformulation of Community Theory," *Human Organization,* 15 (Summer, 1962), pp. 8–11.

on the local level. We find that his concept of a vertical axis of community organization has particular importance for this analysis.

AN EXPLANATION OF DIFFERENTIAL PATTERNS OF COMMUNITY POWER STRUCTURE

Power is defined here as *the capacity to mobilize resources for the accomplishment of intended effects with recourse to some type of sanction(s) to encourage compliance.* This definition includes the elements of both potential and actualized power in that capacity for mobilizing resources refers to potential while the application of sanctions refers to actualized power. *Capacity* also implies a distinction from *right* such that *authority* is not confused with the definition. Following Lasswell and Kaplan, the threat of sanctions, positive or negative, distinguishes *influence* from power—*i.e.*, influence refers only to the capacity to mobilize resources.

Power structure is defined as *the characteristic pattern within a social organization whereby resources are mobilized and sanctions employed in ways that affect the organization as a whole.*

For the sake of simplicity we will deal here with competitive and monopolistic power structures. Monopolistic power structures characterize social organizations in which the capacity for mobilizing resources and recourse to sanctions are the exclusive property of a group with similar interests. In competitive situations the capacity for mobilizing resources and recourse to sanctions are possessed by two or more groups with different interests.

The basic assumption of the theoretical statement to be developed here is that a monopoly of power produces a situation in which consensus is the most important factor underlying the use of power. This consensus may, but need not, imply agreement on values and objectives. What it does imply is agreement concerning the capabilities of those holding power to realize their own intentions over a wide range of community relevant issues. In such a monopolistic situation expectations concerning the norms prescribed by the existing power arrangement tend to be widely recognized. That is, the limits of allowable (nonsanctionable) deviance and opposition are narrow and clear. As a result of these congruent expectations, potential rather than manifest power is more commonly the mechanism by which compliance is encouraged; overt conflict and coercion are relatively infrequent occurrences because compliance can be realized without them. Merriam captured the sense of this assumption when he wrote "Power is not strongest when it uses violence, but weakest."

By contrast, in competitive situations the exercise of power moves from a reliance on consensus to more overt applications of sanctions. This becomes necessary to the extent that competing groups become capable of restricting the scope of each other's sanctions. Claims to power must be supported by effective action. Greater normative diversity, with attendant diversity in expectations, characterizes this situation. Such circumstances result in a greater incidence of conflict stemming from the fact that those who would exercise power are required to make evident their claim through the use of sanctions.

It should be added that each of these circumstances contains elements of the other. Monopolistic power arrangements do, at times, generate divergent norms and expectations just as they occasionally have recourse to overt applications of coercion. More importantly, the role of consensual expectations and potential power are critical to all forms of social organization and can be observed in many of the transactions carried on in competitive power settings. In this connection conflict is probably most characteristic of those transitional periods in which power is becoming more or less diffused since it is at this point that the normative order is most uncertain and expectations least clear. In the event that this transition is one from monopolistic to competitive it may culminate in a new set of rules defining community power arrangements which, while more conducive to conflict than the monopolistic situation, produces less conflict than the transitional phase.

Because at first glance this assumption may appear to be a truism, its nontrivial character will be demonstrated. Presthus' study of two New York communities which differed on a pluralist-elitist continuum is valuable here. Discussing the more elitist of the two, Presthus reasons:

> In Riverview sharper class and economic differences and resulting disparities in expectations, values and consensus seem to have placed a premium on more centralized, imperative leadership. As organizational theory and studies of group behavior suggest, social support, shared values, and common expectations make possible the minimization of overt power and authority. When community consensus is limited, leaders tend to function in a more unilateral manner.

Here the minimization of overt power and authority is equated with a more pluralistic (competitive) power situation. The present argument agrees with the prior notion that common expectations result in a minimization of overt power (and conflict), but this is taken to be characteristic of a monopolistic situation. Thus, when community consensus is limited the leadership process tends to be more competitive.[5]

---

[5]A more precise treatment of this relationship would specify types of conflict and how these are associated with various power arrangements. For example, monopolistic power structures may suppress dissent and conflict, they may manage it within innocuous limits or they may engender revolutionary conflict. Competitive power structures, on the other hand, may encourage conflict which results in a stalemate or ineffective argument and nonrevolutionary change.

Obviously the relationship identified in my assumption may operate in either direction—*i.e.*, changes in the competitiveness of the power situation can produce changes in norms and expectations and, similarly, changes in norms and expectations can lead to changes in power arrangements. In this approach we are concerned with developing an explanation of the change in power structures, that is, in the latter direction of the causal complex.

In this section we have reasoned that normative expectations bear a particular relationship to power structure and that conflict can be taken as an indicator of that relationship. In what follows an attempt will be made to elaborate the connection between normative expectations and types of power structure in terms of the data drawn from existing community studies.

Returning to the data in Table 1, we can now raise the question of how the ideas presented would account for the findings. It will be recalled that the data indicate a relationship between competitive power structures and the presence of absentee-owned corporations, competitive party politics, adequate economic resources and satellite status. Further, in those communities where change was studied, the trend was in the direction of a greater dispersion of power. Do these findings suggest some underlying explanation?

Upon closer examination the evidence does point to an explanation. Each of the variables associated with competitive power structures reflects the interdependence of the community and extracommunity centers of power or increased emphasis on the vertical axis. For example, a high proportion of absentee-owned industry suggests that many community relevant decisions are controlled by the personnel and interests of national corporate bodies whose influence may stem from either a deliberate intervention in local affairs or from the more characteristic aloofness to local responsibility. Similarly competitive political parties may often reflect the involvement of county, state and national party organizations in a struggle for control of local constituencies. While it could be reasonably argued that inadequate economic resources result in substantial intervention and control by state and federal agencies which extend aid to local bodies, the position taken here is that communities with more adequate economic resources maintain a greater number of interdependent ties to extra-community institutions such as the suppliers, markets, investors and other economic units. Finally, in the case of type of city, the connection is apparent. Suburban municipalities and smaller towns which form satellites of large urban centers are interdependent in a variety of economic and political activities including municipal services, jobs, consumer behavior, etc. If, at points, the relationship between each of these variables and community interdependence is not unambiguous, the position taken here is enhanced by the pattern they suggest when taken together.

Drawing together all that has been said up to this point, the proposition which seems best to account for the findings can be stated as follows: to the extent that the local community becomes increasingly interdependent with respect to extra-community institutions (or develops along its vertical axis) the structure of local leadership becomes more competitive.

Theoretically this proposition derives from the more general statement concerning norms and power arrangements. That is, the mechanism by which interdependence, or increasing relevance of the vertical axis of community organization, affects the distribution of community power is the disruption of the local normative order associated with the existing power structure. Development along the vertical axis involves the introduction of new interests and new institutional relationships implying new definitions of the community, and these have the effect of disrupting consensual normative expectations.

In addition to a differentiation of allegiances, these changes include the introduction of new *resources* and *sanctions* into the community. Local organizations with vertical ties to extracommunity institutions frequently share in the capital and human resources of the larger entity making it possible for them to sustain a broader scope of activities than would otherwise be the case. For example, absentee-owned corporations may receive funds and skilled personnel for a desired expansion of local operations making them more important as local tax contributors, employers and suppliers. Such resources carry with them potention sanctions. In the above example some of these would include the threat to locate elsewhere, threat of cutbacks or other actions having an adverse effect on the local economy, support or nonsupport in local elections. What has been said here of absentee-owned corporations could also be said, though perhaps in less dramatic ways, of other vertical community organizations. The point to be emphasized is that these organizations introduce new sources of power into the local picture and, being interdependent, they also have stakes in the local decision-making process which occasionally must be defended. The greater the number of community organizations with vertical ties, the more frequent and the more inclusive are contests surrounding the decision-making process. . . .

Accordingly, variables which reflect the interdependence of the community and the "carrying society"—absentee ownership, party competition, adequate economic resources and satellite status—are associated with competitive power structures; whereas those variables which reflect only intra-community changes—economic diversity, population increase, *etc.*—are not so associated.[6] . . .

---

[6]The point to be emphasized here is that greater complexity and specialization are not necessarily conducive to the changes under consideration, but only insofar as these developments produce greater interdependence. At some point, of course, complexity and specialization do necessitate greater interdependence, but it would seem

The findings on change in Table 1 indicated that community power structures are tending to become more competitive. This trend is a predictable consequence of the spread of "metropolitan dominance" and its implications for greater community interdependence. That is, . . . the spread of metropolitan dominance would lead one to predict a corresponding trend toward competitive power arrangements. Such is, in fact, what the findings indicate. . . .

METROPOLITAN POLITICS AND COMMUNITY ACTION

Since the purpose of this paper was to develop an explanation of how power is distributed in local communities, *and* how power arrangements may account for community action, some comments on the latter question are called for. This may be particularly useful for two reasons; first, the foregoing analysis bears directly on the subject of community action and, second, the discussion serves to integrate another perspective on power and decision-making into this explanation.

In his well known essay describing the local community as an "ecology of games," Norton Long argues that the concept of "power structure" suffers from misplaced concreteness, that when we look more closely at cities we find no such structured decision-making institution.

> What is characteristic of metropolitan areas is the lack of overall decision-making institutions. This does not mean that there are not institutions with power in metropolitan areas. It does mean that there are no institutions with sufficient power and overall responsibility to make decisions settling metropolitan issues and solving metropolitan problems . . .[7]

Rather, Long conceives of metropolitan issues as having careers in which interested and powerful parties—governments, groups and institutions—interact and "develop a system of largely unintended cooperation through which things get done . . ."[8] In this process actors deal with metropolitan problems from a limited point of view: *i.e.* one confined to their particular interest and institutional base.

There are at least two reasons why Long's empirically persuasive ap-

---

that this is not always the case at every level of community development. We would expect that some of these variables are confounded in such a way that increasing size, for example, will be related to competitive power structures at that point in a community's development when size and interdependence vary together. According to this argument, such an association would be spurious. This may be the case though the available data are too crude and provide too few observations to allow an unequivocal solution.

[7]Norton E. Long, *The Polity* (Chicago: Rand McNally, 1962), p. 157.
[8]*Ibid.*

proach has stymied students of community power. One would appear to be the fact that much of this research has been conducted in places other than metropolitan areas where decisions settling local issues are possible. Second, the well known controversy over pluralism and elitism in the literature—because it is a debate over who makes local decisions, a small, cohesive group or a large, diverse one—may have obscured the possibility that no one makes such decisions.

In the present explanation metropolitan areas are prototypes of interdependent, vertically organized communities. Here we would expect a highly fragmented and competitive power arrangement in which the scope of any group or institution would be limited to prime interest areas. That is, the competitive process would militate against generalized influence and require that actors work to maintain their position within the system. Long and Banfield concur with this prediction in the stress they put on metropolitan politics as going systems in which institutions and groups seek to maintain and enhance their power in particular areas, public policy representing the results of their cooperation.

Under these circumstances we would expect to find a fragmented and competitive pattern of community action. Community action in American cities seems increasingly to fit this pattern. The most apparent illustrations are found in the activities of civil rights, anti-poverty and peace groups which often possess resources conferred by extracommunity institutions and which are beginning to seriously involve themselves in the local political process. Here, of course, they encounter opposition from other local and vertically organized groups. As a result coordinated community action becomes more problematic and public policy represents less a reflection of consensus than a byproduct of the competitive process in which power is differentially exercised. . . . In another vein, several studies which have touched on the consequences of increasing involvement of the federal government in local affairs find, contrary to political folklore, an enhancement of competitive processes.[9]

Notable among deviant cases is the Vidich and Bensman study [Ed. See Section III.] where involvement of state and county governments resulted in an abdication of responsibility on the part of local leaders. While it is significant that these changes diluted the power of Springdale's elite, it is also recognized that the consequences of extracommunity involvement were not those we would predict. In this regard the theory presented here may be in need of modification. Recalling that Springdale is a town of 2,500 people and that its extracommunity ties center chiefly around state subsidies, it is reasonable to infer that both the nature of the community and of

[9]Presthus, Men at the Top; William V. D'Antonio, "Community Leadership in an Economic Crisis: Testing Ground for Ideological Cleavage," American Journal of Sociology, 71 (May, 1966), pp. 688–700.

the vertical ties are contingent elements in the theory presented here. Perhaps it is the case, for example, that changes along the vertical axis lead to greater competitiveness only in those communities which possess a certain minimum of institutional viability and that without this the same changes spell the demise of local leadership.

CONCLUSIONS

The explanation offered here represents an attempt to push the study of community power beyond a disproportionate emphasis on technique and toward a concern for testing propositions derived from explicit theoretical statements. There seems little doubt that this alternative is best suited for resolving the controversies over how power is distributed in local communities, and for generalizing research in this area to the larger problems of social organization and change.

The theory developed in this paper states that the introduction into the local community of the institutions and influence of national-urban culture produces a "fragmentation of local normative order" or a disruption of consensual expectations concerning the norms prescribed by existing power arrangements. As expectations are altered and interests are differentiated, new resources are exploited for the creation of competing power groups.

The theory, as we have said, focuses on one direction of influence in what is undoubtedly a complex process. In so doing, however, it has the virtue of generating a number of testable propositions. Future comparative studies could evaluate, on the basis of first-hand data, the fundamental proposition regarding community interdependence and the advent of competitive power arrangements. A sampling of related propositions includes:

1. Changes, other than interdependence, which challenge the local normative order lead to more competitive power arrangements.
2. Intracommunity change which does not challenge the normative order does not lead to greater competitiveness.
3. Vertical ties which do not alter the normative order do not lead to the exploitation of new resources and more competitive power arrangements.
4. Normative diversity within a community leads to a greater frequency of application of overt sanctions. . . .
5. The greater the number of vertical ties in a community, the smaller the scope of local power groups.
6. The greater the number of vertical ties (and competitiveness) the more difficult (less frequent) is coordinated community action.

In addition to suggesting propositions the theory implies a new direction for research in that it locates the source of local change in the relationship between the community and extracommunity institutions. It is expected that researchers will find this theory informative as they become increasingly aware of what it implies for the choice of an appropriate unit of analysis in future community power studies. If the theory is correct the appropriate unit of analysis is not the community per se but, rather, the relationship between the community and the institutions of national-urban culture.

CHAPTER EIGHT

The Cross-Cultural Study
of Community Power

LOCAL POWER AND COMPARATIVE POLITICS:
NOTES TOWARD THE STUDY
OF COMPARATIVE LOCAL POLITICS

Mark Kesselman and Donald B. Rosenthal

*In closing this volume, we remind readers that the search for com-
munity power is but one facet of a larger scholarly study—local politics.
Moreover, as John Walton stressed in the preceding article, local politics must be seen as a part of a national political system and linked
further to processes in other national systems. In this paper, Kesselman
and Rosenthal provide a current roundup of the place of community
power study in this larger framework. In addition, they point clearly to
the most fruitful directions for further study. Particularly important is
their caution about treating communities which actually exist in a na-*

This article was prepared in its present form for this volume. An earlier
version appeared as a paper of the same title and was delivered at the 1972
Annual Meeting of the American Political Science Association and revised for
this volume by the authors.

tional web of extramural influences as though they were autonomous political systems.

They also remind us that political study of any kind eventually can be a contribution to a comparative theory of politics. This was the task Aristotle set himself twenty-five centuries ago and one which contemporary scholars still pursue.

As students of comparative politics and particularly of local government and local political processes outside the United States, we find ourselves discomforted by an existing situation but uncertain of how best to surmount it. That situation may be described as one in which the writing on comparative politics is largely insensitive to matters bearing on local politics and government (although it is aware of what we shall call localism). At the same time, a good deal of research is being conducted into local politics in various political systems, but often on the basis of particular ethnocentric traditions of treating local political phenomena. Little attention is paid in the comparative politics literature to the diverse political consequences for political systems of local politics; equally little interest in cross national comparison has been evinced by research conducted into local politics within particular political systems.

This paper proceeds by first distinguishing among three possible dimensions in the study of comparative local politics—localism; government for the locality; and localistic processes. These three dimensions, we would argue, are present to some degree in every political system large enough to require meaningful territorial differentiation. Varying national traditions of political research have tended to stress one or two of these dimensions rather than taking all three into account. We would hold that systematic comparisons across nations of local political phenomena requires incorporating the three dimensions into a systematic model.

DIMENSIONS FOR ANALYSIS

Whatever else studies of comparative local politics may include they are informed by a concern for notions related to territoriality. Thus, a major focus is *localism*—the political sub-culture(s) within a society linked to space or territoriality. While many comparative studies have concerned themselves with *parochialism* as a deterrent to modernization or a blockage to nation-building, we need to distinguish localism from parochialism.

Parochialism, as the term is generally employed, seems to refer to any subnational identification which impedes the highest possible integration of the constituent elements of a society into a well-coordinated centrally-directed national political system.[1] Parochial forces may include religion, race, ethnicity, language, as well as territorial identifications. It is the last we identify as localism. As we use the term, localism is a system dimension quite distinct from the "modernization" issue. No matter how "modern" a nation is, factors like national size and the imperatives of economic, political and social organization create the conditions for societal differentiation into territorially-based political or governmental units with certain characteristics which distinguish one unit from another. National elites may attempt to shape local units, in an assembly-line fashion, into simple patterns of governmental and political organization. But so long as the territorial unit retains or acquires meaning for residents, localism is a force to be reckoned with in analyzing the larger political system and its operations. It is a psycho-cultural force which may be heightened in significance when it is associated with other factors often identified as parochial (race, language, caste, etc.).

At the same time, national political systems may vary in the extent to which localism is perceived as antagonistic to the goals of the national political system itself. In a country like France, national leaders (following the Jacobin tradition) continue to excoriate localism, although they cannot root it out. The result is a system beset by continuing tensions between national and local political cultures. In both the United States and India, on the other hand, localism is not only praised as part of the "genius" of government, but it is institutionalized in political structures and processes. Localism and parochialism are thus quite distinct. Localism may, but need not, be parochial; parochialism may, but need not, be localistic.

Localistic strains within distinct national traditions create considerable variation among nations in terms of arrangements for local governance. The pattern of government for the locality therefore, forms a second major dimension for the study of comparative local politics. We need to know much more than we do about the historical processes and social correlates of local governmental arrangements. Surprisingly little attention has been given, as well, to the philosophical assumptions, ordering conceptualiza-

[1]In that connection, see the various contributions to Clifford Geertz (ed.) *Old Societies and New States* (New York, Free Press, 1963), especially Geertz' own contribution "The Integrative Revoltuion: Primordial Sentiments and Civic Politics in the New States." The end of the process during which parochialisms are obliterated is by no means clearly indicated in the relevant literature on nation-building. Much of the writing seems to teeter on the brink of advocating a total universalization of societal values—what may represent a "mass society" phenomenon—rather than accepting (or advocating) the possibility of some form of societal pluralism. For an interesting discussion of the universalistic assumptions of liberal theory in American politics with respect to the "community control" debate, see Leonard J. Fein, *The Ecology of the Public Schools* (New York: Pegasus, 1971). The arguments might well be extended to the nation-building literature.

tions and operational theories of local government in most nations, particularly as compared with the extensive literature of a purely descriptive nature available on the legal organization and problems of territorial governance.[2] In addition to studying the institutions themselves, studies of comparative local politics should also indicate why some nations provide essentially local extensions of their national governments for their localities while others allow their localities considerable political autonomy. The concern here is in part with traditional institutional comparisons (for, it should be noted, there have been very few systematic cross-national comparisons of local governmental institutions). However, the additional step we advocate is to relate local governmental institutions in different countries to localistic cleavages and national political forces in those countries.

A third dimension for comparative local politics would be the study of *localistic political processes.* Comparative local politics should be concerned not only with units of local governance and with narrowly-defined local political processes such as local decision-making and community power distributions. It should also take into account how decisions are made for the locality by authorities (sometime including non-governmental authorities) whose constituency is more extensive than the locality itself.

It may be helpful to review very briefly some of the features of the existent literature concerned with local government and politics.

VARYING APPROACHES TO LOCAL POLITICS

Until intellectual cross-pollination began to occur in studies of local politics within political systems, one could identify four different strains within the field, each broadly associated with a different tradition of studying local politics and, to an extent, with a different philosophical understanding of the place of local politics and government in national political life.

One can identify an *administrative tradition* informing much of the writing on local government in Europe, particularly in France with its long

---

[2]Some items that do begin to raise interesting questions about the ways in which local politics and government are thought about include: W. Hardy Wickwar, *The Political Theory of Local Government* (Columbia: University of South Carolina Press, 1969); L. J. Sharpe, "Theories and Values of Local Government," *Political Studies*, 18 (June, 1970), 153–74; Robert A. Dahl, "The City in the Future of Democracy," *American Political Science Review*, 61 (December, 1967), 953–70; and Anwar Syed, *The Political Theory of American Local Government* (New York: Random House, 1966). Among the more useful historical studies are Hugh Tinker, *Foundations of Local Self-Government in India, Pakistan and Burma* (London: Athlone Press, 1954) and Robert C. Fried, *The Italian Prefects* (New Haven and London: Yale University Press, 1963).

administrative history—a history in which local government has been treated as essentially a problem in legal and administrative subordinacy. Studies of local government in France tended to focus on formal institutional relationships and were oblivious to the variance of those relationships from behavioral actuality.

While this tradition continues to be prominent among studies of local government in continental Europe, local-formalism has also been associated in the past with studies of local government in countries like England and nations influenced by British rule like India. Even in the United States, the institutional approach with its emphases on formal governmental powers and on the structure of administrative organization was a common feature of American studies of local politics until the behavioral reorientation of the 1950's.[3]

If a less formalistic approach to local politics is to be found in much writing on the subject in England, that body of literature might better be characterized as a *nuts-and-bolts tradition*. The problems of local government are recognized as both political and administrative but with a definite accent on the latter. Both the problems and the structural arrangements for dealing with them seem to be handled on a case-by-case basis in the literature. The considerable variety of units involved in local decision-making in Great Britain and the variations in national involvement in affecting local decisions through legislation and grants-in-aid may have discouraged the development of a literature that went beyond the particularistic. It is only very recently that English scholars, influenced by American research, have begun to explore the possibilities available for systematic comparisons among local political units.[4] Until these studies began to emerge, the English tended to produce an essentially "pragmatic"

---

[3]Lawrence Herson, "The Lost World of Municipal Government," *American Political Science Review*, 51 (June, 1957), 330–45; Robert Daland, "Political Science and the Study of Urbanism," *American Political Science Review*, 51 (June, 1957), 491–509.

[4]Noel T. Boaden and Robert R. Alford, "Sources of Diversity in English Local Government Decisions," *Public Administration*, 47 (Summer, 1969), 203–23. Typical of the new emphases are Noel T. Boaden, *Urban Policy-Making: Influences on County Boroughs in England and Wales* (Cambridge: Cambridge University Press, 1971); W. P. Grant, " 'Local' Parties in British Local Politics," *Political Studies*, 19 (June, 1971), 201–12; and J. Alt, "Some Social and Political Correlates of County Borough Expenditures," *British Journal of Political Science*, 1 (January, 1971), 49–62. It is notable that these authors still seem to be engaged in a battle to establish the usefulness of a comparative approach to the study of local political systems within Great Britain, the counterassumption apparently being that local government behaviors have been influenced so much by national policies that there is little room for the analysis of variation. Though influenced by studies conducted in the United States, none of these studies evidences much direct concern for cross-national analysis.

literature concerned with description and problem-solving rather than political analysis.[5]

Third, there is the community power and *community decision-making tradition*, first popularized in the United States. By a variety of techniques, and with a variety of findings and interpretations, scholars have studied how power is distributed both formally and informally within communities. Unfortunately, from a cross-national perspective, such studies have largely ignored the extent to which such factors as the relative autonomy of local communities from other levels of government affect the internal distribution of power. If local political processes are intimately linked to extra-community forces, however, assessing who governs (or who has influence to affect those who have formal authority to govern) may be of little intrinsic political interest. Too few of the studies concerned with exporting American power structure methodologies to other countries have concerned themselves with this problem, with the result that such efforts may turn into methodological exercises.

A fourth approach, associated most recently with trends in American political research, emphasizes *public policy-making* at the local level. One major way the question has been approached has been through synchronic correlations of large quantities of political, economic and social data characterizing localities, and (most commonly) financial expenditures.[6] A few studies have attempted to study policy-making processes other than budget-related ones, but they have tended to ignore the problem of local autonomy and, as a result, their comparative value is questionable.[7] Moreover, the nature of the available quantitative data sometimes appears to dictate the character of the studies being conducted. We would argue that among the most interesting questions for comparative local politics are such issues as

[5]For a useful contrast between the American and the British literature, see K. Newton, "City Politics in Britain and the United States," *Political Studies*, 17 (June, 1969), 208–217.

[6]A useful summary of much of the American literature on urban socioeconomic variables and their structural and policy correlates may be found in Brett W. Hawkins, *Politics and Urban Policies* (Indianapolis: Bobbs-Merrill, 1971). Also see, Philip Coulter, "American Community Politics: The Policy Perspective," in James A. Riedel (ed.), *New Perspectives in State and Local Politics* (Waltham: Xerox College Publishing, 1971), pp. 43–70. For an application to the English experience, see Boaden, *op. cit.*, and for Italy, Robert C. Fried, "Communism, Urban Budgets and the Two Italies," *Journal of Politics*, 33 (November, 1971), 1008–51.

[7]Americans, characteristically, have had a hand in applying this approach in the United States and then extending it to other nations. For examples of the comparative policy approach in the United States, see James Q. Wilson (ed.), *City Politics and Public Policy* (New York: John Wiley, 1968); for an English case study done by an American, see Paul E. Peterson, "British Interest Group Theory Reexamined: The Politics of Comprehensive Education in Three British Cities," *Comparative Politics*, 3 (April, 1971), 381–402. A recent British piece based on American sources (without making the extent of that reliance explicit) is J. A. Brand, "The Politics of Fluoridation: A Community Conflict," *Political Studies*, 19 (December, 1971), 430–39.

the nature of societal mobilization, the structure of political repression, and different national styles of political conflict—matters not directly reflected in local budgetary data.

The "traditions" we have identified above appear in studies of local politics conducted *within* nations. Few of these studies reflect a concern with the comparative implications of their findings, although they are suggestive for the study of comparative local politics. Indeed, some of these approaches have been directly applied outside the boundaries of those national traditions in which they originated. In addition, a number of themes can be identified which may prove helpful in bridging the gap between the study of comparative and of local politics:

1) The urbanization approach. Most readily identifiable with the whole-systems comparative politics perspective, urbanization is viewed as a transitional process linking rural underdevelopment and tradition, on the one hand, with modernity and nation-building, on the other. Despite scattered exceptions, however, the linkages between the socioeconomic changes associated with urbanization and the political consequences or correlates of those changes remain to be worked out both theoretically and empirically. Contrary to the implicit assumptions made by some social scientists, the political consequences of different levels of urbanization within nations or across nations are by no means certain.[8] Not only do political responses to given socioeconomic change vary, but micro-studies of urbanization in developing areas indicate the existence of as many continuities as dissonances between city and countryside.[9]

[8]The literature is substantial, but among the more useful items are: Joan Nelson, "The Urban Poor," *World Politics*, 22 (April, 1970), 393–414; Francine F. Rabinovitz, "Urban Development and Political Development in Latin America," in Robert T. Daland (ed.), *Comparative Urban Research* (Beverly Hills: Sage Publications, 1969); Irving Louis Horowitz, "Electoral Politics, Urbanization, and Social Development in Latin America," *Urban Affairs Quarterly*, 2 (March, 1967), 3–35; Clifford Kaufman, "Latin American Urban Inquiry," *Urban Affairs Quarterly*, 5 (June, 1970), 394–411. The "mobilization" literature employing urbanization as a major dimension is also extensive. For an interesting recent approach to the problem which tends to weaken the apparent importance of urbanization as a determinant of participation, see Norman H. Nie, G. Bingham Powell Jr., and Kenneth Prewitt, "Social Structure and Political Participation, Parts I and II," *American Political Science Review*, 63 (June and September, 1969), 361–78 and 808–32.

[9]In this connection, useful studies include William John Hanna and Judith Lynne Hanna, "Polyethnicity and Political Integration in Umuahia and Mbale," in Daland, *op. cit.*, pp. 162–202; Daniel Goldrich, "Political Organization and the Politicization of the Poblador," *Comparative Political Studies*, 3 (July, 1970), 176–202; Abner Cohen, *Custom and Politics in Urban Africa* (Berkeley and Los Angeles: University of California Press, 1969). Also see, Donald B. Rosenthal, "Deurbanization, Elite Displacement and Political Change In India, *Comparative Politics*, 2 (January, 1970), 169–201. It is interesting that these studies, concerned as they are with aspects of urbanization in Africa, Latin America and India all point to the ways by which locally-involved political and parochial organizations may act to smooth the transition from rural to urban settings. In that respect, too, see James C. Scott, "Corruption, Machine Politics and Political Change," *American Political Science Review*, 63 (December, 1969), 1142–58.

We still know little about the variable political processes associated with the movement to the city from rural areas.

2) Distinct from the first approach is that which views local governments as actors having different political characteristics,[10] making decisions and producing outputs which vary within the political system as a whole in response to national socioeconomic and political processes. The problem for the researcher then becomes one of identifying the correlates of decisional outputs. Population characteristics, political structures, and socioeconomic organization may be factors taken into account in assessing variations in budgetary expenditures, policy choices and administrative performances.[11] This approach assumes the availability of relevant quantitative data or necessitates the generation of such data, sometimes at considerable expense and with little assurance of theoretical payoff. For, even if we knew cities with higher-income populations spent proportionately more money on police services than cities with lower-income populations, we might not understand why. As a result, we would soon be back to the problem of examining local decision-making processes directly or we would have to depend on the heady speculations which often follow from having to interpret modest correlations among a variety of socioeconomic and political variables.

3) In contrast to the study of localities through the long end of the telescope of national data, localities may be viewed as analytically autonomous political systems in which government and politics are a function of local preferences and localistic pressures. Most studies of city politics in the United States proceed along these lines. In this respect, both protagonists of the "power structure" and "decision-making" debate have assumed, until recently, that the locality was the crucial decision-making arena. Thus, most of Robert Dahl's references to urban renewal (a federal program) in his study of New Haven allude to the success of the mayor in manipulating the local political elite; little attention is given the means by which the locality manipulated or was affected in turn by national bureaucratic and political leadership. Even less attention is given to national influences over local policy in Hunter's study of Atlanta, although a brief allusion is made to attempts by local elites to affect national policy.[12] There is little sense in either study of the place of these local political systems in the larger context of American political life.

[10]See, for example, Kesselman, *Ambiguous Consensus*, ch. I; Sidney Tarrow, "The Urban-Rural Cleavage in Political Involvement: The Case of France," *American Political Science Review*, 65 (June, 1971), 341–57.

[11]Almost all of the research conducted thus far along these lines is of an intra-system character, but there is no reason to assume that equivalent measures could not be developed for inter-nation comparisons. For examples of American and British studies, see Hawkins, *op. cit.*, and Boaden, *op. cit.*

[12]Robert A. Dahl, *Who Governs?* (New Haven and London: Yale University Press, 1961). Insofar as he mentions relations with the federal government at all, Dahl emphasizes the success of the mayor and his administrative associates in winning renewal resources for New Haven, but he does not explain, in any detail the means by which federal largesse was achieved for New Haven *as compared with other American cities.* Floyd Hunter, *Community Power Structure* (Chapel Hill: University of North Carolina Press, 1953). The national policies mentioned, however, were rather remote from the urban development problems of Atlanta.

Although power structure and decision-making approaches in the United States have been attacked for neglecting the biases inherent in local structural and procedural arrangements, most attacks seem to accept the myth of local autonomy.[13] The reasons why certain issues are prevented from being brought forward for discussion, according to these critiques, seem to derive from patterns of local power rather than from the character of national politics and the biases built into the structure of the American political system. Furthermore, whatever the validity of assuming the existence of local autonomy in decision-making in the past—and some studies would modify even that assumption[14]—the last decade has witnessed an enormous penetration of local political processes by forces operating at the federal level. This is true despite the fact (and perhaps just because of the fact) that localities have played a major role in instigating those changes, shaping their content and administering the new programs. The net change seems to be that some movement away from local autonomy in the definition of choices has occurred, although there continue to be variations in the application of national standards and in decisional outcomes at the local level.[15]

Behavioral studies of local decison-making conducted in a systematic fashion outside the United States are still relatively few in number, although the body of literature would be much larger if one included some items from the nuts-and-bolts tradition. For the most part, however, decision-making studies tend to proceed in a manner which cannot be described as comparative, for either they analyze decision-making in only one community or they pay little attention to inter-nation variations in decision-making processes.[16]

Analyses of role behaviors across political systems should have an important place in the study of comparative local politics. Some efforts in this respect have been undertaken within the United States, but the amount of work done is still very limited. We have only the beginnings of a literature comparing city manager styles,[17] the behaviors of city

[13]Peter Bachrach and Morton S. Baratz, "Two Faces of Power," *The American Political Science Review*, 56 (December, 1962), 947–52 and their "Decisions and Non-decisions," *The American Political Science Review*, 57 (September, 1963), 641–51. Also see, Agger, Goldrich and Swanson, *op. cit.*

[14]Morton Grodzins, *The American System: A New View of Government in the United States*, ed. Daniel J. Elazar (Chicago: Rand McNally, 1966); and Daniel J. Elazar, *American Federalism: A View from the States* (New York: Thomas Y. Crowell, 1966).

[15]Even in such a minor instance as the adoption of fluoridation in the United States, federal and state bureaucracies played a major role in spreading information about the process and in encouraging local health officials to assume a major role in developing support for the measure. Cf. Crain, Katz and Rosenthal, esp. ch. 2.

[16]In addition to Peterson, *op. cit.*, and Brand, *op. cit.*, see such items as Thomas J. Anton, "Incrementalism in Utopia: The Political Integration of Metropolitan Stockholm," *Urban Affairs Quarterly*, 5 (September, 1969), 59–82; and, Jewel Bellush, "Urban Renewal: Utrecht Style," *Urban Affairs Quarterly*, 4 (December, 1968), 167–84. Except for Peterson, these policies are not explicitly comparative with respect to inter-unit differences even within the national political systems that they do examine.

[17]Ronald O. Loveridge, *City Managers in Legislative Politics* (Indianapolis: Bobbs-Merrill, 1971); Robert Paul Boynton and Deil S. Wright, "Mayor-Manager Relationships in Large Council-Manager Cities," *Public Administration Review*, 31 (January–

councilmen,[18] and some suggestions about variations in mayoral behaviors.[19] Outside the United States, we have even fewer leads. The
most obvious problem is how to develop a basis for comparison of roles
across political systems which is also meaningful within each political
system. Certainly, one could compare (in the broadest sense) the behavior of the mayor of a French city with that of a mayor in the
United States or India, but it is an open question whether much of
value would result from a treatment of roles which are in many respects fundamentally different and embedded in different political circumstances.

4) Localities or locally-based groups may be seen as actors in larger political
   arenas associated with regional or national politics. In the formulation
   of policies that affect local jurisdictions, individual local governments
   may participate either as entities in their own right, as collectivities (in
   association with one another),[20] or their constituent actors may be fragmented into specialized interests: teachers, educational bureaucrats,
   local health officials, and other municipal employees.

Thus, at the national level, a kind of "interest group pluralism" may
operate in which local governmental actors constitute some few among the
many interests contending for influence. At the same time, sufficient autonomy may still exist at the local level for the arena of local government
to remain an important focus for understanding variations in the formulation and application of policy. Indeed, unlike the first and second approaches, whose ultimate unit of analysis is the nation as it incorporates
socioeconomic and political diversity, and the third, which focuses on the
local juridical unit as the object of analysis, the accent of the fourth approach is on policy and political process variables not constrained by whatever formal boundaries or hierarchies which may be defined by law.

February, 1971), 28–35; Gladys Kammerer, Charles Farris, John DeGrove, and
Alfred Clubok, *The Urban Political Community* (Boston: Houghton Mifflin, 1963);
and, Williams and Adrian, *op. cit.*

[18]Kenneth Prewitt, *The Recruitment of Political Leaders: A Study of Citizen-
Politicians*, (Indianapolis: Bobbs-Merrill, 1970); Kenneth Prewitt and Heinz Eulau,
"Political Matrix and Political Representation," *American Political Science Review*,
63 (June, 1969), 427–41. Unfortunately, these studies are limited to councilmanic
roles in only one metropolitan region of the United States—the San Francisco metropolitan area—a region in which most local councils operate under non-partisanship
and in conjunction with managers. For the Detroit area, see the brief report by
Wolfgang Pindur, "The Urban Legislator: Problems and Perspectives," in Riedel,
op. cit., pp. 227–246.

[19]Boyton and Wright, *op. cit.*; and Crain, Katz and Rosenthal, *op. cit.* Despite
the considerable anecdotal material in the city politics literature which focusses on
particular mayors, there is little of a systematically comparative nature which
examines the mayoral role. The quality of the available material (or, rather, the lack
of quality) is suggested by the pieces included in Leonard I. Ruchelman, (ed.), *Big
City Mayors* (Bloomington: Indiana University Press, 1969).

[20]Howard Scarrow, "Policy Pressures by British Local Government," *Comparative
Politics*, 4 (October, 1971), 1–28.

A MODEL FOR THE STUDY OF COMPARATIVE LOCAL POLITICS

It remains for us to discuss the features of a paradigm which incorporates the elements of the last two approaches in particular and that might be useful as a starting-point in developing a field of comparative local politics. Following our earlier comments, we feel that comparative local politics may be advanced most fruitfully by emphasizing five components: 1) the political culture of localism; 2) the character of local and locally-relevant institutions; 3) institutional linkages; 4) decision-making and service delivery for the locality; and 5) the performance of systemic functions.

The Political Culture of Localism

While the term "political culture" is widely used, there is a need to focus on the localistic dimensions of political values held within particular societies and, with that as a base, to develop a systematic understanding of localistic values across political systems. Survey research techniques, for example, might be appropriate for identifying the extent of convergence or tension between localistic identifications and national identifications;[21] such techniques might also be valuable for treating variations among localities within and across political systems by examining particular values shared among residents of different localities.[22]

The extreme case is where a localistic political culture reinforces territorial or nationalistic particularisms.[23] Indeed, one of the major questions

[21]The work of the Values Project moves in this direction. Our main objections to that effort relate to its almost total reliance upon data provided by local informants, to the short shrift given to the attitudes of nationally-involved political and administrative actors and to the lack of attention to the structural correlates of differences in local attitudes from nation to nation.

[22]The sort of thing we have in mind follows upon the kinds of typologies developed by Agger, Goldrich and Swanson, *op. cit.*, by Williams and Adrian, *op. cit.*, by Herbert Jacob, "Wage Garnishment and Bankruptcy Proceedings in Four Wisconsin Cities," in Wilson, *op. cit.* and Robert R. Alford, *Bureaucracy and Participation: Political Cultures in Four Wisconsin Cities* (Chicago: Rand McNally, 1969), for comparing community value patterns in the United States.

[23]William R. Keech, "Linguistic Diversity and Political Conflict; Some Observations Based on Four Swiss Cantons," *Comparative Politics*, 4 (April, 1972), 387–404. "Modernity" of socioeconomic arrangements is by no means correlated with the development of nationalistic as opposed to localistic values. The recent problems of Belgium and Canada, which have witnessed severe cleavages based on localistic and parochial factors, indicate some of the difficulties. In that connection, see George Armstrong Kelly, "Belgium: New Nationalism in an Old World," *Comparative Pol-*

to be asked when viewing the localistic dimension of any political system is the degree to which cultural and geographic pluralisms are strengthened or diluted by formal institutional arrangements and informal political practices.[24]

Further along a continuum from territorially-based regional particularisms are those cases where local identities exist alongside but do not directly threaten a relatively homogeneous national political culture. Thus the ways in which a political system resolves the potential conflict among and between local political cultures and an emergent national political culture (or cultures) creates many of the basic terms for the operation of the larger political system. In such cases, local and national loyalties may coexist with the occasional strains between them being accepted as part of the expression of legitimate demands in the political system.

In contrast, there may exist in some nations a relatively homogeneous national political culture fostered by national elites which brands localism and particularism as illegitimate. In such a system, then, localism may be regarded as illegitimate; still, localistic strains may continue to exist within national political systems with strongly assertive national political cultures, as is the case in France.

The Character of Locally-Relevant Political Institutions

While local and national political cultures may provide the bases for certain conflicts in a national political system, the ways in which those conflicts are mediated, exacerbated or suppressed are considerably affected by the formal character of national and local political arrangements. The legal power granted to local governments do not explain everything, but they are one important factor reflecting the nature of the political settlements reached between nationalizing and localizing forces in the society.

This question can be examined by investigating the assumptions which underlie the distribution of authority between national agencies and local elites with respect to local government and administration. Much depends

---

itics, 1 (April, 1969), 343–65; and, W. Dale Posgate, "Social Mobilization and Political Change in Quebec," Unpublished Ph.D. dissertation, State University of New York at Buffalo, 1972.

[24]However, the causes and consequences of federalism are by no means preordained. See, for example, Franz Neumann, "On The Theory of the Federal State," in Arthur MacMahon (ed.), *Federalism Mature and Emergent* (New York: Doubleday, 1955), pp. 44–57. The problematic aspects of political solutions to localistic and parochial conflicts with national values are suggested in Arend Lijphart, *Politics of Accommodation: Pluralism and Democracy in the Netherlands* (Berkeley and Los Angeles: University of California Press, 1968); also see Michael W. Suleiman, *Political Parties in Lebanon: The Challenge of a Fragmented Political Culture* (Ithaca: Cornell University Press, 1967).

on whether local government is perceived as an agent of national or provincial administration in such areas as the delivery of services, the maintenance of local order and the socialization of the young, or whether local government is seen as a vehicle for the participation of citizens in activities which directly affect their lives. Between the two extremes of tight bureaucratic control and largely self-directing systems of local government and administration, there are numerous possible configurations with respect to the "scopes" of local government—the kinds of powers and functions assumed by local governmental agencies and by agencies responsible for administering services to localities under the direction of national or provincial authorities.

While it may be possible to create local institutional arrangements which encourage both high citizen participation and the performance of administrative functions in the fashion of a legal-rational bureaucratic structure, political systems tend to strike different balances with some opting for a participatory emphasis and others for the development of universalistic standards applied locally by local administrative units under the supervision of national bureaucracies. A choice of one set of values rather than the other seems to carry with it a commitment to certain institutional arrangements.

At the same time, formal devices may exist either for insulating local government and politics from national politics or for making the two congruent. Various institutional devices can exert an influence toward convergence or conflict. For example, the nature of electoral laws, in the boundaries of electoral districts, or the timing of elections may be significant.

Institutional Linkages

Equally important to analyzing the functioning of individual institutions is the study of how these are articulated with one another—what might be called the "layering" problem. In studying the processes of political life in nations and across nations, it is frequently misleading to assume *a priori* that those officials associated with national political institutions are automatically more powerful than officials associated with local political institutions. Rather, this is a key question for empirical research. It is mistaken to assume that "levels" exist in every political system in a neat hierarchical fashion.

Even in centralized regimes, decision-making may reflect a good deal of conflict among organized groups having both national and local connections. Because the national bureaucracy and its subordinate units may be influenced by local interests functioning through national parties and nationalized interest groups, local pressures may affect some variation in the application of national rules at the local level. National politics may well be in command but local sources of influence may considerably alter the intentions of national leaders.

In less centralized regimes, administrative and governmental arrangements may more directly reflect local or regional preferences. Where local governmental arenas have sufficient scope for political decision-making in matters of importance to citizens, those local institutions may be so strong that the national political regime may need to bargain for authority. The ideal of American government, and frequently the practice, has often seemed to resemble this picture, for even in those instances where federal programs dominate a field, they have often reflected a certain responsiveness to local preferences.

Notions of hierarchy also imply that various territorial units have an autonomy or integrity which permits one to study processes without examining cross-cutting affiliations. In effect, there is an implicit model operating which assumes that territorial actors (both national and local) are cohesive and monolithic. Decentralized regimes may, in practice, approach the pluralist model of a limited war of all against all in which groups (at whatever "level" they are located) with the most resources and the greatest political skills gain the greatest benefits. The national government may be in no position to impose solutions to problems; indeed, actual administration is often farmed out to governmental, quasi-governmental and non-governmental bodies in a fashion which only serves to reinforce the decentralization of the system.[25]

In contrast to more centralized regimes which retain their superiority by denying autonomy to localities, decentralized systems may actually encourage local actors to employ the resources of central authorities to *strengthen* local autonomy. The result is that rather than localities being dependent on the goodwill of the central government (or of a regional government) for their successful achievement of local goals, it is often the national government—if one can even talk in such monolithic terms when dealing with such decentralized regimes—which is dependent on localities for the achievement of goals. More often, however, there is a mutuality of dependence among units (individuals and groups) at different "levels" of the system which undermines any attempt to enforce a sense of formal hierarchy.

Thus, national political systems may vary along a continuum from: 1) those situations in which local government is clearly seen as part of a

[25]Theodore J. Lowi, *The End of Liberalism* (New York: Norton, 1969); Grant McConnell, *Private Power and American Democracy* (New York: Alfred A. Knopf, 1966).

national hierarchy of governments and government-related political structures; 2) through instances in which greater power may rest with the national government but some authority remains with localities to set priorities within boundaries permitted by national law; 3) to cases in which local institutions have considerable autonomy to raise money and provide services as they see fit.[26] In the less hierarchical situations, local governments are likely to be only one of many structures competing for influence in national political life. Other structures may include political parties, unions, business organizations, farmers' groups and professional associations. In a sense, the participatory component of the regime challenges the hierarchical principle which may exist in law.

The character of systemic linkages among institutions, then, has much to say about the place of local forces in national politics and vice-versa.

Decision-Making Processes for the Locality

It is important to know how institutions are arranged to make decisions, but it is equally important to analyze the ways in which specific decisions are made and which groups are benefited or harmed as a result. Although evaluation of the consequences of programs is by no means easy, it is necessary if we are to understand how differences in the distribution of local power affect individuals and groups in different political systems.

At the most obvious level, we must concern ourselves with identifying those persons and groups who have the formal authority to make major decisions for the locality and those who are able to influence them in the making of decisions.

In sum, we need to identify those responsible for making *general* policy that affects the lives of individuals. But we need to concern ourselves, equally, with the making of those day-to-day decisions in and for the locality which incrementally influence the character of governmental service delivery and the citizen's orientation to that administrative activity. For, citizens' perceptions of the quality of services delivered and their effect toward the systems providing those services constitute important feedbacks into the operation of the larger political system.

---

[26]For an interesting attempt to compare national approaches to the participatory dimension in introducing institutions of local government and administration, see Douglas E. Ashford, *National Development and Local Reform: Political Participation in Morocco, Tunisia, and Pakistan* (Princeton: Princeton University Press, 1967). Lloyd Rodwin, *Nations and Cities* (Boston: Houghton-Mifflin, 1970) is another sensible study employing a particularly useful comparative approach. Rodwin examines the tensions between national and local political forces with respect to urban growth strategies in Venezuela, Turkey, Britain, France and the United States.

Performance of Systemic Functions

Local government and politics are seen here as part of one arena in which conflict is articulated, suppressed, resolved or exacerbated. A central concern is to examine the linkages between this arena and others; this would include the examination of the impact of outputs from the local arena upon other arenas. Among those dimensions which need to be taken into account in assessing the impact of localism, local governance mechanisms and localistic political processes upon the national political system are the following:

1) the extent to which politics within sub-national arenas contributes to increasing or diminishing the load on other arenas, notably, the national government.
2) the implications of the manner in which local politics and government divides national power and resources. The very existence of multiple power centers diffuses responsibility, increases the ability of traditional authorities to maintain control, and thus may weaken protest and inhibit change.[27]
3) the extent to which a distribution of national power which favors subnational authorities may well increase the probability that particularistic demands will be more salient to the political system (e.g., pork barrel legislation) than universalistic ones (class issues).
4) the possibility that political mobilization conducted with the aid of locally-based political and governmental agencies may have different consequences than other kinds of efforts at mobilization.
5) the degree to which local governments provide a channel for innovation and political change within a political system.

TRADITION-MODERNITY, LOCALIZATION-NATIONALIZATION, AND POLITICAL CHANGE

Despite the serious questions which have been raised about the proper usage of the concepts of "tradition" and "modernity,"[28] it is possible to argue that in many societies "tradition" was identified with social organization that stressed localistic attachments. Within localities, at least in an ancient society like India's, the dominant theme was one of social and political hierarchy.

[27]McConnell, *op. cit.*; Lowi, *op. cit.*
[28]Lloyd I. Rudolph and Susanne Hoeber Rudolph, *The Modernity of Tradition* (Chicago and London: University of Chicago Press, 1967).

Distinctions like those between tradition and modernity, on the one hand, and localization and nationalization, on the other, may also be misleading if they equate moves toward socioeconomic pluralism at the local level with nationalizing processes of an inherently centralizing character. Thus, within the United States, the findings of studies of "community power" structures during the past twenty years have suggested the existence of a relationship between the extent of socioeconomic diversity in a community and the presence of societal forces which promote a gradual loosening and decentralizing of power within those local political systems. From tightly integrated local power structures, we are told by these studies, we have witnessed the ebbing of the authority of local elites and, consequently, nationalization of local politics.[29]

At the same time, however, the pluralization characteristic of metropolitan areas, as a whole, and within central cities, has been associated with rapid suburbanization which has had the effect of moving American society toward *greater* segmentation into political communities based on internal equality but external differentiation.[30] As a consequence of what appears almost to be a re-segmentation process, it is possible we are witnessing a "relocalization" of American political life based on political and social formulas different from those formerly identified as localistic. Even in the former small-town and central-city traditions, however, class distinctions often were expressed in American life in spatial terms—a fact which illuminates the intense feelings surrounding current efforts by some to overturn suburban-central city segmentation patterns. Further, and more recently, participatory democracy has been defined in territorial terms as much as in terms of workplace or voluntary association involvements. Issues of education, employment, housing, and transportation are all permeated by the conflict over localistic and nationalizing forces.

Yet, as we suggested earlier, we also find the modernization literature deficient in its handling of the local dimension. Only recently have writings begun to highlight the patron-client relations which operate in many societies as an integral part of the political system. And the patron-client literature has become so enmeshed in the politics of localism that it fails to

---

[29]What sometimes is presented in the literature as pluralism arising out of purely local factors may actually reflect the interventions of a series of extra-local forces into community life. Claire W. Gilbert, "Community Power and Decision-Making," and John Walton, "Differential Patterns of Community Power Structure," both in Terry N. Clark, *Community Structure and Decision-Making: Comparative Analyses,* pp. 139–56 and 441–59. Also see Hawkins, *op. cit.,* esp. pp. 106–11.

[30]Oliver P. Williams, Harold Herman, Charles S. Liebman and Thomas R. Dye, *Suburban Differences and Metropolitan Policies* (Philadelphia: University of Pennsylvania Press, 1965); Oliver P. Williams, *Metropolitan Political Analysis* (New York: Free Press, 1971).

provide an adequate picture of how local patron-client relations affect national politics; moreover, changes within the structure of relations in the two realms are rarely related in a systematic manner.

There also remains an uncertainty about the characteristics appropriately associated with the modernization process. It leaves us unsure in particular about what follows the "transition" to modernity with respect to the localization-nationalization dimension. On the one hand, evidence may point to the increasing bureaucratization of the larger society through such mechanisms as the professionalization of governmental administration and the standardization of sources of information and patterns of socialization. On the other hand, on the basis of recent trends in politics, one may point to an actual increase in the scale and quality of popular participation in political systems and increase of diversity.

CONCLUSIONS

Our framework reflects the concerns we believe most significant in the study of comparative local politics: questions concerning policy and process. Yet to understand political life, more is required than an accumulation of discrete policy studies, no matter how significant the policy or well executed the study. The problem is to integrate studies of policy with analysis of those political processes which affect how individuals and groups in the polity obtain superior political resources—formal political office, informal influence, favorable access to power. Furthermore, neither process should be examined in terms of the dramatic case alone, for much that affects the individual in his daily routine consists of just those behaviors which are patterned out of pressures which have little to do with decisions taken by formal institutions: the "little" favors the police may expect from businessmen on their routes; the behaviors of welfare agency personnel toward their clienteles; the bureaucratic routines adopted by educational administrators to restrain parent participation in educational decision-making.[31]

We believe that the gains from the conversion of the study of local politics and government into a more self-consciously comparative activity will be fruitful for both fields. For the study of local politics, one benefit of a comparative focus may be to help us identify those factors which are often mistakenly considered to be nation-specific but which in fact are the result of more general contextual factors. Thus, for example, the assumption of most American community studies that the local community is autonomous might be challenged when communities outside the United

[31]Wilson, *City Politics and Public Policy.*

States are examined. The results of such studies would be beneficial for distinguishing the contingent from the universal; it might lead to asking questions not being considered at present, such as the consequences of local government activity for the behavior of political systems. At the same time, studying local politics cross-nationally may help us assess better the importance of national variables.

On the other hand, comparative political studies have been so concerned with nation-building and most writers have identified themselves so completely with those political elites attempting to construct national political systems that they have tended to denigrate the localistic in their analyses.[32] If considered at all, localism—like "tradition"—has been viewed as a barrier to political development and nation-building.

Ultimately, we seek a way of conceptualizing comparative local politics which should enrich the study both of local politics and comparative politics, which looks not so much to the formalities of political institutions as to what is consequential in the local political dimension. We do not seek to define the field by reference to a few formal institutions found in every political system, but by identifying the local dimension which plays an integral part in a nation's political life.

[32]One notable exception is Aristide R. Zolberg, *Creating Political Order: The Party-States of West Africa* (Chicago: Rand McNally, 1966), but that work reflects the insights of an African specialist rather than the approach of the "great simplifiers" who have dominated comparative politics.

APPENDIX: Bibliographies
Related to the
Study of Community Power

BECK, CARL and J. THOMAS MCKECHNIE, *Political Elites, A Select Computerized Bibliography* (Cambridge: M.I.T. Press, 1968).
Although the primary focus of this bibliography is the study of political elites in comparative politics, it does include extensive citations of studies of community power structure. The time period covered is 1945–1967.

BELL, WENDELL, RICHARD J. HILL and CHARLES R. WRIGHT, *Public Leadership* (San Francisco: Chandler Publishing Co., 1961) pp. 196–228.
This is a selected bibliography (not annotated) of books, articles, and unpublished documents on public leadership in the United States.

GILBERT, CLAIRE, "The Study of Community Power: A Summary and a Test," in Scott Greer, et. al., eds., *The New Urbanization* (New York: St. Martin's Press, 1968) pp. 222–45.
This article includes an extensive bibliography of community power studies. The listings are not annotated.

HAWLEY, WILLIS D. and JAMES H. SVARA, *The Study of Community Power— A Bibliographic Review* (Santa Barbara: ABC–Clio Inc., 1972).
This bibliography encompasses about 100 pages of annotated citations. References to dissertations are included. In addition, a list of material dealing with more general commentary and study of social power is presented.

KEYNES, EDWARD and DAVID M. RICCI, eds., *Political Power, Community and Democracy* (Chicago: Rand McNally & Co., 1970).
"Selected Bibliography of Community Power and Related Subjects," prepared with the assistance of Gary W. Sykes, pp. 255–77. Some of these items are annotated.

NORVAL, GLENN D., JOHN P. ALSTON and DAVID WEINER, *Social Stratification: A Research Bibliography* (Berkeley, California: The Glendessary Press, Inc., 1970).
With respect to community power research, the authors acknowledge drawing almost exclusively on Pellegrin's bibliography in the *Southwestern Social Science Quarterly*. None of the citations is annotated.

PELLEGRIN, RONALD J., "Selected Bibliography on Community Power Structure," *Southwestern Social Science Quarterly* 48 (December 1967), 451–65.
The items here are not annotated.

PRESS, CHARLES, *Main Street Politics: Policy Making at the Local Level, A Survey of the Periodical Literature Since 1950* (East Lansing: Michigan State University, 1962).
This is an annotated bibliography comprised primarily of journal articles related to community power and to community politics in general, which appeared (for the most part) between 1951 and 1961.